Trübner's Oriental Series

BUDDHIST BIRTH STORIES

Trübner's Oriental Series

BUDDHISM
In 16 Volumes

I	The Life of Hiuen-Tsiang *Samuel Beal*
II	Si-Yu-Ki: Buddhist Records of the Western World Vol I *Samuel Beal*
III	Si-Yu-Ki: Buddhist Records of the Western World Vol II *Samuel Beal*
IV	Texts from the Buddhist Canon *Samuel Beal*
V	The Life or Legend of Gaudama Vol I *P Bigandet*
VI	The Life or Legend of Gaudama Vol II *P Bigandet*
VII	The Life of Gotama the Buddha *E H Brewster*
VIII	The Milinda-Questions *Mrs Rhys Davids*
IX	Buddhist Birth Stories *T W Rhys Davids*
X	Life and Works of Alexander Csoma de Körös *Theodore Duka*
XI	Early Buddhist Monachism *Sukumar Dutt*
XII	Chinese Buddhism *Joseph Edkins*
XIII	A Manual of Buddhist Philosophy *William Montgomery McGovern*
XIV	Udânavarga *W Woodville Rockhill*
XV	The Life of the Buddha *W Woodville Rockhill*
XVI	Tibetan Tales *F Anton von Schiefner*

BUDDHIST BIRTH STORIES

THE OLDEST COLLECTION OF FOLK-LORE EXTANT

T W RHYS DAVIDS

Routledge
Taylor & Francis Group
LONDON AND NEW YORK

First published in 1880 by
Trübner & Co Ltd

Reprinted in 2000 by
Routledge
2 Park Square, Milton Park, Abingdon, Oxon, OX14 4RN

Simultaneously published in the USA and Canada
by Routledge
711 Third Avenue, New York, NY 10017

Routledge is an imprint of the Taylor & Francis Group, an informa business

First issued in paperback 2013

The publishers have made every effort to contact authors/copyright holders of the works reprinted in *Trübner's Oriental Series*. This has not been possible in every case, however, and we would welcome correspondence from those individuals/companies we have been unable to trace.

These reprints are taken from original copies of each book. In many cases the condition of these originals is not perfect. The publisher has gone to great lengths to ensure the quality of these reprints, but wishes to point out that certain characteristics of the original copies will, of necessity, be apparent in reprints thereof.

British Library Cataloguing in Publication Data
A CIP catalogue record for this book
is available from the British Library

Buddhist Birth Stories
ISBN 978-0-415-24476-3 (Hbk)
ISBN 978-0-415-84631-8 (Pbk)
Buddhism: 16 Volumes
ISBN 978-0-415-24286-8
Trübner's Oriental Series
ISBN 978-0-415-23188-6

BUDDHIST BIRTH STORIES;

OR,

JĀTAKA TALES.

THE OLDEST COLLECTION OF FOLK-LORE EXTANT:

BEING

THE JĀTAKATTHAVAṆṆANĀ,

For the first time Edited in the Original Pāli

BY V. FAUSBÖLL,

AND TRANSLATED

BY T. W. RHYS DAVIDS.

TRANSLATION.

VOLUME I.

LONDON:
TRÜBNER & CO., LUDGATE HILL.
1880.

TO

GEHEIM-RATH PROFESSOR DOCTOR

STENZLER

MY FIRST GUIDE IN ORIENTAL STUDIES

IN CONGRATULATION ON HIS 'DOCTOR JUBILÄUM'

AND IN DEEP RESPECT FOR HIS PROFOUND SCHOLARSHIP

THIS WORK IS DEDICATED BY

HIS GRATEFUL PUPIL

THE AUTHOR.

TABLE OF CONTENTS.

INTRODUCTION.

It is well known that amongst the Buddhist Scriptures there is one book in which a large number of old stories, fables, and fairy tales, lie enshrined in an edifying commentary; and have thus been preserved for the study and amusement of later times. How this came about is not at present quite certain. The belief of orthodox Buddhists on the subject is this. The Buddha, as occasion arose, was accustomed throughout his long career to explain and comment on the events happening around him, by telling of similar events that had occurred in his own previous births. The experience, not of one lifetime only, but of many lives, was always present to his mind; and it was this experience he so often used to point a moral, or adorn a tale. The stories so told are said to have been reverently learnt and repeated by his disciples; and immediately after his death 550 of them were gathered together in one collection, called the Book of the 550 Jātakas or Births; the commentary to which gives for each Jātaka, or Birth Story, an account of the event in Gotama's life which led to his first telling that particular story. Both text and commentary were then handed down intact, and in the Pāli language in which they were composed, to the time of the Council of Patna (held in or about the year 250 B.C.); and they were carried in the following year to Ceylon by the great missionary Mahinda. There the commentary was translated into Siṃhalese, the Aryan dialect spoken in Ceylon; and was re-translated into its present form in the Pāli language in the fifth century of our era. But the text of the Jātaka stories themselves has been throughout preserved in its original Pāli form.

Unfortunately this orthodox Buddhist belief as to the history of the Book of Birth Stories rests on a foundation of quicksand. The Buddhist belief, that most of their sacred books were in existence immediately after the Buddha's death, is not only not supported, but is contradicted by the evidence of those books themselves. It may be necessary to state what that belief is, in order to show the importance which the Buddhists attach to the book; but in order to estimate the value we ourselves should give it, it will be necessary by critical, and more roundabout methods, to endeavour to arrive at some more reliable conclusion. Such an investigation cannot, it is true, be completed until the whole series of the Buddhist Birth Stories shall have become accessible in the original Pāli text, and the history of those stories shall have been traced in other sources. With the present inadequate information at our command, it is only possible to arrive at probabilities. But it is therefore the more fortunate that the course of the inquiry will lead to some highly interesting and instructive results.

In the first place, the fairy tales, parables, fables, riddles, and comic and moral stories, of which the Buddhist Collection—known as the Jātaka Book—consists, have been found, in many instances, to bear a striking resemblance to similar ones current in the West. Now in many instances this resemblance is simply due to the fact that the *Western stories were borrowed from the Buddhist ones.*

To this resemblance much of the interest excited by the Buddhist Birth Stories is, very naturally, due. As, therefore, the stories translated in the body of this volume do not happen to contain among them any of those most generally known in England, I insert here one or two specimens which may at the same time afford some amusement, and also enable the reader to judge how far the alleged resemblances do actually exist.

It is absolutely essential for the correctness of such judgment that the stories should be presented exactly as they stand in the original. I am aware that a close and literal translation involves the disadvantage of presenting the stories in a style which will probably seem strange, and even wooden, to the modern reader. But it cannot be admitted that, for even purposes of comparison, it would be sufficient to reproduce the stories in a modern form which should aim at combining substantial accuracy with a pleasing dress.

And the Book of Birth Stories has a value quite independent of the fact that many of its tales have been transplanted to the West. It contains a record of the every-day life, and every-day thought, of the people among whom the tales were told: it is *the oldest, most complete, and most important Collection of Folk-lore extant.*

The whole value of its evidence in this respect would be lost, if a translator, by slight additions in some places, slight omissions in others, and slight modifications here and there, should run the risk of conveying erroneous impressions of early Buddhist beliefs, and habits, and modes of thought. It is important, therefore, that the reader should understand, before reading the stories I intend to give, that while translating sentence by sentence, rather than word by word, I have never lost sight of the importance of retaining in the English version, as far as possible, not only the phraseology, but the style and spirit of the Buddhist story-teller.

The first specimen I propose to give is a half-moral half-comic story, which runs as follows.

The Ass in the Lion's Skin.

SĪHA-CAMMA JĀTAKA.

(Fausböll, No. 189.)

Once upon a time, while Brahma-datta was reigning in Benāres, the future Buddha was born one of a peasant family; and when he grew up, he gained his living by tilling the ground.

At that time a hawker used to go from place to place, trafficking in goods carried by an ass. Now at each place he came to, when he took the pack down from the ass's back, he used to clothe him in a lion's skin, and turn him loose in the rice and barley-fields. And when the watchmen in the fields saw the ass, they dared not go near him, taking him for a lion.

So one day the hawker stopped in a village; and whilst he was getting his own breakfast cooked, he dressed the ass in a lion's skin, and turned him loose in a barley-field. The watchmen in the field dared not go up to him; but going home, they published the news. Then all the villagers came out with weapons in their hands; and blowing chanks, and beating drums, they went near the field and shouted. Terrified with the fear of death, the ass uttered a cry—the cry of an ass!

And when he knew him then to be an ass, the future Buddha pronounced the First Stanza:

"This is not a lion's roaring,
Nor a tiger's, nor a panther's;
Dressed in a lion's skin,
'Tis a wretched ass that roars!"

But when the villagers knew the creature to be an ass, they beat him till his bones broke; and, carrying off the lion's skin, went away. Then the hawker came; and seeing the ass fallen into so bad a plight, pronounced the Second Stanza:

"Long might the ass,
Clad in a lion's skin,
Have fed on the barley green.
But he brayed!
And that moment he came to ruin."

And even whilst he was yet speaking the ass died on the spot!

This story will doubtless sound familiar enough to English ears; for a similar tale is found in our modern collections of so-called 'Æsop's Fables.'[1] Professor Benfey has further traced it in mediæval French, German, Turkish, and Indian literature.[2] But it may have been much older than any of these books; for the fable possibly gave rise to a proverb of which we find traces among the Greeks as early as the time of Plato.[3] Lucian gives the fable in full, localizing it

[1] *James's* 'Æsop's Fables' (London, Murray, 1852), p. 111; *La Fontaine*, Book v. No. 21; Æsop (in Greek text, ed. Furia, 141, 262; ed. Coriæ, 113); *Babrius* (Lewis, vol. ii. p. 43).

[2] *Benfey's* Pancha Tantra, Book iv., No. 7, in the note on which, at vol. i. p. 462, he refers to *Halm*, p. 333; *Robert*, in the 'Fables inédites du Moyen Age, vol. i. p. 360; and the Turkish Tūtī-nāmah (Rosen, vol. ii. p. 149). In India it is found also in the Northern Buddhist Collection called Kathā Sarit Sāgāra, by Somadeva; and in Hitopadesa (iii. 2, Max Müller, p. 110).

[3] Kratylos, 411 (ed. Tauchnitz, ii. 275).

at Kumē, in South Italy,[1] and Julien has given us a Chinese version in his 'Avadānas.'[2] Erasmus, in his work on proverbs,[3] alludes to the fable; and so also does our own Shakespeare in 'King John.'[4] It is worthy of mention that in one of the later story-books—in a Persian translation, that is, of the Hitopadesa—there is a version of our fable in which it is the vanity of the ass in trying to sing which leads to his disguise being discovered, and thus brings him to grief.[5] But Professor Benfey has shown[6] that this version is simply the rolling into one of the present tale and of another, also widely prevalent, where an ass by trying to sing earns for himself, not thanks, but blows.[7] I shall hereafter attempt to draw some conclusions from the history of the story. But I would here point out that the fable could scarcely have originated in any country in which lions were not common; and that the Jātaka story gives a reasonable explanation of the ass being dressed in the skin, instead of saying that he dressed himself in it, as is said in our 'Æsop's Fables.'

The reader will notice that the 'moral' of the tale

1 *Lucian*, Piscator, 32.

2 Vol. ii. No. 91.

3 'Adagia,' under 'Asinus apud Cumanos.'

4 Act ii. scene 1; and again, Act iii. scene 1.

5 *De Sacy*, 'Notes et Extraits,' x. 1, 247.

6 *Loc. cit.* p. 463.

7 Pancha Tantra, v. 7. Prof. Weber (Indische Studien, iii. 352) compares *Phædrus* (Dressler, App. vi. 2) and *Erasmus's* 'Adagia' under 'Asinus ad Lyrum.' See also Tūti-nāmah (Rosen ii. 218); and I would add *Varro*, in Aulus Gellius, iii. 16; and *Jerome*, Ep. 27, 'Ad Marcellam.'

is contained in two stanzas, one of which is put into the mouth of the Bodisat or future Buddha. This will be found to be the case in all the Birth Stories, save that the number of the stanzas differs, and that they are usually all spoken by the Bodisat. It should also be noticed that the identification of the peasant's son with the Bodisat, which is of so little importance to the story, is the only part of it which is essentially Buddhistic. Both these points will be of importance further on.

The introduction of the human element takes this story, perhaps, out of the class of fables in the most exact sense of that word. I therefore add a story containing a fable proper, where animals speak and act like men.

The Talkative Tortoise.

KACCHAPA JĀTAKA.

(Fausböll, No. 215.)

Once upon a time, when Brahma-datta was reigning in Benāres, the future Buddha was born in a minister's family; and when he grew up, he became the king's adviser in things temporal and spiritual.

Now this king was very talkative: while he was speaking, others had no opportunity for a word. And the future Buddha, wanting to cure this talkativeness of his, was constantly seeking for some means of doing so.

At that time there was living, in a pond in the Himālaya mountains, a tortoise. Two young haŋsas (*i.e.* wild ducks[1]) who came to feed there, made friends with him. And one day, when they had become very intimate with him, they said to the tortoise—

"Friend tortoise! the place where we live, at the Golden Cave on Mount Beautiful in the Himālaya country, is a delightful spot. Will you come there with us?"

"But how can I get there?"

"We can take you, if you can only hold your tongue, and will say nothing to anybody."[2]

"O! that I can do. Take me with you."

"That's right," said they. And making the tortoise bite hold of a stick, they themselves took the two ends in their teeth, and flew up into the air.[3]

Seeing him thus carried by the haŋsas, some villagers called out, "Two wild ducks are carrying a tortoise along on a stick!" Whereupon the tortoise wanted to say, "If my friends choose to carry me, what is that to you, you wretched slaves!" So just as the swift flight of the wild ducks had brought him over the king's palace in the city of Benāres, he let go of the stick he was biting, and falling in the open courtyard, split in two! And there arose a universal cry, "A tortoise has fallen in the open courtyard, and has split in two!"

[1] Pronounced hangsa, often rendered swan, a favourite bird in Indian tales, and constantly represented in Buddhist carvings. It is the original Golden Goose. See below, p. 294, and Jātaka No. 136.

[2] There is an old story of a Fellow of Magdalen College, Oxford, who inherited a family living. He went in great trouble to Dr. Routh, the Head of his College, saying that he doubted whether he could hold, at the same time, the Living and the Fellowship. "You can hold anything," was the reply, "if you can only hold your tongue." And he held *all three.*

[3] In the Vinīla Jātaka (No. 160) they similarly carry a crow to the Himālaya mountains.

The king, taking the future Buddha, went to the place, surrounded by his courtiers; and looking at the tortoise, he asked the Bodisat, "Teacher! how comes he to be fallen here?"

The future Buddha thought to himself, "Long expecting, wishing to admonish the king, have I sought for some means of doing so. This tortoise must have made friends with the wild ducks; and they must have made him bite hold of the stick, and have flown up into the air to take him to the hills. But he, being unable to hold his tongue when he hears any one else talk, must have wanted to say something, and let go the stick; and so must have fallen down from the sky, and thus lost his life." And saying, "Truly, O king! those who are called chatter-boxes—people whose words have no end—come to grief like this," he uttered these Verses:

"Verily the tortoise killed himself
Whilst uttering his voice;
Though he was holding tight the stick,
By a word himself he slew.

"Behold him then, O excellent by strength!
And speak wise words, not out of season.
You see how, by his talking overmuch,
The tortoise fell into this wretched plight!"

The king saw that he was himself referred to, and said, "O Teacher! are you speaking of us?"

And the Bodisat spake openly, and said, "O great king! be it thou, or be it any other, whoever talks beyond measure meets with some mishap like this."

And the king henceforth refrained himself, and became a man of few words.

This story too is found also in Greek, Latin, Arabic, Persian, and in most European languages,[1] though, strangely enough, it does not occur in our books of Æsop's Fables. But in the 'Æsop's Fables' is usually included a story of a tortoise who asked an eagle to teach him to fly; and being dropped, split into two![2] It is worthy of notice that in the Southern recension of the Pañca Tantra it is eagles, and not wild ducks or swans, who carry the tortoise;[3] and there can, I think, be little doubt that the two fables are historically connected.

Another fable, very familiar to modern readers, is stated in the commentary to have been first related in ridicule of a kind of Mutual Admiration Society existing among the opponents of the Buddha. Hearing the monks talking about the foolish way in which Devadatta and Kokālika went about among the people ascribing each to the other virtues which neither possessed, he is said to have told this tale.

[1] *Pañca Tantra*, vol. i. p. 13, where Professor Benfey (i. 239–241) traces also the later versions in different languages. He mentions *Wolff's* German translation of the Kalilah and Dimnah, vol. i. p. 91; *Knatchbull's* English version, p. 146; *Simeon Seth's* Greek version, p. 28; *John of Capua's* Directorium Humanæ Vitæ, D. 5 b.; the German translation of this last (Ulm, 1483), F. viii. 6; the Spanish translation, xix a.; *Firenzuola*, 65; *Doni*, 93; *Anvār i Suhaili*, p. 159; *Le Livre des Lumières* (1664, 8vo.), 124; *Le Cabinet des Fées*, xvii. 309. See also Contes et Fables Indiennes de Bidpai et de Lokman, ii. 112; *La Fontaine*, x. 3, where the ducks fly to America (!); and *Bickell's* 'Kalilag und Dimnag,' p. 24. In India it is found in *Somadeva*, and in the *Hitopadesa*, iv. 2 (Max Müller, p. 125). See also *Julien*, i. 71.

[2] This version is found in *Babrius* (Lewis, i. 122); *Phædrus*, ii. 7 and vii. 14 (Orelli, 55, 128); and in the Æsopæan collections (Fur. 193; Coriæ, 61) and in *Abstemius*, 108.

[3] Dubois, p. 109.

The Jackal and the Crow.

JAMBU-KHĀDAKA JĀTAKA.

(Fausböll, No. 294.)

Long, long ago, when Brahma-datta was reigning in Benāres, the Bodisat had come to life as a tree-god, dwelling in a certain grove of Jambu-trees.

Now a crow was sitting there one day on the branch of a Jambu-tree, eating the Jambu-fruits, when a jackal coming by, looked up and saw him.

"Ha!" thought he. "I'll flatter that fellow, and get some of those Jambus to eat." And thereupon he uttered this verse in his praise:

"Who may this be, whose rich and pleasant notes
Proclaim him best of all the singing-birds?
Warbling so sweetly on the Jambu-branch,
Where like a peacock he sits firm and grand!"

Then the crow, to pay him back his compliments, replied in this second verse:

"'Tis a well-bred young gentleman, who understands
To speak of gentlemen in terms polite!
Good Sir!—whose shape and glossy coat reveal
The tiger's offspring—eat of these, I pray!"

And so saying, he shook the branch of the Jambu-tree till he made the fruit to fall.

But when the god who dwelt in that tree saw the two of them, now they had done flattering one another, eating the Jambus together, he uttered a third verse:

"Too long, forsooth, I've borne the sight
Of these poor chatterers of lies—
The refuse-eater and the offal-eater
Belauding each other!"

And making himself visible in awful shape, he frightened them away from the place!

It is easy to understand, that when this story had been carried out of those countries where the crow and the jackal are the common scavengers, it would lose its point; and it may very well, therefore, have been shortened into the fable of the Fox and the Crow and the piece of cheese. On the other hand, the latter is so complete and excellent a story, that it would scarcely have been expanded, if it had been the original, into the tale of the Jackal and the Crow.[1]

The next tale to be quoted is one showing how a wise man solves a difficulty. I am sorry that Mr. Fausböll has not yet reached this Jātaka in his edition of the Pāli text; but I give it from a Siŋhalese version of the fourteenth century, which is nearer to the Pāli than any other as yet known.[2] It is an episode in

[1] See La Fontaine, Book i. No. 2, and the current collections of Æsop's Fables (*e.g.* James's edition, p. 136). It should be added that the Jambu-khādaka-saŋyutta in the Saŋyutta Nikāya has nothing to do with our fable. The Jambu-eater of that story is an ascetic, who lives on Jambus, and is converted by a discussion on Nirvāna.

[2] The Siŋhalese text will be found in the '*Sidat Saŋgarāwa*,' p. clxxvii.

The Birth as 'Great Physician.'[1]

MAHOSADHA JĀTAKA.

A woman, carrying her child, went to the future Buddha's tank to wash. And having first bathed the child, she put on her upper garment and descended into the water to bathe herself.

Then a Yakshiṇī,[2] seeing the child, had a craving to eat it. And taking the form of a woman, she drew near, and asked the mother—

"Friend, this *is* a *very* pretty child, is it one of yours?"

And when she was told it was, she asked if she might nurse it. And this being allowed, she nursed it a little, and then carried it off.

But when the mother saw this, she ran after her, and cried out, "Where are you taking my child to?" and caught hold of her.

The Yakshiṇī boldly said, "Where did you get the child from? It is mine!" And so quarrelling, they passed the door of the future Buddha's Judgment Hall.

He heard the noise, sent for them, inquired into the matter, and asked them whether they would abide by his

[1] Literally 'the great medicine.' The Bodisat of that time received this name because he was born with a powerful drug in his hand,—an omen of the cleverness in device by which, when he grew up, he delivered people from their misfortunes. Compare my 'Buddhism,' p. 187.

[2] The Yakshas, products of witchcraft and cannibalism, are beings of magical power, who feed on human flesh. The male Yaksha occupies in Buddhist stories a position similar to that of the wicked genius in the Arabian Nights; the female Yakshiṇī, who occurs more frequently, usually plays the part of siren.

decision. And they agreed. Then he had a line drawn on the ground; and told the Yakshiṇī to take hold of the child's arms, and the mother to take hold of its legs; and said, "The child shall be hers who drags him over the line."

But as soon as they pulled at him, the mother, seeing how he suffered, grieved as if her heart would break. And letting him go, she stood there weeping.

Then the future Buddha asked the bystanders, "Whose hearts are tender to babes? those who have borne children, or those who have not?"

And they answered, "O Sire! the hearts of mothers are tender."

Then he said, "Whom think you is the mother? she who has the child in her arms, or she who has let go?"

And they answered, "She who has let go is the mother."

And he said, "Then do you all think that the other was the thief?"

And they answered, "Sire! we cannot tell."

And he said, "Verily this is a Yakshiṇī, who took the child to eat it."

And they asked, "O Sire! how did you know it?"

And he replied, "Because her eyes winked not, and were red, and she knew no fear, and had no pity, I knew it."

And so saying, he demanded of the thief, "Who are you?"

And she said, "Lord! I am a Yakshiṇī."

And he asked, "Why did you take away this child?"

And she said, "I thought to eat him, O my Lord!"

And he rebuked her, saying, "O foolish woman! For your former sins you have been born a Yakshiṇī, and now do you still sin!" And he laid a vow upon her to keep the Five Commandments, and let her go.

But the mother of the child exalted the future Buddha, and said, "O my Lord! O Great Physician! may thy life be long!" And she went away, with her babe clasped to her bosom.

The Hebrew story, in which a similar judgment is ascribed to Solomon, occurs in the Book of Kings, which is more than a century older than the time of Gotama. We shall consider below what may be the connexion between the two.

The next specimen is a tale about lifeless things endowed with miraculous powers; perhaps the oldest tale in the world of that kind which has been yet published. It is an episode in

---

Sakka's Presents.

DADHI-VĀHANA JĀTAKA.

(Fausböll, No. 186.)

Once upon a time, when Brahma-datta was reigning in Benāres, four brothers, Brāhmans, of that kingdom, devoted themselves to an ascetic life; and having built themselves huts at equal distances in the region of the Himālaya mountains, took up their residence there.

The eldest of them died, and was re-born as the god Sakka.[1] When he became aware of this, he used to go and render help at intervals every seven or eight days to the others. And one day, having greeted the eldest hermit, and sat down beside him, he asked him, "Reverend Sir, what are you in need of?"

The hermit, who suffered from jaundice, answered, "I want fire!" So he gave him a double-edged hatchet.

But the hermit said, "Who is to take this, and bring me firewood?"

Then Sakka spake thus to him, "Whenever, reverend Sir, you want firewood, you should let go the hatchet from your hand, and say, 'Please fetch me firewood: make me fire!' And it will do so."

So he gave him the hatchet; and went to the second hermit, and asked, "Reverend Sir, what are you in need of?"

Now the elephants had made a track for themselves close to his hut. And he was annoyed by those elephants, and said, "I am much troubled by elephants; drive them away."

Sakka, handing him a drum, said, "Reverend Sir, if you strike on this side of it, your enemies will take to flight; but if you strike on this side, they will become friendly, and surround you on all sides with an army in fourfold array."[2]

[1] Not quite the same as Jupiter. Sakka is a very harmless and gentle kind of a god, not a jealous god, nor given to lasciviousness or spite. Neither is he immortal: he dies from time to time; and, if he has behaved well, is reborn under happy conditions. Meanwhile somebody else, usually one of the sons of men who has deserved it, succeeds, for a hundred thousand years or so, to his name and place and glory. Sakka can call to mind his experiences in his former birth, a gift in which he surpasses most other beings. He was also given to a kind of practical joking, by which he tempted people, and has become a mere beneficent fairy.

[2] That is, infantry, cavalry, chariots of war, and elephants of war. Truly a useful kind of present to give to a pious hermit!

So he gave him the drum; and went to the third hermit, and asked, "Reverend Sir, what are you in need of?"

He was also affected with jaundice, and said, therefore, "I want sour milk."

Sakka gave him a milk-bowl, and said, "If you wish for anything, and turn this bowl over, it will become a great river, and pour out such a torrent, that it will be able to take a kingdom, and give it to you."

And Sakka went away. But thenceforward the hatchet made fire for the eldest hermit; when the second struck one side of his drum, the elephants ran away; and the third enjoyed his curds.

Now at that time a wild boar, straying in a forsaken village, saw a gem of magical power. When he seized this in his mouth, he rose by its magic into the air, and went to an island in the midst of the ocean. And thinking, "Here now I ought to live," he descended, and took up his abode in a convenient spot under an Udumbara-tree. And one day, placing the gem before him, he fell asleep at the foot of the tree.

Now a certain man of the land of Kāsi had been expelled from home by his parents, who said, "This fellow is of no use to us." So he went to a seaport, and embarked in a ship as a servant to the sailors. And the ship was wrecked; but by the help of a plank he reached that very island. And while he was looking about for fruits, he saw the boar asleep; and going softly up, he took hold of the gem.

Then by its magical power he straightway rose right up into the air! So, taking a seat on the Udumbara-tree, he said to himself, "Methinks this boar must have become a sky-walker through the magic power of this gem. That's how he got to be living here! It's plain enough what I ought to do; I'll first of all kill and eat him, and then I can get away!"

So he broke a twig off the tree, and dropped it on his head. The boar woke up, and not seeing the gem, ran about, trembling, this way and that way. The man seated on the tree laughed. The boar, looking up, saw him, and dashing his head against the tree, died on the spot.

But the man descended, cooked his flesh, ate it, and rose into the air. And as he was passing along the summit of the Himālaya range, he saw a hermitage; and descending at the hut of the eldest hermit, he stayed there two or three days, and waited on the hermit; and thus became aware of the magic power of the hatchet.

"I must get that," thought he. And he showed the hermit the magic power of his gem, and said, "Sir, do you take this, and give me your hatchet." The ascetic, full of longing to be able to fly through the air,[1] did so. But the man, taking the hatchet, went a little way off, and letting it go, said, "O hatchet! cut off that hermit's head, and bring the gem to me!" And it went, and cut off the hermit's head, and brought him the gem.

Then he put the hatchet in a secret place, and went to the second hermit, and stayed there a few days. And having thus become aware of the magic power of the drum, he exchanged the gem for the drum; and cut off *his* head too in the same way as before.

[1] The power of going through the air is usually considered in Indian legends to be the result, and a proof, of great holiness and long-continued penance. So the hermit thought he would get a fine reputation cheaply.

Then he went to the third hermit, and saw the magic power of the milk-bowl; and exchanging the gem for it, caused *his* head to be cut off in the same manner. And taking the Gem, and the Hatchet, and the Drum, and the Milk-bowl, he flew away up into the air.

Not far from the city of Benāres he stopped, and sent by the hand of a man a letter to the king of Benāres to this effect, "Either do battle, or give me up your kingdom!"

No sooner had he heard that message, than the king sallied forth, saying, "Let us catch the scoundrel!"

But the man beat one side of his drum, and a fourfold army stood around him! And directly he saw that the king's army was drawn out in battle array, he poured out his milk-bowl; and a mighty river arose, and the multitude, sinking down in it, were not able to escape! Then letting go the hatchet, he said, "Bring me the king's head!" And the hatchet went, and brought the king's head, and threw it at his feet; and no one had time even to raise a weapon!

Then he entered the city in the midst of his great army, and caused himself to be anointed king, under the name of Dadhi-vāhana (The Lord of Milk), and governed the kingdom with righteousness.[1]

The story goes on to relate how the king planted a wonderful mango, how the sweetness of its fruit turned to sourness through the too-close proximity of bitter

[1] Compare Mahā-bhārata, xii. 1796.

herbs, (!) and how the Bodisat, then the king's minister, pointed out that evil communications corrupt good things. But it is the portion above translated which deserves notice as the most ancient example known of those tales in which inanimate objects are endowed with magical powers; and in which the Seven League Boots, or the Wishing Cup, or the Vanishing Hat, or the Wonderful Lamp, render their fortunate possessors happy and glorious. There is a very tragical story of a Wishing Cup in the Buddhist Collection,[1] where the Wishing Cup, however, is turned into ridicule. It is not unpleasant to find that beliefs akin to, and perhaps the result of, fetish-worship, had faded away, among Buddhist story-tellers, into sources of innocent amusement.

In this curious tale the Hatchet, the Drum, and the Milk-bowl are endowed with qualities much more fit for the use they were put to in the latter part of the story, than to satisfy the wants of the hermits. It is common ground with satirists how little, save sorrow, men would gain if they could have anything they chose to ask for. But, unlike the others we have quoted, the tale in its present shape has a flavour distinctively Buddhist in the irreverent way in which it treats the great god Sakka, the Jupiter of the pre-Buddhistic Hindus. It takes for granted, too, that the hero ruled in righteous-

[1] Fausböll, No. 291.

ness; and this is as common in the Jātakas, as the 'lived happily ever after' of modern love stories.

This last idea recurs more strongly in the Birth Story called

---

A Lesson for Kings.

RĀJOVĀDA JĀTAKA.

(Fausböll, No. 151.)

Once upon a time, when Brahma-datta was reigning in Benāres, the future Buddha returned to life in the womb of his chief queen; and after the conception ceremony had been performed, he was safely born. And when the day came for choosing a name, they called him Prince Brahma-datta. He grew up in due course; and when he was sixteen years old, went to Takkasilā,[1] and became accomplished in all arts. And after his father died he ascended the throne, and ruled the kingdom with righteousness and equity. He gave judgments without partiality, hatred, ignorance, or fear.[2] Since he thus reigned with justice, with justice also his ministers administered the law. Lawsuits being thus decided with justice, there were none who brought false cases. And as these ceased, the noise and tumult of litigation ceased in the king's court. Though the judges sat all day in

[1] This is the well-known town in the Panjāb called by the Greeks Taxila, and famed in Buddhist legend as the great university of ancient India, as Nālanda was in later times.

[2] Literally "without partiality and the rest," that is, the rest of the *agatis*, the actions forbidden to judges (and to kings as judges).

the court, they had to leave without any one coming for justice. It came to this, that the Hall of Justice would have to be closed!

Then the future Buddha thought, "From my reigning with righteousness there are none who come for judgment; the bustle has ceased, and the Hall of Justice will have to be closed. It behoves me, therefore, now to examine into my own faults; and if I find that anything is wrong in me, to put that away, and practise only virtue."

Thenceforth he sought for some one to tell him his faults; but among those around him he found no one who would tell him of any fault, but heard only his own praise.

Then he thought, "It is from fear of me that these men speak only good things, and not evil things," and he sought among those people who lived outside the palace. And finding no fault-finder there, he sought among those who lived outside the city, in the suburbs, at the four gates.[1] And there too finding no one to find fault, and hearing only his own praise, he determined to search the country places.

So he made over the kingdom to his ministers, and mounted his chariot; and taking only his charioteer, left the city in disguise. And searching the country through, up to the very boundary, he found no fault-finder, and heard only of his own virtue; and so he turned back from the outermost boundary, and returned by the high road towards the city.

Now at that time the king of Kosala, Mallika by name,

[1] The gates opening towards the four "directions," that is, the four cardinal points of the compass.

was also ruling his kingdom with righteousness; and when seeking for some fault in himself, he also found no fault-finder in the palace, but only heard of his own virtue! So seeking in country places, he too came to that very spot. And these two came face to face in a low cart-track with precipitous sides, where there was no space for a chariot to get out of the way!

Then the charioteer of Mallika the king said to the charioteer of the king of Benāres, "Take thy chariot out of the way!"

But he said, "Take thy chariot out of the way, O charioteer! In this chariot sitteth the lord over the kingdom of Benāres, the great king Brahma-datta."

Yet the other replied, "In this chariot, O charioteer, sitteth the lord over the kingdom of Kosala, the great king Mallika. Take thy carriage out of the way, and make room for the chariot of our king!"

Then the charioteer of the king of Benāres thought, "They say then that he too is a king! What *is* now to be done?" After some consideration, he said to himself, "I know a way. I'll find out how old he is, and then I'll let the chariot of the younger be got out of the way, and so make room for the elder."

And when he had arrived at that conclusion, he asked that charioteer what the age of the king of Kosala was. But on inquiry he found that the ages of both were equal. Then he inquired about the extent of his kingdom, and about his army, and his wealth, and his renown, and about the country he lived in, and his caste and tribe and family. And he found that both were lords of a kingdom three hundred leagues in extent; and that in respect of army and wealth and renown, and the countries in which they lived, and their caste and their tribe and their family, they were just on a par!

Then he thought, "I will make way for the most righteous." And he asked, "What kind of righteousness has this king of yours?"

And the other saying, "Such and such is our king's righteousness," and so proclaiming his king's wickedness as goodness, uttered the First Stanza:

The strong he overthrows by strength,
The mild by mildness, does Mallika;
The good he conquers by goodness,
And the wicked by wickedness too.
Such is the nature of *this* king!
Move out of the way, O charioteer!

But the charioteer of the king of Benāres asked him, "Well, have you told all the virtues of your king?"

"Yes," said the other.

"If these are his *virtues*, where are then his faults?" replied he.

The other said, "Well, for the nonce, they shall be faults, if you like! But pray, then, what is the kind of goodness your king has?"

And then the charioteer of the king of Benāres called unto him to hearken, and uttered the Second Stanza:

Anger he conquers by calmness,
And by goodness the wicked;
The stingy he conquers by gifts,
And by truth the speaker of lies.
Such is the nature of *this* king!
Move out of the way, O charioteer!"

And when he had thus spoken, both Mallika the king

and his charioteer alighted from their chariot. And they took out the horses, and removed their chariot, and made way for the king of Benāres!

But the king of Benāres exhorted Mallika the king, saying, "Thus and thus is it right to do." And returning to Benāres, he practised charity, and did other good deeds, and so when his life was ended he passed away to heaven.

And Mallika the king took his exhortation to heart; and having in vain searched the country through for a fault-finder, he too returned to his own city, and practised charity and other good deeds; and so at the end of his life he went to heaven.

The mixture in this Jātaka of earnestness with dry humour is very instructive. The exaggeration in the earlier part of the story; the hint that law depends in reality on false cases; the suggestion that to decide cases justly would by itself put an end, not only to 'the block in the law courts,' but even to all lawsuits; the way in which it is brought about that two mighty kings should meet, unattended, in a narrow lane; the cleverness of the first charioteer in getting out of his difficulties; the brand-new method of settling the delicate question of precedence—a method which, logically carried out, would destroy the necessity of such questions being raised at all;—all this is the amusing side of the

Jātaka. It throws, and is meant to throw, an air of unreality over the story; and it is none the less humour because it is left to be inferred, because it is only an aroma which might easily escape unnoticed, only the humour of naïve absurdity and of clever repartee.

But none the less also is the story-teller thoroughly in earnest; he really means that justice is noble, that to conquer evil by good is the right thing, and that goodness is the true measure of greatness. The object is edification also, and not amusement only. The lesson itself is quite Buddhistic. The first four lines of the Second Moral are indeed included, as verse 223, in the *Dhammapada* or 'Scripture Verses,' perhaps the most sacred and most widely-read book of the Buddhist Bible; and the distinction between the two ideals of virtue is in harmony with all Buddhist ethics. It is by no means, however, exclusively Buddhistic. It gives expression to an idea that would be consistent with most of the later religions; and is found also in the great Hindu Epic, the Mahā Bhārata, which has been called the Bible of the Hindus.[1] It is true that further on in the same poem is found the opposite sentiment, attributed in our story to the king of Mallika;[2] and that the higher teaching is in one of the latest portions of the Mahā Bhārata, and

[1] Mahā Bhārata, v. 1518. Another passage at iii. 13253 is very similar.

[2] Mahā Bhārata, xii. 4052. See Dr. Muir's "Metrical Translations from Sanskrit Writers" (1879), pp. xxxi, 88, 275, 356.

probably of Buddhist origin. But when we find that the Buddhist principle of overcoming evil by good was received, as well as its opposite, into the Hindu poem, it is clear that this lofty doctrine was by no means repugnant to the best among the Brāhmans.[1]

It is to be regretted that some writers on Buddhism have been led away by their just admiration for the noble teaching of Gotama into an unjust depreciation of the religious system of which his own was, after all, but the highest product and result. There were doubtless among the Brāhmans uncompromising advocates of the worst privileges of caste, of the most debasing belief in the efficacy of rites and ceremonies; but this verse is only one among many others which are incontestable evidence of the wide prevalence also of a spirit of justice, and of an earnest seeking after truth. It is, in fact, inaccurate to draw any hard-and-fast line between the Indian Buddhists and their countrymen of other faiths. After the first glow of the Buddhist reformation had passed away, there was probably as little difference between Buddhist and Hindu as there was between the two kings in the story which has just been told.

[1] Similar passages will also be found in Lao Tse, Douglas's Confucianism, etc., p. 197; Pancha Tantra, i. 247 (277) = iv. 72; in Stobæus, quoted by Muir, p. 356; and in St. Matthew, v. 44–46; whereas the Mallika doctrine is inculcated by Confucius (Legge, Chinese Classics, i. 152).

THE KALILAG AND DAMNAG LITERATURE.

Among the other points of similarity between Buddhists and Hindus, there is one which deserves more especial mention here,—that of their liking for the kind of moral-comic tales which form the bulk of the Buddhist Birth Stories. That this partiality was by no means confined to the Buddhists is apparent from the fact that books of such tales have been amongst the most favourite literature of the Hindus. And this is the more interesting to us, as it is these Hindu collections that have most nearly preserved the form in which many of the Indian stories have been carried to the West.

The oldest of the collections now extant is the one already referred to, the PANCHA TANTRA, that is, the 'Five Books,' a kind of Hindu 'Pentateuch' or 'Pentamerone.' In its earliest form this work is unfortunately no longer extant; but in the sixth century of our era a book very much like it formed part of a work translated into Pahlavi, or Ancient Persian; and thence, about 750 A.D., into Syriac, under the title of 'KALILAG AND DAMNAG,' and into Arabic under the title 'KALILAH AND DIMNAH.'[1]

[1] The names are corruptions of the Indian names of the two jackals, Karaṭak and Damanak, who take a principal part in the first of the fables.

These tales, though originally Buddhist, became great favourites among the Arabs; and as the Arabs were gradually brought into contact with Europeans, and penetrated into the South of Europe, they brought the stories with them; and we soon afterwards find them translated into Western tongues. It would be impossible within the limits of this preface to set out in full detail the intricate literary history involved in this statement; and while I must refer the student to the Tables appended to this Introduction for fuller information, I can only give here a short summary of the principal facts.

It is curious to notice that it was the Jews to whom we owe the earliest versions. Whilst their mercantile pursuits took them much amongst the followers of the Prophet, and the comparative nearness of their religious beliefs led to a freer intercourse than was usually possible between Christians and Moslems, they were naturally attracted by a kind of literature such as this—Oriental in morality, amusing in style, and perfectly free from Christian legend and from Christian dogma. It was also the kind of literature which travellers would most easily become acquainted with, and we need not therefore be surprised to hear that a Jew, named Symeon Seth, about 1080 A.D., made the first translation into a European language, viz. into modern Greek. Another

Jew, about 1250, made a translation of a slightly different recension of the 'Kalilah and Dimnah' into Hebrew; and a third, John of Capua, turned this Hebrew version into Latin between 1263 and 1278. At about the same time as the Hebrew version, another was made direct from the Arabic into Spanish, and a fifth into Latin; and from these five versions translations were afterwards made into German, Italian, French, and English.

The title of the second Latin version just mentioned is very striking—it is "Æsop the Old." To the translator, Baldo, it evidently seemed quite in order to ascribe these new stories to the traditional teller of similar stories in ancient times; just as witty sayings of more modern times have been collected into books ascribed to the once venerable Joe Miller. Baldo was neither sufficiently enlightened to consider a good story the worse for being an old one, nor sufficiently scrupulous to hesitate at giving his new book the advantage it would gain from its connexion with a well-known name.

Is it true, then, that the so-called Æsop's Fables—so popular still, in spite of many rivals, among our Western children—are merely adaptations from tales invented long ago to please and to instruct the child-like people of the East? I think I can give an answer, though not a complete answer, to the question.

Æsop himself is several times mentioned in classical literature, and always as the teller of stories or fables. Thus Plato says that Socrates in his imprisonment occupied himself by turning the stories (literally myths) of Æsop into verse:[1] Aristophanes four times refers to his tales:[2] and Aristotle quotes in one form a fable of his, which Lucian quotes in another.[3] In accordance with these references, classical historians fix the date of Æsop in the sixth century B.C.;[4] but some modern critics, relying on the vagueness and inconsistency of the traditions, have denied his existence altogether. This is, perhaps, pushing scepticism too far; but it may be admitted that he left no written works, and it is quite certain that if he did, they have been irretrievably lost.

Notwithstanding this, a learned monk of Constantinople, named PLANUDES, and the author also of numerous other works, did not hesitate, in the first half of the fourteenth century, to write a work which he called a collection of Æsop's Fables. This was first printed at Milan at the end of the fifteenth century;

[1] Phædo, p. 61. Comp. Bentley, Dissertation on the Fables of Æsop, p. 136.

[2] Vespæ, 566, 1259, 1401, and foll.; and Aves, 651 and foll.

[3] Arist. de part. anim., iii. 2; Lucian Nigr., 32.

[4] Herodotus (ii. 134) makes him contemporary with King Amasis of Egypt, the beginning of whose reign is placed in 569 B.C.; Plutarch (Sept. Sap. Conv., 152) makes him contemporary with Solon, who is reputed to have been born in 638 B.C.; and Diogenes Laertius (i. 72) says that he flourished about the fifty-second Olympiad, *i.e.* 572–569 B.C. Compare *Clinton*, Fast. Hell. i. 237 (under the year B.C. 572) and i. 239 (under B.C. 534).

and two other supplementary collections have subsequently appeared.[1] From these, and especially from the work of Planudes, all our so-called Æsop's Fables are derived.

Whence then did Planudes and his fellow-labourers draw their tales? This cannot be completely answered till the source of each one of them shall have been clearly found, and this has not yet been completely done. But Oriental and classical scholars have already traced a goodly number of them; and the general results of their investigations may be shortly stated.

BABRIUS, a Greek poet, who probably lived in the first century before Christ, wrote in verse a number of fables, of which a few fragments were known in the Middle Ages.[2] The complete work was fortunately discovered by Mynas, in the year 1824, at Mount Athos; and both Bentley and Tyrwhitt from the fragments, and Sir George Cornewall Lewis in his well-known edition of the whole work, have shown that several of Planudes' Fables are also to be found in Babrius.[3]

[1] One at Heidelberg in 1610, and the other at Paris in 1810. There is a complete edition of all these fables, 231 in number, by T. Gl. Schneider, Breslau, 1812.

[2] See the editions by *De Furia*, Florence, 1809; *Schneider*, in an appendix to his edition of Æsop's Fables, Breslau, 1812; *Berger*, München, 1816; *Knoch*, Halle, 1835; and *Lewis*, Philolog. Museum, 1832, i. 280–304.

[3] *Bentley*, loc. cit.; *Tyrwhitt*, De Babrio, etc., Lond., 1776. The editions of the newly-found MS. are by *Lachmann*, 1845; *Orelli* and *Baiter*, 1845; *G. C. Lewis*, 1846; and *Schneidewin*, 1853.

It is possible, also, that the Æsopean fables of the Latin poet PHÆDRUS, who in the title of his work calls himself a freedman of Augustus, were known to Planudes. But the work of Phædrus, which is based on that of Babrius, existed only in very rare MSS. till the end of the sixteenth century,[1] and may therefore have easily escaped the notice of Planudes.

On the other hand, we have seen that versions of Buddhist Birth Stories, and other Indian tales, had appeared in Europe before the time of Planudes in Greek, Latin, Hebrew, and Spanish; and many of his stories have been clearly traced back to this source.[2] Further, as I shall presently show, some of the fables of Babrius and Phædrus, found in Planudes, were possibly derived by those authors from Buddhist sources. And lastly, other versions of the Jātakas, besides those which have been mentioned as coming through the Arabs, had reached Europe long before the time of Planudes; and some more of his stories have been traced back to Buddhist sources through these channels also.

[1] It was first edited by *Pithou*, in 1596; also by *Orelli*, Zürich, 1831. Comp. *Oesterley*, 'Phædrus und die Æsop. Fabel im Mittelalter.'

[2] By *Silvestre de Sacy*, in his edition of Kalilah and Dimnah, Paris, 1816; *Loiseleur Deslongchamps*, in his 'Essai sur les Fables Indiennes, et sur leur Introd. en Europe,' Paris, 1838; Professor *Benfey*, in his edition of the Pañca Tantra, Leipzig, 1859; Professor *Max Müller*, 'On the Migration of Fables,' *Contemporary Review*, July, 1870; Professor *Weber*, 'Ueber den Zusammenhang indischer Fabeln mit Griechischen,' Indische Studien, iii. 337 and foll.; *Adolf Wagener*, 'Essai sur les rapports entre les apologues de l'Inde et de la Grèce,' 1853; *Otto Keller*, 'Ueber die Geschichte der Griechischen Fabeln,' 1862.

What is at present known, then, with respect to the so-called Æsop's fables, amounts to this—that none of them are really Æsopean at all; that the collection was first formed in the Middle Ages; that a large number of them have been already traced back, in various ways, to our Buddhist Jātaka book; and that almost the whole of them are probably derived, in one way or another, from Indian sources.

It is perhaps worthy of mention, as a fitting close to the history of the so-called Æsop's Fables, that those of his stories which Planudes borrowed indirectly from India have at length been restored to their original home, and bid fair to be popular even in this much-altered form. For not only has an Englishman translated a few of them into several of the many languages spoken in the great continent of India,[1] but Narāyan Balkrishṇa Godpole, B.A., one of the Masters of the Government High School at Ahmadnagar, has lately published a second edition of his translation into Sanskrit of the common English version of the successful spurious compilation of the old monk of Constantinople!

[1] *J. Gilchrist*, 'The Oriental Fabulist, or Polyglot Translations of Æsop's and other Ancient Fables from the English Language into Hindustani, Persian, Arabic, Bhakka, Bongla, Sanscrit, etc., in the Roman Character,' Calcutta, 1803.

THE BARLAAM AND JOSAPHAT LITERATURE.

A complete answer to the question with which the last digression started can only be given when each one of the two hundred and thirty-one fables of Planudes and his successors shall have been traced back to its original author. But—whatever that complete answer may be—the discoveries just pointed out are at least most strange and most instructive. And yet, if I mistake not, the history of the Jātaka Book contains hidden amongst its details a fact more unexpected and more striking still.

In the eighth century the Khalif of Bagdad was that Almansur at whose court was written the Arabic book Kalilah and Dimnah, afterwards translated by the learned Jews I have mentioned into Hebrew, Latin, and Greek. A Christian, high in office at his court, afterwards became a monk, and is well known, under the name of St. John of Damascus, as the author in Greek of many theological works in defence of the orthodox faith. Among these is a religious romance called 'Barlaam and Jōasaph,' giving the history of an Indian prince who was converted by Barlaam and became a hermit. This history, the reader will be surprised to learn, is taken from the life of the Buddha; and Joasaph is merely the Buddha under another name, the word Joasaph, or Josaphat, being simply a corruption of the word Bodisat, that title of the future Buddha so constantly repeated in the Buddhist Birth Stories.[1] Now a life of the Buddha forms the introduction to our Jātaka Book, and St. John's romance also contains a number of fables and stories, most of which have been traced back to the same source.[2]

This book, the first religious romance published in a Western language, became very popular indeed, and, like the Arabic Kalilah and Dimnah, was translated into many other European languages. It exists in Latin, French, Italian, Spanish, German, English, Swedish, and Dutch. This will show how widely it was read, and how much its moral tone pleased the taste of the Middle Ages. It was also translated as early as 1204 into Icelandic, and has even been published in the Spanish dialect used in the Philippine Islands!

Now it was a very ancient custom among Christians to recite at the most sacred part of their most sacred service (in the so-called Canon of the Mass, immediately

[1] Joasaph is in Arabic written also Yūdasatf; and this, through a confusion between the Arabic letters *Y* and *B*, is for Bodisat. See, for the history of these changes, Reinaud, 'Memoire sur l'Inde,' 1849, p. 91; quoted with approbation by Weber, 'Indische Streifen,' iii. 57.

[2] The Buddhist origin was first pointed out by Laboulaye in the *Debats*, July, 1859; and more fully by Liebrecht, in the 'Jahrbuch für romanische und englische Literatur,' 1860. See also Littré, *Journal des Savans*, 1865, who fully discusses, and decides in favour of the romance being really the work of St. John of Damascus. I hope, in a future volume, to publish a complete analysis of St. John's work; pointing out the resemblances between it and the Buddhist lives of Gotama, and giving parallel passages wherever the Greek adopts, not only the Buddhist ideas, but also Buddhist expressions.

before the consecration of the Host) the names of deceased saints and martyrs. Religious men of local celebrity were inserted for this purpose in local lists, called Diptychs, and names universally honoured throughout Christendom appeared in all such catalogues. The confessors and martyrs so honoured are now said to be *canonized*, that is, they have become enrolled among the number of Christian saints mentioned in the 'Canon,' whom it is the duty of every Catholic to revere, whose intercession may be invoked, who may be chosen as patron saints, and in whose honour images and altars and chapels may be set up.[1]

For a long time it was permitted to the local ecclesiastics to continue the custom of inserting such names in their 'Diptychs,' but about 1170 a decretal of Pope Alexander III. confined the power of canonization, as far as the Roman Catholics were concerned,[2] to the Pope himself. From the different Diptychs various martyrologies, or lists of persons so to be commemorated in the 'Canon,' were composed to supply the place of the merely local lists or Diptychs. For as time went on, it began to be considered more and more improper

[1] *Pope Benedict XIV.* in 'De servorum Dei beatificatione et beatorum canonisatione,' lib. i. cap. 45; *Regnier*, 'De ecclesiâ Christi,' in Migne's Theol. Curs. Compl. iv. 710.

[2] Decret. Greg., Lib. iii. Tit. xlvi., confirmed and explained by decrees of Urban VIII. (13th March, 1625, and 5th July, 1634) and of Alexander VII. (1659).

to insert new names in so sacred a part of the Church prayers; and the old names being well known, the Diptychs fell into disuse. The names in the Martyrologies were at last no longer inserted in the Canon, but are repeated in the service called the 'Prime'; though the term 'canonized' was still used of the holy men mentioned in them. And when the increasing number of such Martyrologies threatened to lead to confusion, and to throw doubt on the exclusive power of the Popes to canonize, Pope Sixtus the Fifth (1585–1590) authorized a particular Martyrologium, drawn up by Cardinal Baronius, to be used throughout the Western Church. In that work are included not only the saints first canonized at Rome, but all those who, having been already canonized elsewhere, were then acknowledged by the Pope and the College of Rites to be saints of the Catholic Church of Christ. Among such, under the date of the 27th of November, are included "The holy Saints Barlaam and Josaphat, of India, on the borders of Persia, whose wonderful acts Saint John of Damascus has described."[1]

Where and when they were first canonized, I have been unable, in spite of much investigation, to ascertain. Petrus de Natalibus, who was Bishop of Equilium,

[1] p. 177 of the edition of 1873, bearing the official approval of Pope Pius IX., or p. 803 of the Cologne edition of 1610.

the modern Jesolo, near Venice, from 1370 to 1400, wrote a Martyrology called 'Catalogus Sanctorum'; and in it, among the 'saints,' he inserts both Barlaam and Josaphat, giving also a short account of them derived from the old Latin translation of St. John of Damascus.[1] It is from this work that Baronius, the compiler of the authorized Martyrology now in use, took over the names of these two saints, Barlaam and Josaphat. But, so far as I have been able to ascertain, they do not occur in any martyrologies or lists of saints of the Western Church older than that of Petrus de Natalibus.

In the corresponding manual of worship still used in the Greek Church, however, we find, under August 26, the name 'of the holy Iosaph, son of Abenēr, king of India.'[2] Barlaam is not mentioned, and is not therefore recognized as a saint in the Greek Church. No history is added to the simple statement I have quoted; and I do not know on what authority it rests. But there is no doubt that it is in the East, and probably among the records of the ancient church of Syria, that a final solution of this question should be sought.[3]

Some of the more learned of the numerous writers

[1] Cat. Sanct., Leyden ed. 1542, p. cliii.

[2] p. 160 of the part for the month of August of the authorized Μηναῖον of the Greek Church, published at Constantinople, 1843: "Τοῦ ὁσίου Ἰωάσαφ, υἱοῦ Ἀβενὴρ τοῦ βασιλέως τῆς Ἰνδίας."

[3] For the information in the last three pages I am chiefly indebted to my father, the Rev. T. W. Davids, without whose generous aid I should not have attempted to touch this obscure and difficult question.

who translated or composed new works on the basis of the story of Josaphat, have pointed out in their notes that he had been canonized;[1] and the hero of the romance is usually called St. Josaphat in the titles of these works, as will be seen from the Table of the Josaphat literature below. But Professor Liebrecht, when identifying Josaphat with the Buddha, took no notice of this; and it was Professor Max Müller, who has done so much to infuse the glow of life into the dry bones of Oriental scholarship, who first pointed out the strange fact—almost incredible, were it not for the completeness of the proof—that Gotama the Buddha, under the name of St. Josaphat, is now officially recognized and honoured and worshipped throughout the whole of Catholic Christendom as a Christian saint!

I have now followed the Western history of the Buddhist Book of Birth Stories along two channels only. Space would fail me, and the reader's patience perhaps too, if I attempted to do more. But I may mention that the inquiry is not by any means exhausted. A learned Italian has proved that a good many of the stories of the hero known throughout Europe as Sinbad the Sailor are derived from the same inexhaustible treasury of stories witty and wise;[2] and a

[1] See, for instance, Billius, and the Italian Editor of 1734.

[2] *Comparetti*, 'Ricerche intorne al Libro di Sindibad,' Milano, 1869. Compare *Landsberger*, 'Die Fabeln des Sophos,' Posen, 1859.

similar remark applies also to other well-known Tales included in the Arabian Nights.[1] La Fontaine, whose charming versions of the Fables are so deservedly admired, openly acknowledges his indebtedness to the French versions of Kalilah and Dimnah; and Professor Benfey and others have traced the same stories, or ideas drawn from them, to Poggio, Boccaccio, Gower, Chaucer, Spenser, and many other later writers. Thus, for instance, the three caskets and the pound of flesh in 'The Merchant of Venice,' and the precious jewel which in 'As You Like It' the venomous toad wears in his head,[2] are derived from the Buddhist tales. In a similar way it has been shown that tales current among the Hungarians and the numerous peoples of Slavonic race have been derived from Buddhist sources, through translations made by or for the Huns, who penetrated in the time of Genghis Khān into the East of Europe.[3] And finally yet other Indian tales, not included in the Kalilag and Damnag literature, have been brought into the opposite corner of Europe, by the Arabs of Spain.[4]

---

[1] See Benfey, Pantscha Tantra, vol. i., Introduction, *passim*.

[2] Act ii. scene 1. Professor Benfey, in his Pantscha Tantra, i. 213–220, has traced this idea far and wide. Dr. Dennys, in his 'Folklore of China,' gives the Chinese Buddhist version of it.

[3] See Benfey's Introduction to Pañca Tantra, §§ 36, 39, 71, 92, 166, 186. Mr. Ralston's forthcoming translation of Tibetan stories will throw further light on this, at present, rather obscure subject.

[4] See, for example, the Fable translated below, pp. 275–278.

There is only one other point on which a few words should be said. I have purposely chosen as specimens one Buddhist Birth Story similar to the Judgment of Solomon; two which are found also in Babrius; and one which is found also in Phædrus. How are these similarities, on which the later history of Indian Fables throws no light, to be explained?

As regards the cases of Babrius and Phædrus, it can only be said that the Greeks who travelled with Alexander to India may have taken the tales there, but they may equally well have brought them back. We only know that at the end of the fourth, and still more in the third century before Christ, there was constant travelling to and fro between the Greek dominions in the East and the adjoining parts of India, which were then Buddhist, and that the Birth Stories were already popular among the Buddhists in Afghanistan, where the Greeks remained for a long time. Indeed, the very region which became the seat of the Græco-Bactrian kings takes, in all the Northern versions of the Birth Stories, the place occupied by the country of Kāsi in the Pāli text,—so that the scene of the tales is laid in that district. And among the innumerable Buddhist remains still existing there, a large number are connected with the Birth Stories.[1] It is also in this very

[1] The legend of Sumedha's self-abnegation (see below, pp. 11–13) is laid near Jelālabad; and Mr. William Simpson has discovered on the spot two bas-reliefs representing the principal incident in the legend.

district, and under the immediate successor of Alexander, that the original of the 'Kalilah and Dimnah' was said by its Arabian translators to have been written by Bidpai. It is possible that a smaller number of similar stories were also current among the Greeks; and that they not only heard the Buddhist ones, but told their own. But so far as the Greek and the Buddhist stories can at present be compared, it seems to me that the internal evidence is in favour of the Buddhist versions being the originals from which the Greek versions were adapted. Whether more than this can be at present said is very doubtful: when the Jātakas are all published, and the similarities between them and classical stories shall have been fully investigated, the contents of tho stories may enable criticism to reach a more definite conclusion.

The case of Solomon's judgment is somewhat different. If there were only one fable in Babrius or Phædrus identical with a Buddhist Birth Story, we should suppose merely that the same idea had occurred to two different minds; and there would thus be no necessity to postulate any historical connexion. Now the similarity of the two judgments stands, as far as I know, in complete isolation; and the story is not so curious but that two writers may have hit upon the same idea. At the same time, it is just possible that when the Jews were in Babylon they may have told, or heard, the story.

Had we met with this story in a book unquestionably later than the Exile, we might suppose that they heard the story there; that some one repeating it had ascribed the judgment to King Solomon, whose great wisdom was a common tradition among them; and that it had thus been included in their history of that king. But we find it in the Book of Kings, which is usually assigned to the time of Jeremiah, who died during the Exile; and it should be remembered that the chronicle in question was based for the most part on traditions current much earlier among the Jewish people, and probably on earlier documents.

If, on the other hand, they told it there, we may expect to find some evidence of the fact in the details of the story as preserved in the Buddhist story-books current in the North of India, and more especially in the Buddhist countries bordering on Persia. Now Dr. Dennys, in his '*Folklore of China*,' has given us a Chinese Buddhist version of a similar judgment, which is most probably derived from a Northern Buddhist Sanskrit original; and though this version is very late, and differs so much in its details from those of both the Pāli and Hebrew tales that it affords no basis itself for argument, it yet holds out the hope that we may discover further evidence of a decisive character. This hope is confirmed by the occurrence of a similar tale in the *Gesta Romanorum*, a mediæval work which quotes Barlaam and Josaphat, and is otherwise largely indebted in an indirect way to Buddhist sources.[1] It is true that the basis of the judgment in that story is not the love of a mother to her son, but the love of a son to his father. But that very difference is encouraging. The orthodox compilers of the 'Gests of the Romans'[2] dared not have so twisted the sacred record. They could not therefore have taken it from our Bible. Like all their other tales, however, this one was borrowed from somewhere; and its history, when discovered, may be expected to throw some light on this inquiry.

I should perhaps point out another way in which this tale may possibly be supposed to have wandered from the Jews to the Buddhists, or from India to the Jews. The land of Ophir was probably in India. The Hebrew names of the apes and peacocks said to have been brought thence by Solomon's coasting-vessels are merely corruptions of Indian names; and Ophir must therefore have been either an Indian port (and if so, almost certainly at the mouth of the Indus, afterwards a Buddhist country), or an entrepot, further west,

[1] No. xlv. p. 80 of Swan and Hooper's popular edition, 1877; No. xlii. p. 167 of the critical edition published for the Early English Text Society in 1879 by S. J. H. Herrtage, who has added a valuable historical note at p. 477.

[2] This adaptation of the Latin title is worthy of notice. It of course means 'Deeds'; but as most of the stories are more or less humorous, the word *Gest*, now spelt *Jest*, acquired its present meaning.

for Indian trade. But the very gist of the account of Solomon's expedition by sea is its unprecedented and hazardous character; it would have been impossible even for him without the aid of Phœnician sailors; and it was not renewed by the Hebrews till after the time when the account of the judgment was recorded in the Book of Kings. Any intercourse between his servants and the people of Ophir must, from the difference of language, have been of the most meagre extent; and we may safely conclude that it was not the means of the migration of our tale. It is much more likely, if the Jews heard or told the Indian story at all, and before the time of the captivity, that the way of communication was overland. There is every reason to believe that there was a great and continual commercial intercourse between East and West from very early times by way of Palmyra and Mesopotamia. Though the intercourse by sea was not continued after Solomon's time, gold of Ophir,[1] ivory, jade, and Eastern gems still found their way to the West; and it would be an interesting task for an Assyrian or Hebrew scholar to trace the evidence of this ancient overland route in other ways.

[1] Psalm xiv. 9; Isaiah xiii. 12; Job xxii. 24, xxviii. 16.

SUMMARY.

To sum up what can at present be said on the connexion between the Indian tales, preserved to us in the Book of Buddhist Birth Stories, and their counterparts in the West:—

1. In a few isolated passages of Greek and other writers, earlier than the invasion of India by Alexander the Great, there are references to a legendary Æsop, and perhaps also allusions to stories like some of the Buddhist ones.

2. After Alexander's time a number of tales also found in the Buddhist collection became current in Greece, and are preserved in the poetical versions of Babrius and Phædrus. They are probably of Buddhist origin.

3. From the time of Babrius to the time of the first Crusade no migration of Indian tales to Europe can be proved to have taken place. About the latter time a translation into Arabic of a Persian work containing tales found in the Buddhist book was translated by Jews into Greek, Hebrew, and Latin. Translations of these versions afterwards appeared in all the principal languages of Europe.

4. In the eleventh or twelfth century a translation was made into Latin of the legend of Barlaam and

Josaphat, a Greek romance written in the eighth century by St. John of Damascus on the basis of the Buddhist Jātaka book. Translations, poems, and plays founded on this work were rapidly produced throughout Western Europe.

5. Other Buddhist stories not included in either of the works mentioned in the two last paragraphs were introduced into Europe both during the Crusades and also during the dominion of the Arabs in Spain.

6. Versions of other Buddhist stories were introduced into Eastern Europe by the Huns under Genghis Khān.

7. The fables and stories introduced through these various channels became very popular during the Middle Ages, and were used as the subjects of numerous sermons, story-books, romances, poems, and edifying dramas. Thus extensively adopted and circulated, they had a considerable influence on the revival of literature, which, hand in hand with the revival of learning, did so much to render possible and to bring about the Great Reformation. The character of the hero of them—the Buddha, in his last or in one or other of his supposed previous births—appealed so strongly to the sympathies, and was so attractive to the minds of mediæval Christians, that he became, and has ever since remained, an object of Christian worship. And a collection of these and similar stories—wrongly, but very naturally, ascribed to

a famous story-teller of the ancient Greeks—has become the common property, the household literature, of all the nations of Europe; and, under the name of Æsop's Fables, has handed down, as a first moral lesson-book and as a continual feast for our children in the West, tales first invented to please and to instruct our far-off cousins in the distant East.

PART II.

ON THE HISTORY OF THE BIRTH STORIES IN INDIA.

In the previous part of this Introduction I have attempted to point out the resemblances between certain Western tales and the Buddhist Birth Stories, to explain the reason of those resemblances, and to trace the history of the Birth Story literature in Europe. Much remains yet to be done to complete this interesting and instructive history; but the general results can already be stated with a considerable degree of certainty, and the literature in which further research will have to be made is accessible in print in the public libraries of Europe.

For the history in India of the Jātaka Book itself, and of the stories it contains, so little has been done, that one may say it has still to be written; and the authorities for further research are only to be found in manuscripts very rare in Europe, and written in languages for the most part but little known. Much of what follows is necessarily therefore very incomplete and provisional.

In some portions of the Brāhmanical literature, later than the Vedas, and probably older than Buddhism, there are found myths and legends of a character somewhat similar to a few of the Buddhist ones. But, so far as I know, no one of these has been traced either in Europe or in the Buddhist Collection.

On the other hand, there is every reason to hope that in the older portions of the Buddhist Scriptures a considerable number of the tales also included in the Jātaka Book will be found in identical or similar forms; for even in the few fragments of the Piṭakas as yet studied, several Birth Stories have already been discovered.[1] These occur in isolated passages, and, except the story of King Mahā Sudassana, have not as yet become Jātakas,—that is, no character in the story is

[1] Thus, for instance, the Maṇi Kaṇṭha Jātaka (Fausböll, No. 253) is taken from a story which is in both the Pāli and the Chinese versions of the Vinaya Piṭaka (Oldenberg, p. xlvi); the Tittira Jātaka (Fausböll, No. 37, translated below) occurs almost word for word in the Culla Vagga (vi. 6, 3–5); the Khandhavatta Jātaka (Fausböll, No. 203) is a slightly enlarged version of Culla Vagga, v. 6; the Sukhavihāri Jātaka (Fausböll, No. 10, translated below) is founded on a story in the Culla Vagga (vii. 1, 4–6); the Mahā-sudassana Jātaka (Fausböll, No. 95) is derived from the Sutta of the same name in the Dīgha Nikāya (translated by me in 'Sacred Books of the East,' vol. ix.); the Makhā Deva Jātaka (Fausböll, No. 9, translated below) from the Sutta of the same name in the Majjhima Nikāya (No. 83); and the Sakuṇagghi Jātaka (Fausböll, No. 168), from a parable in the Satipaṭṭhāna Vagga of the Saŋyutta Nikāya.

identified with the Buddha in one or other of his supposed previous births. But one book included in the Pāli Piṭakas consists entirely of real Jātaka stories, all of which are found in our Collection.

The title of this work is Cariyā-piṭaka; and it is constructed to show when, and in what births, Gotama had acquired the Ten Great Perfections (Generosity, Goodness, Renunciation, Wisdom, Firmness, Patience, Truth, Resolution, Kindness, and Equanimity), without which he could not have become a Buddha. In striking analogy with the modern view, that true growth in moral and intellectual power is the result of the labours, not of one only, but of many successive generations; so the qualifications necessary for the making of a Buddha, like the characters of all the lesser mortals, cannot be acquired during, and do not depend upon the actions of, one life only, but are the last result of many deeds performed through a long series of consecutive lives.[1]

To each of the first two of these Ten Perfections a whole chapter of this work is devoted, giving in verse ten examples of the previous births in which the Bodisat or future Buddha had practised Generosity and Goodness respectively. The third chapter gives only fifteen

[1] See on this belief below, pp. 54–58, where the verses 259–269 are quotations from the Cariyā Piṭaka.

examples of the lives in which he acquired the other eight of the Perfections. It looks very much as if the original plan of the unknown author had been to give ten Birth Stories for each of the Ten Perfections. And, curiously enough, the Northern Buddhists have a tradition that the celebrated teacher Asvagosha began to write a work giving ten Births for each of the Ten Perfections, but died when he had versified only thirty-four.[1] Now there is a Sanskrit work called JĀTAKA MĀLĀ, as yet unpublished, but of which there are several MSS. in Paris and in London, consisting of thirty-five Birth Stories in mixed prose and verse, in illustration of the Ten Perfections.[2] It would be premature to attempt to draw any conclusions from these coincidences, but the curious reader will find in a Table below a comparative view of the titles of the Jātakas comprised in the Cariyā Piṭaka and in the Jātaka Mālā.[3]

There is yet another work in the Pāli Piṭakas which constantly refers to the Jātaka theory. The BUDDHAVAŊSA, which is a history of all the Buddhas, gives an account also of the life of the Bodisat in the character he

[1] *Tāranātha's* 'Geschichte des Buddhismus' (a Tibetan work of the eighteenth century, translated into German by Schiefner), p. 92.
[2] *Fausböll's* 'Five Jātakas,' pp. 58–68, where the full text of one Jātaka is given, and *Léon Feer*, 'Etude sur les Jātakas,' p. 57.
[3] See Table, below.

filled during the lifetime of each of twenty-four of the previous Buddhas. It is on that work that a great part of the Pāli Introduction to our Jātaka Book is based, and most of the verses in the first fifty pages of the present translation are quotations from the Buddha-vaŋsa. From this source we thus have authority for twenty-four Birth Stories, corresponding to the first twenty-four of the twenty-seven previous Buddhas,[1] besides the thirty-four in illustration of the Perfections, and the other isolated ones I have mentioned.

Beyond this it is impossible yet to state what proportion of the stories in the Jātaka Book can thus be traced back to the earlier Pāli Buddhist literature; and it would be out of place to enter here upon any lengthy discussion of the difficult question as to the date of those earlier records. The provisional conclusions as to the age of the Sutta and Vinaya reached by Dr. Oldenberg in the very able introduction prefixed to his edition of the text of the Mahā Vagga, and summarized at p. xxxviii of that work, will be sufficient for our present purposes. It may be taken as so highly probable as to be almost certain, that all those Birth Stories, which are not only found in the so-called Jātaka Book itself, but are also referred to in these other parts of the

[1] See the list of these Buddhas below, p. 52, where it will be seen that for the last three Buddhas we have no Birth Story.

Pāli Piṭakas, are at least older than the Council of Vesāli.[1]

The Council of Vesāli was held about a hundred years after Gotama's death, to settle certain disputes as to points of discipline and practice which had arisen among the members of the Order. The exact date of Gotama's death is uncertain;[2] and in the tradition regarding the length of the interval between that event and the Council, the 'hundred years' is of course a round number. But we can allow for all possibilities, and still keep within the bounds of certainty, if we fix the date of the Council of Vesāli at within thirty years of 350 B.C.

The members of the Buddhist Order of Mendicants were divided at that Council—as important for the history of Buddhism as the Council of Nice is for the history of Christianity—into two parties. One side advocated the relaxation of the rules of the Order in ten particular matters, the others adopted the stricter view. In the accounts of the matter, which we at present only possess from the successors of the stricter party (or,

[1] This will hold good though the Buddhavaṃsa and the Cariyā Piṭaka should turn out to be later than most of the other books contained in the Three Pāli Piṭakas. That the stories they contain have already become Jātakas, whereas in most of the other cases above quoted the stories are still only parables, would seem to lead to this conclusion; and the fact that they have preserved some very ancient forms (such as locatives in *i*) may merely be due to the fact that they are older, not in matter and ideas, but only in form. Compare what is said below as to the verses in the Birth Stories.

[2] The question is discussed at length in my '*Ancient Coins and Measures of Ceylon*' in 'Numismata Orientalia,' vol. i.

as they call themselves, the orthodox party), it is acknowledged that the other, the laxer side, were in the majority; and that when the older and more influential members of the Order decided in favour of the orthodox view, the others held a council of their own, called, from the numbers of those who attended it, the Great Council.

Now the oldest Ceylon Chronicle, the Dīpavaŋsa, which contains the only account as yet published of what occurred at the Great Council, says as follows:[1]—

"The monks of the Great Council turned the religion upside down;
They broke up the original Scriptures, and made a new recension;
A discourse put in one place they put in another;
They distorted the sense and the teaching of the Five Nikāyas.
Those monks—knowing not what had been spoken at length, and what concisely,
What was the obvious, and what was the higher meaning—
Attached new meaning to new words, as if spoken by the Buddha,
And destroyed much of the spirit by holding to the shadow of the letter.
In part they cast aside the Sutta and the Vinaya so deep,
And made an imitation Sutta and Vinaya, changing this to that.

[1] Dīpavaŋsa, V. 32 and foll.

The Pariwāra abstract, and the Six Books of Abhidhamma;
The Paṭisambhidā, the Niddesa, *and a portion of the Jātaka*—
So much they put aside, and made others in their place!" . . . .

The animus of this description is sufficiently evident; and the Dīpavaŋsa, which cannot have been written earlier than the fourth century after the commencement of our era, is but poor evidence of the events of seven centuries before. But it is the best we have; it is acknowledged to have been based on earlier sources, and it is at least reliable evidence that, according to Ceylon tradition, a book called the Jātaka existed at the time of the Councils of Vesāli.

As the Northern Buddhists are the successors of those who held the Great Council, we may hope before long to have the account of it from the other side, either from the Sanskrit or from the Chinese.[1] Meanwhile it is important to notice that the fact of a Book of Birth Stories having existed at a very early date is confirmed, not only by such stories being found in other parts of the Pāli Piṭakas, but also by ancient monuments.

Among the most interesting and important discoveries

[1] There are several works enumerated by Mr. Beal in his Catalogue of Chinese Buddhistic Works in the India Office Library (see especially pp. 93–97, and pp. 107-109), from which we might expect to derive this information.

which we owe to recent archæological researches in India must undoubtedly be reckoned those of the Buddhist carvings on the railings round the dome-shaped relic shrines of Sānchi, Amaravatī, and Bharhut. There have been there found, very boldly and clearly sculptured in deep bas-relief, figures which were at first thought to represent merely scenes in Indian life. Even so their value as records of ancient civilization would have been of incalculable value; but they have acquired further importance since it has been proved that most of them are illustrations of the sacred Birth Stories in the Buddhist Jātaka book,—are scenes, that is, from the life of Gotama in his last or previous births. This would be incontestable in many cases from the carvings themselves, but it is rendered doubly sure by the titles of Jātakas having been found inscribed over a number of those of the bas-reliefs which have been last discovered — the carvings, namely, on the railing at Bharhut.

It is not necessary to turn aside here to examine into the details of these discoveries. It is sufficient for our present inquiry into the age of the Jātaka stories that these ancient bas-reliefs afford indisputable evidence that the Birth Stories were already, at the end of the third century B.C., considered so sacred that they were chosen as the subjects to be represented round the most sacred Buddhist buildings, and that they were already popularly known under the technical name of 'Jātakas.' A detailed statement of all the Jātakas hitherto discovered on these Buddhist railings, and other places, will be found in one of the Tables appended to this Introduction; and it will be noticed that several of those tales translated below in this volume had thus been chosen, more than two thousand years ago, to fill places of honour round the relic shrines of the Great Teacher.

One remarkable fact apparent from that Table will be that the Birth Stories are sometimes called in the inscriptions over the bas-reliefs by names different from those given to them in the Jātaka Book in the Pāli Piṭakas. This would seem, at first sight, to show that, although the very stories as we have them must have been known at the time when the bas-reliefs were carved, yet that the present collection, in which different names are clearly given at the end of each story, did not then exist. But, on the other hand, we not only find in the Jātaka Book itself very great uncertainty as to the names,—the same stories being called in different parts of the Book by different titles,[1]—but one of these very

[1] Thus, No. 41 is called both LOSAKA JĀTAKA and MITTA-VINDAKA JĀTAKA (Feer, 'Etude sur les Jātakas,' p. 121); No. 439 is called CATUD-VĀRA JĀTAKA and also MITTA-VINDAKA JĀTAKA (*Ibid.* p. 120); No. 57 is called VĀNARINDA JĀTAKA and also KUMBHĪLA JĀTAKA (Fausböll, vol. i.

bas-reliefs has actually inscribed over it two distinct names in full![1]

The reason for this is very plain. When a fable about a lion and a jackal was told (as in No. 157) to show the advantage of a good character, and it was necessary to choose a short title for it, it was called 'The Lion Jātaka,' or 'The Jackal Jātaka,' or even 'The Good Character Jātaka'; and when a fable was told about a tortoise, to show the evil results which follow on talkativeness (as in No. 215), the fable might as well be called 'The Chatterbox Jātaka' as 'The Tortoise Jātaka,' and the fable is referred to accordingly under both those names. It must always have been difficult, if not impossible, to fix upon a short title which should at once characterize the lesson to be taught, and the personages through whose acts it was taught; and different names would thus arise, and become interchangeable. It would be wrong therefore to attach too much importance to the difference of the names on the bas-reliefs and in the Jātaka Book. And in trans-

p. 278, and vol. ii. p. 206); No. 96 is called Telapatta Jātaka and also Takkasīla Jātaka (*Ibid.* vol. i. p. 393, and vol. i. pp. 469, 470); No. 102, there called Paṇṇika Jātaka, is the same story as No. 217, there called Seggu Jātaka; No. 30, there called Muṇika Jātaka, is the same story as No. 286, there called Sālūka Jātaka; No. 215, the Kacchapa Jātaka, is called Bahu-bhāṇi Jātaka in the Dhammapada (p. 419); and No. 157 is called Guṇa Jātaka, Sīha Jātaka, and Sigāla Jātaka.

[1] *Cunningham,* 'The Stupa of Bharhut,' pl. xlvii. The carving illustrates a fable of a cat and a cock, and is labelled both Biḍala Jātaka and Kukkuṭa Jātaka (Cat Jātaka and Cock Jātaka).

lating the titles we need not be afraid to allow ourselves a latitude similar to that which was indulged in by the early Buddhists themselves.

There is yet further evidence confirmatory of the Dīpavaŋsa tradition. The Buddhist Scriptures are sometimes spoken of as consisting of nine different divisions, or sorts of texts (Aŋgāni), of which the seventh is 'Jātakas,' or 'The Jātaka Collection' (Jātakaŋ). This division of the Sacred Books is mentioned, not only in the Dīpavaŋsa itself, and in the Sumaŋgala Vilāsinī, but also in the Aŋguttara Nikāya (one of the later works included in the Pāli Piṭakas), and in the Saddharma Puṇḍarīka (a late, but standard Sanskrit work of the Northern Buddhists).[1] It is common, therefore, to both of the two sections of the Buddhist Church; and it follows that it was probably in use before the great schism took place between them, possibly before the Council of Vesāli itself. In any case it is conclusive as to the existence of a collection of Jātakas at a very early date.

The text of the Jātaka Book, as now received among the Southern Buddhists, consists, as will be seen from the

[1] See the authorities quoted in my manual, 'Buddhism,' pp. 214, 215; and Dr. Morris, in the *Academy* for May, 1880.

translation, not only of the stories, but of an elaborate commentary, containing a detailed Explanation of the verse or verses which occur in each of the stories; an Introduction to each of them, giving the occasion on which it is said to have been told; a Conclusion, explaining the connexion between the personages in the Introductory Story and the characters in the Birth Story; and finally, a long general Introduction to the whole work. It is, in fact, an edition by a later hand of the earlier stories; and though I have called it concisely the Jātaka Book, its full title is 'The Commentary on the Jātakas.'

We do not know either the name of the author of this work, or the date when it was composed. The meagre account given at the commencement of the work itself (below, pp. 1, 2) contains all our present information on these points. Mr. Childers, who is the translator of this passage, has elsewhere ascribed the work to Buddhaghosa;[1] but I venture to think that this is, to say the least, very uncertain.

We have, in the thirty-seventh chapter of the Mahāvaŋsa,[2] a perhaps almost contemporaneous account of Buddhaghosa's literary work; and it is there distinctly stated, that after writing in India the Atthasālinī (a commentary on the Dhammasaŋginī, the first of the Six

[1] In his Dictionary, Preface, p. ix, note. [2] Turnour, pp. 250–253.

Books of the Abhidhamma Piṭaka), he went to Ceylon (about 430 A.D.) with the express intention of translating the Siŋhalese commentaries into Pāli. There he studied under the Thera Saŋghapāli, and having proved his efficiency by his great work 'The Path of Purity' (Visuddhi-Magga, a compendium of all Buddhism), he was allowed by the monks in Ceylon to carry out his wish, and translate the commentaries. The Chronicle then goes on to say that he did render 'the whole Siŋhalese Commentary' into Pāli. But it by no means follows, as has been too generally supposed, that he was the author of all the Pāli Commentaries we now possess. He translated, it may be granted, the Commentaries on the Vinaya Piṭaka and on the four great divisions (Nikāyas) of the Sutta Pitaka; but these works, together with those mentioned above, would amply justify the very general expression of the chronicler. The 'Siŋhalese Commentary' being now lost, it is impossible to say what books were and what were not included under that expression as used in the Mahāvaŋsa; and to assign any Pāli commentary, other than those just mentioned, to Buddhaghosa, some further evidence more clear than the ambiguous words of the Ceylon Chronicle should be required.

What little evidence we have as regards the particular work now in question seems to me to tend very strongly in the other direction. Buddhaghosa could scarcely have commenced his labours on the Jātaka Commentary, leaving the works I have mentioned—so much more important from his point of view—undone. Now I would ask the reader to imagine himself in Buddhaghosa's position, and then to read carefully the opening words of our Jātaka Commentary as translated below, and to judge for himself whether they could possibly be such words as Buddhaghosa would probably, under the circumstances, have written. It is a matter of feeling; but I confess I cannot think it possible that he was the author of them. Three Elders of the Buddhist Order are there mentioned with respect, but neither the name of Revata, Buddhaghosa's teacher in India, nor the name of Saŋghāpali, his teacher in Ceylon, is even referred to; and there is not the slightest allusion either to Buddhaghosa's conversion, his journey from India, the high hopes he had entertained, or the work he had already accomplished! This silence seems to me almost as convincing as such negative evidence can possibly be.

If not however by Buddhaghosa, the work must have been composed after his time; but probably not long after. It is quite clear from the account in the Mahāvaŋsa, that before he came to Ceylon the Siŋhalese commentaries had not been turned into Pāli; and on the other hand, the example he had set so well will almost certainly have been quickly followed. We know one instance at least, that of the Mahāvaŋsa itself, which would confirm this supposition; and had the present work been much later than his time, it would not have been ascribed to Buddhaghosa at all.

It is worthy of notice, perhaps, in this connexion, that the Pāli work is not a translation of the Siŋhalese Commentary. The author three times refers to a previous Jātaka Commentary, which possibly formed part of the Siŋhalese work, as a separate book;[1] and in one case mentions what it says only to overrule it.[2] Our Pāli work may have been based upon it, but cannot be said to be a mere version of it. And the present Commentary agrees almost word for word, from p. 58 to p. 124 of my translation, with the MADHURA-ATTHA-VILĀSINĪ, the Commentary on the 'Buddhavaŋsa' mentioned above, which is not usually ascribed to Buddhaghosa.[3]

The Jātaka Book is not the only Pāli Commentary which has made use of the ancient Birth Stories. They occur in numerous passages of the different exegetical works composed in Ceylon, and the only commentary of which anything is known in print, that on the

[1] Fausböll, vol. i. p. 62 and p. 488; vol. ii. p. 224.
[2] See the translation below, p. 82.
[3] I judge from *Turnour's* analysis of that work in the Journal of the Bengal Asiatic Society, 1839, where some long extracts have been translated, and the contents of other passages given in abstract.

Dhamma-padaŋ or 'Collection of Scripture Verses,' contains a considerable number of them. Mr. Fausböll has published copious extracts from this Commentary, which may be by Buddhaghosa, as an appendix to his edition of the text; and the work by Captain Rogers, entitled 'Buddhaghosa's Parables'—a translation from a Burmese book called 'Dhammapada-vatthu' (that is 'Stories connected with the Dhamma-padaŋ')—consists almost entiṛely of Jātaka tales.

In Siam there is even a rival collection of Birth Stories, which is called PAṆṆĀSA-JĀTAKAŊ ('The Fifty Jātakas'), and of which an account has been given us by M. Léon Feer;[1] and the same scholar has pointed out that isolated stories, not contained in our collection, are also to be found in the Pāli literature of that country.[2] The first hundred and fifty tales in our collection are divided into three *Paṇṇāsas*, or fifties;[3] but the Siamese collection cannot be either of these, as M. Feer has ascertained that it contains no tales beginning in the same way as any of those in either of these three 'Fifties.'

---

1 'Etude sur les Jātakas,' pp. 62-65. 2 *Ibid.* pp. 66–71.

3 This is clear from vol. i. p. 410 of Mr. Fausböll's text, where, at the end of the 100th tale, we find the words *Majjhima-paṇṇāsako nitthito*, that is, 'End of the Middle Fifty.' At the end of the 50th tale (p. 261) there is a corresponding entry, *Paṭhamo paṇṇāso*, 'First Fifty'; and though there is no such entry at the end of the 150th tale, the expression 'Middle Fifty' shows that there must have been, at one time, such a division as is above stated.

In India itself the Birth Stories survived the fall, as some of them had probably preceded the rise, of Buddhism. Not a few of them were preserved by being included in the Mahā Bhārata, the great Hindu epic which became the storehouse of Indian mythology, philosophy, and folk-lore.[1] Unfortunately, the date of the final arrangement of the Mahā Bhārata is extremely uncertain, and there is no further evidence of the continued existence of the Jātaka tales till we come to the time of the work already frequently referred to—the Pancha Tantra.

It is to the history of this book that Professor Benfey has devoted that elaborate and learned Introduction which is the most important contribution to the study of this class of literature as yet published; and I cannot do better than give in his own words his final conclusions as to the origin of this popular story-book:[2]—

"Although we are unable at present to give any certain information either as to the author or as to the date of the work, we receive, as it seems to me, no unimportant compensation in the fact, that it turned out,[3] with a certainty beyond doubt, to have been originally a Buddhist book. This followed especially from the chapter discussed in § 225. But it was already indicated by the considerable number of the fables and

[1] See, for instance, above, p. xxvii; and below, p. 185.
[2] 'Pantscha Tantra,' von *Theodor Benfey*, Leipzig, 1859, p. xi.
[3] That is, in the course of Prof. Benfey's researches.

tales contained in the work, which could also be traced in Buddhist writings. Their number, and also the relation between the form in which they are told in our work, and that in which they appear in the Buddhist writings, incline us—nay, drive us—to the conclusion that the latter were the source from which our work, within the circle of Buddhist literature, proceeded. . . . .

"The proof that our work is of Buddhist origin is of importance in two ways: firstly—on which we will not here further insist—for the history of the work itself; and secondly, for the determination of what Buddhism is. We can find in it one more proof of that literary activity of Buddhism, to which, in my articles on 'India,' which appeared in 1840,[1] I had already felt myself compelled to assign the most important place in the enlightenment and general intellectual development of India. This view has since received, from year to year, fresh confirmations, which I hope to bring together in another place; and whereby I hope to prove that the very bloom of the intellectual life of India (whether it found expression in Brahmanical or Buddhist works) proceeded substantially from Buddhism, and is contemporaneous with the epoch in which Buddhism flourished;—that is to say, from the third century before Christ to the sixth or seventh century after Christ. With that principle, said to have been proclaimed by Buddhism in its earliest years, 'that only *that* teaching of the Buddha's is true which contraveneth not sound reason,'[2] the autonomy of man's Intellect was, we may fairly say, effectively acknowledged; the whole relation between the realms of the knowable and of the unknowable was subjected to its control; and notwithstanding that the actual reasoning powers, to which the ultimate appeal was thus given, were in fact then not altogether

[1] In 'Ersch und Grüber's Encyklopædie,' especially at pp. 255 and 277.
[2] *Wassiliew*, 'Der Buddhismus,' etc., p. 68.

sound, yet the way was pointed out by which Reason could, under more favourable circumstances, begin to liberate itself from its failings. We are already learning to value, in the philosophical endeavours of Buddhism, the labours, sometimes indeed quaint, but aiming at thoroughness and worthy of the highest respect, of its severe earnestness in inquiry. And that, side by side with this, the merry jests of light, and even frivolous poetry and conversation, preserved the cheerfulness of life, is clear from the prevailing tone of our work, and still more so from the probable Buddhist origin of those other Indian story-books which have hitherto become known to us."

Professor Benfey then proceeds to show that the Pancha Tantra consisted originally, not of five, but of certainly eleven, perhaps of twelve, and just possibly of thirteen books; and that its original design was to teach princes right government and conduct.[1] The whole collection had then a different title descriptive of this design; and it was only after a part became detached from the rest that that part was called, for distinction's sake, the Pancha Tantra, or Five Books. When this occurred it is impossible to say. But it was certainly the older and larger collection, not the present Pancha Tantra, which travelled into Persia, and became the source of the whole of the extensive 'Kalilag and Damnag' literature.[2]

[1] Compare the title of the Birth Story above, p. xxii, 'A Lesson for Kings.'
[2] See above, p. xxix.

The Arabian authors of the work translated (through the ancient Persian) from this older collection assign it to a certain Bidpai; who is said to have composed it in order to instruct Dabschelim, the successor of Alexander in his Indian possessions, in worldly wisdom.[1] There may well be some truth in this tradition. And when we consider that the 'Barlaam and Josaphat' literature took its origin at the same time, and in the same place, as the 'Kalilag and Damnag' literature; that both of them are based upon Buddhist originals taken to Bagdad in the sixth century of our era; and that it is precisely such a book as the Book of Birth Stories from which they could have derived all that they borrowed; it is difficult to avoid connecting these facts together by the supposition that the work ascribed to Bidpai may, in fact, have been a selection of those Jātaka stories bearing more especially on the conduct of life, and preceded, like our own collection, by a sketch of the life of the Buddha in his last birth. Such a supposition would afford a reasonable explanation of some curious facts which have been quite inexplicable on the existing theory. If the Arabic 'Kalilah and Dimnah' was an exact translation, in our modern sense of the word translation, of an exact translation of a Buddhist work, how

[1] Knatchbull, p. 29.

comes it that the various copies of the 'Kalilah and Dimnah' differ so greatly, not only among themselves, but from the lately discovered Syriac 'Kalilag and Damnag,' which was also, according to the current hypothesis, a translation of the same original?—how comes it that in these translations from a Buddhist book there are no references to the Buddha, and no expressions on the face of them Buddhistic? If, on the other hand, the later writers had merely derived their subject-matter from a Buddhist work or works, and had composed what were in effect fresh works on the basis of such an original as has been suggested, we can understand how the different writers might have used different portions of the material before them, and might have discarded any expressions too directly in contradiction with their own religious beliefs.

The first three of those five chapters of the work ascribed to Bidpai which make up the Pancha Tantra, are also found in a form slightly different, but, on the whole, essentially the same, in two other Indian Story-books,—the KATHĀ-SARIT-SĀGARA (Ocean of the Rivers of Stories), composed in Sanskrit by a Northern Buddhist named *Somadeva* in the twelfth century, and in the well-known HITOPADESA, which is a much later work. If Somadeva had had the Pancha Tantra in its present form before him, he would probably have included the whole five books in his encyclopædic collection; and the absence from the Kathā-Sarit-Sāgara of the last two books would tend to show that when he wrote his great work the Pancha Tantra had not been composed, or at least had not reached the North of India.

Somadeva derived his knowledge of the three books he does give from the VṚIHAT-KATHĀ, a work ascribed to Guṇādhya, written in the Paiṣāchī dialect, and probably at least as early as the sixth century.[1] This work, on which Somadeva's whole poem is based, is lost. But Dr. Bühler has lately discovered another Sanskrit poem, based on that earlier work, written in Kashmīr by Kshemendra at the end of the eleventh century, and called, like its original, Vṛihat-Kathā; and as Somadeva wrote quite independently of this earlier poem, we may hope that a comparison of the two Sanskrit works will afford reliable evidence of the contents of the Old Vṛihat-Kathā.[2]

I should also mention here that another well-known work, the VETĀLA-PAÑCA-VIṄSATĪ (the Twenty-five Tales of a Demon), is contained in both the Sanskrit poems, and was therefore probably also in Guṇādhya's collection; but as no Jātaka stories have been as yet traced in it, I have simply included it for purposes of

[1] *Dr. Fitz-Edward Hall's* Vāsavadatta, pp. 22–24.
[2] *Dr. Bühler* in the Indian Antiquary, i. 302, v. 29, vi. 269.

reference in Table I., together with the most important of those of the later Indian story-books of which anything certain is at present known.

There remains only to add a few words on the mode in which the stories, whose history in Europe and in India I have above attempted to trace, are presented to us in the Jātaka Book.

Each story is introduced by another explaining where and why it was told by the Buddha; the Birth Story itself being called the *Atīta-vatthu* or Story of the Past, and the Introductory Story the *Paccuppanna-vatthu* or Story of the Present. There is another book in the Pāli Piṭakas called APADĀNAŋ, which consists of tales about the lives of the early Buddhists; and many of the Introductory Stories in the Jātaka Book (such, for instance, as the tale about Little Roadling, No. 4, or the tale about Kumāra Kassapa, No. 12) differ very little from these Apadānas. Other of the Introductory Stories (such, for instance, as No. 17 below) seem to be mere repetitions of the principal idea of the story they introduce, and are probably derived from it. That the Introductory Stories are entirely devoid of credit is clear from the fact that different Birth Stories are introduced as having been told at the same time and place, and in answer to the same question. Thus no less than ten stories are each said to have been told to a certain love-sick monk as a warning to him against his folly;[1] the closely-allied story given below as the Introduction to Birth Story No. 30 appears also as the Introduction to at least four others;[2] and there are many other instances of a similar kind.[3]

After the two stories have been told, there comes a Conclusion, in which the Buddha identifies the personages in the Birth Story with those in the Introductory Story; but it should be noticed that in one or two cases characters mentioned in the Atīta-vatthu are supposed not to have been reborn on earth at the time of the Paccuppanna-vatthu.[4] And the reader must of course avoid the mistake of importing Christian ideas into this Conclusion by supposing that the identity of the persons in the two stories is owing to the passage of a 'soul' from the one to the other. Buddhism does not teach the Transmigration of Souls. Its doctrine (which is somewhat intricate, and for a fuller statement of which I must refer to my Manual of Buddhism[5]) would be better summarized as the Transmigration of Character;

[1] Nos. 61, 62, 63, 147, 159, 193, 196, 198, 199, 263.
[2] Nos. 106, 145, 191, 286.
[3] Nos. 58, 73, 142, 194, 220, and 277, have the same Introductory Story. And so Nos. 60, 104, 116, 161. And Nos. 127, 128, 138, 173, 175.
[4] See the Pāli note at the end of Jātaka No. 91.
[5] pp. 99–106.

for it is entirely independent of the early and widely-prevalent notion of the existence within each human body of a distinct soul, or ghost, or spirit. The Bodisat, for instance, is not supposed to have a Soul, which, on the death of one body, is transferred to another; but to be the inheritor of the Character acquired by the previous Bodisats. The insight and goodness, the moral and intellectual perfection which constitute Buddhahood, could not, according to the Buddhist theory, be acquired in one lifetime: they were the accumulated result of the continual effort of many generations of successive Bodisats. The only thing which continues to exist when a man dies is his *Karma*, the result of his words and thoughts and deeds (literally his 'doing'); and the curious theory that this result is concentrated in some new individual is due to the older theory of soul.

In the case of one Jātaka (Fausböll, No. 276), the Conclusion is wholly in verse; and in several cases the Conclusion contains a verse or verses added by way of moral. Such verses, when they occur, are called *Abhisambuddha-gāthā*, or Verses spoken by the Buddha, not when he was still only a Bodisat, but when he had become a Buddha. They are so called to distinguish them from the similar verses inserted in the Birth Story, and spoken there by the Bodisat. Each story has its verse or verses, either in the *Atīta-vatthu* or in the Conclusion, and sometimes in both. The number of cases in which all the verses are *Abhisambuddha-gāthā* is relatively small (being only one in ten of the Jātakas published[1]); and the number of cases in which they occur together with verses in the *Atīta-vatthu* is very small indeed (being only five out of the three hundred Jātakas published[2]); in the remaining two hundred and sixty-five the verse or verses occur in the course of the Birth Story, and are most generally spoken by the Bodisat himself.

There are several reasons for supposing that these verses are older than the prose which now forms their setting. The Ceylon tradition goes so far as to say that the original Jātaka Book, now no longer extant, consisted of the verses alone; that the Birth Stories are Commentary upon them; and the Introductory Stories, the Conclusions and the '*Pada-gata-sannaya*,' or word-for-word explanation of the verses, are Commentary on this Commentary.[3] And archaic forms and forced

[1] Nos. 1, 2, 3, 4, 5, 28, 29, 37, 55, 56, 68, 85, 87, 88, 97, 100, 114, 136 (total, eighteen in the Eka-Nipāta); 156 (=55, 56), 196, 202, 237 (=68), 241 (total, five in the Duka-Nipāta); 255, 256, 258, 264, 284, 291, 300 (total, seven in the Tika-Nipāta, and thirty altogether).

[2] Nos. 152, 168, 179, 233, 286.

[3] This belief underlies the curious note forming the last words of the Mahāsupina Jātaka, i. 345: "Those who held the Council after the death of the Blessed One placed the lines beginning *usabhā rukkhā* in the Commentary, and then, making the other lines beginning *lābūni* into one verse, they put (the Jātaka) into the Eka-Nipāta (the chapter including all those Jātakas which have only one verse)."

constructions in the verses (in striking contrast with the regularity and simplicity of the prose parts of the book), and the corrupt state in which some of the verses are found, seem to point to the conclusion that the verses are older.

But I venture to think that, though the present form of the verses may be older than the present form of the Birth Stories, the latter, or most of the latter, were in existence first; that the verses, at least in many cases, were added to the stories after they had become current; and that the Birth Stories without verses in them at all —those enumerated in the list in note 1 on the last page, where the verses are found only in the Conclusion —are, in fact, among the oldest, if not the oldest, in the whole collection. For any one who takes the trouble to go through that list seriatim will find that it contains a considerable number of those stories which, from their being found also in the Pāli Piṭakas or in the oldest European collections, can already be proved to belong to a very early date. The only hypothesis which will reconcile these facts seems to me to be that the Birth Stories, though probably originally older than the verses they contain, were handed down in Ceylon till the time of the compilation of our present Jātaka Book, in the Siŋhalese language; whilst the verses on the other hand were not translated, but were preserved as they were received, in Pāli.

There is another group of stories which seems to be older than most of the others; those, namely, in which the Bodisat appears as a sort of chorus, a moralizer only, and not an actor in the play, whose part may have been an addition made when the story in which it occurs was adopted by the Buddhists. Such is the fable above translated of the Ass in the Lion's Skin, and most of the stories where the Bodisat is a *rukkha-devatā*—the fairy or genius of a tree.[1] But the materials are insufficient at present to put this forward as otherwise than a mere conjecture.

The arrangement of the stories in our present collection is a most unpractical one. They are classified, not according to their contents, but according to the number of verses they contain. Thus, the First division (Nipāta) includes those one hundred and fifty of the stories which have only one verse; the Second, one hundred stories, each having two verses; the Third and Fourth, each of them fifty stories, containing respectively three and four verses each; and so on, the number of stories in each division decreasing rapidly after the number of verses exceeds four; and the whole of the five hundred and fifty Jātakas being contained in twenty-two Nipātas. Even this division, depending on so unimportant a factor

[1] See, for instance, below, pp. 212, 228, 230, 317; above, p. xii; and Jātaka, No. 113.

as the number of the verses, is not logically carried out; and the round numbers of the stories in the first four divisions are made up by including in them stories which, according to the principle adopted, should not properly be placed within them. Thus several Jātakas are only mentioned in the first two Nipātas to say that they will be found in the later ones;[1] and several Jātakas given with one verse only in the First Nipāta, are given again with more verses in those that follow;[2] and occasionally a story is even repeated, with but little variation, in the same Nipāta.[3]

On the other hand, several Jātakas, which count only as one story in the present enumeration, really contain several different tales or fables. Thus, for instance, the Kulāvaka Jātaka (On Mercy to Animals)[4] consists of seven stories woven, not very closely, into one. The most striking instance of this is perhaps the Ummagga Jātaka, not yet published in the Pāli, but of which the Siŋhalese translation by the learned Baṭuwan Tudāwa

[1] Nos. 110, 111, 112, 170, 192 in the Ummagga Jātaka, and No. 264 in the Suruci Jātaka.

[2] No. 30 = No. 286. ,, 34 = ,, 216. ,, 46 = ,, 268. ,, 57 = ,, 224. No. 68 = No. 237. ,, 86 = ,, 290. ,, 102 = ,, 217. ,, 145 = ,, 198.

[3] So No. 82 = No. 104. ,, 99 = ,, 101. ,, 134 = ,, 135. ,, 195 = ,, 225. ,, 294 = ,, 295. Compare the two stories Nos. 23 and 24 translated below.

[4] Translated below, pp. 278–290.

occupies two hundred and fifty pages octavo, and consists of a very large number (I have not counted them, and there is no index, but I should think they amount to more than one hundred and fifty) of most entertaining anecdotes. Although therefore the Birth Stories are spoken of as 'The five hundred and fifty Jātakas,' this is merely a round number reached by an entirely artificial arrangement, and gives no clue to the actual number of stories. It is probable that our present collection contains altogether (including the Introductory Stories where they are not mere repetitions) between two and three thousand independent tales, fables, anecdotes, and riddles.

Nor is the number 550 any more exact (though the discrepancy in this case is not so great) if it be supposed to record, not the number of stories, but the number of distinct births of the Bodisat. In the Kulāvaka Jātaka, just referred to (the tale On Mercy to Animals), there are two consecutive births of the future Buddha; and on the other hand, none of the six Jātakas mentioned in note 1, p. lxxx, represents a distinct birth at all—the Bodisat is in them the same person as he is in the later Jātakas in which those six are contained.

From the facts as they stand it seems at present to

be the most probable explanation of the rise of our Jātaka Book to suppose that it was due to the religious faith of the Indian Buddhists of the third or fourth century B.C., who not only repeated a number of fables, parables, and stories ascribed to the Buddha, but gave them a peculiar sacredness and a special religious significance by identifying the best character in each with the Buddha himself in some previous birth. From the time when this step was taken, what had been merely parables or fables became 'Jātakas,' a word invented to distinguish, and used only of, those stories which have been thus sanctified. The earliest use of that word at present known is in the inscriptions on the Buddhist Tope at Bhārhut; and from the way in which it is there used it is clear that the word must have then been already in use for some considerable time. But when stories thus made sacred were popularly accepted among people so accustomed to literary activity as the early Buddhists, the natural consequence would be that the Jātakas should have been brought together into a collection of some kind; and the probability of this having been done at a very early date is confirmed, firstly, by the tradition of the difference of opinion concerning a Jātaka Book at the Councils of Vesāli; and secondly by the mention of a Jātaka Book in the ninefold division of the Scriptures found in the Aŋguttara Nikāya and in the Saddharma Puṇḍarīka. To the compiler of this, or of some early collection, are probably to be ascribed the Verses, which in some cases at least are later than the Stories.

With regard to some of the Jātakas, among which may certainly be included those found in the Pāli Piṭakas, there may well have been a tradition, more or less reliable, as to the time and the occasion at which they were supposed to have been uttered by the Buddha. These traditions will have given rise to the earliest Introductory Stories, in imitation of which the rest were afterwards invented; and these will then have been handed down as commentary on the Birth Stories, till they were finally made part of our present collection by its compiler in Ceylon. That (either through their later origin, or their having been much more modified in transmission) they represent a more modern point of view than the Birth Stories themselves, will be patent to every reader. There is a freshness and simplicity about the 'Stories of the Past' that is sadly wanting in the 'Stories of the Present'; so much so, that the latter (and this is also true of the whole long Introduction containing the life of the Buddha) may be compared more accurately with mediæval Legends of the Saints than with such simple stories as Æsop's Fables, which still bear a likeness to their forefathers, the 'Stories of the Past.'

The Jātakas so constituted were carried to Ceylon in the Pāli language, when Buddhism was first introduced into that island (a date that is not quite certain, but may be taken provisionally as about 200 B.C.); and the whole was there translated into and preserved in the Siŋhalese language (except the verses, which were left untranslated) until the compilation in the fifth century A.D., and by an unknown author, of the Pāli Jātaka Book, the translation of which into English is commenced in this volume.

When we consider the number of elaborate similes by which the arguments in the Pāli Suttas are enforced, there can be no reasonable doubt that the Buddha was really accustomed to teach much by the aid of parables, and it is not improbable that the compiler was quite correct in attributing to him that subtle sense of good-natured humour which led to his inventing, as occasion arose, some fable or some tale of a previous birth, to explain away existing failures in conduct among the monks, or to draw a moral from contemporaneous events. It is even already possible to point to some of the Jātakas as being probably the oldest in the collection; but it must be left to future research to carry out in ampler detail the investigation into the comparative date of each of the stories, both those which are called 'Stories of the Past' and those which are called 'Stories of the Present.'

Besides the points which the teaching of the Jātakas has in common with that of European moralists and satirists, it inculcates two lessons peculiar to itself—firstly, the powerful influence of inherited character; and secondly, the essential likeness between man and other animals. The former of these two ideas underlies both the central Buddhist doctrine of Karma and the theory of the Buddhas, views certainly common among all the early Buddhists, and therefore probably held by Gotama himself. And the latter of the two underlies and explains the sympathy with animals so conspicuous in these tales, and the frequency with which they lay stress upon the duty of kindness, and even of courtesy, to the brute creation. It is curious to find in these records of a strange and ancient faith such blind feeling after, such vague foreshadowing of beliefs only now beginning to be put forward here in the West; but it is scarcely necessary to point out that the paramount value to us now of the Jātaka stories is historical.

In this respect their value does not consist only in the evidence they afford of the intercommunion between East and West, but also, and perhaps chiefly, in the assistance which they will render to the study of folk-lore;—that is, of the beliefs and habits of men in the earlier stages of their development. The researches of Tylor and Waitz and Peschel and Lubbock and Spencer have shown us that it is by this means that it is most easily possible rightly to understand and estimate many of the habits and beliefs still current among ourselves. But the chief obstacle to a consensus of opinion in such studies is the insufficiency and inaccuracy of the authorities on which the facts depend. While the ancient literature of peoples more advanced usually ignores or passes lightly over the very details most important from this point of view, the accounts of modern travellers among the so-called savage tribes are often at best very secondary evidence. It constantly happens that such a traveller can only tell us the impression conveyed to his mind of that which his informant holds to be the belief or custom of the tribe. Such native information may be inaccurate, incomplete, or misleading; and it reaches us only after filtration through a European mind more or less able to comprehend it rightly.

But in the Jātakas we have a nearly complete picture, and quite uncorrupted and unadulterated by European intercourse, of the social life and customs and popular beliefs of the common people of Aryan tribes closely related to ourselves, just as they were passing through the first stages of civilization.

The popularity of the Jātakas as amusing stories may pass away. How can it stand against the rival claims of the fairy tales of science, and the entrancing, many-sided story of man's gradual rise and progress? But though these less fabulous and more attractive stories shall increasingly engage the attention of ourselves and of our children, we may still turn with appreciation to the ancient Book of the Buddhist Jātaka Tales as a priceless record of the childhood of our race.

I avail myself of this opportunity of acknowledging my indebtedness to several friends whose assistance has been too continuous to be specified on any particular page. Professor Childers, whose premature death was so great a blow to Pāli studies, and whose name I never think of without a feeling of reverent and grateful regret, had undertaken the translation of the Jātakas, and the first thirty-three pages are from his pen. They are the last memento of his earnest work: they stand exactly as he left them. Professor Estlin Carpenter, who takes a deep interest in this and cognate subjects, has been kind enough to read through all the proofs, and I owe to his varied scholarship many useful hints. And my especial thanks, and the thanks of any readers this work may meet with, are above all due to Professor Fausböll, without whose *editio princeps* of the Pāli text, the result of self-denying labours spread over many years, this translation would not have been undertaken.

T. W. RHYS DAVIDS.

TABLES ILLUSTRATIVE OF THE HISTORY AND MIGRATIONS OF THE BUDDHIST BIRTH STORIES.

TABLE I.

INDIAN WORKS.

1. The JĀTAKA ATTHAVAṆṆANĀ. A collection, probably first made in the third or fourth century B.C., of stories previously existing, and ascribed to the Buddha, and put into its present form in Ceylon, in the fifth century A.D. The Pāli text is being edited by Professor Fausböll, of Copenhagen; vol. i. 1877, vol. ii. 1878, vol. iii. in the press. English translation in the present work.

1*a*. Siŋhalese translation of No. 1, called PAN SIYA PANAS JĀTAKA POTA. Written in Ceylon in or about 1320 A.D.

1*b*. GUTTILA KĀWYAYA. A poetical version in Elu, or old Siŋhalese, of one of the stories in 1*a*, by *Badawættāwa Unnānse*, about 1415. Edited in Colombo, 1870, with introduction and commentary, by *Baṭuwan Tuḍāwa*.

1*c*. KUSA JĀTAKAYA. A poetical version in Elu, or old Siŋhalese, of one of the stories in 1*a*, by *Alagiawanna Mohoṭṭāle*, 1610. Edited in Colombo, with commentary, 1868.

1*d*. *An Eastern Love Story*. Translation in verse of 1*c*, by *Thomas Steele, C.C.S.*, London, 1871.

1*e*. ASADISA JĀTAKAYA. An Elu poem, by *Rājādhirāja Siṅha*, king of Ceylon in 1780.

2. The CARIYĀ PIṬAKA. A book of the Buddhist Scriptures of the fourth century B.C., containing thirty-five of the oldest above stories. See Table IV.

3. The JĀTAKA MĀLĀ. A Sanskrit work of unknown date, also containing thirty-five of the oldest stories in No. 1. See Table IV.

4. The PAṆṆĀSA-JĀTAKAŊ, or '50 Jātakas.' A Pāli work written in Siam, of unknown date and contents, but apparently distinct from No. 1. See above, p. lxvii.

5. PAÑCHA TANTRA. ? Mediæval. See above, pp. lxviii–lxxii.

Text edited by *Kosegarten*, Bonn, 1848.

Kielhorn and *Bühler*, Bombay, 1868.

6. Translations:—German, by *Benfey*, Leipzig, 1859.

7. French ,, *Dubois*, Paris, 1826.

8. ,, ,, *Lancerau*, Paris, 1871.

9. Greek ,, *Galanos* and *Typaldos*, Athens, 1851.

10. HITOPADESA. Mediæval. Compiled principally from No. 2, with additions from another unknown work.

Text edited by *Carey* and *Colebrooke*, Serampur, 1804.

Hamilton, London, 1810.

Bernstein, Breslau, 1823.

Schlegel and *Lassen*, Bonn, 1829–1831.

Nyālankar, Calcutta, 1830 and 1844.

Johnson, Hertford, 1847 and 1864, with English version.

Yates, Calcutta, 1841.

E. Arnold, Bombay, 1859 ,,

Max Müller, London, 1864–1868 ,,

11. Translations:—English, by *Wilkins*, Bath, 1787; reprinted by Nyālankar in his edition of the text.

12. ,, ,, *Sir W. Jones*, Calcutta, 1816.

12*a*. ,, ,, *E. Arnold*, London, 1861.

13. German ,, *Max Müller*, Leipzig, 1844.

13*a*. ,, ,, *Dursch*, Tübingen, 1853.

14. ,, ,, *L. Fritze*, Breslau, 1874.

15. French ,, *Langlès*, Paris, 1790.

16. ,, ,, *Lancerau*, Paris, 1855.

17. Greek ,, *Galanos* and *Typaldos*, Athens, 1851.

18. VETĀLA PAÑCA VIŊṢATI. Twenty-five stories told by a Vetāla, or demon. Sanskrit text in No. 32, vol. ii. pp. 288–293.

18*a*. Greek version of No. 18 added to No. 17.

19. VETHĀLA KATHEI. Tamil version of No. 18. Edited by *Robertson* in 'A Compilation of Papers in the Tamil Language,' Madras, 1839.

20. No. 19, translated into English by *Babington*, in 'Miscellaneous Translations from Oriental Languages,' London, 1831.

21. No. 18, translated into Brajbakha, by *Surāt*, 1740.

22. BYTAL PACHISI. Translated from No. 21 into English by *Rāja Kāli Krishṇa Bahadur*, Calcutta, 1834. See No. 41*a*.

22*a*. BAITAL PACHISI. Hindustani version of No. 21, Calcutta, 1805. Edited by *Barker*, Hertford, 1855.

22*b*. English versions of 22*a*, by *J. T. Platts*, *Hollings*, and *Barker*.

22*c*. VIKRAM AND THE VAMPIRE, or Tales of Hindu Devilry. Adopted from 22*b* by *Richard F. Burton*, London, 1870.

22*d*. German version of 22*a*, by *H. Oesterley*, in the 'Bibliothek Orientalischer Märchen und Erzählungen,' 1873, with valuable introduction and notes.

23. SSIDDI KÜR. Mongolian version of No. 18.

24. German versions of No. 23, by *Benjamin Bergmann* in *Nomadische Streifereien im Lande der Kalmücken*, i. 247 and foll., 1804; and by *Juelg*, 1866 and 1868.

25. German version of No. 18, by *Dr. Luber*, Görz, 1875.

26. ṢUKA SAPTATI. The seventy stories of a parrot.

27. Greek version of No. 26, by *Demetrios Galanos* and *G. K. Typaldos*, *Psittakou Mythologiai Nukterinai*, included in their version of Nos. 10 and 18.

28. Persian version of No. 26, now lost; but reproduced by *Nachshebi* under the title Tuti Nāmeh.

28*a*. TOTA KAHANI. Hindustāni version of 26. Edited by *Forbes*.

28*b*. English version of 28*a*, by the *Rev. G. Small*.

29. SIṄHĀSANA DVĀTRIṄṢATI. The thirty-two stories of the throne of Vikramāditya; called also *Vikrama Caritra*. Edited in Madras, 1861.

29*a*. SINGHASAN BATTISI. Hindī version of 29. Edited by *Syed Abdoolah*.

30. VATRIṢ SINGHĀSAN. Bengalī version of No. 29, Serampur, 1818.

31. ARJI BORJI CHAN. Mongolian version of No. 29.

32. VṚIHAT-KATHĀ. By *Guṇādhya*, probably about the sixth century; in the Paiṣacī Prākrit. See above, p. lxxiii.

33. KATHĀ SARIT SĀGARA. The Ocean of the Rivers of Tales. It is founded on No. 32. Includes No. 18, and a part of No. 5. The Sanskrit text edited by *Brockhaus*, Leipzig, vol. i. with German translation, 1839; vol. ii. text only, 1862 and 1866. Original by *Ṣrī Somadeva Bhaṭṭa*, of Kashmīr, at the beginning of the twelfth century A.D. See above, pp. lxxii, lxxiii.

34. VṚIHAT-KATHA. A Sanskrit version of No. 34, by *Kshemendra*, of Kashmīr. Written independently of Somadeva's work, No. 32. See above, p. lxxiii.

35. PAÑCA DAṆḌA CHATTRA PRABANDHA. Stories about King Vikramāditya's magic umbrella. Jain Sanskrit. Text and German version by *Weber*, Berlin, 1877.

36. VĀSAVADATTA. By *Subandhu*. Possibly as old as the sixth century. Edited by *Fitz-Edward Hall*, in the *Bibliotheca Indica*, Calcutta, 1859. This and the next are romances, not story-books.

37. KĀDAMBARĪ. By *Bāṇa Bhaṭṭa*, ? seventh century. Edited in Calcutta, 1850; and again, 1872, by *Tarkavacaspati*.

38. Bengali version of No. 37, by *Tāra Shankar Tarkaratna.* Tenth edition, Calcutta, 1868.

39. DASA-KUMĀRA-CARITA. By *Daṇḍin,* ? sixth century. Edited by *Carey,* 1804; *Wilson,* 1846; and by *Bühler,* 1873.

39*a*. HINDOO TALES, founded on No. 39. By *P. W. Jacob,* London, 1873.

39*b*. UNE TÉTRADE. By *Hippolyte Fauche,* Paris, 1861-1863. Contains a translation into French of No. 39.

40. KATHĀRṆAVA, the Stream of Tales. In four Books; the first being No. 18, the second No. 29, the third and fourth miscellaneous.

41. PURUSHA-PARĪKSHĀ, the Adventures of King Hammīra. Probably of the fourteenth century. By *Vidyāpati.*

41*a*. English translation of No. 41, by *Rājā Kāli Krishna,* Serampur, 1830. See No. 22.

42. VĪRA-CARITAṂ, the Adventures of King Ṣālivāhana.

TABLE II.

THE KALILAG AND DAMNAG LITERATURE.

1. A lost Buddhist work in a language of Northern India, ascribed to Bidpai. See above, pp. lxx-lxxii.

2. Pēlvī version, 531–579 A.D. By *Barzūyē*, the Court physician of Khosru Nushirvan. See above, p. xxix.

3. KALILAG UND DAMNAG. Syrian version of No. 2. Published with German translation by *Gustav Bickell*, and Introduction by Professor *Benfey*, Leipzig, 1876. This and No. 15 preserve the best evidence of the contents of No. 2, and of its Buddhist original or originals.

4. KALILAH WĀ DIMNAH (Fables of Bidpai). Arabic version of No. 3, by *Abd-allah*, son of Almokaffa. Date about 750 A.D. Text of one recension edited by *Silvestre de Sacy*, Paris, 1816. Other recensions noticed at length in Ignazio Guidi's 'Studii sul testo Arabo del libro di Calila e Dimna' (Rome, 1873).

5. KALILA AND DIMNA. English version of No. 4, by *Knatchbull*, Oxford, 1819.

6. DAS BUCH DES WEISEN. German version of No. 4, by *Wolff*, Stuttgart, 1839.

7. STEPHANITĒS KAI ICHVĒLATĒS. Greek version of No. 4, by *Simeon Seth*, about 1080 A.D. Edited by *Seb. Gottfried Starke*, Berlin, 1697 (reprinted in Athens, 1851), and by *Aurivillius*, Upsala, 1786.

8. Latin version of No. 7, by *Father Possin*, at the end of his edition of Pachymeres, Rome, 1866.

9. Persian translation of No. 4, by *Abdul Maali Nasr Allah*, 1118–1153. Exists, in MS. only, in Paris, Berlin, and Vienna.

10. ANVĀR I SUHAILI. Persian translation, through the last, of No. 4, by *Husain ben Ali el Vāiz U'l-Kāshifī*; end of the fifteenth century.

11. ANVĀR I SUHÀILI, OR THE LIGHTS OF CANOPUS. English version of No. 10, by *Edward Eastwick*, Hertford, 1854.

11*a*. Another English version of No. 10, by *Arthur N. Wollaston* (London, Allen).

12. LIVRE DES LUMIÈRES. French version of No. 10, by *David Sahid*, d'Ispahan, Paris, 1644, 8vo.

13. DEL GOVERNO DE' REGNI. Italian version of No. 7, Ferrara, 1583; by *Giulio Nūti*. Edited by *Teza*, Bologna, 1872.

14. Hebrew version of No. 4, by *Joel* (?), before 1250. Exists only in a single MS. in Paris, of which the first part is missing.

15. Directorium Humanæ Vitæ. Latin version of No. 14, by *John of Capua.* Written 1263-1278. Printed about 1480, without date or name of place. Next to No. 3 it is the best evidence of the contents of the lost books Nos. 1 and 2.

16. German version of No. 15, also about 1480, but without date or name of place.

17. Version in Ulm dialect of No. 16. Ulm, 1483.

18. *Baldo's* 'Alter Æsopus.' A translation direct from Arabic into Latin (? thirteenth century.) Edited in *du Meril's* 'Poesies inédites du moyen age,' Paris, 1854.

19. Calila é Dymna. Spanish version of No. 4 (? through an unknown Latin version). About 1251. Published in 'Biblioteca de Autores Españoles,' Madrid, 1860, vol. 51.

20. Calila et Dimna. Latin version of the last, by *Raimond de Beziers,* 1313.

21. Conde Lucanor. By *Don Juan Manuel* (died 1347), grandson of St. Ferdinand of Spain. Spanish source not certain.

22. Sinbad the Sailor, or Book of the Seven Wise Masters. See *Comparetti,* 'Ricerche intorno al Libro di Sindibad,' Milano, 1869.

23. Contes et Nouvelles. By *Bonaventure des Periers,* Lyons, 1587.

24. Exemplario contra los Engaños. 1493. Spanish version of the Directorium.

25. Discorse degli Animali. Italian of last, by *Ange Firenzuola,* 1548.

26. La Filosofia Morale. By *Doni,* 1552. Italian of last but one.

27. *North's* English version of last, 1570.

28. Fables by *La Fontaine.*

First edition in vi. books, the subjects of which are mostly taken from classical authors and from Planudes's Æsop, Paris, 1668.

Second edition in xi. books, the five later taken from Nos. 12 and 23, Paris, 1678.

Third edition in xii. books, Paris, 1694.

TABLE III.

THE BARLAAM AND JOSAPHAT SERIES.

1. *St. John of Damascus's Greek Text.* Seventh century A.D. First edited by BOISSONADE, in his 'Anecdota Græca,' Paris, 1832, vol. iv. Reprinted in Migne's 'Patrologia Cursus Completus, Series Græca,' tom. xcvi, pp. 836-1250, with the Latin translation by BILLY[1] in parallel columns. Boissonade's text is reviewed, and its imperfections pointed out, by SCHUBART (who makes use of six Vienna MSS.) in the 'Wiener Jahrbücher,' vol. lxiii.

2. *Syriac version* of No. 1 exists only in MS.

3. *Arabic version* of No. 2 exists only in MS., one MS. being at least as old as the eleventh century.

4. *Latin version* of No. 1, of unknown date and author, of which MSS. of the twelfth century are still extant. There is a black-letter edition (? Spiers, 1470) in the British Museum. It was adopted, with abbreviations in several places, by VINCENTIUS BELLOVICENSIS, in his 'Speculum Historiale' (lib. xv. cap. 1-63); by JACOBUS A VORAGINE, in his 'Legenda Aurea' (ed. *Grässe*, 1846); and was reprinted in full in the editions of the works of St. John of Damascus, published at Basel in the sixteenth century.[2] From this Latin version all the later mediæval works on this subject are either directly or indirectly derived.

4*a*. An abbreviated version in Latin of the fourteenth century in the British Museum. Arundel MS. 330, fol. 51-57. See Koch, No. 9, p. xiv.

German:—

5. *Barlaam und Josaphat.* A poem of the thirteenth century, published from a MS. in the Solms-Laubach Library by L. DIEFENBACH, under the title 'Mittheilungen über eine noch ungedruckte m.h.d. bearbeitung des B. and J.' Giessen, 1836.

6. Another poem, partly published from an imperfect MS. at Zürich, by FRANZ PFEIFFER, in Haupt's 'Zeitsch. f. d. Alterthum,' i. 127-135.

7. *Barlaam und Josaphat.* By RUDOLF VON EMS. Written about 1230. Latest and best edition by FRANZ PFEIFFER, in 'Dichtungen des deutschen

[1] Billy (1535-1577) was Abbot of St. Michael's, in Brittany. Another edition of his Latin version, by Rosweyd, is also reprinted in Migne, 'Series Latina,' tom. lxxiii; and several separate editions have appeared besides (Antwerp, 1602; Cologne, 1624, etc.).

[2] The British Museum copy of the first, undated, edition has the date 1539 written, in ink, on the title-page. Rosweyd, in Note 4 to his edition of Pillius (Migne, vol. lxxiii. p. 606), mentions an edition bearing the date 1548. In the British Museum there is a third, dated 1575 (on the last page).

Mittelalters,' vol. iii., Leipzig, 1843. This popular treatment of the subject exists in numerous MSS.

7. *Die Hÿstorí Josaphat und Barlaam.* Date and author not named. Black-letter. Woodcuts. Title on last page. Fifty-six short chapters. Quaint and forcible old German. A small folio in the British Museum.

8. *Historia von dem Leben der zweien* H. *Beichtiger Barlaam Eremiten, und Josaphat des König's in Indien Sohn, etc.* Translated from the Latin by the Counts of Helffenstein and Hohenzollern, München, 1684. In 40 long chapters, pp. 602, 12mo.

Dutch:—

9. *Het Leven en Bedryf van Barlaam den Heremit, en Josaphat Koning van Indien.* Noo in Nederduits vertaalt door F. v. H., Antwerp, 1593, 12mo.

A new edition of this version appeared in 1672. This is a long and tedious prose version of the holy legend.

French:—

8. Poem by Gui de Cambray (1200-1250). Edited by Hermann Zotenberg and Paul Meyer in the 'Bibliothek des Literarischen Vereins,' in Stuttgart, vol. lxxv., 1864. They mention also (pp. 318-325):—

9. *La Vie de Seint Josaphaz.* Poem by Chardry. Edited by John Koch, Heilbronn, 1879, who confirms the editors of No. 8 as to the following old French versions, 10-15; and further adduces No. 11*a*.

10. A third poem by an unknown author.

11. A prose work by an unknown author—all three being of the 13th cent.

11*a*. Another in MS. Egerton, 745, British Museum.

12. A poem in French of the fifteenth century, based on the abstract in Latin of No. 4, by Jacob de Voragine.

13. A Provençal tale in prose, containing only the story of Josafat and the tales told by Barlaam, without the moralizations.

14. A miracle play of about 1400.

15. Another miracle play of about 1460.

Italian:—

16. *Vita di san Giosafat convertito da Barlaam.* By Geo. Antonio Remondini. Published about 1600, at Venezia and Bassano, 16mo. There is a second edition of this, also without date; and a third, published in Modena in 1768, with illustrations.

17. *Storia de' SS. Barlaam e Giosafatte.* By Bottari, Rome, 1734, 8vo., of which a second edition appeared in 1816.

18. *La santissima vita di Santo Josafat, figluolo del Re Avenero, Re dell' India, da che ei nacque per infino ch'ei morì.* A prose romance, edited by Telesforo Bini from a MS. belonging to the Commendatore Francesco de Rossi, in pp. 124-152 of a collection 'Rime e Prose,' Lucca, 1852, 8vo.

19. A prose *Vita da Santo Josafat.* In MS. Add. 10902 of the British Museum, which Paul Mayer (see No. 8) says begins exactly as No. 18, but ends differently. (See Koch, No. 9 above, p. xiii.)

20. A *Rappresentatione di Barlaam e Josafat* is mentioned by Frederigo Palermo in his 'I manuscritti Palatini de Firenze,' 1860, vol. ii. p. 401.

Skandinavian :—

A full account of all the Skandinavian versions is given in *Barlaam's ok Josaphat's Saga*, by C. R. Unger, Christiania, 1851, 8vo.

Spanish :—

Honesta, etc., historia de la rara vida de los famosos y singulares sanctos Barlaam, etc. By Baltasat de Santa Cruz. Published in the Spanish dialect used in the Philippine Islands at Manila, 1692. A literal translation of Bilius (No. 1).

English :—

In Horstmann's 'Altenglische Legenden,' Paderborn, 1875, an Old English version of the legend is published from the Bodleian MS. No. 779. There is another recension of the same poem in the Harleian MS. No. 4196. Both are of the fourteenth century; and of the second there is another copy in the Vernon MS. See further, Warton's 'History of English Poetry,' i. 271-279, and ii. 30, 58, 308.

Horstmann has also published a Middle English version in the 'Program of the Sagan Gymnasium,' 1877.

The History of the Five Wise Philosophers; or, the Wonderful Relation of the Life of Jehoshaphat the Hermit, Son of Avenerian, King of Barma in India, etc. By N. H. (that is, Nicholas Herick), Gent., London, 1711, pp. 128, 12mo. This is a prose romance, and an abridged translation of the Italian version of 1600 (No. 16), and contains only one fable (at p. 46) of the Nightingale and the Fowler.

The work referred to on p. xlvi, under the title *Gesta Romanorum*, a collection of tales with lengthy moralizations (probably sermons), was made in England about 1300. It soon passed to the Continent, and was repeatedly re-written in numerous MSS., with additions and alterations. Three printed editions appeared between 1472 and 1475; and one of these, containing 181 stories, is the source of the work now known under this title. Tale No. 168 quotes Barlaam. The best edition of the Latin version is by H. Oesterley, Berlin, 1872. The last English translation is Hooper's, Bohn's Antiquarian Library, London, 1877. The Early English versions have been edited by Sir F. Madden; and again, in vol. xxxiii. of the Extra Series of the Early English Text Society, by S. J. H. Herrtage.

The Seven Sages (edited by Thomas Wright for the Percy Society, 1845) also contains some Buddhist tales.

TABLE IV.

COMPARISON OF THE CARIYĀ PIṬAKA AND THE JĀTAKA MĀLĀ.

1. Akitte-cariyaŋ.	Vyāghī-jātakaŋ.
2. Saŋkha-c°.	Ṣivi-j° (8).
3. Danañjaya-c°.	Kulmāsapiṇḍi-j°.
4. Mahā-sudassana-c°.	Ṣreshthi-j° (21).
5. Mahā-govinda-c°.	Avisajyaṣreshthi-j°.
6. Nimi-rāja-c°.	Ṣaṣa-j° (10).
7. Canda-kumāra-c°.	Agastya-j°.
8. Sivi-rāja-c° (2).	Maitribala-j°.
9. Vessantara-c° (9).	Viṣvantara-j° (9).
10. Sasa-paṇḍita-c° (6).	Yajña-j°.
11. Sīlava-nāga-c° (J. 72).	Ṣakra-j°.
12. Bhuridatta-c°.	Brāhmaṇa-j°.
13. Campeyya-nāga-c°.	Ummādayanti-j°.
14. Cūla-bodhi-c°.	Suparāga-j°.
15. Mahiŋsa-rāja-c° (27).	Matsya-j° (30).
16. Ruru-rāja-c°.	Vartaka-potaka-j° (29).
17. Mātaŋga-c°.	Kacchapa-j°.
18. Dhammādhamma-devaputta-c°.	Kumbha-j°.
19. Jayadisa-c°.	Putra-j°.
20. Saŋkhapāla-c°.	Visa-j°.
21. Yudañjaya-c°.	Ṣreshthi-j° (4).
22. Somanassa-c°.	Buddhabodhi-j°.
23. Ayoghara-c° (33).	Haŋsa-j°.
24. Bhisa-c°.	Mahābodhi-j°.
25. Soma-paṇḍita-c° (32).	Mahākapi-j° (27, 28).
26. Temiya-c°.	Ṣarabha-j°.
27. Kapi-rāja-c° (25, 28).	Ruru-j° (16).
28. Saccahvaya-paṇḍita-c°.	Mahākapi-j° (25, 27).
29. Vaṭṭaka-potaka-c° (16).	Kshānti-j°.
30. Maccha-rāja-c° (15).	Brahma-j°.
31. Kaṇha-dipāyana-c°.	Hasti-j°.
32. Sutasoma-c° (25, 32).	Sutasoma-j° (25, 32).
33. Suvaṇṇa-sāma-c°.	Ayogṛiha-j° (23).
34. Ekarāja-c°.	Mahisha-j°.
35. Mahā-lomahaŋsa-c° (J. 94).	Ṣatapatra-j°.

For the above lists see *Feer*, 'Etude sur les Jatakas,' p. 58; *Gogerly*, Journal of the Ceylon Branch of the Royal Asiatic Society, 1853; and *Fausböll*, 'Five Jātakas,' p. 59; and also above, pp. liii, liv. It will be seen that there are seven tales with identical, and one or two more with similar titles, in the two collections. Editions of these two works are very much required. The Cambridge University Library possesses a MS. of the former, with the various readings of several other MSS. noted, for me, by Dewa Arānolis.

TABLE V.

ALPHABETICAL LIST OF JĀTAKA STORIES IN THE MAHĀVASTU.

Arranged from Cowell and Eggeling's 'Catalogue of Buddhist Sanskrit MSS. in the Possession of the Royal Asiatic Society (Hodgson Collection).'

Amarāye karmārakādhītāye jātakaŋ.
Arindama-j°.
Asthisenasya-j°.
Bhadravargikānaŋ-j°.
Campaka-nāgarāja-j°.
Godhā-j°.
Hastinī-j°.
Kāka-j°.
Uruvilva-kāṣyapādi-kāṣyapānaŋ-j°.
Ājnāta-Kauṇḍinya-j°.
Kinnarī-j°.[1]
Kṛicchapa-j°.
Kuṣa-j°.
Mañjerī-j°.
Markaṭa-j°.
Mṛigarājño surūpasya-j°.
Nalinīye rājakumārīye-j°.
Puṇyavanta-j°.
Pūrṇasya Maitrāyaṇī-putrasya j°.
Rakshito-nāma-ṛishi-j°.
Ṛishabasya-j°.
Ṣakuntaka-j°. (Two with this title.)
Ṣarakshepanaŋ-j°.
Ṣaratāŋ-j°.
Sārthavāhasya-j°.
Ṣirī-j°.
Ṣirī-prabhasya mṛiga-rājasya j°.
Ṣyāma-j°.[1] (Car. Piṭ. 33.)
Ṣyāmaka-j°.
Triṇakunīyaŋ nāma j°.
Upali gaṅga palānaŋ-j°.
Vānarādhipa-j°.
Vara-j°.
Vijītāvasya Vaideha-rājño-j°.
Yaṣoda-j°.
Yosodharāye hārapradāna-j°.
,, vyaghrībhūtāya-j°.

[1] These two Jatakas also form the contents of a separate MS. in the Royal Asiatic Society's Library (Catalogue, p 14).

TABLE VI.

PLACES AT WHICH THE TALES WERE TOLD.

M. Léon Feer has taken the trouble to count the number of times each of the following places is mentioned at the commencement of the Commentary.

Jetavana monastery	410	416
Sāvatthi	6	
Veḷmana	49	55
Rājagaha	5	
Laṭṭhivanuyyāna	1	
Vesāli		4
Kosambi		5
Āḷavī		3
Kuṇḍāladaha		3
Kusa		2
Magadha		2
Dakkhiṇāgiri		1
Migadāya		1
Mithila		1
By the Ganges		1
		494
To which we may add from pp. 124-128 below—		
Kapilavatthu		4
		498

TABLE VII.

THE BODISATS.

At his request the Rev. Spence Handy's 'paṇḍit' made an analysis of the number of times in which the Bodisat appears in the Buddhist Birth Stories in each of the following characters:—

An ascetic	83	An iguana	3
A king	85	A fish	2
A tree god	43	An elephant driver	2
A teacher	26	A rat	2
A courtier	24	A jackal	2
A brāhman	24	A crow	2
A king's son	24	A woodpecker	2
A nobleman	23	A thief	2
A learned man	22	A pig	2
Sakka	20	A dog	1
A monkey	18	A curer of snake bites	1
A merchant	13	A gambler	1
A man of property	12	A mason	1
A deer	11	A smith	1
A lion	10	A devil dancer	1
A wild duck	8	A student	1
A snipe	6	A silversmith	1
An elephant	6	A carpenter	1
A cock	5	A water-fowl	1
A slave	5	A frog	1
An eagle	5	A hare	1
A horse	4	A kite	1
A bull	4	A jungle cock	1
Brahma	4	A fairy	1
A peacock	4		
A serpent	4		
A potter	3		530
An outcast	3		

TABLE VIII.

JĀTAKAS ILLUSTRATED IN BAS-RELIEF ON THE ANCIENT MONUMENTS.

Arranged from *General Cunningham's* 'Stūpa of Bharhut.'

No.	Plate	Title inscribed on the stone.	Title in the Jātaka Book.
1.	xxv.	Miga Jātaka.	Nigrodha-miga Jātaka.[1]
2.	,,	Nāga[2] ,,	Kakkaṭaka ,,
3.	,,	Yava-majhakiya Jātaka.	?[3]
4.	,,	Muga-pakhaya ,,	Muga-pakkha ,,
5.	xxvi.	Laṭuwa ,,	Laṭukikā ,,
6.	,,	Cha-dantiya ,,	Chad-danta ,,
7.	,,	Isi-siŋgiya ,,	Isa-siŋga ,,
8.	,, (?)	Ya*mb*uma*ne*-ayavesi ,,	Andha-bhūta ,,
9.	xxvii.	?[4]	Kuruŋga-miga ,,
10.	,,	Haŋsa ,,	Nacca ,,[5]
11.	,,	Kinara ,,	Canda-kinnara ,,[6]
12.	,,	?[4]	Asadisa ,,
13.	,,	?[4] ,,	Dasaratha ,,
14.	xliii.	Isi-migo ,,	?[7]
15.	xlvi.	Uda ,,	?[7]
16.	,,	Secha ,,	Dūbhiya-makkaṭa.
17.	xlvii.	Sujāto gahuto ,,	Sujāta ,,
18.	,,	{ Biḍala ,,	
		{ Kukuṭa ,,	Kukkuṭa ,,
19.	xlviii.	Maghā-deviya ,,	Makhā-deva ,,[8]
20.	,,	Bhisa-haraniya ,,	?[7]
21.	xviii.	Vitura-panakaya ,,[9]	Vidhūra ,,
22.	xxviii.	{ Janako Rāja ,,	Janaka ,,
		{ Sivala Devi ,,	

[1] Translated below, pp. 205, and foll. This is one of those which General Cunningham was unable to identify.

[2] General Cunningham says (p. 52): "The former [Nāga Jātaka, *i.e.* Elephant Jātaka] is the correct name, as in the legend here represented Buddha is the King of the Elephants, and therefore the Jātaka, or Birth, must of necessity have been named after him." As I have above pointed out (p. xli), the title of each Jātaka, or Birth Story, is chosen, not by any means from the character which the Bodisat fills in it, but indifferently from a variety of other reasons. General Cunningham himself gives the story called Isī-singga Jātaka (No. 7 in the above list), in which the ascetic after whom the Jātaka is named is not the Bodisat.

[3] Not as yet found in the Jātaka Book; but Dr. Bühler has shown in the 'Indian Antiquary,' vol. i. p. 305, that it is the first tale in the 'Vrihat Kathā' of Kshemendra (Table I. No. 34), and in the 'Kathā Sarit Sāgara' of Somadeva (Table I. No. 33), and was therefore probably included in the 'Vrihat Kathā' of Guṇadhya (Table I. No. 32).

[4] The part of the stone supposed to have contained the inscription is lost.

[5] Translated below, pp. 292, 293.

[6] It is mentioned below, p. 128, and is included in the Mahāvastu (Table V.), and forms the subject of the carving on one of the rails at Buddha Gayā (Rajendra Lāl Mitra, pl. xxxiv. fig. 2).

[7] Not as yet found in the Jātaka Book.

[8] Translated below, pp. 186-188. See also above, p. lxiv.

[9] There are four distinct bas-reliefs illustrative of this Jātaka.

There are numerous other scenes without titles, and not yet identified in the Jātaka Book, but which are almost certainly illustrative of Jātaka Stories; and several scenes with titles illustrative of passages in the Nidāna Kathā of the Jātaka Book. So, for instance, Pl. xvi. fig. 1 is the worship in heaven of the Buddha's Head-dress, whose reception into heaven is described below, p. 86; and the heavenly mansion, the Palace of Glory, is inscribed *Vejayanto Pāsādo*, the origin of which name is explained below, p. 287. Plate xxviii. has a scene entitled '*Bhagavato Okkanti*' (The Descent of the Blessed One),[1] in illustration of Māyā Devi's Dream (below, pp. 62, 63); and Plate lvii. is a representation of the Presentation of the Jetavana Monastery (below, pp. 130-133). The identifications of Nos. 12 and 13 in the above list are very doubtful.

Besides the above, Mr. Fergusson, in his 'Tree and Serpent Worship,' has identified bas-reliefs on the Sanchi Tope in illustration of the Sama and Asadisa Jātakas (Pl. xxxvi. p. 181) and of the Vessantara Jātaka (Pl. xxiv. p. 125); and there are other Jātaka scenes on the Sanchi Tope not yet identified.

Mr. Simpson also has been kind enough to show me drawings of bas-reliefs he discovered in Afghanistān, two of which I have been able to identify as illustrations of the Sumedha Jātaka (below, p. 11-13), and another as illustrative of the scene described below on pp. 125, 126.

[1] General Cunningham's reading of this inscription as *Bhagavato rukdanta* seems to me to be incorrect, and his translation of it ('Buddha as the sounding elephant') to be grammatically impossible.

THE NIDĀNAKATHĀ

OR

THE THREE EPOCHS.

[vv. 1-11.] The Apa*nn*aka and other Births, which in times gone by were recounted on various occasions by the great illustrious Sage, and in which during a long period our Teacher and Leader, desirous of the salvation of mankind, fulfilled the vast conditions of Buddhahood,[1] were all collected together and added to the canon of Scripture by those who made the recension of the Scriptures, and rehearsed by them under the name of THE JĀTAKA. Having bowed at the feet of the Great Sage, the lord of the world, by whom in innumerable existences[2] boundless benefits were conferred upon mankind, and having paid reverence to the Law, and ascribed honour to the Clergy, the receptacle of all honour; and having removed all dangers by the efficacy of that meritorious act of veneration and honour referring to the Three Gems, I proceed to recite a Commentary upon this Jātaka, illustrating as it does the infinite efficacy of the actions of great men—a commentary based upon the method of exposition current among the inmates of the Great Monastery. And I do so at the personal request of the elder Atthadassin, who lives apart from the world and

[1] Lit. perfected the vast constituents of Buddhahood, the Pāramitās are meant.

[2] Lit. in thousands of koṭis of births; a koṭi is ten millions.

ever dwells with his fraternity, and who desires the perpetuation of this chronicle of Buddha; and likewise of Buddhamitta the tranquil and wise, sprung from the race of Mahiṃsāsaka, skilled in the canons of interpretation; and moreover of the monk Buddhadeva of clear intellect. May all good men lend me their favourable attention while I speak![1]

Inasmuch as this comment on the Jātaka, if it be expounded after setting forth the three Epochs, the distant, the middle, and proximate, will be clearly understood by those who hear it by being understood from the beginning, therefore I will expound it after setting forth the three Epochs. Accordingly from the very outset it will be well to determine the limits of these Epochs. Now the narrative of the Bodhisatta's existence, from the time that at the feet of Dīpankara he formed a resolution to become a Buddha to his rebirth in the Tusita heaven after leaving the Vessantara existence, is called the Distant Epoch. From his leaving the Tusita heaven to his attainment of omniscience on the throne of Knowledge, the narrative is called the Intermediate Epoch. And the Proximate Epoch is to be found in the various places in which he sojourned (during his ministry on earth). The following is

THE DISTANT EPOCH.

Tradition tells us that four asankheyyas[2] and a hundred thousand cycles ago there was a city called Amaravatī. In this city there dwelt a brahmin named Sumedha, of good family on both sides, on the father's and the

[1] The above lines in the original are in verse. I have found it impossible to follow the arrangement of the stanzas, owing to the extreme involution of the style.

[2] An asankheyya is a period of vast duration, lit. an incalculable.

mother's side, of pure conception for seven generations back, by birth unreproached and respected, a man comely, well-favoured and amiable, and endowed with remarkable beauty. He followed his brahminical studies without engaging in any other pursuit. His parents died while he was still young. A minister of state, who acted as steward of his property, bringing forth the roll-book of his estate, threw open the stores filled with gold and silver, gems and pearls, and other valuables, and said, "So much, young man, belonged to your mother, so much to your father, so much to your grandparents and great-grand-parents," and pointing out to him the property inherited through seven generations, he bade him guard it carefully. The wise Sumedha thought to himself, "After amassing all this wealth my parents and ancestors when they went to another world took not a farthing with them, can it be right that I should make it an object to take my wealth with me when I go?" And informing the king of his intention, he caused proclamation to be made[1] in the city, gave largess to the people, and embraced the ascetic life of a hermit.

To make this matter clear the STORY OF SUMEDHA must here be related. This story, though given in full in the Buddhava*m*sa, from its being in a metrical form, is not very easy to understand. I will therefore relate it with sentences at intervals explaining the metrical construction.

Four asankheyyas and a hundred thousand cycles ago there was a city called Amaravatī or Amara, resounding with the ten city cries, concerning which it is said in Buddhava*m*sa,

12. Four asankheyyas and a hundred thousand cycles ago
A city there was called Amara, beautiful and pleasant,
Resounding with the ten cries, abounding in food and drink.[2]

[1] Lit. "caused the drums to be beat."

[2] Here a gloss in the text enumerates the whole ten cries.

Then follows a stanza of Buddhavaṃsa enumerating some of these cries,

13. The trumpeting of elephants, the neighing of horses, (the sound of) drums, trumpets, and chariots,
And viands and drinks were cried, with the invitation, "Eat and drink."

It goes on to say,

14. A city supplied with every requisite, engaged in every sort of industry,
Possessing the seven precious things, thronged with dwellers of many races;
The abode of devout men, like the prosperous city of the angels.
15. In the city of Amaravatī dwelt a brahmin named Sumedha,
Whose hoard was many tens of millions, blest with much wealth and store;
16. Studious, knowing the Mantras, versed in the three Vedas,
Master of the science of divination and of the traditions and observances of his caste.

Now one day the wise Sumedha, having retired to the splendid upper apartment of his house, seated himself cross-legged, and fell a thinking. "Oh! wise man,[1] grievous is rebirth in a new existence, and the dissolution of the body in each successive place where we are reborn. I am subject to birth, to decay, to disease, to death,—it is right, being such, that I should strive to attain the great deathless Nirvāṇa, which is tranquil, and free from birth, and decay, and sickness, and grief and joy; surely there must be a road that leads to Nirvāṇa and releases man from existence." Accordingly it is said,

17. Seated in seclusion, I then thought as follows:
Grievous is rebirth and the breaking up of the body.
18. I am subject to birth, to decay, to disease,
Therefore will I seek Nirvāṇa, free from decay and death, and secure.
19. Let me leave this perishable body, this pestilent congregation of vapours,
And depart without desires and without wants.
20. There is, there must be a road, it cannot but be:
I will seek this road, that I may obtain release from existence.

[1] The Bodhisatta is frequently called paṇḍita, e.g. *sasapaṇḍito* (Five Jāt. 52), *Rāmapaṇḍito* (Dasaratha Jāt. 1).

Further he reasoned thus, "For as in this world there is pleasure as the correlative of pain, so where there is existence there must be its opposite the cessation of existence; and as where there is heat there is also cold which neutralizes it, so there must be a Nirvāṇa[1] that extinguishes (the fires of) lust and the other passions; and as in opposition to a bad and evil condition there is a good and blameless one, so where there is evil Birth there must also be Nirvāṇa, called the Birthless, because it puts an end to all rebirth." Therefore it is said,

21. As where there is suffering there is also bliss,
So where there is existence we must look for non-existence.
22. And as where there is heat there is also cold,
So where there is the threefold fire of passion extinction must be sought.
23. And as coexistent with evil there is also good,
Even so where there is birth[2] the cessation of birth should be sought.

Again he reasoned thus, "Just as a man who has fallen into a heap of filth, if he beholds afar off a great pond covered with lotuses of five colours, ought to seek that pond, saying, 'By what way shall I arrive there?' but if he does not seek it the fault is not that of the pond; even so where there is the lake of the great deathless Nirvāṇa for the washing of the defilement of sin, if it is not sought it is not the fault of the lake. And just as a man who is surrounded by robbers, if when there is a way of escape he does not fly it is not the fault of the way but of the man; even so when there is a blessed road leading to Nirvāṇa for the man who is encompassed and held fast by sin, its not being sought is not the fault of the road but of the person. And as a man who is oppressed with sickness, there being a physician who can heal his disease, if he does not get

[1] Lit. "Extinction."
[2] Mr. Fausböll points out to me that in *tividhaggi* and *jāti* we have Vedic abbreviations.

cured by going to the physician that is no fault of the physician; even so if a man who is oppressed by the disease of sin seeks not a spiritual guide who is at hand and knows the road which puts an end to sin, the fault lies with him and not with the sin-destroying teacher." Therefore it is said,

24. As a man fallen among filth, beholding a brimming lake,
If he seek not that lake, the fault is not in the lake;
25. So when there exists a lake of Nirvāna that washes the stains of sin,
If a man seek not that lake, the fault is not in the lake of Nirvāna.
26. As a man beset with foes, there being a way of escape,
If he flee not away, the fault is not with the road;
27. So when there is a way of bliss, if a man beset with sin
Seek not that road, the fault is not in the way of bliss.
28. And as one who is diseased, there being a physician at hand,
If he bid him not heal the disease, the fault is not in the healer:
29. So if a man who is sick and oppressed with the disease of sin
Seek not the spiritual teacher, the fault is not in the teacher.

And again he argued, "As a man fond of gay clothing, throwing off a corpse bound to his shoulders, goes away rejoicing, so must I, throwing off this perishable body, and freed from all desires, enter the city of Nirvāna. And as men and women depositing filth on a dung-heap do not gather it in the fold or skirt of their garments, but loathing it, throw it away, feeling no desire for it; so shall I also cast off this perishable body without regret, and enter the deathless city of Nirvāna. And as seamen abandon without regret an unseaworthy ship and escape, so will I also, leaving this body, which distils corruption from its nine festering apertures, enter without regret the city of Nirvāna. And as a man carrying various sorts of jewels, and going on the same road with a band of robbers, out of fear of losing his jewels withdraws from them and gains a safe road; even so this impure body is like a jewel-plundering robber, if I set my affections thereon the precious spiritual jewel of the sublime path of holiness will be lost to me, therefore ought I to enter the city of Nirvā*n*a, forsaking this robber-like body." Therefore it is said,

30. As a man might with loathing shake off a corpse bound upon his shoulders,
And depart secure, independent, master of himself;
31. Even so let me depart, regretting nothing, wanting nothing,
Leaving this perishable body, this collection of many foul vapours.
32. And as men and women deposit filth upon a dungheap,
And depart regretting nothing, wanting nothing,
33. So will I depart, leaving this body filled with foul vapours,
As one leaves a cesspool after depositing ordure there.
34. And as the owners forsake the rotten bark that is shattered and leaking,
And depart without regret or longing,
35. So shall I go, leaving this body with its nine apertures ever running,
As its owners desert the broken ship.
36. And as a man carrying wares, walking with robbers,
Seeing danger of losing his wares, parts company with the robbers and gets him gone,
37. Even so is this body like a mighty robber,—
Leaving it I will depart through fear of losing good.

Having thus in nine similes pondered upon the advantages connected with retirement from the world, the wise Sumedha gave away at his own house, as aforesaid, an immense hoard of treasure to the indigent and wayfarers and sufferers, and kept open house. And renouncing all pleasures, both material and sensual, departing from the city of Amara, away from the world in Himavanta he made himself a hermitage near the mountain called Dhammaka, and built a hut and a perambulation hall free from the five defects which are hindrances (to meditation). And with a view to obtain the power residing in the supernatural faculties, which are characterized by the eight causal qualities described in the words beginning "With a mind thus tranquillised,"[1] he embraced in that

[1] *Evaṁ samāhite citte parisuddhe pariyodāte anaṅgaṇe vigatūpakkilese mudubhūte kammaniye ṭhite ānejjappatte ñāṇadassanāya cittaṁ abhinīharati* (Sāmaññaphala Sutta, see Lotus, p. 476, line 14).

hermitage the ascetic life of a Ṛishi, casting off the cloak with its nine disadvantages, and wearing the garment of bark with its twelve advantages. And when he had thus given up the world, forsaking this hut, crowded with eight drawbacks, he repaired to the foot of a tree with its ten advantages, and rejecting all sorts of grain lived constantly upon wild fruits. And strenuously exerting himself both in sitting and in standing and in walking, within a week he became the possessor of the eight Attainments, and of the five Supernatural Faculties; and so, in accordance with his prayer, he attained the might of supernatural knowledge. Therefore it is said,

38. Having pondered thus I gave many thousand millions of wealth
To rich and poor, and made my way to Himavanta.
39. Not far from Himavanta is the mountain called Dhammaka,
Here I made an excellent hermitage, and built with care a leafy hut.
40. There I built me a cloister, free from five defects,
Possessed of the eight good qualities, and attained the strength of the supernatural Faculties.
41. Then I threw off the cloak possessed of the nine faults,
And put on the raiment of bark possessed of the twelve advantages.
42. I left the hut, crowded with the eight drawbacks,
And went to the tree-foot possessed of ten advantages.[1]
43. Wholly did I reject the grain that is sown and planted,
And partook of the constant fruits of the earth, possessed of many advantages.
44. Then I strenuously strove, in sitting, in standing, and in walking,
And within seven days attained the might of the Faculties.[2]

Now while the hermit Sumedha, having thus attained the strength of supernatural knowledge, was living in the bliss of the (eight) Attainments, the Teacher Dīpankara appeared in the world. At the moment of his conception, of his birth, of his attainment of Buddhahood, of his preaching his first discourse, the whole universe

[1] Mr. Fausböll writes to me that *guṇe* for guṇehi must be viewed as an old Pali form originating in the Sanskrit guṇaih.

[2] Here follow four pages of later commentary or gloss, which I leave untranslated.

of ten thousand worlds trembled, shook and quaked, and gave forth a mighty sound, and the thirty-two prognostics showed themselves. But the hermit Sumedha, living in the bliss of the Attainments, neither heard that sound nor beheld those signs. Therefore it is said,

> 45. Thus when I had attained the consummation, while I was subjected to the Law,
> The Conqueror named Dīpankara, chief of the universe, appeared.
> 46. At his conception, at his birth, at his Buddhahood, at his preaching,
> I saw not the four signs, plunged in the blissful trance of meditation.

At that time Dīpankara Buddha, accompanied by a hundred thousand saints, wandering his way from place to place, reached the city of Ramma, and took up his residence in the great monastery of Sudassana. And the dwellers of the city of Ramma heard it said, "Dīpankara, lord of ascetics, having attained supreme Buddhaship, and set on foot the supremacy of the Law, wandering his way from place to place, has come to the town of Ramma, and dwells at the great monastery of Sudassana." And taking with them ghee and butter and other medicinal requisites and clothes and raiment, and bearing perfumes and garlands and other offerings in their hands, their minds bent towards the Buddha, the Law, and the Clergy, inclining towards them, hanging upon them, they approached the Teacher and worshipped him, and presenting the perfumes and other offerings, sat down on one side. And having heard his preaching of the Law, and invited him for the next day, they rose from their seats and departed. And on the next day, having prepared almsgiving for the poor, and having decked out the town, they repaired the road by which the Buddha was to come, throwing earth in the places that were worn away by water and thereby levelling the surface, and scattering sand that looked like strips of silver. And they sprinkled fragrant roots and flowers, and raised aloft flags and banners of many-coloured cloths, and set up banana arches and rows of brimming jars. Then the hermit Sumedha, ascending from his hermitage, and proceeding through the air till he was above those men, and beholding the joyous multitude, exclaimed, "What can be the reason?" and alighting stood on one side and questioned the people, "Tell me, why are you adorning this road?" Therefore it is said,

47. In the region of the border districts, having invited the Buddha,
With joyful hearts they are clearing the road by which he should come.
48. And I at that time leaving my hermitage,
Rustling my barken tunic, departed through the air.
49. And seeing an excited multitude joyous and delighted,
Descending from the air I straightway asked the men,
50. The people is excited, joyous and happy,
For whom is the road being cleared, the path, the way of his coming?

And the men replied, "Lord Sumedha, dost thou not know? Dīpankara Buddha, having attained supreme Knowledge, and set on foot the reign of the glorious Law, travelling from place to place, has reached our town, and dwells at the great monastery Sudassana; we have invited the Blessed One, and are making ready for the blessed Buddha the road by which he is to come." And the hermit Sumedha thought, "The very sound of the word Buddha is rarely met with in the world, much more the actual appearance of a Buddha; it behoves me to join these men in clearing the road." He said therefore to the men, "If you are clearing this road for the Buddha, assign to me a piece of ground, I will clear the ground in company with you." They consented, saying, "It is well;" and perceiving the hermit Sumedha to be possessed of supernatural power, they fixed upon a swampy piece of ground, and assigned it to him, saying, "Do thou prepare this spot." Sumedha, his heart filled with joy of which the Buddha was the cause, thought within himself, "I am able to prepare this piece of ground by supernatural power, but if so prepared it will give me no satisfaction; this day it behoves me to perform menial duties;" and fetching earth he threw it upon the spot.

But ere the ground could be cleared by him,—with a train of a hundred thousand miracle-working saints endowed with the six supernatural faculties, while angels offered celestial wreaths and perfumes, while celestial hymns rang forth, and men paid their homage with earthly perfumes and with flowers and other offerings, Dīpankara endowed with the ten Forces, with all a Buddha's transcendant majesty, like a lion rousing himself to seek his prey on the Vermilion plain, came down into the road all decked and made ready for him. Then the hermit Sumedha—as the Buddha with unblenching eyes approached along the road prepared for him, beholding that form endowed with the perfection of beauty, adorned with the thirty-two characteristics of a great man, and marked with the eighty minor beauties, attended by a halo of a fathom's depth, and sending forth in streams the six-hued Buddha-rays, linked in pairs of different colours, and wreathed like the varied lightnings that flash in the gem-studded vault of heaven—exclaimed, "This day it behoves me to make sacrifice of my life for the Buddha: let not the Blessed one walk in the mire—nay, let him advance with his four hundred thousand saints trampling on my body as if walking upon a bridge of jewelled planks, this deed will long be for my good and my happiness." So saying, he loosed his hair, and spreading in the inky mire his hermit's skin mantle, roll of matted hair and garment of bark, he lay down in the mire like a bridge of jewelled planks. Therefore it is said,

51. Questioned by me they replied, An incomparable Buddha is born into the world,
The Conqueror named Dīpankara, lord of the universe,
For him the road is cleared, the way, the path of his coming.

52. When I heard the name of Buddha joy sprang up forthwith within me,
Repeating, a Buddha, a Buddha! I gave utterance to my joy.
53. Standing there I pondered, joyful and excited,
Here I will sow the seed, may the happy moment not pass away.
54. If you clear a path for the Buddha, assign to me a place,
I also will clear the road, the way, the path of his coming.
55. Then they gave me a piece of ground to clear the pathway;
Then repeating within me, a Buddha, a Buddha! I cleared the road.
56. But ere my portion was cleared, Dīpankara the great sage,
The Conqueror, entered the road with four hundred thousand saints like himself,
Possessed of the six supernatural attributes, pure from all taint of sin.
57. On every side men rise to receive him, many drums send forth their music,
Men and angels overjoyed, shout forth their applause.
58. Angels look upon men, men upon angels,
And both with clasped hands upraised approach the great Being.
59. Angels with celestial music, men with earthly music,
Both sending forth their strains approach the great Being.
60. Angels floating in the air sprinkle down in all directions
Celestial Erythrina flowers, lotuses and coral flowers.
61. Men standing on the ground throw upwards in all directions
Champac and Salala flowers, Cadamba and fragrant Mesua, Punnaga, and Ketaka.
62. Then I loosed my hair, and spreading in the mire
Bark robe and mantle of skin, lay prone upon my face.
63. Let the Buddha advance with his disciples, treading upon me;
Let him not tread in the mire, it will be for my blessing.

And as he lay in the mire, again beholding the Buddha-majesty of Dīpankara Buddha with his unblenching gaze, he thought as follows: "Were I willing, I could enter the city of Ramma as a novice in the priesthood, after having destroyed all human passions; but why should I disguise myself[1] to attain Nirvāṇa after the destruction

[1] The following is what I take to be the meaning of this passage: "If I chose I could at once enter the Buddhist priesthood, and by the practice of ecstatic meditation (Jhāna) free myself from human passion, and become an Arhat or saint. I should then at death at once attain Nirvāṇa and cease to exist. But this would be a selfish course to pursue, for thus I should benefit myself only. Why should I thus slip unobserved and in the humble garb of a monk into Nirvāṇa? Nay, let me rather qualify myself to become a Buddha, and so save others as well as myself." This is the great ACT OF RENUNCIATION by which the Bodhisattva, when Nirvāṇa was within his grasp, preferred to endure ages of heroic trials in the exercise of the Pāramitās, that he might be enabled to become a Buddha, and so redeem mankind. See D'Alwis's Introduction to Kachchāyana's Grammar, p. vi.

of human passion? Let me rather, like Dīpankara, having risen to the supreme knowledge of the Truth, enable mankind to enter the Ship of the Truth and so carry them across the Ocean of Existence, and when this is done afterwards attain Nirvā*n*a; this indeed it is right that I should do." Then having enumerated the eight conditions (necessary to the attainment of Buddhahood), and having made the resolution to become Buddha, he laid himself down. Therefore it is said,

64. As I lay upon the ground this was the thought of my heart,
If I wished it I might this day destroy within me all human passions.
65. But why should I in disguise arrive at the knowledge of the Truth?
I will attain omniscience and become a Buddha, and (save) men and angels.
66. Why should I cross the ocean resolute but alone?
I will attain omniscience, and enable men and angels to cross.
67. By this resolution of mine, I a man of resolution
Will attain omniscience, and save men and angels,
68. Cutting off the stream of transmigration, annihilating the three forms of existence,
Embarking in the ship of the Truth, I will carry across with me men and angels.[1]

And the blessed Dīpankara having reached the spot stood close by the hermit Sumedha's head. And opening his eyes possessed of the five kinds of grace as one opens a jewelled window, and beholding the hermit Sumedha lying in the mire, thought to himself, "This hermit who lies here has formed the resolution to be a Buddha; will his prayer be fulfilled or not?" And casting forward his prescient gaze into the future, and considering, he perceived that four asankheyyas and a hundred thousand cycles from that time he would become a Buddha named Gotama. And standing there in the midst of the assembly he delivered this prophecy, "Behold ye this austere hermit lying in the mire?" "Yes, Lord," they answered.

[1] What follows from *yasmā* to *nipajji* belongs to a later commentary. I resume the translation with p. 15, line 11.

"This man lies here having made the resolution to become a Buddha, his prayer will be answered; at the end of four asankheyyas and a hundred thousand cycles hence he will become a Buddha named Gotama, and in that birth the city Kapilavatthu will be his residence, Queen Māyā will be his mother, King Suddhodana his father, his chief disciple will be the thera Upatissa, his second disciple the thera Kolita, the Buddha's servitor will be Ānanda, his chief female disciple the nun Khemā, the second the nun Uppalava*nn*ā. When he attains to years of ripe knowledge, having retired from the world and made the great exertion, having received at the foot of a banyan-tree a meal of rice milk, and partaken of it by the banks of the Neranjarā, having ascended the throne of Knowledge, he will, at the foot of an Indian fig-tree, attain Supreme Buddhahood. Therefore it is said,

70. Dīpankara, knower of all worlds, receiver of offerings,
Standing by that which pillowed my head, spoke these words:
71. See ye this austere hermit with his matted hair,
Countless ages hence he will be a Buddha in this world.
72. Lo, the great Being departing from pleasant Kapila,
Having fought the great fight, performed all manner of austerities,
73. Having sat at the foot of the Ajapāla tree, and there received rice pottage,
Shall approach the Neranjarā river.
74. Having received the rice pottage on the banks of the Neranjarā, the Conqueror
Shall come by a fair road prepared for him to the foot of the Bodhi-tree.
75. Then, unrivalled and glorious, reverentially saluting the throne of Bodhi,
At the foot of an Indian fig-tree he shall attain Buddhahood.
76. The mother that bears him shall be called Māyā,
His father will be Suddhodana, he himself will be Gotama.
77. His chief disciples will be Upatissa and Kolita,
Void of human passion, freed from desire, calm-minded and tranquil.
78. The servitor Ānanda will attend upon the Conqueror,
Khemā and Uppalava*nn*ā will be his chief female disciples,
79. Void of human passion, freed from desire, calm-minded and tranquil.
The sacred tree of this Buddha is called Assattha.

The hermit Sumedha, exclaiming, "My prayer, it seems, will be accomplished," was filled with happiness. The multitudes, hearing the words of Dīpankara Buddha, were joyous and delighted, exclaiming, "The hermit Sumedha, it seems, is an embryo Buddha, the tender shoot that will grow up into a Buddha." For thus they thought, "As a man fording a river, if he is unable to cross to the ford opposite him, crosses to a ford lower down the stream, even so we, if under the dispensation of Dīpankara Buddha we fail to attain the Paths and their fruition, yet when thou shalt become Buddha we shall be enabled in thy presence to make the paths and their fruition our own,"—and so they recorded their prayer (for future sanctification). And Dīpankara Buddha also having praised the Bodhisatta, and made an offering to him of eight handfuls of flowers, reverentially saluted him and departed. And the Arhats also, four hundred thousand in number, having made offerings to the Bodhisatta of perfumes and garlands, reverentially saluted him and departed. And the angels and men having made the same offerings, and bowed down to him, went their way.

And the Bodhisatta, when all had retired, rising from his seat and exclaiming, "I will investigate the Perfections," sat himself down cross-legged on a heap of flowers. And as the Bodhisatta sat thus, the angels in all the ten thousand worlds assembling shouted applause. "Venerable hermit Sumedha," they said, "all the auguries which have manifested themselves when former Bodhisattas seated themselves cross-legged, saying, 'We will investigate the Perfections,'—all these this day have appeared: assuredly thou shalt become Buddha. This we know, to whom these omens appear, he surely will become Buddha; do thou make a strenuous effort and exert thyself." With these words they lauded the Bodhisatta with varied praises. Therefore it is said,

80. Hearing these words of the incomparable Sage,
Angels and men delighted, exclaimed, This is an embryo Buddha.
81. A great clamour arises, men and angels in ten thousand worlds
Clap their hands, and laugh, and make obeisance with clasped hands.
82. "Should we fail," they say, "of this Buddha's dispensation,
Yet in time to come we shall stand before him.
83. As men crossing a river, if they fail to reach the opposite ford,
Gaining the lower ford cross the great river,
84. Even so we all, if we lose this Buddha,
In time to come shall stand before him."
85. The world-knowing Dīpankara, the receiver of offerings,
Having celebrated my meritorious act, went his way.[1]
86. All the disciples of the Buddha that were present saluted me with reverence,
Men, Nāgas, and Gandhabbas bowed down to me and departed.
87. When the Lord of the world with his following had passed beyond my sight,
Then glad, with gladsome heart, I rose up from my seat.
88. Joyful I am with a great joy, glad with a great gladness;
Flooded with rapture then I seated myself cross-legged.
89. And even as thus I sat I thought within myself,
I am subject to ecstatic meditation, I have mastered the supernatural Faculties.
90. In a thousand worlds there are no sages that rival me,
Unrivalled in miraculous powers I have reached this bliss.
91. When thus they beheld me sitting,[2] the dwellers of ten thousand worlds
Raised a mighty shout, Surely thou shalt be a Buddha!
92. The omens[3] beheld in former ages when Bodhisatta sat cross-legged,
The same are beheld this day.
93. Cold is dispelled and heat ceases,
This day these things are seen,—verily thou shalt be Buddha.
94. A thousand worlds are stilled and silent,
So are they seen to-day,—verily thou shalt be Buddha.
95. The mighty winds blow not, the rivers cease to flow,
These things are seen to-day,—verily thou shalt be Buddha.
96. All flowers blossom on land and sea,
This day they all have bloomed,—verily thou shalt be Buddha.
97. All creepers and trees are laden with fruit,
This day they all bear fruit,—verily thou shalt be Buddha.
98. Gems sparkle in earth and sky,
This day all gems do glitter,—verily thou shalt be Buddha.

[1] Lit. "raised his right foot (to depart)."
[2] Lit. "at my sitting cross-legged."
[3] Mr. Fausböll writes that *yaṁ* is a mistake of the copyist for *yá*=*yáni*.

99. Music earthly and celestial sounds,
Both these to-day send forth their strains,—verily thou shalt be Buddha.
100. Flowers of every hue rain down from the sky,
This day they are seen,—verily thou shalt be Buddha.
101. The mighty ocean bends itself, ten thousand worlds are shaken,
This day they both send up their roar,—verily thou shalt be Buddha.
102. In hell the fires of ten thousand worlds die out,
This day these fires are quenched,—verily thou shalt be Buddha.
103. Unclouded is the sun and all the stars are seen,
These things are seen to-day,—verily thou shalt be Buddha.
104. Though no water fell in rain, vegetation burst forth from the earth,
This day vegetation springs from the earth,—verily thou shalt be Buddha.
105. The constellations are all aglow, and the lunar mansions in the vault of heaven,
Visākhā is in conjunction with the moon,—verily thou shalt be Buddha.
106. Those creatures that dwell in holes and caves depart each from his lair,
This day these lairs are forsaken,—verily thou shalt be Buddha.
107. There is no discontent among mortals, but they are filled with contentment,
This day all are content,—verily thou shalt be Buddha.
108. Then diseases are dispelled and hunger ceases,
This day these things are seen,—verily thou shalt be Buddha.
109. Then Desire wastes away, Hate and Folly perish,
This day all these are dispelled,—verily thou shalt be Buddha.
110. No danger then comes near; this day this thing is seen,
By this sign we know it,—verily thou shalt become Buddha.
111. No dust flies abroad; this day this thing is seen,
By this sign we know it, verily thou shalt be Buddha.
112. All noisome odours flee away, celestial fragrance breathes around,
Such fragrance breathes this day,—verily thou shalt be Buddha.
113. All the angels are manifested, the Formless only excepted,
This day they all are seen,—verily thou shalt be Buddha.
114. All the hells become visible,
These all are seen this day,—verily thou shalt be Buddha.
115. Then walls, and doors, and rocks are no impediment,
This day they have melted into air,[1]—verily thou shalt be Buddha.
116. At that moment death and birth do not take place,
This day these things are seen,—verily thou shalt be Buddha.
117. Do thou make a strenuous effort, hold not back, go forward,
This thing we know,—verily thou shalt be Buddha.

[1] Or "have risen into the air"?

And the Bodhisatta, having heard the words of Dīpankara Buddha, and of the angels in ten thousand worlds, filled with immeasurable resolution, thought thus within himself, "The Buddhas are beings whose word cannot fail; there is no deviation from truth in their speech. For as the fall of a clod thrown into the air, as the death of a mortal, as the sunrise at dawn, as a lion's roaring when he leaves his lair, as the delivery of a woman with child, as all these things are sure and certain,—even so the word of the Buddhas is sure and cannot fail, verily I shall become a Buddha." Therefore it is said,

118. Having heard the words of Buddha and of the angels of ten thousand worlds,
Glad, joyous, delighted, I then thought thus within myself:

119. The Buddhas speak not doubtful words, the Conquerors speak not vain words,
There is no falsehood in the Buddhas,—verily I shall become a Buddha.

120. As a clod cast into the air doth surely fall to the ground,
So the word of the glorious Buddhas is sure and everlasting.

121. As the death of all mortals is sure and constant,
So the word of the glorious Buddhas is sure and everlasting.

122. As the rising of the sun is certain when night has faded,
So the word of the glorious Buddhas is sure and everlasting.

123. As the roaring of a lion who has left his den is certain,
So the word of the glorious Buddhas is sure and everlasting.

124. As the delivery of women with child is certain,
So the word of the glorious Buddhas is sure and everlasting.

And having thus made the resolution, "I shall surely become Buddha," with a view to investigating the conditions that constitute a Buddha, exclaiming, "Where are the conditions that make the Buddha, are they found above or below, in the principal or the minor directions?" investigating successively the principles of all things, and beholding the first Perfection of Almsgiving, practised and followed by former Bodhisattas, he thus admonished his own soul: "Wise Sumedha, from this time forth thou must fulfil the perfection of Almsgiving; for as a water-jar overturned discharges the water so that none remains, and cannot recover it, even so if thou, indifferent to wealth and fame, and wife and child, and goods great and small, give away to all who come and ask everything that they require till nought remains, thou shalt seat thyself at the foot of the tree of Bodhi and become a Buddha." With these words he strenuously resolved to attain the first perfection of Almsgiving. Therefore it is said,

125. Come, I will search the Buddha-making conditions, this way and that,
Above and below, in all the ten directions, as far as the principles of things extend.
126. Then, as I made my search, I beheld the first Gift-perfection,
The high road followed by former sages.
127. Do thou strenuously taking it upon thyself advance
To this first perfection of almsgiving, if thou wilt attain Buddhaship.
128. As a brimming water-jar, overturned by any one,
Discharges entirely all the water, and retains none within,
129. Even so, when thou seest any that ask, great, small, and middling,
Do thou give away all in alms, as the water-jar overthrown.

But considering further, "There must be beside this other conditions that make a Buddha," and beholding the second Perfection of Moral Practice, he thought thus, "O wise Sumedha, from this day forth mayest thou fulfil the perfection of Morality; for as the Yak ox, regardless of his life, guards his bushy tail, even so thou shalt become Buddha, if from this day forward regardless of thy life thou keepest the moral precepts." And he strenuously resolved to attain the second perfection of Moral Practice. Therefore it is said,

130. For the conditions of a Buddha cannot be so few,
Let me investigate the other conditions that bring Buddhaship to maturity.
131. Then investigating I beheld the second Perfection of Morality
Practised and followed by former sages.

132. This second one do thou strenuously undertake,
And reach the perfection of Moral Practice if thou wilt attain Buddhahood.
133. And as the Yak cow, when her tail has got entangled in anything,
Then and there awaits death, and will not injure her tail,[1]
134. So also do thou, having fulfilled the moral precepts in the four stages,
Ever guard the Sīla as the Yak guards her tail.

But considering further, "These cannot be the only Buddha-making conditions," and beholding the third Perfection of Self-abnegation, he thought thus, "O wise Sumedha, mayest thou henceforth fulfil the perfection of Abnegation; for as a man long the denizen of a prison feels no love for it, but is discontented, and wishes to live there no more, even so do thou, likening all births to a prison-house, discontented with all births, and anxious to get rid of them, set thy face toward abnegation, thus shalt thou become Buddha." And he strenuously made the resolution to attain the third perfection of Self-abnegation. Therefore it is said,

135. For the conditions that make a Buddha cannot be so few,
I will investigate others, the conditions that bring Buddhaship to maturity.
136. Investigating then I beheld the third Perfection of Abnegation
Practised and followed by former sages.
137. This third one do thou strenuously undertake,
And reach the perfection of abnegation, if thou wilt attain Buddhahood.
138. As a man long a denizen of the house of bonds, oppressed with suffering,
Feels no pleasure therein, but rather longs for release,
139. Even so do thou look upon all births as prison-houses,
Set thy face toward self-abnegation, to obtain release from Existence.

But considering further, "These cannot be the only Buddha-making conditions," and beholding the fourth Perfection of Wisdom, he thought thus, "O wise Sumedha,

[1] Viz., I suppose, by dragging it forcibly away. This metaphor, which to us appears wanting in dignity, is a favourite one with the Hindus. The tail of the Yak or Tibetan ox (*Bos Grunniens*) is a beautiful object, and one of the insignia of Hindu royalty.

do thou from this day forth fulfil the perfection of Wisdom, avoiding no subject of knowledge, great, small, or middling,[1] do thou approach all wise men and ask them questions; for as the mendicant friar on his begging rounds, avoiding none of the families, great and small, that he frequents,[2] and wandering for alms from place to place, speedily gets food to support him, even so shalt thou, approaching all wise men, and asking them questions, become a Buddha." And he strenuously resolved to attain the fourth perfection of Wisdom. Therefore it is said,

140. For the conditions that make a Buddha cannot be so few,
I will investigate the other conditions that bring Buddhaship to maturity.
141. Investigating then I beheld the fourth Perfection of Wisdom
Practised and followed by former sages.
142. This fourth do thou strenuously undertake,
And reach the perfection of wisdom, if thou wilt attain Buddhahood.
143. And as a monk on his begging rounds avoids no families,
Either small, or great, or middling, and so obtains subsistence,
144. Even so thou, constantly questioning wise men,
And reaching the perfection of wisdom, shalt attain supreme Buddhaship.

But considering further, "These cannot be the only Buddha-making conditions," and seeing the fifth Perfection of Exertion, he thought thus, "O wise Sumedha, do thou from this day forth fulfil the perfection of Exertion. As the lion, the king of beasts, in every action[3] strenuously exerts himself, so if thou in all existences and in all thy acts art strenuous in exertion, and not a laggard, thou shalt become a Buddha." And he made a firm resolve to attain the fifth perfection of Exertion. Therefore it is said,

[1] Lit. "not avoiding anything among things great, small, and middling."
[2] After *kiñci* understand *kulaṁ*, as will be seen from v. 143.
[3] Lit. in all postures, walking, standing, etc.

145. For the conditions of a Buddha cannot be so few,
I will investigate the other conditions which bring Buddhaship to maturity.
146. Investigating then I beheld the fifth Perfection of Exertion
Practised and followed by former sages.
147. This fifth do thou strenuously undertake,
And reach the perfection of exertion, if thou wilt attain Buddhahood.
148. As the lion, king of beasts, in lying, standing and walking,
Is no laggard, but ever of resolute heart,
149. Even so do thou also in every existence strenuously exert thyself,
And reaching the perfection of exertion, thou shalt attain the supreme Buddhaship.

But considering further, "These cannot be the only Buddha-making conditions," and beholding the sixth Perfection of Patience, he thought to himself, "O wise Sumedha, do thou from this time forth fulfil the perfection of Longsuffering; be thou patient in praise and in reproach. And as when men throw things pure or foul upon the earth, the earth does not feel either desire or repulsion towards them, but suffers them, endures them and acquiesces in them, even so thou also, if thou art patient in praise and reproach, shalt become Buddha." And he strenuously resolved to attain the sixth perfection of Longsuffering. Therefore it is said,

150. For the conditions of a Buddha cannot be so few,
I will seek other conditions also which bring about Buddhaship.
151. And seeking then I beheld the sixth Perfection of Longsuffering
Practised and followed by former Buddhas.
152. Having strenuously taken upon thee this sixth perfection,
Then with unwavering mind thou shalt attain supreme Buddhaship.
153. And as the earth endures all that is thrown upon it,
Whether things pure or impure, and feels neither anger nor pity,
154. Even so enduring the praises and reproaches of all men,
Going on to perfect longsuffering, thou shalt attain supreme Buddhaship.

But further considering, "These cannot be the only conditions that make a Buddha," and beholding the seventh Perfection of Truth, he thought thus within himself, "O wise Sumedha, from this time forth do thou fulfil the perfection of Truth; though the thunderbolt descend upon thy head, do thou never under the influence of desire and other passions utter a conscious lie, for the sake of wealth or any other advantage. And as the planet Venus at all seasons pursues her own course, nor ever goes on another course forsaking her own, even so, if thou forsake not truth and utter no lie, thou shalt become Buddha." And he strenuously turned his mind to the seventh perfection of Truth. Therefore it is said,

155. For these are not all the conditions of a Buddha,
I will seek other conditions which bring about Buddhaship.
156. Seeking then I beheld the seventh Perfection of Truth
Practised and followed by former Buddhas.
157. Having strenuously taken upon thyself this seventh perfection,
Then free from duplicity of speech thou shalt attain supreme Buddhaship.
158. And as the planet Venus, balanced in all her times and seasons,
In the world of men and devas, departs not from her path,
159. Even so do thou not depart from the course of truth,[1]
Advancing to the perfection of truth, thou shalt attain supreme Buddhaship.

But further considering, "These cannot be the only conditions that make a Buddha," and beholding the eighth Perfection of Resolution, he thought thus within himself, "O wise Sumedha, do thou from this time forth fulfil the perfection of Resolution; whatsoever thou resolvest be thou unshaken in that resolution. For as a mountain, the wind beating upon it in all directions, trembles not, moves not, but stands in its place, even so thou, if unswerving in thy resolution, shalt become Buddha." And he strenuously resolved to attain the eighth perfection of Resolution. Therefore it is said,

160. For these are not all the conditions of a Buddha,
I will seek out other conditions that bring about Buddhaship.

[1] Lit. depart from thy course in the matter of truthful things.

161. Seeking then I beheld the eighth Perfection of Resolution
Practised and followed by former Buddhas.
162. Do thou resolutely take upon thyself this eighth perfection,
Then thou being immovable shalt attain supreme Buddhaship.
163. And as the rocky mountain, immovable, firmly based,
Is unshaken by many winds, and stands in its own place,
164. Even so do thou also remain ever immovable in resolution,
Advancing to the perfection of resolution, thou shalt attain supreme Buddhaship.

But further considering, "These cannot be the only conditions that make a Buddha," and beholding the ninth Perfection of Good-will, he thought thus within himself, "O wise Sumedha, do thou from this time forth fulfil the perfection of Good-will, mayest thou be of one mind towards friends and foes. And as water fills with its refreshing coolness good men and bad alike,[1] even so, if thou art of one mind in friendly feeling towards all mortals, thou shalt become Buddha." And he strenuously resolved to attain the ninth perfection of Good-will. Therefore it is said,

165. For these are not all the conditions of a Buddha,
I will seek out other conditions that bring about Buddhaship.
166. Seeking I beheld the ninth Perfection of Good-will
Practised and followed by former Buddhas.
167. Do thou, taking resolutely upon thyself this ninth perfection,
Become unrivalled in kindness, if thou wilt become Buddha.
168. And as water fills with its coolness
Good men and bad alike, and carries off all impurity,
169. Even so do thou look with friendship alike on the evil and the good,
Advancing to the perfection of kindness, thou shalt attain supreme Buddhaship.

But further considering, "These cannot be the only conditions that make a Buddha," and beholding the tenth Perfection of Equanimity, he thought thus within himself, "O wise Sumedha, from this time do thou fulfil the

[1] Lit. having made its coldness exactly alike for bad people and good people, pervades them.

perfection of Equanimity, be thou of equal mind in prosperity and adversity. And as the earth is indifferent when things pure or impure are cast upon it, even so, if thou art indifferent in prosperity and adversity, thou shalt become Buddha." And he strenuously resolved to attain the tenth perfection of Equanimity. Therefore it is said,

170. For these cannot be all the conditions of a Buddha,
I will seek other conditions that bring about Buddhaship.
171. Seeking then I beheld the tenth Perfection of Equanimity
Practised and followed by former Buddhas.
172. If thou take resolutely upon thyself this tenth perfection,
Becoming well-balanced and firm, thou shalt attain supreme Buddhaship.
173. And as the earth is indifferent to pure and impure things cast upon her,
To both alike, and is free from anger and favour,
174. Even so do thou ever be evenly-balanced in joy and grief,
Advancing to the perfection of equanimity, thou shalt attain supreme Buddhaship.

Then he thought, "These are the only conditions in this world that, bringing Buddhaship to perfection and constituting a Buddha, have to be fulfilled by Bodhisattas; beside the ten Perfections there are no others. And these ten Perfections are neither in the heaven above nor in the earth below, nor are they to be found in the east or the other quarters, but reside in my heart of flesh." Having thus realized that the Perfections were established in his heart, having strenuously resolved to keep them all, grasping them again and again, he mastered them forwards and backwards;[1] taking them at the end he went backward to the beginning, taking them at the beginning he placed them at the end,[2] taking them at the middle he carried them to the two ends, taking them at both ends he carried them to the middle.

[1] *i.e.* alternately from the first to the tenth and from the tenth to the first.
[2] *i.e.* put the first last.

Repeating, "The Perfections are the sacrifice of limbs, the Lesser Perfections are the sacrifice of property, the Unlimited Perfections are the sacrifice of life," he mastered them as the Perfections, the Lesser Perfections and the Unlimited Perfections,—like one who converts two kindred oils into one,[1] or like one who, using Mount Meru for his churning-rod, churns the great Cakkavāla ocean. And as he grasped again and again the ten Perfections, by the power of his piety this earth, four nahutas and eight hundred thousand leagues in breadth, like a bundle of reeds trodden by an elephant, or a sugar-mill in motion, uttering a mighty roar, trembled, shook and quaked, and spun round like a potter's wheel or the wheel of an oil-mill. Therefore it is said,

175. These are all the conditions in the world that bring Buddhaship to perfection:
Beyond these are no others, therein do thou stand fast.
176. While he grasped these conditions natural and intrinsic,[2]
By the power of his piety the earth of ten thousand worlds quaked.
177. The earth sways and thunders like a sugar-mill at work,
Like the wheel of an oil-mill so shakes the earth.

And while the earth was trembling the people of Ramma, unable to endure it, like great Sāl-trees overthrown by the wind that blows at the end of a cycle, fell swooning here and there, while waterpots and other vessels, revolving like a jar on a potter's wheel, struck against each other and were dashed and ground to pieces. The multitudes in fear and trembling approaching the Teacher said, "Tell us, Blessed one, is this turmoil caused by dragons, or is it caused by either demons, or ogres, or by celestial beings?—for this we know not, but truly this whole multitude is grievously afflicted. Pray does

[1] Vijesinha.

[2] Vijesinha writes to me, "Natural and intrinsic virtues. The Sinhalese gloss says: *paramārthavū rasasahitavū lakshaṇa-æti nohot svabhāvalakshaṇa hā sarvadharmasādhāraṇalakshaṇa-æti.* In the latter case it would mean, having the quality of conformity with all laws."

this portend evil to the world or good?—tell us the cause of it." The Teacher hearing their words said, "Fear not nor be troubled, there is no danger to you from this. The wise Sumedha, concerning whom I predicted this day, 'Hereafter he will be a Buddha named Gotama,' is now mastering the Perfections, and while he masters them and turns them about, by the power of his piety the whole ten thousand worlds with one accord quake and thunder." Therefore it is said,

178. All the multitude that was there in attendance on the Buddha,
Trembling, fell swooning there upon the ground.
179. Many thousands of waterpots and many hundred jars
Were crushed and pounded there and dashed against each other.
180. Excited, trembling, terrified, confused, their sense disordered,
The multitudes assembling, approached the Buddha.
181. Say, will it be good or evil to the world?
The whole world is afflicted, ward off this (danger), thou Omniscient One.
182. Then the Great Sage Dīpankara enjoined upon them,
Be confident, be not afraid at this earthquaking:
183. He concerning whom I predicted this day, He will be a Buddha in this world,
The same is investigating the time-honoured Conditions followed by the Buddhas.
184. Therefore while he is investigating fully these Conditions, the groundwork of a Buddha,
The earth of ten thousand worlds is shaken in the world of men and of angels.

And the people hearing the Buddha's words, joyful and delighted, taking with them garlands, perfumes and unguents, left the city of Ramma, and went to the Bodhisatta. And having offered their flowers and other presents, and bowed to him and respectfully saluted him, they returned to the city of Ramma. And the Bodhisatta, having made a strenuous exertion and resolve, rose from the seat on which he sat. Therefore it is said,

185. Having heard the Buddha's word, their minds were straightway calmed,
All of them approaching me again paid me their homage.

186. Having taken upon me the Perfections of a Buddha, having made firm my resolve,
Having bowed to Dīpankara, I rose from my seat.

And as the Bodhisatta rose from his seat, the angels in all the ten thousand worlds having assembled and offered him garlands and perfumes, uttered these and other words of praise and blessing, "Venerable hermit Sumedha, this day thou hast made a mighty resolve at the feet of Dīpankara Buddha, mayest thou fulfil it without let or hindrance: fear not nor be dismayed, may not the slightest sickness visit thy frame, quickly exercise the Perfections and attain supreme Buddhaship. As the flowering and fruit-bearing trees bring forth flowers and fruit in their season, so do thou also, not letting the right season pass by, quickly reach the supreme knowledge of a Buddha." And thus having spoken, they returned each one to his celestial home. Then the Bodhisatta, having received the homage of the angels, made a strenuous exertion and resolve, saying, "Having fulfilled the ten Perfections, at the end of four asankheyyas and a hundred thousand cycles I shall become a Buddha." And rising into the air he returned to Himavanta. Therefore it is said,

187. As he rose from his seat both angels and men
Sprinkle him with celestial and earthly flowers.
188. Both angels and men pronounce their blessing,
A great prayer thou hast made, mayest thou obtain it according to thy wish.
189. May all dangers be averted, may every sickness vanish,
Mayest thou have no hindrance,—quickly reach the supreme knowledge of a Buddha.
190. As when the season is come the flowering trees do blossom,
Even so do thou, O mighty One, blossom with the wisdom of a Buddha.
191. As all the Buddhas have fulfilled the ten Perfections,
Even so do thou, O mighty One, fulfil the ten Perfections.
192. As all the Buddhas are enlightened on the throne of knowledge,
Even so do thou, O mighty One, receive enlightenment in the wisdom of a Buddha.

193. As all the Buddhas have established the supremacy of the Law,
Even so do thou, O mighty One, establish the supremacy of the Law.
194. As the moon on the mid-day of the month shines in her purity,
Even so do thou, with thy mind at the full, shine in ten thousand worlds.
195. As the sun released by Rāhu glows fervently in his heat,
Even so, having redeemed mankind, do thou shine in all thy majesty.
196. As all the rivers find their way to the great ocean,
Even so may the worlds of men and angels take refuge in thee.
197. The Bodhisatta extolled with these praises, taking on himself the ten Conditions,
Commencing to fulfil these Conditions, entered the forest.

End of the Story of Sumedha.

And the people of the city of Ramma, having returned to the city, kept open house to the priesthood with the Buddha at their head. The Teacher having preached the Law to them, and established them in the three Refuges and the other branches of the Faith, departing from the city of Ramma, living thereafter his allotted span of life, having fulfilled all the duties of a Buddha, in due course attained Nirvā*n*a in that element of annihilation in which no trace of existence remains. On this subject all that need be said can be learnt from the narrative in the Buddhava*m*sa, for it is said in that work,

198. Then they, having entertained the Chief of the world with his clergy,
Took refuge in the Teacher Dīpankara.
199. Some the Buddha established in the Refuges,
Some in the five Precepts, others in the ten.
200. To some he gives the privilege of priesthood, the four glorious Fruitions,
On some he bestows those peerless qualities the analytical Knowledges.
201. To some the Lord of men grants the eight sublime Acquisitions,
On some he bestows the three Wisdoms and the six supernatural Faculties.
202. In this order[1] the Great Sage exhorts the multitude.
Therewith the commandment of the world's Protector was spread wide abroad.

[1] Vij. says, "In that order, viz. in the *Saraṇāgamana* first, then in the *Pañcasīla*, then in the *Dasasīla*, and so on."

203. He of the mighty jaw, of the broad shoulder, Dīpankara by name,
Procured the salvation of many men, warded off from them future punishment.

204. Beholding persons ripe for salvation, reaching them in an instant,
Even at a distance of four hundred thousand leagues, the Great Sage awakened them (to the knowledge of the truth).

205. At the first conversion the Buddha converted a thousand millions.
At the second the Protector converted a hundred thousand.

206. When the Buddha preached the truth in the angel world,
There took place a third conversion of nine hundred millions.

207. The Teacher Dīpankara had three assemblies,
The first was a meeting of a million millions.

208. Again when the Conqueror went into seclusion at Nārada Kū*t*a,
A thousand million spotless Arhats met together.

209. When the Mighty One dwelt on the lofty rock Sudassana,
Then the Sage surrounded himself with nine hundred thousand millions.

210. At that time I was an ascetic wearing matted hair, a man of austere penances,
Moving through the air, accomplished in the five supernatural Faculties.

211. The (simultaneous) conversion of tens of thousands, of twenties of thousands, took place,
Of ones and twos the conversions were beyond computation.[1]

212. Then did the pure religion of Dīpankara Buddha become widely spread,
Known to many men prosperous and flourishing.

213. Four hundred thousand saints, possessed of the six Faculties, endowed with miraculous powers,
Ever attend upon Dīpankara, knower of the three worlds.

214. Blameworthy are all they who at that time leave the human existence,
Not having obtained final sanctity, still imperfect in knowledge.

215. The word of Buddha shines in the world of men and angels, made to blossom by saints such as these,
Freed from human passion, void of all taint (of sin).

216. The city of Dīpankara Buddha was called Rammavatī,
The khattiya Sumedha was his father, Sumedhā his mother.

217. Sumangala and Tissa were his chief disciples,
And Sāgata was the servitor of Dīpankara Buddha.

218. Nandā and Sunandā were his chief female disciples.
The Bodhi-tree of this Buddha is called the Pipphali.[2]

219. Eighty cubits in height the Great Sage Dīpankara
Shone conspicuous as a Deodar pine, or as a noble Sāl-tree in full bloom.

[1] Lit. "arithmetically innumerable."
[2] The Banyan-tree.

220. A hundred thousand years was the age of this Great Sage,
And so long as he was living on earth he brought many men to salvation.
221. Having made the Truth to flourish, having saved great multitudes of men,
Having flamed like a mass of fire, he died together with his disciples.
222. And all this power, this glory, these jewel-wheels on his feet,
All is wholly gone,—are not all existing things vanity!
223. After Dīpankara was the Leader named Ko*nd*añña,
Of infinite power, of boundless renown, immeasurable, unrivalled.

Next to the Dīpankara Buddha, after the lapse of one asankheyya, the Teacher Ko*nd*añña appeared. He also had three assemblies of saints, at the first assembly there were a million millions, at the second ten thousand millions, at the third nine hundred millions. At that time the Bodhisatta, having been born as a universal monarch named Vijitāvin, kept open house to the priesthood with the Buddha at their head, in number a million of millions. The Teacher having predicted of the Bodhisatta, "He will become a Buddha," preached the Law. He having heard the Teacher's preaching gave up his kingdom and became a Buddhist monk. Having mastered the three Treasuries,[1] having obtained the six supernatural Faculties, and having practised without failure the ecstatic meditation, he was reborn in the Brahma heavens. The city of Ko*nd*añña Buddha was Rammavatī, the khattiya Sunanda was his father, his mother was queen Sujātā, Bhadda and Subhadda were his two chief disciples, Anuruddha was his servitor, Tissā and Upatissā his chief female disciples, his Bodhi-tree was the Sālakalyā*n*i, his body was eighty-eight cubits high, and the duration of his life was a hundred thousand years.

After him, at the end of one asankheyya, in one and the same cycle four Buddhas were born, Mangala, Sumana, Revata and Sobhita. Mangala Buddha had three assemblies of saints, of these at the first there were

[1] The three divisions of the Buddhist Scriptures.

a million million priests, at the second ten thousand millions, at the third nine hundred millions. It is related that a step-brother of his, prince Ānanda, accompanied by an assembly of nine hundred millions, went to the Teacher to hear him preach the Law. The Teacher gave a discourse dealing successively with his various doctrines, and Ānanda and his whole retinue attained Arhatship together with the analytical Knowledges. The Teacher looking back upon the meritorious works done by these men of family in former existences, and perceiving that they had merit to acquire the robe and bowl by miraculous means, stretching forth his right hand exclaimed, "Come, priests."[1] Then straightway all of them having become equipped with miraculously obtained robes and bowls, and perfect in decorum,[2] as if they were elders of sixty years standing, paid homage to the Teacher and attended upon him. This was his third assembly of saints. And whereas with other Buddhas a light shone from their bodies to the distance of eighty cubits on every side, it was not so with this Buddha, but the light from his body permanently filled ten thousand worlds, and trees, earth, mountains, seas and all other things, not excepting even pots and pans and such-like articles, became as it were overspread with a film of gold. The duration of his life was ninety thousand years, and during the whole of this period the sun, moon and other heavenly bodies could not shine by their own light, and there was no distinction between night and day. By day all living beings went about in the light of the Buddha as if in the light of the sun, and men ascertained the limits of night and day only by the flowers that blossomed in the evening and by the birds and other animals that uttered their cries in the morning. If I am asked, "What, do not other Buddhas also possess this power?" I reply, Cer-

[1] The formula by which a Buddha admits a layman to the priesthood.
[2] Vijesinha.

tainly they do, for they might at will fill with their lustre ten thousand worlds or more. But in accordance with a prayer made by him in a former existence, the lustre of Mangala Buddha permanently filled ten thousand worlds, just as the lustre of the others permanently extended to the distance of a fathom.[1] The story is that when he was performing the duties of a Bodhisatta,[2] being in an existence corresponding to the Vessantara existence,[3] he dwelt with his wife and children on a mountain like the Vanka mountain (of the Vessantara Jātaka). One day a demon named Kharadāṭhika,[4] hearing of the Bodhisatta's inclination to giving, approached him in the guise of a brahmin, and asked the Bodhisatta for his two children. The Bodhisatta, exclaiming, "I give my children to the brahmin," cheerfully and joyfully gave up both the children, thereby causing the ocean-girt earth to quake.[5] The demon, standing by the bench at the end of the cloistered walk, while the Bodhisatta looked on, devoured the children like a bunch of roots. Not a particle of sorrow[6] arose in the Bodhisatta as he looked on the demon, and saw his mouth as soon as he opened it disgorging streams of blood like flames of fire, nay, a great joy and satisfaction welled within him as he thought, "My gift was well given." And he put up the prayer, "By the merit of this deed may rays of light one day issue from me in this very way." In consequence of this prayer of his it was that the rays emitted from his body when he became Buddha filled so vast a space. There was also another deed done by him in a former existence. It is related that, when a Bodhisatta, having visited the relic shrine of a Buddha, he exclaimed, "I

[1] Lit. "like the fathom-light of the others, so the personal lustre of Mangala Buddha remained constantly pervading ten thousand worlds."
[2] *i.e.* the Pāramitās.
[3] *i.e.* his last birth before attaining Buddhahood.
[4] This name means "sharp-fanged."
[5] In approval of his act of faith.
[6] Lit. "no grief as big as the tip of a hair."

ought to sacrifice my life for this Buddha," and having wrapped round the whole of his body in the same way that torches are wrapped, and having filled with clarified butter a golden vessel with jewelled wick-holders, worth a hundred thousand pieces, he lit therein a thousand wicks, and having set fire to the whole of his body beginning with his head, he spent the whole night in circumambulating the shrine. And as he thus strove till dawn not the root of a hair of his head was even heated, 'twas as one enters the calyx of a lotus, for the Truth guards him who guards himself. Therefore has the Blessed One said,

224. Religion verily protects him who walks according thereto,
Religion rightly followed brings happiness.
This blessing is then in rightly following the Law,
The righteous man goes not to a state of punishment.

And through the merit of this work also the bodily lustre of this Buddha constantly extended through ten thousand worlds. At this time our Bodhisatta,[1] having been born as the brahmin Suruci, approached the Teacher with the view of inviting him to his house, and having heard his sweet discourse, said, "Lord, take your meal with me to-morrow." "Brahmin, how many monks do you wish for?" "Nay but how many monks have you in your escort?" At that time was the Teacher's first assembly, and accordingly he replied, "A million millions." "Lord, bring them all with you and come and take your meal at my house." The Teacher consented. The Brahmin having invited them for the next day, on his way home thought to himself, "I am perfectly well able to supply

[1] Viz. Gotama Bodhisatta.

all these monks with broth and rice and clothes and such-like necessaries, but how can there be room for them to sit down?" This thought of his caused the marble throne of the archangel Indra, three hundred and thirty-six thousand leagues away, to become warm.[1] Indra exclaiming, "Who wishes to bring me down from my abode?" and looking down with the divine eye beheld the Bodhisatta, and said, "The brahmin Suruci having invited the clergy with the Buddha at their head is perplexed for room to seat them, it behoves me also to go thither and obtain a share of his merit." And having miraculously assumed the form of a carpenter, axe in hand he appeared before the Bodhisatta and said, "Has any one got a job to be done for hire?" The Bodhisatta seeing him said, "What sort of work can you do?" "There's no art that I do not know; any house or hall that anybody orders me to build, I'll build it for him." "Very well, I've got a job to be done." "What is it, sir?" "I've invited a million million priests for to-morrow, will you build a hall to seat them all?" "I'll build one with pleasure if you've the means of paying me." "I have, my good man." "Very well, I'll build it." And he went and began looking out for a site. There was a spot some fifty leagues in extent[2] as level as a kasi*n*a circle.[3] Indra fixed his eyes upon it, while he thought to himself, "Let a hall made of the seven precious stones rise up over such and such an extent of ground." Immediately the edifice bursting through the ground rose up. The golden pillars of this hall had silver capitals,[4] the silver pillars had golden capitals, the gem pillars had coral capitals, the coral pillars had gem capitals, while those pillars which were made of all the

[1] When a good man is in difficulty, Indra is apprised of it by his marble throne becoming warm.

[2] Lit. twelve or thirteen yojanas; a yojana is four leagues.

[3] Used in the ecstatic meditation.

[4] The Pali word for the capital of a column is gha*t*aka, "little pot."

seven precious stones had capitals of the same. Next he said, "Let the hall have hanging wreaths of little bells at intervals," and looked again. The instant he looked a fringe of bells hung down, whose musical tinkling, as they were stirred by a gentle breeze, was like a symphony of the five sorts of instruments, or as when the heavenly choirs are going on. He thought, "Let there be hanging garlands of perfumes and flowers," and there the garlands hung. He thought, "Let seats and benches for a million million monks rise up through the earth," and straightway they appeared. He thought, "Let water vessels rise up at each corner of the building," and the water vessels arose. Having by his miraculous power effected all this, he went to the brahmin and said, "Come, sir, look at your hall, and pay me my wages." The Bodhisatta went and looked at the hall, and as he looked his whole frame was thrilled in every part with fivefold joy. And as he gazed on the hall he thought thus within himself, "This hall was not wrought by mortal hands, but surely through my good intention, my good action, the palace of Indra became hot, and hence this hall must have been built by the archangel Indra; it is not right that in such a hall as this I should give alms for a single day, I will give alms for a whole week." For the gift of external goods, however great, cannot give satisfaction to the Bodhisattas, but the Bodhisattas feel joy at their self-renunciation when they sever the crowned head, put out the henna-anointed eyes, cut out the heart and give it away. For when our Bodhisatta in the Sivijātaka gave alms in the middle of his capital, at the four gates of the city, at a daily expenditure of five bushels of gold coins, this liberality failed to arouse within him a feeling of satisfaction at his renunciation. But on the other hand, when the archangel Indra came to him in the disguise of a brahmin, and asked for his eyes, then indeed, as he took them out and gave them away, laughter rose within him, nor did his heart swerve a hair's breadth from its purpose. And hence we see that as regards almsgiving the Bodhisattas can have no satiety. Therefore this Bodhisatta also thinking, "I ought to give alms for seven days to a million million priests," seated them in that hall, and for a week gave them the alms called gavapâna.[1] Men alone were not able to wait upon them, but the angels themselves, taking turns with men, waited upon them. A space of fifty leagues or more sufficed not to contain the monks, yet they seated themselves each by his own supernatural power. On the last day, having caused the bowls of all the monks to be washed, and filled them with butter clarified and unclarified, honey and molasses, for medicinal use, he gave them back to them, together with the three robes. The robes and cloaks received by novices and ordained priests were worth a hundred thousand. The Teacher, when he returned thanks, considering, "This man has given such great alms, who can he be?" and perceiving that at the end of two asankheyyas and four thousand cycles he would become a Buddha named Gotama, addressing the Bodhisatta, made this prediction: "After the lapse of such and such a period thou shalt become a Buddha named Gotama." The Bodhisatta, hearing the prediction, thought, "It seems that I am to become a Buddha, what good can a householder's life do me? I will give up the world," and, treating all this prosperity like so much drivel, he received ordination at the hands of the Teacher. And having embraced the ascetic life and learnt the word of Buddha, and having attained the supernatural Faculties and the Attainments, at the end of his life he was reborn in the Brahma heavens. The city of Mangala Buddha was called Uttara, his father was the khattiya Uttara; his mother was Uttarā, Sudeva and Dhammasena were his two chief

[1] According to the gloss printed in the text it is a compound of milk, rice, honey, sugar and clarified butter.

disciples, Pālita was his servitor, Sīvalī and Asokā his two chief female disciples. The Nāga was his Bodhi-tree, his body was eighty-eight cubits high. When his death took place, after he had lived ninety thousand years, at the same instant ten thousand worlds were involved in darkness, and in all worlds there was a great cry and lamentation of men.

225. After Ko*nd*añña the Leader named Mangala,
Dispelling darkness in the world, held aloft the torch of truth.

And after the Buddha had died, shrouding in darkness ten thousand worlds, the Teacher named Sumana appeared. He also had three great assemblies of saints, at the first assembly the priests were a million millions, at the second, on the Golden Mountain, ninety million of millions, at the third eighty million of millions. At this time the Bodhisatta was the Nāga king Atula, mighty and powerful. And he, hearing that a Buddha had appeared, left the Nāga world, accompanied by his assembled kinsmen, and, making offerings with celestial music to the Buddha, whose retinue was a million million of monks, and having given great gifts, bestowing upon each two garments of fine cloth, he was established in the Three Refuges. And this Teacher also foretold of him, "One day he will be a Buddha." The city of this Buddha was named Khema, Sudatta was his father, Sirimā his mother, Sara*n*a and Bhāvitatta his chief disciples, Udena his servitor, So*n*ā and Upaso*n*ā his chief female disciples. The Nāga was his Bodhi-tree, his body was ninety cubits high, and his age ninety thousand years.

226. After Mangala came the Leader named Sumana,
In all things unequalled, the best of all beings.

After him the Teacher Revata appeared. He also had

three assemblies of saints. At the first assembly the priests were innumerable, at the second there were a million millions, so also at the third. At that time the Bodhisatta having been born as the brahmin Atideva, having heard the Teacher's preaching, was established in the Three Refuges. And raising his clasped hands to his head, having praised the Teacher's abandonment of human passion, presented him with a monk's upper robe. And he also made the prediction, "Thou wilt become a Buddha." Now the city of this Buddha was called Sudhaññavatī, his father was the khattiya Vipula, his mother Vipulā, Varuṇa and Brahmadeva his chief disciples, Sambhava his servitor, Bhaddā and Subhaddā his chief female disciples, and the Nāga-tree his Bo-tree. His body was eighty cubits high, and his age sixty thousand years.

227. After Sumana came the Leader named Revata,
The Conqueror unequalled, incomparable, unmatched, supreme.

After him appeared the Teacher *Sobhita*. He also had three assemblies of saints; at the first assembly a thousand million monks were present, at the second nine hundred millions, at the third eight hundred millions. At that time the Bodisat having been born as *the brahman Ajita*, and having heard the Teacher's preaching, was established in the Three Refuges, and gave a great donation to the Order of monks, with the Buddha at their head. To this man also he prophesied, saying, "Thou shalt become a Buddha." Sudhamma was the name of the city of this Blessed One, Sudhamma the king was his father, Sudhammā his mother, Asama and Sunetta his chief disciples, Anoma his servitor, Nakulā and Sujātā his chief female disciples, and the Nāga-tree his Bo-tree; his body was fifty-eight cubits high, and his age ninety thousand years.

228. After Revata came the Leader named Sobhita,
Subdued and mild, unequalled and unrivalled.

After him, when an asaṇkheyya had elapsed, three Buddhas were born in one kalpa—Anomadassin, Paduma, and Nārada. Anomadassin had three assemblies of saints; at the first eight hundred thousand monks were present, at the second seven, at the third six. At that time the Bodisat was a *Yakkha chief*, mighty and powerful, the lord of many millions of millions of yakkhas. He, hearing that a Buddha had appeared, came and gave a great donation to the Order of monks, with the Buddha at their head. And the Teacher prophesied to him too, saying, "Hereafter thou shalt be a Buddha." The city of Anomadassin the Blessed One was called Candavatī, Yasava the king was his father, Yasodharā his mother, Nisabha and Anoma his chief disciples, Varuṇa his servitor, Sundarī and Sumanā his chief female disciples, the Arjuna-tree his Bo-tree; his body was fifty-eight cubits high, his age a hundred thousand years.

229. After Sobhita came the perfect Buddha—the best of men—
Anomadassin, of infinite fame, glorious, difficult to surpass.

After him appeared the Teacher named *Paduma*. He too had three assemblies of saints; at the first assembly a million million monks were present, at the second three hundred thousand, at the third two hundred thousand of the monks who dwelt at a great grove in the uninhabited forest. At that time, whilst the Tathāgata was living in that grove, the Bodisat having been born as *a lion*, saw the Teacher plunged in ecstatic trance, and with trustful heart made obesiance to him, and walking round him with reverence, experienced great joy, and thrice uttered a mighty roar. For seven days he laid not aside the bliss arising from the thought of the Buddha, but through joy and gladness, seeking not after prey, he kept in attendance there, offering up his life. When the Teacher, after seven days, aroused himself from his trance, he looked upon the lion and thought, "He will put trust in the Order of monks and make obeisance to them; let them draw near." At that very moment the monks drew near, and the lion put faith in the Order. The Teacher, knowing his thoughts, prophesied, saying, "Hereafter he shall be a Buddha." Now the city of Paduma the Blessed One was called Champaka, his father was Paduma the king, his mother Asamā, Sāla and Upasāla were his chief disciples, Varuṇa his servitor, Rāmā and Uparāmā his chief female disciples, the Crimson-tree his Bo-tree; his body was fifty-eight cubits high, and his age was a hundred thousand years.

230. After Anomadassin came the perfect Buddha, the best of men,
Paduma by name, unequalled, and without a rival.

After him appeared the Teacher named *Nārada.* He also had three assemblies of saints; at the first assembly a million million monks were present, at the second ninety million million, at the third eighty million million. At that time the Bodisat, having taken the vows as *a sage*, acquired the five kinds of Wisdom and the eight sublime Acquisitions, and gave a great donation to the Order, with the Buddha at their head, making an offering of red sandal wood. And to him also he prophesied, "Hereafter thou shalt be a Buddha." The city of this Blessed One was called Dhaññavati, his father was Sumedha the warrior, his mother Anomā, Bhaddasāla and Jetamitta his chief disciples, Vāseṭṭha his servitor, Uttarā and Pagguṇī his chief female disciples, the great Crimson-tree was his Bo-tree; his body was eighty-eight cubits high, and his age was ninety thousand years.

231. After Paduma came the perfect Buddha, the best of men,
Nārada by name, unequalled, and without a rival.

After Nārada the Buddha a hundred thousand world-cycles ago there appeared in one kalpa only one Buddha called *Padumuttara.* He also had three assemblies of saints; at the first a million million monks were present, at the second, on the Vebhāra Mountain, nine hundred thousand million, at the third eight hundred thousand million. At that time the Bodisat, born as the *Mahratta of the name of Jaṭila,* gave an offering of robes to the Order, with the Buddha at their head. And to him also he announced, "Hereafter thou shalt be a Buddha." And at the time of Padumuttara the Blessed One there were no infidels, but all, men and angels, took refuge in the Buddha. His city was called Haŋsavatī, his father was Ānanda the warrior, his mother Sujātā, Devala and Sujāta his chief disciples, Sumana his servitor, Amitā and Asamā his chief female disciples, the Sāla-tree his Bo-tree; his body was eighty-eight cubits high, the light from his body extended twelve leagues, and his age was a hundred thousand years.

232. After Nārada came the perfect Buddha, the best of men,
Padumuttara by name, the Conqueror unshaken, like the sea.

After him, when thirty thousand world-cycles had elapsed, two Buddhas, Sumedha and Sujāta, were born in one kalpa. *Sumedha* also had three assemblies of his saints; at the first assembly, in the city Sudassana, a thousand million sinless ones were present, at the second nine hundred, at the third eight hundred. At that time the Bodisat, born as *the brahman youth named Uttara,* lavished eight hundred millions of money he had saved in giving a great donation to the Order, with the Buddha at their head. And he then listened to the Law, and accepted the Refuges, and abandoned his home, and took the vows. And to him also the Buddha prophesied, saying, "Hereafter thou shalt be a Buddha." The city of Sumedha the Blessed One was called Sudassana, Sudatta the king was his father, Sudattā his mother, Sarana and Sabbakāma his two chief disciples, Sāgara his servitor, Rāmā and Surāmā his two chief female disciples, the great Champaka-tree his Bo-tree; his body was eighty-eight cubits high, and his age was ninety thousand years.

233. After Padumuttara came the Leader named Sumedha,
The Sage hard to equal, brilliant in glory, supreme in all the world.

After him appeared the Teacher *Sujāta.* He also had three assemblies of his saints; at the first assembly sixty thousand monks were present, at the second fifty, at the third forty. At that time the Bodisat was a *universal monarch;* and hearing that a Buddha was born he went to him and heard the Law, and gave to the Order, with the Buddha at their head, his kingdom of the four continents with its seven treasures, and took the vows under the Teacher. All the dwellers in the land, taking advantage of the birth of a Buddha in their midst, did duty as servants in the monasteries, and continually gave great donations to the Order, with the Buddha at their head. And to him also the Teacher prophesied. The city of this Blessed One was called Sumangala, Uggata the king was his father, Pabhāvatī his mother, Sudassana and

Deva his chief disciples, Nārada his servitor, Nāgā and Nāgasamālā his chief female disciples, and the great Bambu-tree his Bo-tree; this tree, they say, had smaller hollows and thicker wood than ordinary bambus have,[1] and in its mighty upper branches it was as brilliant as a bunch of peacocks' tails. The body of this Blessed One was fifty cubits high, and his age was ninety thousand years.

234. In that age, the Maṇḍakalpa, appeared the Leader Sujāta,
Mighty jawed and grandly framed, whose measure none can take, and hard to equal.

After him, when eighteen hundred world-cycles had elapsed, three Buddhas, Piyadassin, Atthadassin, and Dhammadassin, were born in one kalpa. *Piyadassin* also had three assemblies of his saints; at the first a million million monks were present, at the second nine hundred million, at the third eight hundred million. At that time the Bodisat, as *a young brahman called Kassapa,* who had thoroughly learnt the three Vedas, listened to the Teacher's preaching of the Law, and built a monastery at a cost of a million million, and stood firm in the Refuges and the Precepts. And to him the Teacher prophesied, saying, "After the lapse of eighteen hundred kalpas thou shalt become a Buddha." The city of this Blessed One was called Anoma, his father was Sudinna the king, his mother Candā, Pālita and Sabbadassin his chief disciples, Sobhita his servitor, Sujātā and Dhammadinnā his chief female disciples, and the Priyaŋgu-tree his Bo-tree. His body was eighty cubits high, and his age ninety thousand years.

[1] Compare Jātaka No. 20 below.

235. After Sujāta came Piyadassin, Leader of the world,
Self-taught, hard to match, unequalled, of great glory.

After him appeared the Teacher called *Atthadassin.* He too had three assemblies of his saints; at the first nine million eight hundred thousand monks were present, at the second eight million eight hundred thousand, and the same number at the third. At that time the Bodisat, as the mighty *ascetic Susima,* brought from heaven the sunshade of Mandārava flowers, and offered it to the Teacher, who prophesied also to him. The city of this Blessed One was called Sobhita, Sāgara the king was his father, Sudassanā his mother, Santa and Apasanta his chief disciples, Abhaya his servitor, Dhammā and Sudhammā his chief female disciples, and the Champaka his Bo-tree. His body was eighty cubits high, the glory from his body always extended over a league, and his age was a hundred thousand years.

236. In the same Maṇḍakalpa Atthadassin, best of men,
Dispelled the thick darkness, and attained supreme Enlightenment.

After him appeared the Teacher named *Dhammadassin.* He too had three assemblies of his saints; at the first a thousand million monks were present, at the second seven hundred millions, at the third eight hundred millions. At that time the Bodisat, as *Sakka the king of the gods,* made an offering of sweet-smelling flowers from heaven, and heavenly music. And to him too the Teacher prophesied. The city of this Blessed One was called Saraṇa, his father was Saraṇa the king, his mother Sunandā, Paduma and Phussadeva his chief disciples, Sunetta his servitor, Khemā and Sabbanāmā his chief female disciples, and the red Kuravaka-tree (called also

Bimbijāla) his Bo-tree. His body was eighty cubits high, and his age a hundred thousand years.

> 237. In the same Maṇḍakalpa the far-famed Dhammadassin
> Dispelled the thick darkness, illumined earth and heaven.

After him, ninety-four world-cycles ago, only one Buddha, by name *Siddhattha*, appeared in one kalpa. Of his disciples too there were three assemblies; at the first assembly a million million monks were present, at the second nine hundred millions, at the third eight hundred millions. At that time the Bodisat, as the *ascetic Mangala* of great glory and gifted with the powers derived from the Higher Wisdom, brought a great jambu fruit and presented it to the Tathāgata. The Teacher, having eaten the fruit, prophesied to the Bodisat, saying, "Ninety-four kalpas hence thou shalt become a Buddha." The city of this Blessed One was called Vebhāra, Jayasena the king was his father, Suphassā his mother, Sambala and Sumitta his chief disciples, Revata his servitor, Sīvalī and Surāmā his chief female disciples, and the Kaṇikāra-tree his Bo-tree. His body was sixty cubits high, and his age a hundred thousand years.

> 238. After Dhammadassin, the Leader named Siddhattha
> Rose like the sun, bringing all darkness to an end.

After him, ninety-two world-cycles ago, two Buddhas, Tissa and Phussa by name, were born in one kalpa. *Tissa* the Blessed One had three assemblies of his saints; at the first a thousand millions of monks were present, at the second nine hundred millions, at the third eight hundred millions. At that time the Bodisat was born as the wealthy and famous *warrior-chief Sujāta*. When he had taken the vows and acquired the wonderful powers of a rishi, he heard that a Buddha had been born; and taking a heaven-grown Mandārava lotus, and flowers of the Pāricchattaka-tree (which grows in Indra's heaven), he offered them to the Tathāgata as he walked in the midst of his disciples, and he spread an awning of flowers in the sky. To him, too, the Teacher prophesied, saying, "Ninety-two kalpas hence thou shalt become a Buddha." The city of this Blessed One was called Khema, Janasandha the warrior-chief was his father, Padumā his mother, the god Brahmā and Udaya his chief disciples, Sambhava his servitor, Phussā and Sudattā his chief female disciples, and the Asana-tree his Bo-tree. His body was sixty cubits high, and his age a hundred thousand years.

239. After Siddhattha, Tissa, the unequalled and unrivalled,
Of infinite virtue and glory, was the chief Guide of the world.

After him appeared the Teacher named *Phussa*. He too had three assemblies of his saints; at the first assembly six million monks were present, at the second five, at the third three million two hundred thousand. At that time the Bodisat, born as the *warrior-chief Vijitavī*, laid aside his kingdom, and, taking the vows under the Teacher, learnt the three Piṭakas, and preached the Law to the people, and fulfilled the Perfection of Morality.[1] And the Buddha prophesied to him in the same manner. The city of this Blessed One was called Kāsi (Benares), Jayasena the king was his father, Sirimā his mother, Surakkhita and Dhammasena his chief disciples, Sabhiya his servitor, Cālā and Upacālā his chief female disciples,

[1] Comp. pp. 19–20, verses 130–134.

and the Āmalaka-tree his Bo-tree. His body was fifty-eight cubits high, and his age ninety thousand years.

240. In the same Maṇḍakalpa Phussa was the Teacher supreme,
Unequalled, unrivalled, the chief Guide of the world.

After him, ninety world-cycles ago, appeared the Blessed One named *Vipassin.* He too had three assemblies of his saints; at the first assembly six million eight hundred thousand monks were present, in the second one hundred thousand, in the third eighty thousand. At that time the Bodisat, born as the mighty and powerful *snake king Atula*, gave to the Blessed One a golden chair, inlaid with the seven kinds of gems. To him also he prophesied, saying, "Ninety-one world-cycles hence thou shalt become a Buddha." The city of this Blessed One was called Bandhumatī, Bandhumā the king was his father, Bandhumatī his mother, Khandha and Tissa his chief disciples, Asoka his servitor, Candā and Candamittā his chief female disciples, and the Bignonia (or Pāṭali-tree) his Bo-tree. His body was eighty cubits high, the effulgence from his body always reached a hundred leagues, and his age was a hundred thousand years.

241. After Phussa, the Supreme Buddha, the best of men,
Vipassin by name, the far-seeing, appeared in the world.

After him, thirty-one world-cycles ago, there were two Buddhas, called Sikhin and Vessabhū. *Sikhin* too had three assemblies of his saints; at the first assembly a hundred thousand monks were present, at the second eighty thousand, at the third seventy. At that time the

Bodisat, born as *king Arindama*, gave a great donation of robes and other things to the Order with the Buddha at their head, and offered also a superb elephant, decked with the seven gems and provided with all things suitable. To him too he prophesied, saying, "Thirty-one world-cycles hence thou shalt become a Buddha." The city of that Blessed One was called Aruṇavatī, Aruṇa the warrior-chief was his father, Pabhāvatī his mother, Abhibhū and Sambhava his chief disciples, Khemaŋkura his servitor, Makhelā and Padumā his chief female disciples, and the Puṇḍarīka-tree his Bo-tree. His body was thirty-seven cubits high, the effulgence from his body reached three leagues, and his age was thirty-seven thousand years.

242. After Vipassin came the Supreme Buddha, the best of men,
Sikhin by name, the Conqueror, unequalled and unrivalled.

After him appeared the Teacher named *Vessabhū*. He also had three assemblies of his saints; at the first eight million priests were present, at the second seven, at the third six. At that time the Bodisat, born as the *king Sudassana*, gave a great donation of robes and other things to the Order, with the Buddha at their head. And taking the vows at his hands, he became righteous in conduct, and found great joy in meditating on the Buddha. To him too the Blessed One prophesied, saying, "Thirty-one world-cycles hence thou shalt be a Buddha." The city of this Blessed One was called Anopama, Suppatīta the king was his father, Yasavatī his mother, Soṇa and Uttara his chief disciples, Upasanta his servitor, Dāmā and Sumālā his chief female disciples, and the Sal-tree his Bo-tree. His body was sixty cubits high, and his age sixty thousand years.

243. In the same Maṇḍakalpa, the Conqueror named Vessabhū,
Unequalled and unrivalled, appeared in the world.

After him, in this world-cycle, four Buddhas have appeared—Kakusandha, Koṇāgamana, Kassapa, and our Buddha. *Kakusandha* the Blessed One had one assembly, at which forty thousand monks were present. At that time the Bodisat, as *Kshema the king*, gave a great donation, including robes and bowls, to the Order, with the Buddha at their head, and having given also collyriums and drugs, he listened to the Law preached by the Teacher, and took the vows. And to him also the Buddha prophesied. The city of Kakusandha the Blessed One was called Khema, Aggidatta the Brāhman was his father, Visākhā the Brahman woman his mother, Vidhura and Sanjīva his chief disciples, Buddhija his servitor, Sāmā and Campakā his chief female disciples, and the great Sirīsa-tree his Bo-tree. His body was forty cubits high, and his age forty thousand years.

244. After Vessabhū came the perfect Buddha, the best of men,
Kakusandha by name, infinite and hard to equal.

After him appeared the Teacher *Koṇāgamana*. Of his disciples too there was one assembly, at which thirty thousand monks were present. At that time the Bodisat, as *Pabbata the king*, went, surrounded by his ministers, to the Teacher, and listened to the preaching of the Law. And having given an invitation to the Order, with the Buddha at their head, he kept up a great donation, giving cloths of silk, and of fine texture, and woven with gold. And he took the vows from the Teacher's hands. And to him too the Buddha prophesied. The city of this Blessed One was called Sobhavatī, Yaññadatta the Brahman was his father, Uttarā the Brahman woman his mother, Bhiyyosa and Uttara his chief disciples, Sotthija his servitor, Samuddā and Uttarā his chief female disciples, and the Udumbara-tree his Bo-tree. His body was twenty cubits high, and his age was thirty thousand years.

245. After Kakusandha came the Perfect Buddha, the best of men,
Koṇāgamana by name, Conqueror, chief of the world, supreme among men.

After him the Teacher named *Kassapa* appeared in the world. Of his disciples too there was one assembly, at which twenty thousand monks were present. At that time the Bodisat, as the *Brahman youth Jotipāla*, accomplished in the three Vedas, was well known on earth and in heaven as the friend of the potter Ghaṭīkāra. Going with him to the Teacher and hearing the Law, he took the vows; and zealously learning the three Piṭakas, he glorified, by faithfulness in duty and in works of supererogation, the religion of the Buddhas. And to him too the Buddha prophesied. The birthplace of the Blessed One was called Benāres, Brahmadatta the brahman was his father, Dhanavatī of the brahman caste his mother, Tissa and Bhāradvāja his chief disciples, Sabbamitta his servitor, Anuḷā and Uruveḷā his chief female disciples, and the Nigrodha-tree his Bo-tree. His body was twenty cubits high, and his age was twenty thousand years.

246. After Koṇāgamana came the Perfect Buddha, best of men,
Kassapa by name, that Conqueror, king of Righteousness, and giver of Light.

Again, in the kalpa in which Dīpaŋkara the Buddha

appeared, three other Buddhas appeared also. On their part no prophecy was made to the Bodisat, they are therefore not mentioned here; but in the commentary, in order to mention all the Buddhas from this kalpa, it is said,

247. Taṇhaŋkara and Medhaŋkara, and Saranaŋkara,
And the perfect Buddha Dīpaŋkara, and Kondañña best of men,

248. And Maŋgala, and Sumana, and Revata, and Sobhita the sage,
Anomadassin, Paduma, Nārada, Padumuttara,

249. And Sumedha, and Sujāta, Piyadassin the famous one,
Atthadassin, Dhammadassin, Siddhattha guide of the world,

250. Tissa, and Phussa the perfect Buddha, Vipassin, Sikhin, Vessabhū,
Kakusandha, Koṇāgamana, and Kassapa too the Guide,—

251. These were the perfect Buddhas, the sinless ones, the well-controlled;
Appearing like suns, dispelling the thick darkness;
They, and their disciples too, blazed up like flames of fire and went out.

Thus our Bodisat has come down to us through four *asaŋkheyyas* plus one hundred thousand *kalpas*, making resolve in the presence of the twenty-four Buddhas, beginning with Dīpaŋkara. Now after Kassapa there is no other Buddha beside the present supreme Buddha. So the Bodisat received a prophecy from each of the twenty-four Buddhas, beginning at Dīpaŋkara.

And furthermore in accordance with the saying,

"The resolve (to become a Buddha) only succeeds

> by the combination of eight qualifications: being a man, and of the male sex, and capable of attaining arahatship, association with the Teachers, renunciation of the world, perfection in virtue, acts of self-sacrifice, and earnest determination,"

he combined in himself these eight qualifications. And exerting himself according to the resolve he had made at the feet of Dīpaŋkara, in the words,

> "Come, I will search for the Buddha-making conditions, this way and that;"[1]

and beholding the Perfections of Almsgiving and the rest to be the qualities necessary for the making of a Buddha, according to the words,

> "Then, as I made my search, I beheld the first Perfection of Almsgiving;"[2]

he came down through many births, fulfilling these Perfections, even up to his last appearance as Vessantara. And the rewards which fell to him on his way, as they fall to all the Bodisats who have resolved to become Buddhas, are lauded thus:

252. So the men, perfect in every part, and destined to Buddhahood,
Traverse the long road through thousands of millions of ages.

253. They are not born in hell, nor in the space between the worlds;
They do not become ghosts consumed by hunger, thirst, and want,
And they do not become small animals, even though born to sorrow.

254. When born among men they are not blind by birth,

[1] See verse 125, above p. 19. [2] See verse 126, above p. 19.

They are not hard of hearing, they are not classed among the dumb.

255. They do not become women; among hermaphrodites and eunuchs
They are not found,—these men destined to Buddhahood.

256. Free from the deadly sins, everywhere pure-living,
They follow not after vain philosophy, they perceive the working of Karma.

257. Though they dwell in heaven, they are not born into the Unconscious state,
Nor are they destined to rebirth among the angels in the Pure Abodes.[1]

258. Bent upon renunciation, holy in the world and not of it,
They walk as acting for the world's welfare, fulfilling all perfection.

While he was thus fulfilling the Perfections, there was no limit to the existences in which he fulfilled the Perfection of Almsgiving. As, for instance, in the times when he was the brahman Akitti, and the brahmin Saŋkha, and the king Dhanañjaya, and Mahā-sudassana, and Mahagovinda, and the king Nimi, and the prince Canda, and the merchant Visayha, and the king Sivi, and Vessantara. So, certainly, in the Birth as the Wise Hare, according to the words,[2]

259. When I saw one coming for food, I offered my own self,
There is no one like me in giving, such is my Perfection of Almsgiving,

[1] In the four highest of the thirty-one spheres of existence the angels are unconscious, and the five worlds below these are called the Pure Abodes.

[2] All the following verses down to verse 269 are quotations from the Cariyāpiṭaka.

he, offering up his own life, acquired the Supreme Perfection called the Perfection of Almsgiving.

In like manner there is no limit to the existences—as, for instance, in the times when he was the snake king Sīlava, and the snake king Campeyya, the snake king Bhūridatta, the snake king Chaddanta, and the prince Alīnasaṭṭu, son of king Jayaddisa—in which he fulfilled the Perfection of Goodness. So, certainly, in the Saŋkhapāla Birth, according to the words,

> 260. Even when piercing me with stakes, and striking me with javelins,
> I was not angry with the sons of Bhoja, such is my Perfection of Goodness,

he, offering up himself, acquired the Supreme Perfection, called the Perfection of Goodness.

In like manner there is no limit to existences—as, for instance, in the times when he was the prince Somanassa, and the prince Hatthipāla, and the wise man Ayoghara—in which, forsaking his kingdom, he fulfilled the Perfection of Renunciation. So, certainly, in the Cūla-Sutasoma Birth, according to the words,

> 261. The kingdom, which was in my power, like spittle I rejected it,
> And, rejecting, cared not for it, such is my Perfection of Renunciation,

he, renouncing the kingdom for freedom from the ties of sin,[1] acquired the Supreme Perfection, called the Perfection of Renunciation.

In like manner, there is no limit to the existences—as,

[1] The Saŋgas, of which there are five—lust, hate, ignorance, pride, and false doctrine.

for instance, in the times when he was the wise man Vidhūra, and the wise man Mahā-govinda, and the wise man Kuddāla, and the wise man Araka, and the ascetic Bodhi, and the wise man Mahosadha—in which he fulfilled the Perfection of Wisdom. So, certainly, in the time when he was the wise man Senaka in the Sattubhatta Birth, according to the words,

262. Searching the matter out by wisdom, I set the brahman free from pain,
There is no one like me in wisdom; such is my Perfection of Wisdom,

he, pointing out the snake which had got into the bellows, acquired the Supreme Perfection called the Perfection of Wisdom.

So, certainly, in the Mahā-Janaka Birth, according to the words,

263. Out of sight of the shore, in the midst of the waters, all men are as if dead,
There is no other way of thinking; such is my Perfection of Resolution,

he, crossing the Great Ocean, acquired the Supreme Perfection called the Perfection of Resolution.

And so in the Khantivāda Birth, according to the words,

264. Even when he struck me with a sharp axe, as if I were a senseless thing,
I was not angry with the king of Kāsi; such is my Perfection of Patience,

he, enduring great sorrow as if he were a senseless thing, acquired the Perfection of Patience.

And so in the Mahā-Sutasoma Birth, according to the words,

265. Guarding the word of Truth, and offering up my life,
I delivered the hundred warriors; such is my Perfection of Truth,

he, offering up his life, and observing truth, obtained the Perfection of Truth.

And in the Mūgapakkha Birth, according to the words,

266. Father and mother I hated not, reputation I hated not,
But Omniscience was dear to me, therefore was I firm in duty,

offering up even his life, and being resolute in duty, he acquired the Perfection of Resolution.

And so in the Ekarāja Birth, according to the words,

267. No man terrifies me, nor am I in fear of any man;
Firm in the power of kindness, in purity I take delight,

regarding not even his life while attaining to kindness, he acquired the Perfection of Good-will.

So in the Somahaŋsa Birth, according to the words,

268. I lay me down in the cemetery, making a pillow of dead bones:
The village children mocked and praised: to all I was indifferent,

he was unshaken in equanimity, even when the villagers tried to vex or please him by spitting or by offering garlands and perfumes, and thus he acquired the Perfection of Equanimity.

This is a summary only, the account will be found at length in the Cariyā Piṭaka.

Having thus fulfilled the Perfections, in his birth as Vessantara, according to the words,

> 269. This earth, unconscious though she be and ignorant of joy or grief,
> E'en she by my free-giving's mighty power was shaken seven times,

he performed such mighty acts of virtue as made the earth to shake. And when, in the fullness of time, he had passed away, he reassumed existence in the Tusita heaven.

Thus should be understood the period, called Dūrenidāna, from the Resolution at the feet of Dīpaŋkara down to this birth in the City of Delight.

II.—AVIDŪRE NIDĀNA.

It was when the Bodisat was thus dwelling in the City of Delight, that the so-called "Buddha proclamation" took place. For three such "Proclamations" take place on earth. These are the three. When they realize that at the end of a hundred thousand years a new dispensation will begin, the angels called Loka-byūhā, with their hair flying and dishevelled, with weeping faces, wiping away their tears with their hands, clad in red garments, and with their clothes all in disorder, wander among men, and make proclamation, saying,

"Friends, one hundred thousand years from now there will be a new dispensation; this system of worlds will be destroyed; even the mighty ocean will dry up; this great earth, with Sineru the monarch of mountains, will be burned up and destroyed; and the whole world, up to the realms of the immaterial angels, will pass away. Therefore, O friends, do mercy, live in kindness, and sympathy, and peace, cherish your mothers, support your fathers, honour the elders in your tribes." This is called the proclamation of a new Age [Kappahalāhalaŋ].

Again, when they realize that at the end of a thousand years an omniscient Buddha will appear on earth, the angel-guardians of the world go from place to place and make proclamation, saying, "Friends, at the end of a thousand years from this time a Buddha will appear on earth." This is called the proclamation of a Buddha [Buddha-halāhalaŋ].

Again, when the angels realize that at the end of a hundred years a universal monarch will appear, they go from place to place and make proclamation, saying, "Friends, at the end of a hundred years from this time a universal monarch will appear on earth." This is called the proclamation of a Universal monarch [Cakka-vatti-halāhalaŋ]. These are the three great proclamations.

When of these three they hear the Buddha-proclamation, the deities of the ten thousand world-systems assemble together; and having ascertained which of the then living beings will become the Buddha, they go to him and beseech him to do so,—so beseeching him when the first signs appear that his present life is drawing to its close. Accordingly on this occasion they all, with the archangels in each world-system,[1] assembled in one world, and going to the future Buddha in the Heaven of Delight, they besought him, saying,

"O Blessed One, when thou wast fulfilling the Ten Perfections, thou didst not do so from a desire for the

[1] The names are given in the text; the four Mahārājas, Sakka, Suyāma, Santusita, Paranimitta-vasavatti, and Mahā-Brahma. They are the arch-angels in the different heavenly seats in each world-system (Cakkavāla) of the Buddhist cosmogony.

glorious state of an archangel—Sakka, or Māra, or Brahma—or of a mighty king upon earth; thou wast fulfilling them with the hope of reaching Omniscience for the sake of the Salvation of mankind! Now has the moment come, O Blessed One, for thy Buddhahood; now has the time, O Blessed One, arrived!"

But the Great Being, as if he had not granted the prayer of the deities, reflected in succession on the following five important points, viz. the time of his advent; the continent and country where he should appear; the tribe in which he should be born; the mother who should bear him, and the time when her life should be complete.

Of these he first reflected on the TIME, thinking, "Is this the time or not?" And on this point he thought, "When the duration of human existence is more than a hundred thousand years, the time has not arrived. Why not? Because in such a period men perceive not that living beings are subject to birth, decay, and death; the threefold pearl of the preaching of the Gospel of the Buddhas is unknown; and when the Buddhas speak of the impermanence of all things, of the universality of sorrow, and of the delusion of individuality, people will neither listen nor believe, saying, 'What is this they talk of?' At such a time there can be no perception of the truth, and without that the gospel will not lead to salvation. That therefore is not the time. Neither is it the right time when the term of human existence is under one hundred years. Why not? Because then sin is rife among men; and admonition addressed to the sinners finds no place for edification, but like a streak drawn on the water vanishes quickly away. That therefore is not the time. When, however, the term of human existence is under a hundred thousand and over a hundred years, that is the proper time." Now at that time the age of man was one hundred years.

The Great Being therefore saw that the time of his advent had arrived.

Then reflecting upon THE CONTINENT, and considering the four great continents with their surrounding islands,[1] he thought, "In three of the continents the Buddhas do not—but in Jambudvīpa they do—appear," and thus he decided on the continent.

Then reflecting upon THE DISTRICT, and thinking, "Jambudvīpa indeed is large, ten thousand leagues in extent; now in which district of it do the Buddhas appear?" he fixed upon the Middle Country.[2] And calling to mind that the town named Kapilavastu was in that country, he concluded that he ought to be born in it.

Then reflecting on THE TRIBE, he thought, "The Buddhas are not born in the Vaisya caste, nor the Sūdra caste; but either in the Brāhmana or in the Kshatriya caste, whichever is then held in the highest repute. The Kshatriya caste is now predominant, I must be born in it, and Suddhodana the chief shall be my father." Thus he decided on the tribe.

Then reflecting on THE MOTHER, he thought, "The mother of a Buddha is not eager for love, or cunning after drink, but has fulfilled the Perfections for a hundred thousand ages, and from her birth upwards has kept the five Precepts unbroken. Now this lady Mahā Māyā is

[1] In the seas surrounding each continent (Mahādīpa) there are five hundred islands. See Hardy's Manual of Buddhism, p. 13.

[2] *Majjhima-desa*, of which the commentator adds, "This is the country thus spoken of in the Vinaya," quoting the passage at Mahāvagga, v. 13, 12, which gives the boundaries as follows: "To the E. the town Kajaŋgala, and beyond it Mahāsālā; to the S.E. the river Salalavatī; to the S. the town Setakaṇṇika; to the W. the brāhman town and district Thūṇa; and to the N. the Usīraddhaja Mountain." These are different from the boundaries of the Madhya Desa of later Brahminical literature, on which see Lassen's 'Indische Alterthumskunde,' vol. i. p. 119 (2nd edition). This sacred land was regarded as the centre of Jambudvīpa; that is, of the then known world—just as the Chinese talk of China as the Middle Country, and as other people have looked on their own capital as the navel or centre of the world, and on their world as the centre of the universe.

such a one, she shall be my mother." And further considering how long her life should last, he foresaw that it would still last ten months and seven days.

Having thus reflected on these five important points, he favoured the deities by granting their prayer, saying, "The time has arrived, O Blessed Ones, for me to become a Buddha." He then dismissed them with the words, "You may depart;" and attended by the angels of the heaven of Joy, he entered the grove of Gladness in the City of Delight.

Now in each of the angel-heavens (Devalokas) there is such a grove of Gladness; and there the angels are wont to remind any one of them who is about to depart of the opportunities he has gained by good deeds done in a former birth, saying to him, "When fallen hence, mayest thou be reborn in bliss." And thus He also, when walking about there, surrounded by angels reminding him of his acquired merit, departed thence; and was conceived in the womb of the Lady Mahā Māyā.

In order to explain this better, the following is the account in fuller detail. At that time, it is said, the Midsummer festival was proclaimed in the City of Kapilavastu, and the people were enjoying the feast. During the seven days before the full moon the Lady Mahā Māyā had taken part in the festivity, as free from intoxication as it was brilliant with garlands and perfumes. On the seventh day she rose early and bathed in perfumed water: and she distributed four hundred thousand pieces in giving great largesse. Decked in her richest attire she partook of the purest food: and vowing to observe the Eight Commandments, she entered her beautiful chamber, and lying on her royal couch she fell asleep and dreamt this dream.

The four archangels, the Guardians of the world, lifting her up in her couch, carried her to the Himālaya mountains, and placing her under the Great Sāla-tree, seven leagues high, on the Crimson Plain, sixty yojanas broad, they stood respectfully aside. Their queens then came toward her, and taking her to the lake of Anotatta, bathed her to free her from human stains; and dressed her in heavenly garments; and anointed her with perfumes; and decked her with heavenly flowers. Not far from there is the Silver Hill, within which is a golden mansion; in it they spread a heavenly couch, with its head towards the East, and on it they laid her down. Then the future Buddha, who had become a superb white elephant, and was wandering on the Golden Hill, not far from there, descended thence, and ascending the Silver Hill, approached her from the North. Holding in his silvery trunk a white lotus flower, and uttering a far-reaching cry, he entered the golden mansion, and thrice doing obeisance to his mother's couch, he gently struck her right side, and seemed to enter her womb.[1]

Thus was he conceived at the end of the Midsummer festival. And the next day, having awoke from her sleep, she related her dream to the rāja. The rāja had sixty-four eminent Brāhmans summoned, and had costly seats spread on a spot made ready for the state occasion with green leaves and dalbergia flowers, and he had vessels of gold and silver filled with delicate milk-rice compounded with ghee and sweet honey, and covered with gold and silver bowls. This food he gave them, and he satisfied them with gifts of new garments and of tawny cows. And when he had thus satisfied their every desire, he had the dream told to them, and then he asked them, "What will come of it?"

The Brāhmans said, "Be not anxious, O king! your queen has conceived: and the fruit of her womb will be a man-child; it will not be a woman-child. You will

[1] It is instructive to notice that in later accounts it is soberly related as actual fact that the Bodisat entered his mother's womb as a white elephant: and the Incarnation scene is occasionally so represented in Buddhist sculptures.

have a son. And he, if he adopts a householder's life, will become a king, a Universal Monarch; but if, leaving his home, he adopt the religious life, he will become a Buddha, who will remove from the world the veils of ignorance and sin."

Now at the moment when the future Buddha made himself incarnate in his mother's womb, the constituent elements of the ten thousand world-systems quaked, and trembled, and were shaken violently. The Thirty-two Good Omens also were made manifest. In the ten thousand world-systems an immeasurable light appeared. The blind received their sight (as if from very longing to behold this his glory). The deaf heard the noise. The dumb spake one with another. The crooked became straight. The lame walked. All prisoners were freed from their bonds and chains. In each hell the fire was extinguished. The hungry ghosts received food and drink. The wild animals ceased to be afraid. The illness of all who were sick was allayed. All men began to speak kindly. Horses neighed, and elephants trumpeted gently. All musical instruments gave forth each its note, though none played upon them. Bracelets and other ornaments jingled of themselves. All the heavens became clear. A cool soft breeze wafted pleasantly for all. Rain fell out of due season. Water, welling up from the very earth, overflowed.[1] The birds forsook their flight on high. The rivers stayed their waters' flow. The waters of the mighty ocean became fresh. Everywhere the earth was covered with lotuses of every colour. All flowers blossomed on land and in water. The trunks, and branches, and twigs of trees were covered with the bloom appropriate to each. On earth tree-lotuses sprang up by sevens together, breaking even through

[1] I think this is the meaning of the passage, though Prof. Childers has a different rendering of the similar phrase at verse 104, where I would read "it" instead of "vegetation." Compare Dāṭhāvaŋsa, i. 45.

the rocks; and hanging-lotuses descended from the skies. The ten-thousand world-systems revolved, and rushed as close together as a bunch of gathered flowers; and became as it were a woven wreath of worlds, as sweet-smelling and resplendent as a mass of garlands, or as a sacred altar decked with flowers.

From the moment of the incarnation, thus brought about, of the future Buddha, four angels, with swords in their hands, stood guard over the Bodisat and his mother, to shield them from all harm. Pure in thought, having reached the highest aim and the highest honour, the mother was happy and unwearied; and she saw the child within her as plainly as one could see a thread passed through a transparent gem.[1] But as a womb in which a future Buddha has dwelt, like a sacred relic shrine, can never be occupied by another; the mother of the Bodisat, seven days after his birth, died, and was reborn in the City of Delight.

Now other women give birth, some before, some after, the completion of the tenth month, some sitting, and some lying down. Not so the mother of a Bodisat. She gives birth to the Bodisat, standing, after she has cherished him in her womb for exactly ten months. This is a distinctive quality of the mother of a Buddha elect.

And queen Mahā Māyā, when she too had thus cherished the Bodisat in her womb, like oil in a vessel, for ten months, felt herself far gone with child: and wishing to go to her family home she spake to King Suddhodana, and said,

"O king! I wish to go to Devadaha, to the city of my people."

The king, saying, "It is good," consented, and had the road from Kapilavastu to Devadaha made plain, and decked

[1] I once saw a notice of some mediæval frescoes in which the Holy Child was similarly represented as visible within the Virgin's womb, but have unfortunately mislaid the reference.

with arches of plaintain-trees, and well-filled water-pots, and flags, and banners. And seating the queen in a golden palanquin carried by a thousand attendants, he sent her away with a great retinue.

Now between the two towns there is a pleasure-grove of sāla-trees belonging to the people of both cities, and called the Lumbini grove. At that time, from the roots to the topmost branches, it was one mass of fruits and flowers; and amidst the blossoms and branches swarms of various-coloured bees, and flocks of birds of different kinds, roamed, warbling sweetly. The whole of the Lumbini grove was like a wood of variegated creepers, or the well-decorated banqueting hall of some mighty king. The queen beholding it was filled with the desire of besporting herself in the sal-tree grove; and the attendants, carrying the queen, entered the wood. When she came to the monarch sal-tree of the glade, she wanted to take hold of a branch of it, and the branch bending down, like a reed heated by steam, approached within reach of her hand. Stretching out her hand she took hold of the branch, and then her pains came upon her. The people drawing a curtain round her, retired. Standing, and holding the branch of the sal-tree, she was delivered.

That very moment the four pure-minded Mahā Brahma angels came there bringing a golden net; and receiving the future Buddha on that net, they placed him before his mother, saying, "Be joyful, O Lady! a mighty son is born to thee!"

Now other living things, when they leave their mother's womb, leave it smeared with offensive and impure matter. Not so a Bodisat. The future Buddha left his mother's womb like a preacher descending from a pulpit or a man from a ladder, erect, stretching out his hands and feet, unsoiled by any impurities from contact with his mother's womb, pure and fair, and shining like a gem placed on fine muslin of Benares. But though this was so, two showers of water came down from heaven in honour of them and refreshed the Bodisat and his mother.

From the hands of the angels who had received him in the golden net, four kings received him on cloth of antelope skins, soft to the touch, such as are used on occasions of royal state. From their hands men received him on a roll of fine cloth; and on leaving their hands he stood up upon the ground and looked towards the East. Thousands of world-systems became visible to him like a single open space. Men and angels offering him sweet-smelling garlands, said, "O great Being, there is no other like thee, how then a greater?" Searching the ten directions (the four points of the compass, the four intermediate points, the zenith and the nadir), and finding no one like himself, he took seven strides, saying, "This is the best direction." And as he walked the archangel Brahma held over him the white umbrella, and the archangel Suyāma followed him with the fan, and other deities with the other symbols of royalty in their hands. Then stopping at the seventh step, he sent forth his noble voice and shouted the shout of victory, beginning with, "I am the chief of the world."[1]

Now the future Buddha in three births thus uttered his voice immediately on leaving his mother's womb; in his birth as Mahosadha, in his birth as Vessantara, and in this birth. In the Mahosadha birth the archangel Sakka came to him as he was being born, and placing some fine sandal-wood in his hand, went away. He came out from the womb holding this in his fist. His mother asked him, "What is it you hold, dear, as you come?" He answered, "Medicine, mother!" So because he came holding medicine, they gave him the name of Medicine-child (Osadhadāraka). Taking the medicine they kept

[1] The Madurattha Vilāsinī adds the rest, "I am supreme in the world; this is my last birth; henceforth there will be no rebirth for me."

it in a chatty (an earthenware water-pot); and it became a drug by which all the sickness of the blind and deaf and others, as many as came, was healed. So the saying sprang up, "This is a powerful drug, this is a powerful drug;" and hence he was called Mahosadha (The Great Medicine Man).

Again, in the Vessantara birth, as he left his mother's womb, he stretched out his right hand, saying, "But is there anything in the house, mother? I would give a gift." Then his mother, saying, "You are born, dear, in a wealthy family," took his hand in hers, and placed on it a bag containing a thousand.

Lastly, in this birth he sang the song of victory. Thus the future Buddha in three births uttered his voice as he came out of his mother's womb. And as at the moment of his conception, so at the moment of his birth, the thirty-two Good Omens were seen.

Now at the very time when our Bodisat was born in the Lumbini grove, the lady, the mother of Rāhula, Channa the attendant, Kāḷudāyi the minister, Kanthaka the royal horse, the great Bo-tree, and the four vases full of treasure, also came into being. Of these last, one was two miles, one four, one six, and one eight miles in size. These seven are called the Sahajātā, the Connatal Ones.[1]

The people of both towns took the Bodisat and went to Kapilavastu. On that day too, the choirs of angels in the Tāvatiŋsa heaven were astonished and joyful; and waved their cloaks and rejoiced, saying, "In Kapilavastu,

[1] There is some mistake here, as the list contains nine—or if the four treasures count as one, only six—Connatal Ones. I think before Kaḷudāyi we should insert Ānanda, the loving disciple. So Alabaster and Hardy (Wheel of the Law, p. 106; Manual of Buddhism, p. 146). Bigandet also adds Ānanda, but calls him the son of Amittodana, which is against the common tradition (Life or Legend of Guadama, p. 36, comp. my Buddhism, p. 52). The legend is certainly, as to its main features, an early one, for it is also found, in greatly exaggerated and contradictory terms, in the books of Northern Buddhists (Lalita Vistara, Foucaux, p. 97, Beal, p. 53, comp. Senart, p. 294).

to Suddhodana the king, a son is born, who, seated under the Bo-tree, will become a Buddha."

At that time an ascetic named Kāḷa Devala (a confidential adviser of Suddhodana the king, who had passed through the eight stages of religious attainment)[1] had eaten his mid-day meal, and had gone to the Tāvatiŋsa heaven, to rest through the heat of the day. Whilst there sitting resting, he saw these angels, and asked them, "Why are you thus glad at heart and rejoicing? Tell me the reason of it."

The angels replied, "Sir, to Suddhodana the king is born a son, who seated under the Bo-tree will become a Buddha, and will found a Kingdom of Righteousness.[2] To us it will be given to see his infinite grace and to hear his word. Therefore it is that we are glad!"

The ascetic, hearing what they said, quickly came down from the angel-world, and entering the king's house, sat down on the seat set apart for him, and said, "A son they say is born to you, O king! let me see him."

The king ordered his son to be clad in splendour and brought in to salute the ascetic. But the future Buddha turned his feet round, and planted them on the matted hair of the ascetic.[3] For in that birth there was no one worthy to be saluted by the Bodisat, and if those ignorant ones had placed the head of the future Buddha at the feet of the ascetic, assuredly the ascetic's head would have split in two. The ascetic rose from his seat, and saying, "It is not right for me to work my own destruction," he did homage to the Bodisat. And the king also seeing this wonder did homage to his own son.

[1] *Samāpatti.*

[2] *Dhammacakkaŋ pavattessati.* See my "Buddhism," p. 45.

[3] It was considered among the Brāhmans a sign of holiness to wear matted or platted hair. This is referred to in the striking Buddhist verse (Dhammapada, v. 394), "What is the use of platted hair, O fool! What of a garment of skins! Your low yearnings are within you, and the outside thou makest clean!"

Now the ascetic had the power of calling to mind the events of forty ages (kalpas) in the past, and of forty ages in the future. Looking at the marks of future prosperity on the Bodisat's body, he considered with himself, "Will he become a Buddha or not?" And perceiving that he would most certainly become a Buddha, he smiled, saying, "This is a wonderful child." Then reflecting, "Will it be given to me to behold him when he has become a Buddha?" he perceived that it would not. "Dying before that time I shall be reborn in the Formless World; so that while a hundred or perhaps a thousand Buddhas appear among men, I shall not be able to go and be taught by them. And it will not be my good fortune to behold this so wonderful child when he has become a Buddha. Great, indeed, is my loss!" And he wept.

The people seeing this, asked, saying, "Our master just now smiled, and has now begun to weep! Will, sir, any misfortune befall our master's little one?" [1]

"There is no misfortune in him; assuredly he will become a Buddha," was the reply.

"Why then do you weep?"

"It will not be granted to me," he said, "to behold so great a man when he has become a Buddha. Great, indeed, is my loss! bewailing myself, I weep."

Then reflecting, "Will it be granted or not to any one of my relatives to see him as a Buddha?" he saw it would be granted to his nephew Nālaka. So he went to his sister's house, and said to her, "Where is your son Nālaka?"

"In the house, brother."

"Call him," said he. When he came he said to him, "In the family of Suddhodana the king, dear, a son is

[1] "Our master" is here, of course, the sage. It is a pretty piece of politeness, not unfrequent in the Jātakas, to address a stranger as a relation. See below, Jātaka No. 3.

born, a young Buddha. In thirty-five years he will become a Buddha, and it will be granted you to see him. This very day give up the world!"

Bearing in mind that his uncle was not a man to urge him without a cause, the young man, though born in a family of incalculable wealth,[1] straightway took out of the inner store a yellow suit of clothes and an earthenware pot, and shaved his head and put on the robes. And saying, "I take the vows for the sake of the greatest Being upon earth," he prostrated himself on the ground and raised his joined hands in adoration towards the Bodisat. Then putting the begging bowl in a bag, and carrying it on his shoulder, he went to the Himālaya mountains, and lived the life of a monk.

When the Tathāgata had attained to complete Enlightenment, Nālaka went to him and heard the way of salvation.[2] He then returned to the Himālayas, and reached Arahatship. And when he had lived seven months longer as a pilgrim along the most excellent Path, he past away when standing near a Golden Hill, by that final extinction in which no part or power of man remains.[3]

Now on the fifth day they bathed the Bodisat's head, saying, "Let us perform the rite of choosing a name for him." So they perfumed the king's house with four kinds of odours, and decked it with Dalbergia flowers, and made ready rice well cooked in milk. Then they sent for one hundred and eight Brāhmans who had mastered the three Vedas, and seated them in the king's house, and gave them the pleasant food to eat, and did

[1] Literally "worth eighty and seven times a koṭi," both eighty and seven being lucky numbers.

[2] Literally, "and caused him to declare, 'The way of salvation for Nālaka.'" Perhaps some Sutta is so called. Tathāgata, "gone, or come, in like manner; subject to the fate of all men," is an adjective applied originally to all mortals, but afterwards used as a favourite epithet of Gotama. Childers compares the use of 'Son of Man.'

[3] *Anupādisesāya Nibbāna-dhātuyā parinibbāyi.* In the translator's "Buddhism," p. 113, an analysis of this phrase will be found.

them great honour, and asked them to recognize the signs of what the child should be.

Among them—

270. Rāma, and Dhaja, and Lakkhaṇa, and Mantin,
Kondanya and Bhoja, Suyāma and Sudatta,
These eight Brāhmans then were there,
Their senses all subdued; and they declared the charm.

Now these eight Brāhmans were recognizers of signs; it was by them that the dream on the night of conception had been interpreted. Seven of them holding up two fingers prophesied in the alternative, saying, "If a man having such marks should remain a householder, he becomes a Universal Monarch; but if he takes the vows, he becomes a Buddha." And, so saying, they declared all the glory and power of a Cakkavatti king.

But the youngest of all of them, a young Brāhman whose family name was Kondanya, beholding the perfection of the auspicious marks on the Bodisat, raised up one finger only, and prophesied without ambiguity, and said, "There is no sign of his remaining amidst the cares of household life. Verily, he will become a Buddha, and remove the veils of sin and ignorance from the world."

This man already, under former Buddhas, had made a deep resolve of holiness, and had now reached his last birth. Therefore it was that he surpassed the other seven in wisdom; that he perceived how the Bodisat would only be subject to this one life; and that, raising only one finger, he so prophesied, saying, "The lot of one possessed of these marks will not be cast amidst the cares of household life. Verily he will become a Buddha!"

Now those Brāhmans went home, and addressed their

sons, saying, "We are old, beloved ones; whether or not we shall live to see the son of Suddhodana the king after he has gained omniscience, do you, when he has gained omniscience, take the vows according to his religion." And after they all seven had lived out their span of life, they passed away and were reborn according to their deeds.

But the young Brāhman Kondanya was free from disease; and for the sake of the wisdom of the Great Being he left all that he had and made the great renunciation. And coming in due course to Uruvela, he thought, "Behold how pleasant is this place! how suitable for the exertions of a young man desirous of wrestling with sin." So he took up his residence there.

And when he heard that the Great Being had taken the vows, he went to the sons of those Brāhmans, and said to them, "Siddhattha the prince has taken the vows. Assuredly he will become a Buddha. If your fathers were in health they would to-day leave their homes, and take the vows: and now, if you should so desire, come, I will take the vows in imitation of him." But all of them were not able to agree with one accord; three did not give up the world; the other four made Kondanya the Brāhman their leader, and took the vows. It was those five who came to be called "the Company of the Five Elders."

Then the king asked, "After seeing what, will my son forsake the world?"

"The four Omens," was the reply.

"Which four?"

"A man worn out by age, a sick man, a dead body, and a monk."

The king thought, "From this time let no such things come near my son. There is no good of my son's becoming a Buddha. I should like to see my son exercising rule and sovereignty over the four great continents and the two thousand islands that surround them; and walking, as it were, in the vault of heaven, surrounded by an innumerable retinue."[1] Then, so saying, he placed guards two miles apart in the four directions to prevent men of those four kinds coming to the sight of his son.

That day also, of eighty thousand clansmen assembled in the festival hall, each one dedicated a son, saying, "Whether this child becomes a Buddha or a king, we give each a son; so that if he shall become a Buddha, he shall live attended and honoured by Kshatriya monks, and if he shall become a king, he shall live attended and honoured by Kshatriya nobles."[2] And the rāja appointed nurses of great beauty, and free from every fault, for the Bodisat. So the Bodisat grew up in great splendour and surrounded by an innumerable retinue.

Now one day the king held the so-called Ploughing Festival. On that day they ornament the town like a palace of the gods. All the slaves and servants, in new garments and crowned with sweet-smelling garlands, assemble in the king's house. For the king's work a thousand ploughs are yoked. On this occasion one hundred and eight minus one were, with their oxen-reins and cross-bars, ornamented with silver. But the plough for the king to use was ornamented with red gold; and so also the horns and reins and goads of the oxen.

The king, leaving his house with a great retinue, took his son and went to the spot. There there was a Jambu-tree thick with leaves and giving a dense shade. Under it the rāja had the child's couch laid out; and over the couch a canopy spread inlaid with stars of gold, and round it a curtain hung. Then leaving a guard there, the rāja, clad in splendour and attended by his ministers, went away to plough.

[1] Literally 'a retinue thirty-six leagues in circumference,' where 'thirty-six' is a mere sacred number.

[2] Kshatriya was the warrior caste.

At such a time the king takes hold of a golden plough, the attendant ministers one hundred and eight minus one silver ploughs, and the peasants the rest of the ploughs. Holding them they plough this way and that way. The rāja goes from one side to the other, and comes from the other back again.

On this occasion the king had great success; and the nurses seated round the Bodisat, thinking, "Let us go to see the king's glory," came out from within the curtain, and went away. The future Buddha, looking all round, and seeing no one, got up quickly, seated himself cross-legged, and holding his breath, sank into the first Jhāna.[1]

The nurses, engaged in preparing various kinds of food, delayed a little. The shadows of the other trees turned round, but that of the Jambu-tree remained steady and circular in form. The nurses, remembering their young master was alone, hurriedly raised the curtain and returned inside it. Seeing the Bodisat sitting cross-legged, and that miracle of the shadow, they went and told the rāja, saying, "O king! the prince is seated in such and such a manner; and while the shadows of the other trees have turned, that of the Jambu-tree is fixed in a circle!"

And the rāja went hurriedly and saw that miracle, and did homage to his son, saying, "This, Beloved One, is the second homage paid to thee!"

But the Bodisat in due course grew to manhood. And the king had three mansions made, suitable for the three seasons, one nine stories high, one seven stories high, and one five stories high; and he provided him with forty thousand dancing girls. So the Bodisat, surrounded by well-dressed dancing girls, like a god surrounded by troops of houris, and attended by musical instruments which played of themselves, lived, as the seasons changed,

[1] A state of religious meditation. A full explanation is given in the translator's "Buddhism," pp. 174–176.

in each of these mansions in enjoyment of great majesty. And the mother of Rāhula was his principal queen.

Whilst he was thus in the enjoyment of great prosperity the following talk sprang up in the public assembly of his clansmen: "Siddhattha lives devoted to pleasure; not one thing does he learn; if war should break out, what would he do?"

The king sent for the future Buddha, and said to him, "Your relations, Beloved One, say that you learn nothing, and are given up to pleasure: now what do you think you should do about this?"

"O king! there is no art it is necessary for me to learn. Send the crier round the city, that I may show my skill. Seven days from now I will show my kindred what I can do."

The king did so. The Bodisat assembled those so skilled in archery that they could split even a hair, and shoot as quick as lightning; and then, in the midst of the people, he showed his relatives his twelve-fold skill, and how unsurpassed he was by other masters of the bow.[1] So the assembly of his clansmen doubted no longer.

Now one day the future Buddha, wanting to go to his pleasure ground, told his charioteer to harness his chariot. The latter accordingly decked the gloriously beautiful chariot with all its trappings, and harnessed to it four state horses of the Sindhi breed, and white as the leaves of the white lotus flower. And he informed the Bodisat. So the Bodisat ascended the chariot, resplendent like a mansion in the skies, and went towards the garden.

The angels thought, "The time for young Siddhattha to attain Enlightenment is near, let us show him the Omens." And they did so by making a son of the gods represent a man wasted by age, with decayed teeth

[1] A gloss adds, "This should be understood as is related at full in the Sarabhaṇga Jātaka."

and grey hair, bent and broken down in body, and with a stick in his hand. But he was only visible to the future Buddha and his charioteer.

Then the Bodisat asked his charioteer, as is told in the Mahāpadāna, "What kind of man is this, whose very hair is not as that of other men?" When he heard his servant's answer, he said, "Shame then be to life! since the decay of every living being is notorious!" and with agitated heart he turned back at that very spot and re-entered his palace.

The king asked, "Why does my son turn back so hurriedly?"

"He has seen an old man," they said; "and having seen an old man, he will forsake the world."

"By this you ruin me," exclaimed the rāja; "quickly get ready concerts and plays to be performed before my son. So long as he continues in the enjoyment of pleasure, he will not turn his thoughts to forsaking the world!" Then increasing the guards, he placed them at each point of the compass, at intervals of half a league.

Again, one day, when the future Buddha, as he was going to his pleasure ground, saw a sick man represented by the gods, he made the same inquiry as before; and then, with agitated heart, turned back and re-entered his palace. The king also made the same inquiry, and gave the same orders as before; and again increasing the guard, placed them all round at a distance of three-quarters of a league.

Once more, when the future Buddha, as he was going to his pleasure ground, saw a dead man represented by the gods, he made the same inquiry as before; and then, with agitated heart, turned back and re-entered his palace. The king also made the same inquiry, and gave the same orders as before; and again increasing the guard, placed them all round at a distance of a league.

Once again, when the future Buddha, as he was going to his pleasure ground, saw one who had abandoned the world, carefully and decently clad, he asked his charioteer, "Friend, what kind of man is that?" As at that time there was no Buddha at all in the world, the charioteer understood neither what a mendicant was nor what were his distinguishing characteristics; but nevertheless, inspired by the gods, he said, "That is a mendicant friar;" and described the advantages of renouncing the world. And that day the future Buddha, cherishing the thought of renouncing the world, went on to his pleasure ground.

The repeaters of the Dīgha Nikāya,[1] however, say that he saw all the four Omens on the same day, and then went to his pleasure ground. There he enjoyed himself during the day and bathed in the beautiful lake; and at sunset seated himself on the royal resting stone to be robed. Now his attendants brought robes of different colours, and various kinds of ornaments, and garlands, and perfumes, and ointments, and stood around him.

At that moment the throne on which Sakka was seated became warm.[2] And thinking to himself, "Who is it now who wants me to descend from hence?" he perceived that the time for the adornment of the future Buddha had come. And he said to Vissakamma, "Friend Vissakamma, the young noble Siddhattha, to-day, at midnight, will carry out the Great Renunciation. This is the last time he will be clad in splendour. Go to the pleasure ground and adorn him with heavenly array."

By the miraculous power which angels have, he ac-

[1] The members of the Buddhist Order of mendicant friars were in the habit of selecting some book or books of the Buddhist Scriptures, which it was their especial duty to learn by heart, repeat to their pupils, study, expound, and preach from. Thus the Dīgha Nikāya, or collection of long treatises, had a special school of "repeaters" (*bhāṇakā*) to itself.

[2] At critical moments in the lives of persons of importance in the religious legends of Buddhist India, the seat of the Archangel Sakka becomes warm. Fearful of losing his temporary bliss, he then descends himself, or sends Vissakamma, the Buddhist Vulcan, to act as a *deus ex machinâ*, and put things straight.

cordingly, that very moment, drew near in the likeness of the royal barber; and taking from the barber's hand the material for the turban, he arranged it round the Bodisat's head. At the touch of his hand the Bodisat knew, "This is no man, it is a son of the gods." When the first round of the turban was put on, there arose, by the appearance of the jewelry on the diadem, a thousand folds; when the turban was wrapt the second time round, a thousand folds arose again; when ten times, ten thousand folds appeared. How so many folds could seem to rise on so small a head is beyond imagination; for in size the largest of them were as the flower of the Black Priyaŋgu creeper, and the rest even as Kutumbaka blossoms. And the head of the future Buddha became like a Kuyyaka flower in full bloom.

And when he was arrayed in all his splendour,—the musicians the while exhibiting each one his peculiar skill, the Brāhmans honouring him with words of joy and victory, and the men of lower castes with festive cries and shouts of praise;—he ascended his superbly decorated car.

At that time Suddhodana the king, who had heard that the mother of Rāhula had brought forth a son, sent a message, saying, "Make known my joy to my son!" The future Buddha, hearing this, said, "An impediment has come into being, a bond has come into being." When the king asked, "What did my son say?" and heard that saying; he gave command, "From henceforth let Rāhula (impediment) be my grandson's name." But the Bodisat, riding in his splendid chariot, entered the town with great magnificence and exceeding glory.

At that time a noble virgin, Kisā Gotamī by name, had gone to the flat roof of the upper story of her palace, and she beheld the beauty and majesty of the Bodisat as he was proceeding through the city. Pleased and delighted at the sight, she burst forth into this song of joy:—

271. Blessed indeed is that mother,—
Blessed indeed is that father,—
Blessed indeed is that wife,—
Who owns this Lord so glorious!

Hearing this, the Bodisat thought to himself, "On catching sight of such a one the heart of his mother is made happy, the heart of his father is made happy, the heart of his wife is made happy! This is all she says. But by what can every heart attain to lasting happiness and peace?" And to him whose mind was estranged from sin the answer came, "When the fire of lust is gone out, then peace is gained; when the fires of hatred and delusion are gone out, then peace is gained; when the troubles of mind, arising from pride, credulity, and all other sins, have ceased, then peace is gained! Sweet is the lesson this singer makes me hear, for the Nirvāna of Peace is that which I have been trying to find out. This very day I will break away from household cares! I will renounce the world! I will follow only after the Nirvāna itself![1]

Then loosing from his neck a string of pearls worth a hundred thousand, he sent it to Kisā Gotamī as a teacher's fee. Delighted at this, she thought, "Prince Siddhattha has fallen in love with me, and has sent me a present." But the Bodisat, on entering his palace in great splendour, reclined on a couch of state.

Thereupon women clad in beautiful array, skilful in

[1] The force of this passage is due to the fullness of meaning which, to the Buddhist, the words NIBBUTA and NIBBĀNAŊ convey. No words in Western languages cover exactly the same ground, or connote the same ideas. To explain them fully to any one unfamiliar with Indian modes of thought would be difficult anywhere, and impossible in a note; but their meaning is pretty clear from the above sentences. Where in them, in the song, the words *blessed*, *happy*, *peace*, and the words *gone out*, *ceased*, occur, NIBBUTA stands in the original in one or other of its two meanings; where in them the words *Nirvāna*, *Nirvāna of Peace* occur, NIBBĀNAŊ stands in the original. *Nirvāna* is a lasting state of happiness and peace, to be reached here on earth by the extinction of the 'fires' and 'troubles' mentioned in this passage.

the dance and song, and lovely as heavenly virgins, brought their musical instruments, and ranging themselves in order, danced, and sang, and played delightfully. But the Bodisat, his heart being estranged from sin, took no pleasure in the spectacle, and fell asleep.

And the women, saying, "He, for whose sake we were performing, is gone to sleep? Why should we play any longer?" laid aside the instruments they held, and lay down to sleep. The lamps fed with sweet-smelling oil were just burning out. The Bodisat, waking up, sat cross-legged on the couch, and saw them with their stage properties laid aside and sleeping—some foaming at the mouth, some grinding their teeth, some yawning, some muttering in their sleep, some gaping, and some with their dress in disorder—plainly revealed as mere horrible sources of mental distress.

Seeing this woful change in their appearance, he became more and more disgusted with lusts. To him that magnificent apartment, as splendid as Sakka's residence in heaven, began to seem like a charnel-house full of loathsome corpses. Life, whether in the worlds subject to passion, or in the worlds of form, or in the formless worlds, seemed to him like staying in a house that had become the prey of devouring flames.[1] An utterance of intense feeling broke from him—"It all oppresses me! It is intolerable!" and his mind turned ardently to the state of those who have renounced the world. Resolving that very day to accomplish the Great Renunciation, he rose from his couch, went to the door and called out, "Who is there?"

Channa, who had been sleeping with his head on the threshold, answered, "It is I, sir, Channa."

[1] Literally, "The three Bhavas seemed like houses on fire." The three Bhavas are Existence in the Kāma-loka, the Rūpa-loka, and the Arūpa-loka respectively: that is, existence in the worlds whose inhabitants are subject to passion, have material forms, and have immaterial forms respectively.

Then said he, "I am resolved to-day to accomplish the Great Renunciation—saddle me a horse."

So Channa went to the stable-yard, and entering the stables saw by the light of the lamps the mighty steed Kanthaka, standing at a pleasant spot under a canopy of cloth, beautified with a pattern of jasmine flowers. "This is the very one I ought to saddle to-day," thought he; and he saddled Kanthaka.

Even whilst he was being saddled the horse knew, "He is saddling me so tightly, and not as on other days for such rides as those to the pleasure grounds, because my master is about to-day to carry out the Great Renunciation." Then, glad at heart, he neighed a mighty neigh; and the sound thereof would have penetrated over all the town, had not the gods stopped the sound, and let no one hear it.

Now after the Bodisat had sent Channa on this errand, he thought, "I will just look at my son." And rising from his couch he went to the apartments of Rāhula's mother, and opened her chamber door. At that moment a lamp, fed with sweet-smelling oil, was burning dimly in the inner chamber. The mother of Rāhula was asleep on a bed strewn with many jasmine flowers,[1] and resting her hand on the head of her son. Stopping with his foot on the threshold, the Bodisat thought, "If I lift her hand to take my son, she will awake; and that will prevent my going away. I will come back and see him when I have become a Buddha." And he left the palace.

Now what is said in the Jātaka commentary, "At that time Rāhula was seven days old," is not found in the other commentaries. Therefore the view given above should be accepted.[2]

And when the Bodisat had left the palace, he went to his horse, and said, "My good Kanthaka, do thou save me this

[1] Literally, "about an ammaṇa (*i.e.* five or six bushels) of the large jasmine and the Arabian jasmine."

[2] The Jātaka Commentary here referred to is, no doubt, the older commentary in Elu, or old Siŋhalese, on which the present work is based.

once to-night; so that I, having become a Buddha by your help, shall save the world of men, and that of angels too." Then leaping up, he seated himself on Kanthaka's back.

Kanthaka was eighteen cubits in length from the nape of his neck, and of proportionate height; he was strong and fleet, and white all over like a clean chank shell. If he should neigh or paw the ground, the sound would penetrate through all the town. Therefore the angels so muffled the sound of his neighing that none could hear it; and placed, at each step, the palms of their hands under his feet.

The Bodisat rode on the mighty back of the mighty steed; told Channa to catch hold of its tail, and arrived at midnight at the great gate of the city.

Now the king thinking, "In that way the Bodisat will not be able at any time to open the city gate and get away," had placed a thousand men at each of the two gates to stop him. The Bodisat was mighty and strong according to the measure of elephants as ten thousand million elephants, and according to the measure of men as a million million men. He thought, "If the door does not open, sitting on Kanthaka's back with Channa holding his tail, I will press Kanthaka with my thighs, and jumping over the city rampart, eighteen cubits high, I will get away!" Channa thought, "If the door is not opened, I will take my master on my neck, and putting my right hand round Kanthaka's girth, I will hold him close to my waist, and so leap over the rampart and get away!" Kanthaka thought, "If the door is not opened, I will spring up with my master seated as he is on my back, and Channa holding by my tail, and will leap over the rampart and get away!" And if the door had not been opened, verily one or other of those three would have accomplished that whereof he had thought. But the angel residing at the gate opened it.

At that moment Māra came there with the intention

of stopping the Bodisat; and standing in the air, he exclaimed, "Depart not, O my lord! in seven days from now the wheel of empire will appear, and will make you sovereign over the four continents and the two thousand adjacent isles. Stop, O my lord!"

"Who are you?" said he.

"I am Vasavatti," was the reply.

"Māra! Well do I know that the wheel of empire would appear to me; but it is not sovereignty that I desire. I will become a Buddha, and make the ten thousand world-systems shout for joy."

Then thought the Tempter to himself: "Now, from this time forth, whenever a thought of lust or anger or malice shall arise within you, I will get to know of it." And he followed him, ever watching for some slip, as closely as a shadow which never leaves its object.

But the future Buddha, making light of the kingdom of the world, thus within his reach,—casting it away as one would saliva,—left the city with great honour on the full-moon day of Āsāḷhi, when the moon was in the Uttarāsāḷha lunar mansion (*i.e.* on the 1st July). And when he had left the city a desire sprang up within him to gaze upon it; and the instant he did so the broad earth revolved like a potter's wheel, and was stayed: saying as it were to him, "O Great Being, there is no need for you to stop in order to fulfil your wish." So the Bodisat, with his face towards the city, gazed at it; and he fixed at that place a spot for the Kanthaka-Nivattana Cetiya (that is, The Shrine of Kanthaka's Staying—a Dāgaba afterwards built where this miracle was believed to have happened). And keeping Kanthaka in the direction in which he was going, he went on with great honour and exceeding glory.

For then, they say, angels in front of him carried sixty thousand torches, and behind him too, and on his right hand, and on his left. And while some deities, undefined on the edge of the horizon, held torches aloft; other deities, and the Nāgas, and Winged Creatures, and other superhuman beings, bore him company—doing homage with heavenly perfumes, and garlands, and sandal-wood powder, and incense. And the whole sky was full of Paricchātaka flowers from Indra's heaven, as with the pouring rain when thick clouds gather. Heavenly songs floated around; and on every side thousands of musical instruments sounded, as when the thunder roars in the midst of the sea, or the great ocean heaves against the boundaries of the world!

Advancing in this pomp and glory, the Bodisat, in that one night, passed beyond three kingdoms, and arrived, at the end of thirty leagues, at the bank of the river called Anomā. But why could not the horse go still further? It was not through want of power: for he could go from one edge of the round world to the other, as easily as one could step across the circumference of a wheel lying on its side;—and doing this in the forenoon, he could return and eat the food prepared for him. But on this occasion he was constantly delayed by having to drag himself along, and break his way through the mass of garlands and flowers, cast down from heaven in such profusion by the angels, and the Snakes, and the Winged Creatures, that his very flanks were hid. Hence it was that he only got over thirty leagues.

Now the Bodisat, stopping at the river side, asked Channa, "What is this river called?"

"Its name, my lord, is Anomā."

"And so also our renunciation of the world shall be called Anomā (illustrious)," said he; and signalling to his horse, by pressing it with his heel, the horse sprang over the river, five or six hundred yards in breadth, and stood on the opposite bank.

The Bodisat, getting down from the horse's back, stood on the sandy beach, extending there like a sheet of silver, and said to Channa, "Good Channa, do thou now go back, taking my ornaments and Kanthaka. I am going to become a hermit."

"But I also, my lord, will become a hermit."

"You cannot be allowed to renounce the world, you must go back," he said. Three times he refused this request of Channa's; and he delivered over to him both the ornaments and Kanthaka.

Then he thought, "These locks of mine are not suited for a mendicant. Now it is not right for any one else to cut the hair of a future Buddha, so I will cut them off myself with my sword." Then, taking his sword in his right hand, and holding the plaited tresses, together with the diadem on them, with his left, he cut them off. So his hair was thus reduced to two inches in length, and curling from the right, it lay close to his head. It remained that length as long as he lived, and the beard the same. There was no need at all to shave either hair or beard any more.

The Bodisat, saying to himself, "If I am to become a Buddha, let it stand in the air; if not, let it fall to the ground;" threw the hair and diadem together as he held them towards the sky. The plaited hair and the jewelled turban went a league off and stopped in the air. The archangel Sakka caught sight of it with his divine eye, and receiving it into a jewel casket, a league high, he placed it in the Tāvatiŋsa heaven, in the Dāgaba of the Diadem.

272. Cutting off his hair, with pleasant perfumes sweet,
The Lordly Being cast it to the sky.
The thousand-eyed one, Sakka, the sky God,
Received it humbly in a golden casket.

Again the Bodisat thought, "This my raiment of Benares muslin is not suitable for a mendicant." Now the archangel Ghaṭikāra, who had formerly been his friend in the time of Kassapa Buddha, was led by his friendship, which had not grown old in that long interval, to think, "To-day my friend is accomplishing the Great Renunciation, I will go and provide him with the requisites of a mendicant."

273. The three robes, and the alms bowl,
Razor, needle, and girdle,
And a water strainer—these eight
Are the wealth of the monk devout.

Taking these eight requisites of a mendicant, he gave them to him. The Bodisat dressed himself in the outward signs of an Arahat, and adopted the sacred garb of Renunciation; and he enjoined upon Channa to go and, in his name, assure his parents of his safety. And Channa did homage to the Bodisat reverently, and departed.

Now Kanthaka stood listening to the Bodisat as he talked with Channa. And thinking, "From this time forth I shall never see my master more!" he was unable to bear his grief. And going out of their sight, he died of a broken heart; and was reborn in the Tāvatiŋsa heaven as an angel, with the name of Kanthaka. So far the sorrow of Channa had been but single; now torn with the second sorrow of Kanthaka's death, he returned, weeping and bewailing, to the city.

But the Bodisat, having renounced the world, spent seven days in a mango grove called Anūpiya, hard by that spot, in the joy of salvation. Then he went on foot in one day to Rājagaha, a distance of thirty leagues,[1]

[1] The word rendered league is *yojana*, said by Childers (Dictionary, s. v.) to be twelve miles, but really only between seven and eight miles. See my Ancient Coins and Measures, pp. 16, 17. The thirty yojanas here mentioned, together with the thirty from Kapilavastu to the river Anomā, make together sixty, or four hundred and fifty miles from Kapilavastu to Rājagaha, which is far too much for the direct distance. There is here, I think, an undesigned coincidence between Northern and Southern accounts; for the Lalita Vistara (Chap. xvi. at the commencement) makes the Bodisat go to Rājagaha *viâ* Vesāli, and this would make the total distance exactly sixty yojanas.

and entering the city, begged his food from door to door. The whole city at the sight of his beauty was thrown into commotion, like that other Rājagaha by the entrance of Dhana-pālaka, or like heaven itself by the entrance of the Ruler of the Gods.

The guards went to the king and said, describing him, "O king! such and such a being is begging through the town. We cannot tell whether he is a god, or a man, or a Nāga, or a Supaṇṇa,[1] or what he is."

The king, watching the Great Being from his palace, became full of wonder, and gave orders to his guards, saying, "Go, my men, and see. If it is a superhuman being, it will disappear as soon as it leaves the city; if a god, it will depart through the air; if a snake, it will dive into the earth; if a man, it will eat the food just as it is."

But the Great Being collected scraps of food. And when he perceived there was enough to support him, he left the city by the gate at which he had entered. And seating himself, facing towards the East, under the shadow of the Paṇḍava rock, he began to eat his meal. His stomach, however, turned, and made as if it would come out of his mouth. Then, though distressed by that revolting food, for in that birth he had never even beheld such food with his eyes, he himself admonished himself, saying, "Siddhattha, it is true you were born in a family where food and drink were easily obtainable, into a state of life where your food was perfumed third-season's rice, with various curries of the finest kinds. But ever since you saw one clad in a mendicant's garb, you have been thinking, 'When shall I become like him, and live by begging my food? would that that time were come!' And now that you have left all for that very purpose, what is this that you are doing?" And overcoming his feelings, he ate the food.

[1] These are the superhuman Snakes and Winged Creatures, who were supposed, like the gods or angels, to be able to assume the appearance of men.

The king's men saw this, and went and told him what had happened. Hearing what his messengers said, the king quickly left the city, and approaching the Bodisat, was so pleased at the mere sight of his dignity and grace, that he offered him all his kingdom.

The Bodisat said, "In me, O king! there is no desire after wealth or sinful pleasures. It is in the hope of attaining to complete enlightenment that I have left all." And when the king gained not his consent, though he asked it in many ways, he said, "Assuredly thou wilt become a Buddha! Deign at least after thy Buddhahood to come to my kingdom first."

This is here concisely stated; but the full account, beginning, "I sing the Renunciation, how the Wise One renounced the world," will be found on referring to the Pabbajjā Sutta and its commentary.

And the Bodisat, granting the king's request, went forward on his way. And joining himself to Āḷāra Kāḷāma, and to Uddaka, son of Rāma, he acquired their systems of ecstatic trance. But when he saw that that was not the way to wisdom, he left off applying himself to the realization of that system of Attainment.[1] And with the intention of carrying out the Great Struggle against sin, and showing his might and resolution to gods and men, he went to Uruvela. And saying, "Pleasant, indeed, is this spot!" he took up his residence there, and devoted himself to the Great Struggle.[2]

[1] Samāpatti.

[2] The Great Struggle played a great part in the Buddhist system of moral training; it was the wrestling with the flesh by which a true Buddhist overcame delusion and sin, and attained to Nirvāna. It is best explained by its four-fold division into 1. Mastery over the passions. 2. Suppression of sinful thoughts. 3. Meditation on the seven kinds of Wisdom (Bodhi-angā, see 'Buddhism,' p. 173); and 4. Fixed attention, the power of preventing the mind from wandering. It is also called Sammappadhāna, Right Effort, and forms the subject of the Mahā-Padhāna Sutta, in the Dīgha Nikāya. The system was, of course, not worked out at the time here referred to; but throughout the chronicle the biographer ascribes to Gotama, from the beginning, a knowledge of the whole Buddhist theory as afterwards elaborated. For to our author that theory had no development, it was Eternal and Immutable Truth already revealed by innumerable previous Buddhas.

And those five mendicants, Kondanya and the rest, begging their way through villages, market towns, and royal cities, met with the Bodisat there. And for six years they stayed by him and served him, while he was carrying out the Great Struggle, with different kinds of service, such as sweeping out the hermitage, and so on; thinking the while, "Now he will become a Buddha! now he will become a Buddha!"

Now the Bodisat thought, "I will perform the uttermost penance." And he brought himself to live on one seed of the oil plant, or one grain of rice, and even to fast entirely; but the angels gathered the sap of life and infused it into him through the pores of his skin. By this fasting, however, he became as thin as a skeleton; the colour of his body, once fair as gold, became dark; and the Thirty-two signs of a Great Being disappeared. And one day, when walking up and down, plunged in intense meditation, he was overcome by severe pain; and he fainted, and fell.

Then certain of the angels began to say, "The mendicant Gotama is dead." But others said, "Such is the condition of Arahats (saints)." And those who thought he was dead went and told Suddhodana the king, saying, "Your son is dead."

"Did he die after becoming a Buddha, or before?"

"He was unable to attain to Buddhahood, and fell down and died in the midst of the Great Struggle."

When the king heard this, he refused to credit it, saying, "I do not believe it. My son could never die without attaining to Wisdom!"

If you ask, "Why did not the king believe it?" it was because he had seen the miracles at the foot of the Jambu-tree, and on the day when Kāḷa Devala had been compelled to do homage to the Bodisat.

And the Bodisat recovered consciousness again, and stood up. And the angels went and told the king, "Your son, O king, is well." And the king said, "I knew my son was not dead."

And the Great Being's six years' penance became noised abroad, as when the sound of a great bell is heard in the sky. But he perceived that penance was not the way to Wisdom; and begging through the villages and towns, he collected ordinary material food, and lived upon it. And the Thirty-two signs of a Great Being appeared again upon him, and his body became fair in colour, like unto gold.

Then the five attendant mendicants thought, "This man has not been able, even by six years' penance, to attain Omniscience; how can he do so now, when he goes begging through the villages, and takes material food? He is altogether lost in the Struggle. To think of getting spiritual advantage from him is like a man, who wants to bathe his head, thinking of using a dewdrop. What is to be got from him?" And leaving the Great Being, they took each his robes and begging bowl, and went eighteen leagues away, and entered Isipatana (a suburb of Benāres, famous for its schools of learning).

Now at that time, at Uruvela, in the village Senāni, there was a girl named Sujātā, born in the house of Senāni the landowner, who, when she had grown up, prayed to a Nigrodha-tree, saying, "If I am married into a family of equal rank, and have a son for my first-born child, then I will spend every year a hundred thousand on an offering to thee." And this her prayer took effect.

And in order to make her offering, on the full-moon day of the month of May, in the sixth year of the Great Being's penance, she had driven in front of her a thousand cows into a meadow of rich grass. With their milk she had fed five hundred cows, with theirs two hundred and fifty, and so on down to eight. Thus aspiring after quantity, and sweetness, and strength, she did what is called, "Working the milk in and in."

And early on the full-moon day in the month of May, thinking, "Now I will make the offering," she rose up in the morning early and milked those eight cows. Of their own accord the calves kept away from the cows' udders, and as soon as the new vessels were placed ready, streams of milk poured into them. Seeing this miracle, Sujātā, with her own hands, took the milk and poured it into new pans; and with her own hands made the fire and began to cook it. When that rice-milk was boiling, huge bubbles rising, turned to the right and ran round together; not a drop fell or was lost; not the least smoke rose from the fireplace.

At that time the four guardian angels of the world came from the four points of the compass, and kept watch by the fireplace. The archangel Brahmā held over it a canopy of state. The archangel Sakka put the sticks together and lighted the fire. By their divine power the gods, gathering so much of the Sap of life as would suffice for the support of all the men and angels of the four continents, and their circumjacent two thousand isles—as easily as a man crushing the honey-comb formed round a stick would take the honey—they infused it into the milk-rice. At other times the gods infused the Sap of life into each mouthful of rice as he took it; but on the day of his Buddhahood, and on the day of his Death, they infused it into the very vessel-full of rice itself.

Sujātā, seeing that so many wonders appeared to her on this one day, said to her slave-girl Puṇṇā, "Friend Puṇṇā! Very gracious is our god to-day! Never before have I seen such a wonder. Go at once and keep watch by the holy place." "Very good, my lady," replied she; and ran and hastened to the foot of the tree.

Now the Bodisat had seen that night five dreams, and on considering their purport he had drawn the conclusion, "Verily this day I shall become a Buddha." And at the end of the night he washed and dressed himself, and waiting till the time should come to go round begging his food, he went early, and sat at the foot of that tree, lighting it all up with his glory.

And Puṇṇā coming there saw the Bodisat sitting at the foot of the tree and lighting up all the region of the East; and she saw the whole tree in colour like gold from the rays issuing from his body. And she thought, "To-day our god, descending from the tree, is seated to receive our offering in his own hand." And excited with joy, she returned quickly, and announced this to Sujātā. Sujātā, delighted at the news, gave her all the ornaments befitting a daughter, saying, "To-day, from this time forth, be thou to me in the place of an elder daughter!"

And since, on the day of attaining Buddhahood, it is proper to receive a golden vessel worth a hundred thousand, she conceived the idea, "We will put the milk-rice into a vessel of gold." And sending for a vessel of gold worth a hundred thousand, she poured out the well-cooked food to put it therein. All the rice-milk flowed into the vessel, like water from a lotus leaf, and filled the vessel full. Taking it she covered it with a golden dish, and wrapped it in a cloth. And adorning herself in all her splendour, she put the vessel on her head, and went with great dignity to the Nigrodha-tree. Seeing the Bodisat, she was filled with exceeding joy, taking him for the tree-god; and advanced, bowing, from the spot whence she saw him. Taking the vessel from her head, she uncovered it; and fetching sweet-scented water in a golden vase, she approached the Bodisat, and stood by.

The earthenware pot given him by the archangel Ghaṭikāra, which had never till then left him, disappeared at that moment. Not seeing his pot, the Bodisat stretched out his right hand, and took the water. Sujātā placed the vessel, with the milk-rice in it, in the hand of the Great Being. The Great Being looked at her. Pointing to the food, she said, "O, my lord! accept what I have offered thee, and depart withersoever seemeth to thee good." And adding, "May there arise to thee as much joy as has come to me!" she went away, valuing her golden vessel, worth a hundred thousand, at no more than a dried leaf.

But the Bodisat rising from his seat, and leaving the tree on the right hand, took the vessel and went to the bank of the Neranjara river, down into which on the day of their complete Enlightenment so many thousand Bodisats had gone. The name of that bathing place is the Supatiṭṭhita ferry. Putting the vessel on the bank, he descended into the river and bathed.

And having dressed himself again in the garb of the Arahats worn by so many thousand Buddhas, he sat down with his face to the East; and dividing the rice into forty-nine balls of the size of so many single-seeded Palmyra fruits, he ate all that sweet milk-rice without any water.[1] Now that was the only food he had for forty-nine days, during the seven times seven days he spent, after he became a Buddha, at the foot of the Tree of Wisdom. During all that time he had no other food; he did not bathe; nor wash his teeth; nor feel the cravings of nature. He lived on the joy arising from intense Meditation, on the joy arising from the Noble Path, on the joy arising from the Fruit thereof.

But when he had finished eating that milk-rice, he took the golden vessel, and said, "If I shall be able to-day to become a Buddha, let this pot go up the stream; if not, let it go down the stream!" and he threw it into the water. And it went, in spite of the stream, eighty cubits up the river in the middle of the stream, all the way as quickly as a fleet horse. And diving into a whirlpool it went to the palace of Kāḷa Nāgarāja (the Black Snake King); and striking against the bowls from which the three previous

[1] The fruit of the Palmyra (Borassus Flabelliformis) has always three seeds. I do not understand the allusion to a one-seeded Palmyra.

Buddhas had eaten, it made them sound "click! click!" and remained stationary as the lowest of them. Kāḷa, the snake-king, hearing the noise, exclaimed, "Yesterday a Buddha arose, now to-day another has arisen;" and he continued to praise him in many hundred stanzas.

But the Bodisat spent the heat of the day in a grove of sāla-trees in full bloom on the bank of the river. And in the evening, when the flowers droop on the stalks, he proceeded, like a lion when it is roused, towards the Tree of Wisdom, along a path five or six hundred yards wide, decked by the gods. The Snakes, and Genii, and Winged Creatures,[1] and other superhuman beings, offered him sweet-smelling flowers from heaven, and sang heavenly songs. The ten thousand world-systems became filled with perfumes and garlands and shouts of approval.

At that time there came from the opposite direction a grass-cutter named Sotthiya, carrying grass; and recognizing the Great Being, he gave him eight bundles of grass. The Bodisat took the grass; and ascending the rising ground round the Bo-tree, he stood at the South of it, looking towards the North. At that moment the Southern horizon seemed to descend below the level of the lowest hell, and the Northern horizon mounting up seemed to reach above the highest heaven.

The Bodisat, saying, "This cannot, I think, be the right place for attaining Buddhahood," turned round it, keeping it on the right hand; and went to the Western side, and stood facing the East. Then the Western horizon seemed to descend beneath the lowest hell, and the Eastern horizon to ascend above the highest heaven; and to him, where he was standing, the earth seemed

[1] Nāgas, Yakkhas and Supaṇṇas. The Yakkhas are characterized throughout the Jātaka stories by their cannibalism; the female Yakkhas as sirens luring men on to destruction. They are invisible till they assume human shape; but even then can be recognized by their red eyes. That the Ceylon aborigines are called Yakkhas in the Mahāvaŋsa probably results from a tradition of their cannibalism. On the others, see above, p. 88.

to bend up and down like a great cart wheel lying on its axis when its circumference is trodden on.

The Bodisat, saying, "This cannot, I think, be the right place for attaining Buddhahood," turned round it, keeping it on the right hand; and went to the Northern side, and stood facing the South. Then the Northern horizon seemed to descend beneath the lowest hell, and the Southern horizon to ascend above the highest heaven.

The Bodisat, saying, "This cannot, I think, be the right place for attaining Buddhahood," turned round it, keeping it on the right hand; and went to the Western side, and stood facing towards the East. Now in the East is the place where all the Buddhas have sat cross-legged; and that place neither trembles nor shakes.

The Great Being, perceiving, "This is the steadfast spot chosen by all the Buddhas, the spot for the throwing down of the temple of sin," took hold of the grass by one end, and scattered it there. And immediately there was a seat fourteen cubits long. For those blades of grass arranged themselves in such a form as would be beyond the power of even the ablest painter or carver to design.

The Bodisat turning his back upon the trunk of the Bo-tree, and with his face towards the East, made the firm resolve, "My skin, indeed, and nerves, and bones, may become arid, and the very blood in my body may dry up; but till I attain to complete insight, this seat I will not leave!" And he sat himself down in a cross-legged position, firm and immovable, as if welded with a hundred thunderbolts.

At that time the angel Māra, thinking, "Siddhattha the prince wants to free himself from my dominion. I will not let him get free yet!" went to the hosts of his angels, and told the news. And sounding the drum, called "Satan's War-cry," he led forth the army of Satan.

That army of Māra stretches twelve leagues before him,

twelve leagues to right and left of him, behind him it reaches to the rocky limits of the world, above him it is nine leagues in height; and the sound of its war-cry is heard, twelve leagues away, even as the sound of an earthquake.

Then Māra, the angel, mounted his elephant, two hundred and fifty leagues high, named, "Girded with mountains." And he created for himself a thousand arms, and seized all kinds of weapons. And of the remainder, too, of the army of Māra, no two took the same weapon; but assuming various colours and various forms, they went on to overwhelm the Great Being.

But the angels of the ten thousand world-systems continued speaking the praises of the Great Being. Sakka, the king of the angels, stood there blowing his trumpet Vijayuttara. Now that trumpet is a hundred and twenty cubits long, and can itself cause the wind to enter, and thus itself give forth a sound which will resound for four months, when it becomes still. The Great Black One, the king of the Nāgas, stood there uttering his praises in many hundred stanzas. The archangel Mahā Brahma stood there, holding over him the white canopy of state. But as the army approached and surrounded the seat under the Bo-tree, not one of the angels was able to stay, and they fled each one from the spot where the army met them. The Black One, the king of the Nāgas, dived into the earth, and went to Manjerika, the palace of the Nāgas, five hundred leagues in length, and lay down, covering his face with his hands. Sakka, taking the Vijayuttara trumpet on his back, stopped on the rocky verge of the world. Mahā Brahma, putting the white canopy of state on to the summit of the rocks at the end of the earth, went to the world of Brahma. Not a single deity was able to keep his place. The Great Being sat there alone.

But Māra said to his host, "Friends! there is no other man like Siddhattha, the son of Suddhodana. We cannot give him battle face to face. Let us attack him from behind!" The Great Being looked round on three sides, and saw that all the gods had fled, and their place was empty. Then beholding the hosts of Māra coming thick upon him from the North, he thought, "Against me alone this mighty host is putting forth all its energy and strength. No father is here, nor mother, nor brother, nor any other relative to help me. But those ten cardinal virtues have long been to me as retainers fed from my store. So, making the virtues my shield, I must strike this host with the sword of virtue, and thus overwhelm it!" And so he sat meditating on the Ten Perfections.[1]

Then Māra the angel, saying, "Thus will I drive away Siddhattha," caused a whirlwind to blow. And immediately such winds rushed together from the four corners of the earth as could have torn down the peaks of mountains half a league, two leagues, three leagues high—could have rooted up the shrubs and trees of the forest—and could have made of the towns and villages around one heap of ruins. But through the majesty of the goodness of the Great Being, they reached him with their power gone, and even the hem of his robe they were unable to shake.

Then saying, "I will overwhelm him with water and so slay him," he caused a mighty rain to fall. And the clouds gathered, overspreading one another by hundreds and by thousands, and poured forth rain; and by the violence of the torrents the earth was saturated; and a great flood, overtopping the trees of the forest, approached the Great Being. But it was not able to wet on his robe even the space where a dew-drop might fall.

Then he caused a storm of rocks to fall. And mighty, mighty, mountain peaks came through the air, spitting

[1] His acquisition of the Ten Perfections, or Cardinal Virtues, is described above, pp. 54–58.

forth fire and smoke. But as they reached the Great Being, they changed into bouquets of heavenly flowers.

Then he raised a storm of deadly weapons. And they came—one-edged, and two-edged swords, and spears, and arrows—smoking and flaming through the sky. But as they reached the Great Being, they became flowers from heaven.

Then he raised a storm of charcoal. But the embers, though they came through the sky as red as red Kiŋsuka flowers, were scattered at the feet of the future Buddha as heavenly flowers.

Then he raised a storm of ashes; and the ashes came through the air exceeding hot, and in colour like fire; but they fell at the feet of the future Buddha as the dust of sandal-wood.

Then he raised a storm of sand; and the sand, exceeding fine, came smoking and flaming through the air; but it fell at the feet of the future Buddha as heavenly flowers.

Then he raised a storm of mud. And the mud came smoking and flaming through the air; but it fell at the feet of the future Buddha as heavenly perfume.

Then saying, "By this I will terrify Siddhattha, and drive him away!" he brought on a thick darkness. And the darkness became fourfold: but when it reached the future Buddha, it disappeared as darkness does before the brightness of the sun.

Thus was Māra unable by these nine—the wind, and the rain, and the rocks, and the weapons, and the charcoal, and the ashes, and the sand, and the mud, and the darkness—to drive away the future Buddha. So he called on his host, and said, "Why stand you still? Seize, or slay, or drive away this prince!" And himself mounted the Mountain-girded, and seated on his back, he approached the future Buddha, and cried out, "Get up, Siddhattha, from that seat! It does not belong to thee! It is meant for me!"

The Great Being listened to his words, and said, "Māra! it is not by you that the Ten Cardinal Virtues have been perfected, nor the lesser Virtues, nor the higher Virtues. It is not you who have sacrificed yourself in the five great Acts of Self-renunciation, who have diligently sought after Knowledge, and the Salvation of the world, and the attainment of Wisdom. This seat does not belong to thee, it is to me that it belongs."

Then the enraged Māra, unable to endure the vehemence of his anger, cast at the Great Being that Sceptre-javelin of his, the barb of which was in shape as a wheel. But it became a garland of flowers, and remained as a canopy over him, whose mind was bent upon good.

Now at other times, when that Wicked One throws his Sceptre-javelin, it cleaves asunder a pillar of solid rock as if it were the tender shoot of a bambū. When, however, it thus turned into a garland-canopy, all the host of Māra shouted, "Now he shall rise from his seat and flee!" and they hurled at him huge masses of rock. But these too fell on the ground as bouquets at the feet of Him whose mind was bent upon good!

And the angels stood on the edge of the rocks that encircle the world; and stretching forwards in amazement, they looked on, saying, "Lost! lost is Siddhattha the Prince, the glorious and beautiful! What can he do to save himself!"

Then the Great Being exclaimed, "I have reached the throne on which sit the Buddhas-to-be when they are perfect in all goodness, on that day when they shall reach Enlightenment."

And he said to Māra, standing there before him, "Māra, who is witness that thou hast given alms?"

And Māra stretched forth his hand to the hosts of his followers, and said, "So many are my witnesses."

And that moment there arose a shout as the sound of

an earthquake from the hosts of the Evil One, saying, "I am his witness! I am his witness!"

Then the Tempter addressed the Great Being, and said, "Siddhattha! who is witness that thou hast given alms?"

And the Great Being answered, "Thou hast living witnesses that thou hast given alms: and I have in this place no living witness at all. But not counting the alms I have given in other births, let this great and solid earth, unconscious though it be, be witness of the seven hundredfold great alms I gave when I was born as Wessantara!"

And withdrawing his right hand from beneath his robe, he stretched it forth towards the earth, and said, "Are you, or are you not witness of the seven hundredfold great gift I gave in my birth as Wessantara?"

And the great Earth uttered a voice, saying, "I am witness to thee of that!" overwhelming as it were the hosts of the Evil One as with the shout of hundreds of thousands of foes.

Then the mighty elephant "Girded with mountains," as he realized what the generosity of Wessantara had been, fell down on his knees before the Great Being. And the army of Māra fled this way and that way, so that not even two were left together: throwing off their clothes and their turbans, they fled, each one straight on before him.

But the heavenly hosts, when they saw that the army of Māra had fled, cried out, "The Tempter is overcome! Siddhattha the Prince has prevailed! Come, let us honour the Victor!" And the Nāgas, and the Winged Creatures, and the Angels, and the Archangels, each urging his comrades on, went up to the Great Being at the Bo-tree's foot, and as they came,

274. At the Bo-tree's foot the Nāga bands
Shouted, for joy that the Sage had won;
"The Blessed Buddha—he hath prevailed!
And the Tempter is overthrown!"

275. At the Bo-tree's foot the Winged Ones
Shouted, for joy that the Sage had won;
"The Blessed Buddha—he hath prevailed!
And the Tempter is overthrown!"
276. At the Bo-tree's foot the Angel hosts
Shouted, for joy that the Sage had won;
"The Blessed Buddha—he hath prevailed!
And the Tempter is overthrown!"
277. At the Bo-tree's foot the Brahma Gods
Shouted, for joy that the Sage had won;
"The Blessed Buddha—he hath prevailed!
And the Tempter is overthrown!"

The other gods, too, in the ten thousand world-systems, offered garlands and perfumes and uttered his praises aloud.

It was while the sun was still above the horizon, that the Great Being thus put to flight the army of the Evil One. Then, whilst the Bo-tree paid him homage, as it were, by its shoots like sprigs of red coral falling over his robe, he acquired in the first watch of the night the Knowledge of the Past, in the middle watch the Knowledge of the Present, and in the third watch the Knowledge of the Chain of Causation which leads to the Origin of Evil.[1]

Now on his thus revolving this way and that way, and tracing backwards and forwards, and thoroughly realizing the twelvefold Chain of Causation, the ten thousand world-systems quaked twelve times even to their ocean boundaries. And again, when the Great Being, making the ten thousand world-systems to shout for joy, attained at break of day to complete Enlightenment, the whole ten thousand world-systems became glorious as on a festive day. The streamers of the flags and banners raised on the edge of the rocky boundary to the East of the world

[1] Pubbe-nivāsa-ñāna, Dibba-cakkhu, and Paticca-samuppāda.

reached to the very West; and so those on the West and North, and South, reached to the East, and South, and North; while in like manner those of flags and banners on the surface of the earth reached to the highest heaven, and those of flags and banners in heaven swept down upon the earth. Throughout the universe flowering trees put forth their blossoms, and fruit-bearing trees were loaded with clusters of fruit; the trunks and branches of trees, and even the creepers, were covered with bloom; lotus wreaths hung from the sky; and lilies by sevens sprang, one above another, even from the very rocks. The ten thousand world-systems as they revolved seemed like a mass of loosened wreaths, or like a nosegay tastefully arranged: and the great Voids between them, the hells whose darkness the rays of seven suns had never been able to disperse, became filled with light. The waters of the Great Ocean became sweet, down to its profoundest depths; and the rivers were stayed in their course. The blind from birth received their sight; the deaf from birth heard sound; the lame from birth could use their feet; and chains and bonds were loosed, and fell away.[1]

It was thus in surpassing glory and honour, and with many wonders happening around, that he attained Omniscience, and gave vent to his emotion in the Hymn of Triumph, sung by all the Buddhas.

278. Long have I wandered! long!
Bound by the Chain of Life,
Through many births:
Seeking thus long, in vain,
"Whence comes this Life in man, his Consciousness, his Pain!"
And hard to bear is Birth,
When pain and death but lead to Birth again.

[1] Compare the Thirty-two Good Omens at the Buddha's Birth, above, p. 64.

Found! It is found!
O Cause of Individuality!
No longer shalt thou make a house for me:
Broken are all thy beams.
Thy ridge-pole shattered!
Into Nirvāna now my mind has past:
The end of cravings has been reached at last! [1]

[1] The train of thought is explained at length in my "Buddhism," pp. 100–112. Shortly, it amounts to this. The Unconscious has no pain: without Consciousness, Individuality, there would be no pain. What gives men Consciousness? It is due to a grasping, craving, sinful condition of heart. The absence of these cravings is Nirvāna. Having reached Nirvāna, Consciousness endures but for a time (until the body dies), and it will then no longer be renewed. The beams of sin, the ridge-pole of care, give to the house of individuality its seeming strength: but in the peace of Nirvāna they have passed away. The Bodisat is now Buddha: he has reached Nirvāna: he has solved the great mystery; the jewel of salvation sought through so many ages has been found at last; and the long, long struggle is over.

The following is Spence Hardy's literal translation given in his "Manual of Buddhism," p. 180, where similar versions by Gogerly and Turnour will be found: but they scarcely seem to me to express the inner meaning of these difficult and beautiful verses:—

Through many different births
I have run (to me not having found),
Seeking the architect of the desire resembling house,
Painful are repeated births!

O house-builder! I have seen (thee).
Again a house thou canst not build for me.
I have broken thy rafters,
Thy central support is destroyed.
To Nirvāna my mind has gone.
I have arrived at the extinction of evil-desire.

The figure of the house is found also in Manu (vi. 79–81); in the "Lalita Vistara" (p. 107 of Foucaux's Gya Tcher Rol Pa); and in the Ādi Granth (Trumpp, pp. 215, 216, 471). The last passage is as follows:—

A storm of divine knowledge has come!
The shutters of Delusion all are blown away—are there no longer;
The posts of Double-mindedness are broken down; the ridge-pole of spiritual Blindness is shattered;
The roof of Craving has fallen on the ground; the vessel of Folly has burst!

THE PROXIMATE OR LAST EPOCH.[1]

Now whilst he was still seated there, after he had sung the Hymn of Triumph, the Blessed One thought, "It is in order to attain to this throne of triumph that I have undergone successive births for so long a time,[2] that I severed my crowned head from my neck and gave it away, that I tore out my darkened eyes and my heart's flesh and gave them away, that I gave away to serve others such sons as Jāli the Prince, and such daughters as Kaṇhā Jinā the Princess, and such wives as Maddī the Queen. This seat is a throne of triumph to me, and a throne of glory; while seated on it my aims have been fulfilled: I will not leave it yet." And he sat there absorbed in many thoughts[3] for those seven days referred to in the text, beginning, "And then the Blessed One sat motionless for seven days, realizing the bliss of Nirvāna."

Now certain of the angels began to doubt, thinking, "There must be something more Siddhattha has to do this day, for he still lingers seated there." The Master, knowing their thoughts, and to appease their doubts, rose into the air, and performed the miracle of making another appearance like unto himself.[4]

And the Master having thus by this miracle dispelled the angels' doubts, stood a little to the North-east of the

[1] See above, p. 2. A similar explanation is here repeated in a gloss.

[2] Literally for four *asaŋkheyyas* and a hundred thousand *kalpas*.

[3] Anekakoṭi-sata-sahassā samāpattiyo samāpajjanto.

[4] Yamaka-pāṭihāriyaŋ; literally 'twin-miracle.' Comp. pp. 88, 193, of the text, and Mah. p. 107. I am not sure of the meaning of the expression. Bigandet, p. 93, has 'performed a thousand wonders.' Hardy, p. 181, omits the clause; and Beal omits the whole episode. A gloss here adds that the Buddha performed a similar miracle on three other occasions.

throne, thinking, "It was on that throne that I attained omniscience." And he thus spent seven days gazing steadfastly at the spot where he had gained the result of the deeds of virtue fulfilled through such countless years. And that spot became known as the Dāgaba of the Steadfast Gaze.

Then he created between the throne and the spot where he had stood a cloistered walk, and he spent seven days walking up and down in that jewelled cloister which stretched from East to West. And that spot became known as the Dāgaba of the Jewelled Cloister.

But for the fourth week the angels created to the North-west of the Bo-tree a house of gems; and he spent the week seated there cross-legged, and thinking out the Abhidhamma Pitaka both book by book and generally in respect of the origin of all things as therein explained. (But the Abhidhammikas[1] say that House of Gems here means either a mansion built of the seven kinds of jewels, or the place where the seven books were thought out: and as they give these two explanations of the passage, both should be accepted as correct.)

Having thus spent four weeks close to the Bo-tree, he went, in the fifth week, to the Shepherd's Nigrodha-tree: and sat there meditating on the Truth, and enjoying the sweetness of Nirvāna.[2]

Now at that time the angel Māra thought to himself, "So long a time have I followed this man seeking some fault in him, and find no sin in him; and now, indeed, he is beyond my power." And overcome with sorrow he sat down on the highway, and as he thought of the following sixteen things he drew sixteen lines on the ground. Thinking, "I did not attain, as he did, to the perfection of

[1] The monks whose duty it is to learn by heart, repeat, and commentate upon the seven books in the Abhidhamma Pitaka. See above, p. 78.

[2] *Vimutti*. Perhaps the clause should be rendered: Realizing the sweet sense of salvation gained, and the Truth (Dhamma) may be used in contradistinction to Abhidharma of the rest of the Scriptures.

Charity; therefore I have not become like him," he drew one line. Then thinking, "I did not attain, as he did, to the Perfections of Goodness, and Self-sacrifice, and Wisdom, and Exertion, and Longsuffering, and Truth, and Resolution, and Kindness, and Equanimity;[1] therefore I have not become like him," he drew nine more lines. Then thinking, "I did not attain the Ten Perfections, the conditions precedent to the acquisition of the extraordinary knowledge of the objects of sense, and therefore I have not become like him," he drew the eleventh line. Then thinking, "I did not attain to the Ten Perfections, the conditions precedent to the acquisition of the extraordinary knowledge of inclinations and dispositions, of the attainment of compassion, of the double miracle, of the removal of hindrances, and of omniscience; therefore I have not become like him," he drew the five other lines. And so he sat on the highway, drawing sixteen lines for these sixteen thoughts.

At that time Craving, Discontent, and Lust,[2] the three daughters of Māra, could not find their father, and were looking for him, wondering where he could be. And when they saw him, sad at heart, writing on the ground, they went up to him, and asked, "Why, dear, are you sad and sorrowful?"

And he answered, "Beloved, this illustrious mendicant is escaping from my power. Long have I watched, but in vain, to find some fault in him. Therefore it is that I am sad and sorrowful."

"Be that as it may," replied they, "think not so. We will subject him to our influence, and come back bringing him captive with us."

"Beloved," said he, "you cannot by any means bring him under your influence; he stands firm in faith, unwavering."

[1] On these Ten Perfections, see above, pp. 15–18, and pp. 54–58.

[2] Taṇhā, Aratī, and Ragā.

"But we are women," was the reply; "this moment we will bring him bound by the allurements of passion. Do not you be so grieved."

So they approached the Blessed One, and said, "O, holy man, upon thee we humbly wait!"

But the Blessed One neither paid any attention to their words, nor raised his eyes to look at them. He sat plunged in the joy of Nirvāna, with a mind made free by the complete extinction of sin.

Then the daughters of Māra considered with themselves: "Various are men's tastes. Some fall in love with virgins, some with young women, some with mature women, some with older women. We will tempt him in various forms." So each of them assumed the appearance of a hundred women,—virgins, women who had never had a child, or only once, or only twice, middle-aged women, older women,—and six times they went up to the Blessed One, and professed themselves his humble handmaidens; and to that even the Blessed One paid no attention, since he was made free by the complete extinction of sin.

Now, some teachers say that when the Blessed One saw them approaching in the form of elderly women, he commanded, saying, "Let these women remain just as they are, with broken teeth and bald heads." This should not be believed, for the Master issues not such commands.

But the Blessed One said, "Depart ye! Why strive ye thus? Such things might be done in the presence of men who linger in the paths of sin; but I have put away lust, have put away ill-will, have put away folly." And he admonished them in those two verses from the Chapter on the Buddha in the Scripture Verses:

280. No one can e'er disturb his self-control
Whose inward victories, once gained, are never lost.

That Sinless One, the Wise, whose mind embraces all—
How—by what guile—what sin—can you allure him to his fall?

281. He who has no ensnaring, venomous desire;
No craving wants to lead him aught astray:
The Sinless One, the Wise, whose mind embraces all—
How—by what guile—what sin—can you allure him to his fall?[1]

And thus these women returned to their father, confessing that he had spoken truth when he had said that the Blessed One was not by any means to be led away by any unholy desire.

But the Blessed One, when he had spent a week at that spot, went on to the Mucalinda-tree. There he spent a week, Mucalinda, the snake-king, when a storm arose, shielding him with seven folds of his hood, so that the Blessed One enjoyed the bliss of salvation as if he had been resting in a pleasant chamber, remote from all disturbance. Thence he went away to a Rājāyatana-tree, and there also sat down enjoying the bliss of salvation. And so seven weeks passed away, during which he experienced no bodily wants, but fed on the joy of Meditation, the joy of the Paths, and the joy of the Fruit thereof (that is, of Nirvāna).[2]

Now, as he sat there on the last day of the seven weeks —the forty-ninth day—he felt a desire to bathe his face. And Sakka, the king of the gods, brought a fruit of the Myrobolan-tree, and gave him to eat. And Sakka, too, provided a tooth-cleanser of the thorns of the snake-creeper, and water to bathe his face. And the Master

[1] Dhammapada, verses 179, 180. [2] See "Buddhism," pp. 108-110.

used the tooth-cleanser, and bathed his face, and sat him down there at the foot of the tree.

At that time two merchants, Tapassu and Bhalluka by name, were travelling from Orissa to Central India[1] with five hundred carts. And an angel, a blood relation of theirs, stopped their carts, and moved their hearts to offer food to the Master. And they took a rice cake, and a honey cake, and went up to the Master, and said, "O, Blessed One! have mercy upon us, and accept this food."

Now, on the day when he had received the sweet rice-milk, his bowl had disappeared;[2] so the Blessed One thought, "The Buddhas never receive food in their hands. How shall I take it?" Then the four Guardian Angels knew his thought, and, coming from the four corners of heaven, they brought bowls made of sapphire. And the Blessed One accepted them. Then they brought four other bowls, made of jet; and the Blessed One, out of kindness to the four angels, received the four, and, placing them one above another, commanded, saying, "Let them become one." And the four closed up into one of medium size, becoming visible only as lines round the mouth of it. The Blessed One received the food into that new-created bowl, and ate it, and gave thanks.

The two brothers took refuge in the Buddha, the Truth, and the Order, and became professed disciples. Then, when they asked him, saying, "Lord, bestow upon us something to which we may pay reverence," with his own right hand he tore from his head, and gave to them, the Hair-relics. And they built a Dāgaba in their own city, and placed the relics within it.[3]

[1] Ukkala to Majjhima-desa. The latter included all the Buddhist Holy Land, from the modern Pātnā to Allahabād. See above, p. 61, note.

[2] See above, p. 93.

[3] We have here an interesting instance of the growth of legend to authenticate and add glory to local relics, of which other instances will be found in "Buddhism," p. 195. The ancient form of this legend, as found here, must

But the Perfectly Enlightened One rose up thence, and returned to the Shepherd's Nigrodha-tree, and sat down at its foot. And no sooner was he seated there, considering the depth of the Truth which he had gained, than there arose in his mind a doubt (felt by each of the Buddhas as he became aware of his having arrived at Truth) that he had not that kind of ability necessary to explain that Truth to others.

Then the great Ruler of the Brahma heavens, exclaiming, "Alas! the world is lost! Alas! the world will be altogether lost!" brought with him the rulers and archangels of the heavens in tens of thousands of world-systems, and went up to the Master, and said, "O Blessed Lord, mayst thou proclaim the Truth! Proclaim the Truth, O Blessed Lord!" and in other words of like purport begged from him the preaching of the Truth.

Then the Master granted his request. And considering to whom he should first reveal the Truth, thought at first of Aḷāra, his former teacher, as one who would quickly comprehend it. But, on further reflection, he perceived that Aḷāra had been dead seven days. So he fixed on Uddaka, but perceived that he too had died that very evening. Then he thought of the five mendicants, how faithfully they had served him for a time; and casting about in his mind where they then might be, he perceived they were at the Deer-forest in Benares. And he determined, saying, "There I will go to inaugurate the King-

have arisen when the relics were still in Orissa. Both the Burmese and Ceylonese now claim to possess them. The former say that the two merchants were Burmese, and that the Dāgaba above referred to is the celebrated sanctuary of Shooay Dagob (Bigandet, p. 101, 2nd ed.). The latter say that the Dāgaba was in Orissa, and that the hair-relics were brought thence to Ceylon in 490 A.D., in the manner related in the Kesa Dhātu Vaŋsa, and referred to in the Mahā Vaŋsa. (See verses 43–56 of my edition of the 39th chap. of the M. V. in the J. R. A. S. 1875.) The legend in the text is found in an ancient inscription on the great bell at Rangoon (Hough's version in the Asiatic Researches, vol. xvi.; comp. Hardy, M. B. p. 183; Beal, Rom. Leg.) p. 240.

dom of Righteousness." But he delayed a few days, begging his daily food in the neighbourhood of the Bo-tree, with the intention of going to Benares on the full-moon day of the month of May.

And at dawn of the fourteenth day of the month, when the night had passed away, he took his robe and his bowl; and had gone eighteen leagues, just half way, when he met the Hindu mendicant Upaka. And he announced to him how he had become a Buddha; and on the evening of that day he arrived at the hermitage near Benares.[1]

The five mendicants, seeing already from afar the Buddha coming, said one to another, "Friend, here comes the mendicant Gotama. He has turned back to a free use of the necessaries of life, and has recovered roundness of form, acuteness of sense, and beauty of complexion. We ought to pay him no reverence; but as he is, after all, of a good family, he deserves the honour of a seat. So we will simply prepare a seat for him."

The Blessed One, casting about in his mind (by the power that he had of knowing what was going on in the thoughts of all beings) as to what they were thinking, knew their thoughts. Then, concentrating that feeling of his love which was able to pervade generally all beings in earth and heaven, he directed it specially towards them. And the sense of his love diffused itself through their hearts; and as he came nearer and nearer, unable any longer to adhere to their resolve, they rose from their seats, and bowed down before him, and welcomed him with every mark of reverence and respect. But, not knowing that he had become a Buddha, they addressed him, in everything they said, either by name, or as "Brother." Then the Blessed One announced to them his Buddhahood, saying, "O mendicants, address not a Buddha by his name, or as 'brother.'

[1] Isipatana, the hermitage in the Deer-forest close to Benares. See above, p. 91.

And I, O mendicants, am a Buddha, clear in insight, as those who have gone before."[1]

Then, seated on the place prepared for him, and surrounded by myriads of angels, he addressed the five attendant elders, just as the moon was passing out of conjunction with the lunar mansion in June, and taught them in that discourse which was *The Foundation of the Kingdom of Righteousness.*

Of the five Elders, Kondanya the Believer[2] gained in knowledge as the discourse went on; and as it concluded, he, with myriads of angels, had arrived at the Fruit of the First Path.[3] And the Master, who remained there for the rainy season, sat in the *wihāra* the next day, when the other four had gone a-begging, talking to Vappa: and Vappa that morning attained to the Fruit of the First Path. And, in a similar manner, Bhaddiya on the next day, and Mahā Nāma on the next, and Assaji on the next, attained to the Fruit of the First Path. And, on the fifth day, he called all five to his side, and preached to them the discourse *On the Non-existence of the Soul;* and at the end of that discourse all the five elders attained to Nirvāna.

Then the Master perceived that Yasa, a young man of good family, was capable of entering the Paths. And at night-time, as he was going away, having left his home in weariness of the world, the Master called him, saying, "Follow me, Yasa!" and on that very night he attained to the Fruit of the First Path, and on the next day to Arahatship. And He received also the other fifty-four, his companions, into the order, with the formula, "Follow me!" and caused them to attain to Arahatship.

Now when there were thus in the world sixty-one persons who had become Arahats, the Master, after the rainy season

[1] Tathāgato Sammāsambuddho.

[2] So called from his action on this occasion. See above, pp. 72, 73.

[3] That is, became free from the delusion of soul, from doubt, and from belief in the efficacy of rites and ceremonies. "Buddhism," pp. 95, 108.

and the Feast with which it closes were over, sent out the sixty in different directions, with the words, "Go forth, O mendicants, preaching and teaching." And himself going towards Uruvela, overcame at the Kappāsiya forest, half way thither, the thirty young Bhadda-vaggiyan nobles. Of these the least advanced entered the First, and the most advanced the Third Path: and he received them all into the Order with the formula, "Follow me!" And sending them also forth into the regions round about, he himself went on to Uruvela.

There he overcame, by performing three thousand five hundred miracles, the three Hindu ascetics, brothers,—Uruvela Kassapa and the rest,—who had one thousand disciples. And he received them into the Order with the formula, "Follow me!" and established them in Arahatship by his discourse, when they were seated on the Gayā-sīsa hill, "*On the Lessons to be drawn from Fire.*" And attended by these thousand Arahats, he went to the grove called the Palm-grove, hard by Rājagaha, with the object of redeeming the promise he had made to Bimbisāra the king.[1]

When the king heard from the keeper of the grove the saying, "The Master is come," he went to the Master, attended by innumerable priests and nobles, and fell down at the feet of the Buddha,—those sacred feet, which bore on their surface the mystic figure of the sacred wheel, and gave forth a halo of light like a canopy of cloth of gold. Then he and his retinue respectfully took their seats on one side.

Now the question occurred to those priests and nobles, "How is it, then? has the Great Mendicant entered as a student in religion under Uruvela Kassapa, or Uruvela Kassapa under the Great Mendicant?" And the Blessed One, becoming aware of their thus doubting within themselves, addressed the Elder in the verse—

[1] See above p. 89.

282. What hast thou seen, O dweller in Uruvela,
That thou hast abandoned the Fire God, counting thyself poor?
I ask thee, Kassapa, the meaning of this thing:
How is it thou hast given up the sacrifice of fire?

And the Elder, perceiving what the Blessed One intended, replied in the verse—

283. Some men rely on sights, and sounds, and taste,
Others on sensual love, and some on sacrifice;
But this, I see, is dross so long as sin remains.
Therefore I find no charm in offerings great or small.

And (in order to make known his discipleship) he bowed his head to the Buddha's feet, saying, "The Blessed Lord is my master, and I am the disciple!" And seven times he rose into the air up to the height of one, two, three, and so on, up to the height of seven palm-trees; and descending again, he saluted the Buddha, and respectfully took a seat aside. Seeing that wonder, the multitude praised the Master, saying, "Ah! how great is the power of the Buddhas! Even so mighty an infidel as this has thought him worthy! Even Uruvela Kassapa has broken through the net of delusion, and has yielded to the successor of the Buddhas!"

But the Blessed One said, "Not now only have I overcome Uruvela Kassapa; in former ages, too, he was conquered by me." And he uttered in that connexion the *Mahā Nārada Kassapa Jātaka*, and proclaimed the Four Truths. And the king of Magadha, with nearly all his retinue, attained to the Fruit of the First Path, and the rest became lay disciples (without entering the Paths).[1]

[1] Upāsakas; that is, those who have taken the Three Refuges and the vow to keep the Five Commandments ("Buddhism," pp. 139, 160).

And the king still sitting near the Master told him of the five wishes he had had; and then, confessing his faith, he invited the Blessed One for the next day, and rising from his side, departed with respectful salutation.

The next day all the men who dwelt in Rājagaha, eighteen *koṭis* in number, both those who had already seen the Blessed One, and those who had not, came out early from Rājagaha to the Grove of Reeds to see the successor of the Buddhas. The road, six miles long, could not contain them. The whole of the Grove of Reeds became like a basket packed quite full. The multitude, beholding the exceeding beauty of Him whose power is Wisdom, could not contain their delight. Vaṇṇabhū was it called (that is, the Place of Praise), for at such spots all the greater and lesser characteristics of a Buddha, and the glorious beauty of his person, are fated to be sung. There was not room for even a single mendicant to get out on the road, or in the grove, so crowded was it with the multitude gazing at the beautiful form of the Being endowed with the ten-fold power of Wisdom.

So that day they say the throne of Sakka felt hot, to warn him that the Blessed One might be deprived of nourishment, which should not be. And, on considera-tion, he understood the reason; and he took the form of a young Brāhman, and descended in front of the Buddha, and made way for him, singing the praises of the Buddha, the Truth, and the Order. And he walked in front, mag-nifying the Master in these verses:

284. He whose passions are subdued has come to Rāja-gaha
Glorious as Singī gold,—the Blessed One;
And with him those who once were mere as-cetics,
Now all subdued in heart and freed from sin.

285. He who is free from sin has come to Rājagaha
Glorious as Singī gold,—the Blessed One;
And with him those who once were mere ascetics,
Now freed from sin and saved.

286. He who has crossed the flood[1] has come to Rājagaha
Glorious as Singī gold,—the Blessed One;
And with him those who once were mere ascetics,
But now crossed o'er the flood and freed from sin.

287. He whose dwelling and whose wisdom are tenfold;
He who has seen and gained ten precious things;[2]
Attended by ten hundred as a retinue,—
The Blessed One,—has come to Rājagaha.

The multitude, seeing the beauty of the young Brāhman, thought, "This young Brāhman is exceeding fair, and yet we have never yet beheld him." And they said, "Whence comes the young Brāhman, or whose son is he?" And the young Brāhman, hearing what they said, answered in the verse,

288. He who is wise, and all subdued in heart,
The Buddha, the unequalled among men,
The Arahat, the most happy upon earth!—
His servant am I.

Then the Master entered upon the path thus made free by the Archangel, and entered Rājagaha attended by a

[1] Tiṇṇo, crossed the ocean of transmigration.
[2] That is, the Four Paths, the Four Fruits thereof, Nirvāna, and the Scriptures (or the Truth, Dhamma).

thousand mendicants. The king gave a great donation to the Order with the Buddha at their head; and had water brought, bright as gems, and scented with flowers, in a golden goblet. And he poured the water over the hand of the Buddha, in token of the presentation of the Bambu Grove, saying, "I, my lord, cannot live without the Three Gems (the Buddha, the Order, and the Faith). In season and out of season I would visit the Blessed One. Now the Grove of Reeds is far away; but this Grove of mine, called the Bambu Grove, is close by, is easy of resort, and is a fit dwelling-place for a Buddha. Let the Blessed One accept it of me!"

At the acceptance of this monastery the broad earth shook, as if it said, "Now the Religion of Buddha has taken root!" For in all India there is no dwelling-place, save the Bambu Grove, whose acceptance caused the earth to shake: and in Ceylon there is no dwelling-place, save the Great Wihāra, whose acceptance caused the earth to shake.

And when the Master had accepted the Bambu Grove Monastery, and had given thanks for it, he rose from his seat and went, surrounded by the members of the Order, to the Bambu Grove.

Now at that time two ascetics, named Sāriputta and Moggallāna, were living near Rājagaha, seeking after salvation. Of these, Sāriputta, seeing the Elder Assaji on his begging round, was pleasurably impressed by him, and waited on him, and heard from him the verse beginning,—

"What things soever are produced from causes."[1]

And he attained to the blessings which result from con-

[1] The celebrated verse here referred to has been found inscribed several times in the ruins of the great Dāgaba at Isipatana, and facsimiles are given in Cunningham's Archæological Reports, plate xxxiv. vol. i. p. 123. The text is given by Burnouf in the Lotus de la Bonne Loi, p. 523; and in the Mahā Vagga, pp. 40, 41. See also Hardy's Manual, p. 196.

version; and repeated that verse to his companion Moggallāna the ascetic. And he, too, attained to the blessings which first result from conversion. And each of them left Sanjaya,[1] and with his attendants took orders under the Master. Of these two, Moggallāna attained Arahatship in seven days, and Sāriputta the Elder in half a month. And the Master appointed these two to the office of his Chief Disciples; and on the day on which Sāriputta the Elder attained Arahatship, he held the so-called Council of the Disciples.[2]

Now whilst the Successor of the Buddhas was dwelling there in the Bambu Grove, Suddhodana the king heard that his son, who for six years had devoted himself to works of self-mortification, had attained to Complete Enlightenment, had founded the Kingdom of Righteousness, and was then dwelling at the Bambu Grove near Rājagaha. So he said to a certain courtier, "Look you, Sir; take a thousand men as a retinue, and go to Rājagaha, and say in my name, 'Your father, Suddhodana the king, desires to see you;' and bring my son here."

And he respectfully accepted the king's command with the reply, "So be it, O king!" and went quickly with a thousand followers the sixty leagues distance, and sat down amongst the disciples of the Sage, and at the hour of instruction entered the Wihāra. And thinking, "Let the king's message stay awhile," he stood just beyond the disciples and listened to the discourse. And as he so stood he attained to Arahatship, with his whole retinue, and asked to be admitted to the Order. And the Blessed One stretched forth his hand and said, "Come among us, O mendicants." And all of them that moment appeared there, with robes and bowls created by miracle, like Elders of a hundred years' standing.

[1] Their then teacher.

[2] Or perhaps, "He formed the Corporation of the Disciples," that is, the Order of Mendicants.

Now from the time when they attain Arahatship the Arahats become indifferent to worldly things: so he did not deliver the king's message to the Sage. The king, seeing that neither did his messenger return, nor was any message received from him, called another courtier in the same manner as before, and sent him. And he went, and in the same manner attained Arahatship with his followers, and remained silent. Then the king in the same manner sent nine courtiers each with a retinue of a thousand men. And they all, neglecting what they had to do, stayed away there in silence.

And when the king found no one who would come and bring even a message, he thought, "Not one of these brings back, for my sake, even a message: who will then carry out what I say?" And searching among all his people he thought of Kāḷa Udāyin. For he was in everything serviceable to the king,—intimate with him, and trustworthy. He was born on the same day as the future Buddha, and had been his playfellow and companion.

So the king said to him, "Friend Kāḷa Udāyin, as I wanted to see my son, I sent nine times a thousand men; but there is not one of them who has either come back or sent a message. Now the end of my life is not far off, and I desire to see my son before I die. Can you help me to see my son?"

"I can, O king!" was the reply, "if I am allowed to become a recluse."

"My friend," said the king, "become a recluse or not as you will, but help me to see my son!"

" And he respectfully received the king's message, with the words, "So be it, O king!" and went to Rājagaha; and stood at the edge of the disciples at the time of the Master's instruction, and heard the gospel, and attained Arahatship with his followers, and was received into the Order.

The Master spent the first Lent after he had become

Buddha at Isipatana; and when it was over went to Uruvela and stayed there three months and overcame the three brothers, ascetics. And on the full-moon day of the month of January, he went to Rājagaha with a retinue of a thousand mendicants, and there he dwelt two months. Thus five months had elapsed since he left Benāres, the cold season was past, and seven or eight days since the arrival of Udāyin, the Elder.

And on the full-moon day of March Udāyin thought, "The cold season is past; the spring has come; men raise their crops and set out on their journeys; the earth is covered with fresh grass; the woods are full of flowers; the roads are fit to walk on; now is the time for the Sage to show favour to his family." And going to the Blessed One, he praised travelling in about sixty stanzas, that the Sage might revisit his native town.

289. Red are the trees with blossoms bright,
They give no shade to him who seeks for fruit;
Brilliant they seem as glowing fires.
The very season's full, O Great One, of delights.
290. 'Tis not too hot; 'tis not too cold;
There's plenty now of all good things;
The earth is clad with verdure green,
Fit is the time, O mighty Sage!

Then the Master said to him, "But why, Udāyin, do you sing the pleasures of travelling with so sweet a voice?"

"My lord!" was the reply, "your father is anxious to see you once more; will you not show favour to your relations?"

"'Tis well said, Udāyin! I will do so. Tell the Order that they shall fulfil the duty laid on all its members of journeying from place to place."

Kāḷa Udāyin accordingly told the brethren. And the Blessed One, attended by twenty thousand mendicants free from sin—ten thousand from the upper classes in Magadha and Anga, and ten thousand from the upper classes in Kapila-vatthu—started from Rājagaha, and travelled a league a day; going slowly with the intention of reaching Kapila-vatthu, sixty leagues from Rājagaha, in two months.

And the Elder, thinking, "I will let the king know that the Blessed One has started," rose into the air and appeared in the king's house. The king was glad to see the Elder, made him sit down on a splendid couch, filled a bowl with the delicious food made ready for himself, and gave to him. Then the Elder rose up, and made as if he would go away.

"Sit down and eat," said the king.

"I will rejoin the Master, and eat then," said he.

"Where is the Master now?" asked the king.

"He has set out on his journey, attended by twenty thousand mendicants, to see you, O king!" said he.

The king, glad at heart, said, "Do you eat this; and until my son has arrived at this town, provide him with food from here."

The Elder agreed; and the king waited on him, and then had the bowl cleansed with perfumed chunam, and filled with the best of food, and placed it in the Elder's hand, saying, "Give it to the Buddha."

And the Elder, in the sight of all, threw the bowl into the air, and himself rising up into the sky, took the food again, and placed it in the hand of the Master.

The Master ate it. Every day the Elder brought him food in the same manner. So the Master himself was fed, even on the journey, from the king's table. The Elder, day by day, when he had finished his meal, told the king, "To-day the Blessed One has come so far, to-day so far." And by talking of the high character of the Buddha, he made all the king's family delighted with the Master, even before they saw him. On that account the Blessed

One gave him pre-eminence, saying, "Pre-eminent, O mendicants, among all those of my disciples who gained over my family, was Kāḷa Udāyin."

The Sākyas, as they sat talking of the prospect of seeing their distinguished relative, considered what place he could stay in; and deciding that the Nigrodha Grove would be a pleasant residence, they made everything ready there. And with flowers in their hands they went out to meet him; and sending in front the little children, and the boys and girls of the village, and then the young men and maidens of the royal family; they themselves, decked of their own accord with sweet-smelling flowers and chunam, came close behind, conducting the Blessed One to the Nigrodha Grove. There the Blessed One sat down on the Buddha's throne prepared for him, surrounded by twenty thousand Arahats.

The Sākyas are proud by nature, and stubborn in their pride. Thinking, "Siddattha is younger than we are, standing to us in the relation of younger brother, or nephew, or son, or grandson," they said to the little children and the young people, "Do you bow down before him, we will seat ourselves behind you." The Blessed One, when they had thus taken their seats, perceived what they meant; and thinking, "My relations pay me no reverence; come now, I must force them to do so," he fell into the ecstasy depending on wisdom, and rising into the air as if shaking off the dust of his feet upon them, he performed a miracle like unto that double miracle at the foot of the Gaṇḍamba-tree.[1]

The king, seeing that miracle, said, "O Blessed One! When you were presented to Kāḷa Devala to do obeisance to him on the day on which you were born, and I saw your feet turn round and place themselves on the

[1] See above, p. 105. The Dhammapada Commentary, p. 334, has a different account of the miracle performed on this occasion. It says he made a jewelled terrace (ratana-caŋkamaŋ) in the sky, and walking up and down in it, preached the Faith (Dhammaŋ).

Brāhman's head, I did obeisance to you. That was my first obeisance. When you were seated on your couch in the shade of the Jambu-tree on the day of the ploughing festival, I saw how the shadow over you did not turn, and I bowed down at your feet. That was my second obeisance. Now, seeing this unprecedented miracle, I bow down at your feet. This is my third obeisance."

Then, when the king did obeisance to him, there was not a single Sākya who was able to refrain from bowing down before the Blessed One; and all of them did obeisance.

So the Blessed One, having compelled his relatives to bow down before him, descended from the sky, and sat down on the seat prepared for him. And when the Blessed One was seated, the assembly of his relatives yielded him pre-eminence; and all sat there at peace in their hearts.

Then a thunder-cloud poured forth a shower of rain, and the copper-coloured water went away rumbling beneath the earth. He who wished to get wet, did get wet; but not even a drop fell on the body of him who did not wish to get wet. And all seeing it became filled with astonishment, and said one to another, "Lo! what miracle! Lo! what wonder!"

But the Teacher said, "Not now only did a shower of rain fall upon me in the assembly of my relations, formerly also this happened." And in this connexion he pronounced the story of his Birth as Wessantara.

When they had heard his discourse they rose up, and paid reverence to him, and went away. Not one of them, either the king or any of his ministers, asked him on leaving, "To-morrow accept your meal of us."

So on the next day the Master, attended by twenty thousand mendicants, entered Kapilavatthu to beg. Then also no one came to him or invited him to his house, or took his bowl. The Blessed One, standing at the gate, considered, "How then did the former Buddhas go on their begging rounds in their native town? Did they go direct to the houses of the kings, or did they beg straight on from house to house?" Then, not finding that any of the Buddhas had gone direct, he thought, "I, too, must accept this descent and tradition as my own; so shall my disciples in future, learning of me, fulfil the duty of begging for their daily food." And beginning at the first house, he begged straight on.

At the rumour that the young chief Siddhattha was begging from door to door, the windows in the two-storied and three-storied houses were thrown open, and the multitude was transfixed at the sight. And the lady, the mother of Rāhula, thought, "My lord, who used to go to and fro in this very town with gilded palanquin and every sign of royal pomp, now with a potsherd in his hand begs his food from door to door, with shaven hair and beard, and clad in yellow robes. Is this becoming?" And she opened the window, and looked at the Blessed One; and she beheld him glorious with the unequalled majesty of a Buddha, distinguished with the Thirty-two characteristic signs and the eighty lesser marks of a Great Being, and lighting up the street of the city with a halo resplendent with many colours, proceeding to a fathom's length all round his person.

And she announced it to the king, saying, "Your son is begging his bread from door to door;" and she magnified him with the eight stanzas on "The Lion among Men," beginning—

291. Glossy and dark and soft and curly is his hair;
Spotless and fair as the sun is his forehead;
Well-proportioned and prominent and delicate is his nose;
Around him is diffused a network of rays;—
The Lion among Men!

The king was deeply agitated; and he departed instantly, gathering up his robe in his hand, and went quickly and stood before the Blessed One, and said, "Why, Master, do you put us to shame? Why do you go begging for your food? Do you think it impossible to provide a meal for so many monks?"

"This is our custom, O king!" was the reply.

"Not so, Master! our descent is from the royal race of the Great Elected;[1] and amongst them all not one chief has ever begged his daily food."

"This succession of kings is your descent, O king! but mine is the succession of the prophets (Buddhas), from Dīpaŋkara and Kondanya and the rest down to Kassapa. These, and thousands of other Buddhas, have begged their daily food, and lived on alms." And standing in the middle of the street he uttered the verse—

292. Rise up, and loiter not!
Follow after a holy life!
Who follows virtue rests in bliss,
Both in this world and in the next."

And when the verse was finished the king attained to the Fruit of the First, and then, on hearing the following verse, to the Fruit of the Second Path—

293. Follow after a holy life!
Follow not after sin!
Who follows virtue rests in bliss,
Both in this world and in the next.

And when he heard the story of the Birth as the Keeper of Righteousness,[2] he attained to the Fruit of the Third Path. And just as he was dying, seated on the royal couch under the white canopy of state, he attained to

[1] Mahā Sammata, the first king among men. [2] Dhammapāla Jātaka.

Arahatship. The king never practised in solitude the Great Struggle.[1]

Now as soon as he had realized the Fruit of Conversion, he took the Buddha's bowl, and conducted the Blessed One and his retinue to the palace, and served them with savoury food, both hard and soft. And when the meal was over, all the women of the household came and did obeisance to the Blessed One, except only the mother of Rāhula.

But she, though she told her attendants to go and salute their lord, stayed behind, saying, "If I am of any value in his eyes, my lord will himself come to me; and when he has come I will pay him reverence."

And the Blessed One, giving his bowl to the king to carry, went with his two chief disciples to the apartments of the daughter of the king, saying, "The king's daughter shall in no wise be rebuked, howsoever she may be pleased to welcome me." And he sat down on the seat prepared for him.

And she came quickly and held him by his ankles, and laid her head on his feet, and so did obeisance to him, even as she had intended. And the king told of the fullness of her love for the Blessed One, and of her goodness of heart, saying, "When my daughter heard, O Master, that you had put on the yellow robes, from that time forth she dressed only in yellow. When she heard of your taking but one meal a day, she adopted the same custom. When she heard that you renounced the use of elevated couches, she slept on a mat spread on the floor. When she heard you had given up the use of garlands and unguents, she also used them no more. And when her relatives sent a message, saying, 'Let us take care of you,' she paid them no attention at all. Such is my daughter's goodness of heart, O Blessed One!"

[1] See above, p. 89.

"'Tis no wonder, O king!" was the reply, "that she should watch over herself now that she has you for a protector, and that her wisdom is mature; formerly, even when wandering among the mountains without a protector, and when her wisdom was not mature, she watched over herself." And he told the story of his Birth as the Moonsprite;[1] and rose from his seat, and went away.

On the next day the festivals of the coronation, and of the housewarming, and of the marriage of Nanda, the king's son, were being celebrated all together. But the Buddha went to his house, and gave him his bowl to carry; and with the object of making him abandon the world, he wished him true happiness; and then, rising from his seat, departed. And (the bride) Janapada Kalyāṇī, seeing the young man go away, gazed wonderingly at him, and cried out, "My Lord, whither go you so quickly?" But he, not venturing to say to the Blessed One, "Take your bowl," followed him even unto the Wihāra. And the Blessed One received him, unwilling though he was, into the Order.

It was on the third day after he reached Kapilapura that the Blessed One ordained Nanda. On the second day the mother of Rāhula arrayed the boy in his best, and sent him to the Blessed One, saying, "Look, dear, at that monk, attended by twenty thousand monks, and glorious in appearance as the Archangel Brahma! That is your father. He had certain great treasures, which we have not seen since he abandoned his home. Go now, and ask for your inheritance, saying, 'Father, I am your son. When I am crowned, I shall become a king over all the earth. I have need of the treasure. Give me the treasure; for a son is heir to his father's property.'"

The boy went up to the Blessed One, and gained the love of his father, and stood there glad and joyful, saying,

[1] Candakinnara Jātaka.

"Happy, O monk, is thy shadow!" and adding many other words befitting his position. When the Blessed One had ended his meal, and had given thanks, he rose from his seat, and went away. And the child followed the Blessed One, saying, "O monk! give me my inheritance! give me my inheritance!"

And the Blessed One prevented him not. And the disciples, being with the Blessed One, ventured not to stop him. And so he went with the Blessed One even up to the grove. Then the Blessed One thought, "This wealth, this property of his father's, which he is asking for, perishes in the using, and brings vexation with it! I will give him the sevenfold wealth of the Arahats which I obtained under the Bo-tree, and make him the heir of a spiritual inheritance!" And he said to Sāriputta, "Well, then, Sāriputta, receive Rāhula into the Order."

But when the child had been taken into the Order the king grieved exceedingly. And he was unable to bear his grief, and made it known to the Blessed One, and asked of him a boon, saying, "If you so please, O Master, let not the Holy One receive a son into the Order without the leave of his father and mother." And the Blessed One granted the boon.

And the next day, as he sat in the king's house after his meal was over, the king, sitting respectfully by him, said, "Master! when you were practising austerities, an angel came to me, and said, 'Your son is dead!' And I believed him not, and rejected what he said, answering, 'My son will not die without attaining Buddhahood!'"

And he replied, saying, "Why should you now have believed? when formerly, though they showed you my bones and said your son was dead, you did not believe them." And in that connexion he told the story of his Birth as the Great Keeper of Righteousness.[1] And when the story was ended, the king attained to the Fruit of the

[1] Mahādhammapāla Jātaka. See above, p. 126.

Third Path. And so the Blessed One established his father in the Three Fruits; and he returned to Rājagaha attended by the company of the brethren, and resided at the Grove of Sītā.

At that time the householder Anātha Piṇḍika, bringing merchandise in five hundred carts, went to the house of a trader in Rājagaha, his intimate friend, and there heard that a Blessed Buddha had arisen. And very early in the morning he went to the Teacher, the door being opened by the power of an angel, and heard the Truth and became converted. And on the next day he gave a great donation to the Order, with the Buddha at their head, and received a promise from the Teacher that he would come to Sāvatthi.

Then along the road, forty-five leagues in length, he built resting-places at every league, at an expenditure of a hundred thousand for each. And he bought the Grove called Jetavana for eighteen koṭis of gold pieces, laying them side by side over the ground, and erected there a new building. In the midst thereof he made a pleasant room for the Sage, and around it separately constructed dwellings for the eighty Elders, and other residences with single and double walls, and long halls and open roofs, ornamented with ducks and quails; and ponds also he made, and terraces to walk on by day and by night.

And so having constructed a delightful residence on a pleasant spot, at an expense of eighteen koṭis, he sent a message to the Sage that he should come.

The Master, hearing the messenger's words, left Rājagaha attended by a great multitude of monks, and in due course arrived at the city of Sāvatthi. Then the wealthy merchant decorated the monastery; and on the day on which the Buddha should arrive at Jetavana he arrayed his son in splendour, and sent him on with five hundred youths in festival attire. And he and his retinue, holding five hundred flags resplendent with cloth of five different colours, appeared before the Sage. And behind him Mahā-Subhaddā and Cūla-Subhaddā, the two daughters of the merchant, went forth with five hundred damsels carrying water-pots full of water. And behind them, decked with all her ornaments, the merchant's wife went forth, with five hundred matrons carrying vessels full of food. And behind them all the great merchant himself, clad in new robes, with five hundred traders also dressed in new robes, went out to meet the Blessed One.

The Blessed One, sending this retinue of lay disciples in front, and attended by the great multitude of monks, entered the Jetavana monastery with the infinite grace and unequalled majesty of a Buddha, making the spaces of the grove bright with the halo from his person, as if they were sprinkled with gold-dust.

Then Anātha Piṇḍika asked him, "How, my Lord, shall I deal with this Wihāra?"

"O householder," was the reply, "give it then to the Order of Mendicants, whether now present or hereafter to arrive."

And the great merchant, saying, "So be it, my Lord," brought a golden vessel, and poured water over the hand of the Sage, and dedicated the Wihāra, saying, "I give this Jetavana Wihāra to the Order of Mendicants with the Buddha at their head, and to all from every direction now present or hereafter to come."[1]

And the Master accepted the Wihāra, and giving thanks, pointed out the advantages of monasteries, saying,—

294. Cold they ward off, and heat;
So also beasts of prey,
And creeping things, and gnats,
And rains in the cold season.
And when the dreaded heat and winds
Arise, they ward them off.

[1] This formula has been constantly found in rock inscriptions in India and Ceylon over the ancient cave-dwellings of Buddhist hermits.

295. To give to monks a dwelling-place,
Wherein in safety and in peace
To think till mysteries grow clear,
The Buddha calls a worthy deed.

296. Let therefore a wise man,
Regarding his own weal,
Have pleasant monasteries built,
And lodge there learned men.

297. Let him with cheerful mien
Give food to them, and drink,
And clothes, and dwelling-places
To the upright in mind.

298. Then they shall preach to him the Truth,—
The Truth, dispelling every grief,—
Which Truth, when here a man receives,
He sins no more, and dies away!

Anātha Piṇḍika began the dedication festival from the second day. The festival held at the dedication of Visākhā's building ended in four months, but Anātha Piṇḍika's dedication festival lasted nine months. At the festival, too, eighteen koṭis were spent; so on that one monastery he spent wealth amounting to fifty-four koṭis.

Long ago, too, in the time of the Blessed Buddha Vipassin, a merchant named Punabbasu Mitta bought that very spot by laying golden bricks over it, and built a monastery there a league in length. And in the time of the Blessed Buddha Sikhin, a merchant named Sirivaḍḍha bought that very spot by standing golden ploughshares over it, and built there a monastery three-quarters of a league in length. And in the time of the Blessed Buddha Vessabhū, a merchant named Sotthiya bought that very spot by laying golden elephant feet along it, and built a monastery there half a league in length. And in the time of the Blessed Buddha Kakusandha, a merchant named Accuta also bought that very spot by laying golden bricks over it, and built there a monastery a quarter of a league in length. And in the time of the Blessed Buddha Koṇāgamana, a merchant named Ugga bought that very spot by laying golden tortoises over it, and built there a monastery half a league in length. And in the time of the Blessed Buddha Kassapa, a merchant named Sumaŋgala bought that very spot by laying golden bricks over it, and built there a monastery sixty acres in extent. And in the time of our Blessed One, Anātha Piṇḍika the merchant bought that very spot by laying kahāpaṇas over it, and built there a monastery thirty acres in extent. For that spot is a place which not one of all the Buddhas has deserted. And so the Blessed One lived in that spot from the attainment of omniscience under the Bo-tree till his death. This is the Proximate Epoch. And now we will tell the stories of all his Births.

END OF THE ACCOUNT OF THE CAUSES THAT LEAD TO THE ATTAINMENT OF BUDDHAHOOD.

GLORY BE TO THE BLESSED, THE HOLY, THE ALL-WISE ONE.

BOOK I.

No. 1.—Holding to the Truth.[1]

THIS discourse on the True (Apaṇṇaka), the Blessed One delivered while at the Jetavana Wihāra, near Sāvatthi.

What was the circumstance concerning which this tale arose? About the five hundred heretics, friends of the Merchant.

For one day, we are told, Anātha Piṇḍika the merchant took five hundred heretics, friends of his, and had many garlands and perfumes and ointments and oil and honey and molasses and clothes and vestments brought, and went to Jetavana. And saluting the Blessed One, he offered him garlands and other things, and bestowed medicines and clothes on the Order of Mendicants, and sat down in a respectful and becoming manner on one side of the Teacher.[2] And those followers of wrong belief also saluted the Blessed One, and sat down close to Anātha Piṇḍika. And they beheld the countenance of the Teacher like the full moon in glory; and his person

[1] Apaṇṇaka Jātaka.
[2] Literally, sat down on one side, avoiding the six improper ways of doing so.

endowed with all the greater and lesser marks of honour, and surrounded to a fathom's length with brightness; and also the clustering rays (the peculiar attribute of a Buddha), which issued from him like halos, and in pairs. Then, though mighty in voice like a young lion roaring in his pride in the Red Rock Valley,[1] or like a monsoon thunder-cloud, he preached to them in a voice like an archangel's voice, perfect and sweet and pleasant to hear, a discourse varied with many counsels,—as if he were weaving a garland of pearls out of the stars in the Milky Way!

When they had heard the Teacher's discourse, they were pleased at heart; and rising up, they bowed down to the One Mighty by Wisdom, and giving up the wrong belief as their refuge, they took refuge in the Buddha. And from that time they were in the habit of going with Anātha Piṇḍika to the Wihāra, taking garlands and perfumes with them, and of hearing the Truth, and of giving gifts, and of keeping the Precepts, and of making confession.

Now the Blessed One went back again from Sāvatthi to Rājagaha. And they, as soon as the Successor of the Prophets was gone, gave up that faith; and again put their trust in heresy, and returned to their former condition.

And the Blessed One, after seven or eight months, returned to Jetavana. And Anātha Piṇḍika again brought those men with him, and going to the Teacher honoured him with gifts as before, and bowing down to him, seated himself respectfully by his side. Then he told the Blessed One that when the Successor of the Prophets had left, those men had broken the faith they had taken, had returned to their trust in heresy, and had resumed their former condition.

And the Blessed One, by the power of the sweet words he had continually spoken through countless ages, opened

[1] A famous haunt of lions in the Himālaya Mountains.

his lotus mouth as if he were opening a jewel-casket scented with heavenly perfume, and full of sweet-smelling odours; and sending forth his pleasant tones, he asked them, saying, "Is it true, then, that you, my disciples, giving up the Three Refuges,[1] have gone for refuge to another faith?"

And they could not conceal it, and said, "It is true, O Blessed One!"

And when they had thus spoken, the Teacher said, "Not in hell beneath, nor in heaven above, nor beyond in the countless world-systems of the universe, is there any one like to a Buddha in goodness and wisdom—much less, then, a greater." And he described to them the qualities of the Three Gems as they are laid down in the Scripture passages beginning, "Whatever creatures there may be, etc., the Successor of the Prophets is announced to be the Chief of all." And again, "Whatsoever treasure there be here or in other worlds," etc. And again, "From the chief of all pleasant things," etc.

And he said, "Whatever disciples, men or women, have taken as their refuge the Three Gems endowed with these glorious qualities, they will never be born in hell; but freed from birth in any place of punishment, they will be reborn in heaven, and enter into exceeding bliss. You, therefore, by leaving so safe a refuge, and placing your reliance on other teaching, have done wrong."

And here the following passages should be quoted to show that those who, for the sake of Perfection and Salvation, have taken refuge in the Three Gems, will not be reborn in places of punishment:—

> Those who have put their trust in Buddha,
> They will not go to a world of pain:
> Having put off this mortal coil,
> They will enter some heavenly body!

[1] Trust in the Buddha, in the Order, and in the Truth, which are the 'Three Gems.'

Those who have put their trust in the Truth,
They will not go to a world of pain:
Having put off this mortal coil,
They will enter some heavenly body!

Those who have put their faith in the Order,
They will not go to a world of pain:
Having put off this mortal coil,
They will enter some heavenly body!

They go to many a refuge—
To the mountains and the forest . . . .
(and so on down to)
Having gone to this as their refuge,
They are freed from every pain.[1]

The above was not all the discourse which the Teacher uttered to them. He also said, "Disciples! the meditation on the Buddha, the Truth, and the Order, gives the Entrance and the Fruit of the First Path, and of the Second, and of the Third, and of the Fourth." And having in this way laid down the Truth to them, he added, "You have done wrong to reject so great salvation!"

And here the fact of the gift of the Paths to those who meditate on the Buddha, the Order, and the Truth, might be shown from the following and other similar passages: "There is one thing, O mendicants, which, if practised with increasing intensity, leads to complete weariness of the vanities of the world, to the end of longings, to the destruction of excitement, to peace of mind, to higher knowledge, to complete enlightenment, to Nirvāṇa. What is that one thing? The meditation on the Buddhas."

Having thus exhorted the disciples in many ways, the Blessed One said, "Disciples! formerly, too, men trusting

[1] This last quotation is from Dhammapada, verses 188–192.

to their own reason foolishly mistook for a refuge that which was no refuge, and becoming the prey of demons in a wilderness haunted by evil spirits, came to a disastrous end. Whilst those who adhered to the absolute, the certain, the right belief, found good fortune in that very desert." And when he had thus spoken, he remained silent.

Then Anātha Piṇḍika, the house-lord, arose from his seat, and did obeisance to the Blessed One, and exalted him, and bowed down before him with clasped hands, and said, "Now, at least, O Lord! the foolishness of these disciples in breaking with the best refuge is made plain to us. But how those self-sufficient reasoners were destroyed in the demon-haunted desert, while those who held to the truth were saved, is hid from us, though it is known to you. May it please the Blessed One to make this matter known to us, as one causing the full moon to rise in the sky!"

Then the Blessed One said, "O householder! it was precisely with the object of resolving the doubts of the world that for countless ages I have practised the Ten Cardinal Virtues,[1] and have so attained to perfect knowledge. Listen, then, and give ear attentively, as if you were filling up a golden measure with the most costly essence!" Having thus excited the merchant's attention, he made manifest that which had been concealed by change of birth,—setting free, as it were, the full moon from the bosom of a dark snow-cloud.

Once upon a time in the country of Kāsi and the city of Benares, there was a king called Brahma-datta. The Bodisat was at that time born in a merchant's family;

[1] See above, pp. 54–58, for an explanation of this.

and in due course he grew up, and went about trafficking with five hundred bullock-carts. Sometimes he travelled from east to west, and sometimes from west to east. At Benares too there was another young merchant, stupid, dull, and unskilful in resource.

Now the Bodisat collected in Benares merchandise of great value, and loaded it in five hundred bullock-carts, and made them ready for a journey. And that foolish merchant likewise loaded five hundred carts, and got them ready to start.

Then the Bodisat thought, "If this foolish young merchant should come with me, the road will not suffice for the thousand carts, all travelling together; the men will find it hard to get wood and water, and the bullocks to get grass. Either he or I ought to go on first."

And sending for him he told him as much; saying, "We two can't go together. Will you go on in front, or come on after me?"

And that other thought, "It will be much better for me to go first. I shall travel on a road that is not cut up, the oxen will eat grass that has not been touched, and for the men there will be curry-stuffs, of which the best have not been picked; the water will be undisturbed; and I shall sell my goods at what price I like." So he said, "I, friend, will go on first."

But the Bodisat saw that it would be better to go second: for thus it occurred to him, "Those who go in front will make the rough places plain, whilst I shall go over the ground they have traversed:—the old rank grass will have been eaten by the oxen that have gone first, whilst my oxen will eat the freshly grown and tender shoots:—for the men there will be the sweet curry-stuffs that have grown where the old was picked:—where there is no water these others will dig and get supplies, whilst we shall drink from the wells that they have dug:—and haggling about prices too is killing work; whereas by going afterwards, I shall sell my goods at the prices they have established." So seeing all these advantages, he said, "Well, friend, you may go on first."

The foolish merchant said, "Very well, then!" yoked his waggons and started; and in due course passed beyond the inhabited country, and came to the border of the wilderness.

Now there are five kinds of wildernesses, those that have become so by reason of thieves, of wild beasts, of the want of water, of the presence of demons, and of insufficiency of food; and of these this wilderness was demon-haunted and waterless.[1] So the merchant placed great water-pots on his carts, and filled them with water, and then entered the desert, which was sixty leagues across.

But, when he had reached the middle of the desert, the demon who dwelt there thought, "I will make these fellows throw away the water they have brought; and having thus destroyed their power of resistance, I will eat them every one!"

So he created a beautiful carriage drawn by milk-white bulls; and attended by ten or twelve demons with bows and arrows, and swords and shields, in their hands, he went to meet the merchant, seated like a lord in his carriage,—but adorned with a garland of water-lilies, with his hair and clothes all wet, and his carriage wheels begrimed with mud. His attendants too went before

[1] A gloss repeats these descriptions at somewhat greater length.

and after him, with their hair and clothes all wet, decked with garlands of white lotuses, carrying bunches of red lotuses, eating the edible stalks of water-plants, and with drops of water and mud trickling from them.

Now the chiefs of trading caravans, whenever a headwind blows, ride in their carriage in front, surrounded by their attendants, and thus escape the dust; and when it blows from behind, they, in the same manner, ride behind. At that time there was a headwind, so the merchant went in front.

As the demon saw him coming, he turned his carriage out of the way, and greeted him kindly, saying, "Where are you going to?"

And the merchant hurrying his carriage out of the way, made room for the carts to pass, and waiting beside him, said to the demon, "We have come thus far from Benares. And you I see with lotus wreaths, and water-lilies in your hands, eating lotus stalks, soiled with dirt, and dripping with water and mud. Pray, does it rain on the road you have come by, and are there tanks there covered with water-plants?"

No sooner had the demon heard that, than he answered; "What is this that you say? Yonder streak is green forest; from thence onwards the whole country abounds with water, it is always raining, the pools are full, and here and there are ponds covered with lotuses." And as the carts passed by one after another, he asked, "Where are you going with these carts?"

"To such and such a country," was the reply.

"And in this cart, and in this, what have you got?" said he.

"Such and such things."

"This cart coming last comes along very heavily, what is there in this one?"

"There's water in that."

"You have done right to bring water as far as this; but further on there's no need of it. In front of you there's plenty of water. Break the pots and pour away the water, and go on at your ease." Then he added, "Do you go on, we have already delayed too long!" and himself went on a little, and as soon as he was out of sight, went back to the demons' home.

And that foolish merchant, in his folly, accepted the demon's word, and had his pots broken, and the water poured away (without saving even a cupful), and sent on the carts. And before them there was not the least water. And the men, having nothing to drink, became weary. And journeying on till sunset, they unyoked the waggons, and ranged them in a circle, and tied the oxen to the wheels. And there was neither water for the oxen, nor could the men cook their rice. And the worn-out men fell down here and there and slept.

And at the end of the night the demons came up from their demon city, and slew them all, both men and oxen, and ate their flesh, and went away leaving their bones behind. So on account of one foolish young merchant these all came to destruction, and their bones were scattered to all the points of the compass! And the five hundred carts stood there just as they had been loaded!

Now for a month and a half after the foolish merchant had started, the Bodisat waited; and then left the city, and went straight on till he came to the mouth of the desert. There he filled the vessels, and laid up a plentiful store of water, and had the drum beaten in the encampment to call the men together, and addressed them thus: "Without asking me, let not even a cupful of water be used! There are poisonous trees in the wilderness: without asking me, let not a leaf nor a flower nor a fruit you have not eaten before, be eaten!" And when he had thus exhorted his followers, he entered the desert with his five hundred waggons.

When he had reached the middle of the desert, that demon, in the same way as before, showed himself to the Bodisat as if he were coming from the opposite direction. The Bodisat knew him as soon as he saw him, thinking thus: "There is no water in this wilderness; its very name is the arid desert. This fellow is red-eyed and bold, and throws no shadow. The foolish merchant who went on before me will doubtless have been persuaded by this fellow to throw away all his water; will have been wearied out; and, with all his people, have fallen a prey. But he doesn't know, methinks, how clever I am, and how fertile in resource."

Then he said to him, "Begone! We are travelling merchants, and don't throw away the water we've got till we see some more; and as soon as we do see it, we understand quite well how to lighten carts by throwing ours away!"

The demon went on a little way, and when he got out of sight, returned to his demon city. When the demons were gone, his men said to the Bodisat, "Sir! those men told us that yonder was the beginning of the green forest, and from there onwards it was always raining. They had all kinds of lotuses with them in garlands and branches, and were chewing the edible lotus-stalks; their clothes and hair were all wet, and they came dripping with water.

Let us throw away the water, and go on quickly with light carts!"

And when he heard what they said, the Bodisat made the waggons halt, and collecting all his men, put the question to them, "Have you ever heard anybody say that there was any lake or pond in this desert?"

"We never heard so."

"And now some men are saying that it rains on the other side of that stretch of green forest. How far can a rain-wind be felt?"

"About a league, Sir."

"Now does the rain-wind reach the body of any one of you?"

"No, Sir."

"And how far off is the top of a rain-cloud visible?"

"About a league, Sir."

"Now does any one of you see the top of a single cloud?"

"No one, Sir."

"How far off can a flash of lightning be seen?"

"Four or five leagues, Sir."

"Now has the least flash of lightning been seen by any one of you?"

"No, Sir."

"How far off can thunder be heard?"

"A league or two, Sir."

"Now has any of you heard the thunder?"

"No, Sir."

"These fellows are not men, they are demons! They must have come to make us throw away our water with the hope of destroying us in our weakness. The foolish young merchant who went on before us had no power of resource. No doubt he has let himself be persuaded to throw away his supply of water, and has fallen a prey to these fellows. His waggons will be standing there just as they were loaded. We shall find them to-day. Go on as quickly as you can, and don't throw away a single half-pint of water!"

With these words he sent them forward; and going on he found the five hundred carts as they had been loaded, and the bones of men and oxen scattered about. And he had his waggons unyoked, and ranged in a circle so as to form a strong encampment; and he had the men and oxen fed betimes, and the oxen made to lie down in the midst of the men. And he himself took the overseers of the company, and stood on guard with a drawn sword through the three watches of the night, and waited for the dawn. And quite early the next day he saw that everything that should be done was done, and the oxen fed; and leaving such carts as were weak he took strong ones, and throwing away goods of little value he loaded goods of greater value. And arriving at the proposed mart, he sold his merchandise for two or three times the cost price, and with all his company returned to his own city.

And when he had told this story, the Teacher added, "Thus, O householder, long ago those who relied on their own reason came to destruction, while those who held to the truth escaped the hands of the demons, went whither they had wished to go, and got back again to their own place." And it was when he had become a Buddha that he uttered the following verse belonging to this lesson on Holding to the Truth; and thus uniting the two stories, he said—

1. Some speak that which none can question;
   Mere logicians speak not so.
   The wise man knows that this is so,
   And takes for true what is the truth!

Thus the Blessed One taught those disciples the lesson regarding truth. "Life according to the Truth confers the three happy conditions of existence here below, and the six joys of the Brahmalokas in the heaven of delight, and finally leads to the attainment of Arahatship; but life according to the Untrue leads to rebirth in the four hells and among the five lowest grades of man." He also proclaimed the Four Truths in sixteen ways. And at the end of the discourse on the Truths all those five hundred disciples were established in the Fruit of Conversion.

The Teacher having finished the discourse, and told the double narrative, established the connexion,[1] and summed up the Jātaka by concluding, "The foolish young merchant of that time was Devadatta, his men were Devadatta's followers. The wise young merchant's men were the attendants of the Buddha, and the wise young merchant was I myself."

END OF THE STORY ON HOLDING TO THE TRUTH.

[1] That is, I think, between the persons in the story on the one hand, and the Buddha and his contemporaries on the other: not, as Childers says (under *anusandhi*), between the story and the maxim.

No. 2.

VAṆṆUPATHA JĀTAKA.

The Sandy Road.

"*The Determined Ones,*" *etc.*—This discourse was uttered by the Blessed One while at Sāvatthi. About what? About a mendicant who had no perseverance.

For whilst the Successor of the Prophets, we are told, was staying at Sāvatthi, a young man of good family dwelling there went to Jetavana, and heard a discourse from the Teacher. And with converted heart he saw the evil result of lusts, and entered the Order. When he had passed the five years of noviciate, he learnt two summaries of doctrine, and applied himself to the practice of meditation. And receiving from the Teacher a suitable subject as a starting-point for thought, he retired to a forest. There he proceeded to pass the rainy season; but after three months of constant endeavour, he was unable to obtain even the least hint or presentiment of the attainment of insight.[1] Then it occurred to him, "The

[1] The Buddhists had no prayer; their salvation consisting in a self-produced inward change. This could be brought about in various ways, one of which was the kind of meditation here referred to (*Kammaṭṭhāna*), leading to a firm conviction of the impermanence of all finite things. As every road leads to Rome, so any finite object may be taken as the starting-point from which thought may be taken, by gradually increasing steps, near to the infinite; and so acquire a sense of the proportion of things, and realize the insignificance of the individual. The unassisted mind of the ignorant would naturally find difficulty in doing this; and certain examples of the way in which it might be done were accordingly worked out; and a disciple would go to his teacher, and ask him to recommend which way he should adopt. But the disciple must work out his own enlightenment.

Teacher said there were four kinds of men; I must belong to the lowest class. In this birth there will be, I think, neither Path nor Fruit for me. What is the good of my dwelling in the forest? Returning to the Teacher, I will live in the sight of the glorious person of the Buddha, and within hearing of the sweet sound of the Law." And he returned to Jetavana.

His friends and intimates said to him, "Brother, you received from the Teacher a subject of meditation, and left us to devote yourself to religious solitude; and now you have come back, and have given yourself up again to the pleasures of social intercourse. Have you then really attained the utmost aim of those who have given up the world? Have you escaped transmigration?"[1]

"Brethren! I have gained neither the Path nor the Fruit thereof. I have come to the conclusion that I am fated to be a useless creature; and so have come back and given up the attempt."

"You have done wrong, Brother! after taking vows according to the religion of the Teacher whose firmness is so immovable, to have given up the attempt. Come, let us show this matter to the Buddha." And they took him to the Teacher.

When the Teacher saw them, he said, "I see, O mendicants! that you have brought this brother here against his will. What has he done?"

"Lord! this brother having taken the vows in so sanctifying a faith, has abandoned the endeavour to accomplish the aim of a member of the Order, and has come back to us."

Then the Teacher said to him, "Is it true you have given up trying?"

[1] A successful *Kammaṭṭhāna*, a complete realization of the relation of the individual to the great Sum of all things, will lead to that sense of brotherhood, of humility, of holy calm, which is the "utmost aim," viz. Nirvāna, and involves, as its result, escape from transmigration.

"It is true, O Blessed One!" was the reply.

"How is it, brother, that you, who have now taken the vows according to such a system, have proved yourself to be—not a man of few desires, contented, separate from the world, persevering in effort—but so irresolute! Why, formerly you were full of determination. By *your* energy alone the men and bullocks of five hundred waggons obtained water in the sandy desert, and were saved. How is it that you give up trying, now?"

Then by those few words that brother was established in resolution!

But the others, hearing that story, besought of the Blessed One, saying, "Lord! We know that this brother has given up trying now; and yet you tell how formerly by his energy alone the men and bullocks of five hundred waggons obtained water in the sandy desert, and were saved. Tell us how this was."

"Listen, then, O mendicants!" said the Blessed One: and having thus excited their attention, he made manifest a thing concealed through change of birth.

Once upon a time, when Brahma-datta was reigning in Benares, in the country of Kāsi, the future Buddha was born in a merchant's family; and when he grew up, he went about trafficking with five hundred carts.

One day he arrived at a sandy desert twenty leagues across. The sand in that desert was so fine, that when taken in the closed fist, it could not be kept in the hand. After the sun had risen it became as hot as a mass of charcoal, so that no man could walk on it. Those, therefore, who had to travel over it took wood, and water, and oil, and rice in their carts; and travelled during the night. And at daybreak they formed an encampment, and spread an awning over it, and taking their meals early, they passed the day sitting in the shade. At sunset they supped; and when the ground had become cool, they yoked their oxen and went on. The travelling was like a voyage over the sea: a so-called land-pilot had to be chosen, and he brought the caravan safe to the other side by his knowledge of the stars.

On this occasion the merchant of our story traversed the desert in that way. And when he had passed over fifty-nine leagues he thought, "Now in one more night we shall get out of the sand," and after supper he directed the wood and water to be thrown away, and the waggons to be yoked; and so set out. The pilot had cushions arranged on the foremost cart, and lay down looking at the stars, and directing them where to drive. But worn out by want of rest during the long march, he fell asleep, and did not perceive that the oxen had turned round and taken the same road by which they had come.

The oxen went on the whole night through. Towards dawn the pilot woke up, and, observing the stars, called out, "Stop the waggons, stop the waggons!" The day broke just as they had stopped, and were drawing up the carts in a line. Then the men cried out, "Why, this is the very encampment we left yesterday! Our wood and water is all gone! We are lost!" And unyoking the oxen, and spreading the canopy over their heads, they lay down, in despondency, each one under his waggon.

But the Bodisat, saying to himself, "If I lose heart, all these will perish," walked about while the morning was yet cool. And on seeing a tuft of Kusa-grass, he thought,

"This must have grown by attracting some water which there must be beneath it."

And he made them bring a hoe and dig in that spot. And they dug sixty cubits deep. And when they had got thus far, the spade of the diggers struck on a rock: and as soon as it struck, they all gave up in despair.

But the Bodisat thought, "There *must* be water under that rock," and descending into the well, he got upon the stone, and, stooping down, applied his ear to it, and tested the sound of it. And he heard the sound of water gurgling beneath. And he got out, and called his page. "My lad, if you give up now, we shall all be lost. Don't you lose heart. Take this iron hammer, and go down into the pit, and give the rock a good blow."

The lad obeyed, and though they all stood by in despair, he went down full of determination, and struck at the stone. And the rock split in two, and fell below, and no longer blocked up the stream. And water rose till its brim was the height of a palm-tree in the well. And they all drank of the water, and bathed in it. Then they split up their extra yokes and axles, and cooked rice, and ate it, and fed their oxen with it. And when the sun set, they put up a flag by the well, and went to the place appointed. There they sold their merchandise at double and treble profit, and returned to their own home, and lived to a good old age, and then passed away according to their deeds. And the Bodisat gave gifts, and did other virtuous acts, and passed away according to his deeds.

When the Buddha had told the story, he, as Buddha, uttered the verse—

2. The men of firm resolve dug on into the sand,
Till in the very road they found whereof to drink.
And so the wise, strong by continuing effort,
Finds—if he weary not—Rest for his heart!

When he had thus discoursed, he declared the Four Truths. And when he had concluded, the despairing priest was established in the highest Fruit, in Arahatship (which is Nirvāna).

After the Teacher had told the two stories, he formed the connexion, and summed up the Jātaka, by saying, in conclusion, "The page who at that time despaired not, but broke the stone, and gave water to the multitude, was this brother without perseverance: the other men were the attendants on the Buddha; and the caravan leader was I myself."

END OF THE STORY OF THE SANDY ROAD.

No. 3.

SERI-VĀNIJA JĀTAKA.

The Merchant of Sēri.

"*If you fail here,*" *etc.*—This discourse, too, the Blessed One uttered, while staying at Sāvatthi, about a monk who was discouraged in his efforts to obtain spiritual enlightenment.

For we are told that when he too was brought up by the brethren in the same manner as before, the Teacher said, "Brother! you who have given up trying, after taking the vows according to a system so well fitted to lead you to the Paths and Fruit thereof, will sorrow long, like the Seriva trader when he had lost the golden vessel worth a hundred thousand."

The monks asked the Blessed One to explain to them the matter. The Blessed One made manifest that which had been hidden by change of birth.

Long ago, in the fifth dispensation before the present one, the Bodisat was a dealer in tin and brass ware, named Seriva, in the country of that name. This Seriva, together with another dealer in tin and brass ware, who was an avaricious man, crossed the river Tēla-vāha, and entered the town called Andha-pura. And dividing the streets of the city between them, the Bodisat went round selling his goods in the street allotted to him, while the other took the street that fell to him.

Now in that city there was a wealthy family reduced to abject poverty. All the sons and brothers in the family had died, and all its property had been lost. Only one girl and her grandmother were left; and those two gained their living by serving others for hire. There was indeed in the house the vessel of gold out of which the head of the house used to eat in the days of its prosperity; but it was covered with dirt, and had long lain neglected and unused among the pots and pans. And they did not even know that it was of gold.

At that time the avaricious hawker, as he was going along, calling out, "Buy my water-pots! Buy my water-pots!" came to the door of their house. When the girl saw him, she said to her grandmother, "Mother! do buy me an ornament."

"But we are poor, dear. What shall we give in exchange for it?"

"This dish of ours is no use to us; you can give that away and get one."

The old woman called the hawker, and after asking him to take a seat, gave him the dish, and said, "Will you take this, Sir, and give something to your little sister[1] for it?"

The hawker took the dish, and thought, "This must be gold!" And turning it round, he scratched a line on its back with a needle, and found that it was so. Then hoping to get the dish without giving them anything, he said, "What is this worth? It is not even worth a half-

[1] On this mode of politeness see above, p. 70.

penny." And throwing it on the ground, he got up from his seat, and went away.

Now, it was allowed to either hawker to enter the street which the other had left. And the Bodisat came into that street, and calling out, "Buy my water-pots," came up to the door of that very house. And the girl spoke to her grandmother as before. But the grandmother said, "My child, the dealer who came just now threw the dish on the floor, and went away; what have I now got to give him in exchange?"

"That merchant, mother dear, was a surly man; but this one looks pleasant, and has a kind voice: perchance he may take it."

"Call him, then," said she.

So she called him. And when he had come in and sat down, they gave him the dish. He saw that it was gold, and said, "Mother! this dish is worth a hundred thousand. All the goods in my possession are not equal to it in value!"

"But, Sir, a hawker who came just now threw it on the ground, and went away, saying it was not worth a half-penny. It must have been changed into gold by the power of your virtue, so we make you a present of it. Give us some trifle for it, and take it."

The Bodisat gave them all the cash he had in hand (five hundred pieces), and all his stock-in-trade, worth five hundred more. He asked of them only to let him keep eight pennies, and the bag and the yoke that he used to carry his things with. And these he took and departed.

And going quickly to the river-side, he gave those eight pennies to a boatman, and got into the boat.

But that covetous hawker came back to the house, and said: "Bring out that dish, I'll give you something for it!"

Then she scolded him, and said, "You said our gold dish, worth a hundred thousand, was not worth a half-penny. But a just dealer, who seems to be your master,[1] gave us a thousand for it, and has taken it away."

When he heard this he called out, "Through this fellow I have lost a golden pot worth—O, worth a hundred thousand! He has ruined me altogether!" And bitter sorrow overcame him, and he was unable to retain his presence of mind; and he lost all self-command. And scattering the money he had, and all the goods, at the door of the house, he seized as a club the yoke by which he had carried them, and tore off his clothes, and pursued after the Bodisat.

When he reached the river-side, he saw the Bodisat going away, and he cried out, "Hallo, Boatman! stop the boat!"

But the Bodisat said, "Don't stop!" and so prevented that. And as the other gazed and gazed at the departing Bodisat, he was torn with violent grief; his heart grew hot, and blood flowed from his mouth until his heart broke—like tank-mud in the heat of the sun!

Thus harbouring hatred against the Bodisat, he brought about on that very spot his own destruction. This was the first time that Devadatta harboured hatred against the Bodisat.

But the Bodisat gave gifts, and did other good acts, and passed away according to his deeds.

[1] The reader will not take this too seriously. The old lady's scorn turns as easily here to irony as her gratitude above finds expression in flattery.

It was when the Buddha had finished this discourse, that he, as Buddha, uttered the following verse—

> 3. If in this present time of Grace,
> You fail to reach the Happy State;[1]
> Long will you suffer deep Remorse
> Like this trading man of Seriva.

So the Teacher, discoursing in such a manner as to lead up to the subject of Arahatship, dwelt on the Four Truths. And at the end of the discourse the monk who had given up in despondency was established in the highest Fruit—that is, in Nirvāna.

And when the Teacher had told the double story, he made the connexion, and summed up the Jātaka by concluding, "The then foolish dealer was Devadatta, but the wise dealer was I myself."

END OF THE STORY OF THE MERCHANT OF SĒRI.

[1] What the Happy State is will perhaps best be understood from the enumeration of its six divisions: 1. Faith. 2. Modesty. 3. Fear of sinning. 4. Learning. 5. Energy. 6. Presence of Mind. This Happy State can only be reached in a birth as a man. If being born as a man, one neglects the salvation then within one's reach, one may pass many ages in other births before a "time of grace" comes round again. It is folly to expect salvation in some other and future world; it can only be gained here, and now.

No. 4.

CULLAKA-SEṬṬHI JĀTAKA.

The Story of Chullaka the Treasurer.

"*The wise, far-seeing man*," *etc.*—This discourse the Blessed One uttered, while at Jīvaka's Mango-grove near Rājagaha, concerning the Elder whose name was Roadling the Younger.

Now here it ought to be explained how Roadling the Younger came to be born. The daughter of a wealthy house in Rājagaha, they say, had contracted an intimacy with a slave, and being afraid that people would find out what she had done, she said to him, "We can't stay here. If my parents discover this wrongdoing, they will tear us in pieces. Let us go to some far-off country, and dwell there." So, taking the few things they had, they went out privately together to go and dwell in some place, it did not matter where, where they would not be known.

And settling in a certain place, they lived together there, and she conceived. And when she was far gone with child, she consulted with her husband, saying, "I am far gone with child; and it will be hard for both of us if the confinement were to take place where I have no friends and relations. Let us go home again!"

But he let the days slip by, saying all the while, "Let us go to-day; let us go to-morrow."

[1] The introductory story to this Jātaka is used in Rogers's *Buddhagosha's Parables*, pp. 61–68, as the introduction to a different Birth Story. Verse 25 of the *Dhammapada* is said by the Commentator on that book (Fausböll, p. 181) to have been spoken of Little Roadling, and it would fit very aptly to the present story about him.

Then she thought, "This silly fellow dares not go home because his offence has been so great. But parents are, after all, true friends. Whether he goes or not, it will be better for me to go."

So, as soon as he had gone out, she set her house in order, and telling her nearest neighbours that she was going to her own home, she started on her way. The man returned to the house; and when he could not find her, and learned on inquiry from the neighbours that she had gone home, he followed her quickly, and came up to her halfway on the road. There the pains of labour had just seized her. And he accosted her, saying, "Wife, what is this?"

"Husband, I have given birth to a son," replied she.

"What shall we do now?" said he.

"The very thing we were going home for has happened on the road. What's the use of going there? Let us stop!"

So saying, they both agreed to stop. And as the child was born on the road, they called him Roadling. Now not long after she conceived again, and all took place as before; and as that child too was born on the road, they called the firstborn Great Roadling, and the second Little Roadling. And taking the two babies with them, they went back to the place where they were living.

And whilst they were living there this child of the road heard other children talking about uncles, and grandfathers, and grandmothers; and he asked his mother, saying, "Mother, the other boys talk of their uncles, and grandfathers, and grandmothers. Have we no relations?"

"Certainly, my dear! You have no relations here, but you have a grandfather, a rich gentleman, at Rājagaha; and there you have plenty of relations."

"Then why don't we go there, mother?" said he.

Then she told him the reason of their not going. But

when the children spoke to her again and again about it, she said to her husband, "These children are continually troubling me. Can our parents kill us and eat us when they see us? Come, let us make the boys acquainted with their relatives on the grandfather's side."

"Well, I myself daren't meet them face to face, but I will take you there."

"Very well, then; any way you like: the children ought to be made acquainted with their grandfather's family."

So they two took the children, and in due course arrived at Rājagaha, and put up at a chowltrie (a public resting-place) at the gate of the town. And the mother, taking the two boys, let her parents know of her arrival. When they heard the message, they sent her back word to the following effect: "To be without sons and daughters is an unheard-of thing among ordinary people;[1] but these two have sinned so deeply against us, that they cannot stand in our sight. Let them take such and such a sum, and go and dwell wherever they two may like. But the children they may send here." And their daughter took the money her parents sent, and handing over her children to the messengers, let them go.

And the children grew up in their grandfather's house. Little Roadling was much the younger of the two, but Great Roadling used to go with his grandfather to hear the Buddha preach; and by constantly hearing the Truth from the mouth of the Teacher himself, his mind turned towards renunciation of the world. And he said to his grandfather, "If you would allow it, I should enter the Order."

"What are you saying, my child?" answered the old man. "Of all persons in the world I would rather have you enter the Order. Become a monk by all means, if

[1] Literally, "those subject to transmigration," that is, those who are not Arahats, whose natural desires have not given way before intense religious conviction.

you feel yourself able to do so." So, granting his request, he took him to the Teacher.

The Teacher said, "What, Sir, have you then a son?"

"Yes, my Lord, this lad is my grandson, and he wants to take the vows under you."

The Teacher called a monk, and told him to ordain the lad: and the monk, repeating to him the formula of meditation on the perishable nature of the human body,[1] received him as a novice into the Order. After he had learnt by heart much scripture, and had reached the full age required, he was received into full membership; and applying himself to earnest thought, he attained the state of an Arahat. And whilst he was thus himself enjoying the delight which arises from wise and holy thoughts, and wise and holy life, he considered whether he could not procure the same bliss for Little Roadling.

So he went to his grandfather, and said: "If, noble Sir, you will grant me your consent, I will receive Little Roadling into the Order!"

"Ordain him, reverend Sir," was the reply. The Elder accordingly initiated Little Roadling, and taught him to live in accordance with the Ten Commandments. But though he had reached the noviciate, Little Roadling was dull, and in four months he could not get by heart even this one verse—

> As a sweet-smelling Kokanada lily
> Blooming all fragrant in the early dawn,
> Behold the Sage, bright with exceeding glory
> E'en as the burning sun in the vault of heaven!

For long ago, we are told, in the time of Kassapa the Buddha, he had been a monk, who, having acquired learning himself, had laughed to scorn a dull brother as

[1] *Taca-pañcaka-kammaṭṭhānaŋ*, a formula always repeated at the ordination of a novice. The words of it will be found in Dickson's *Upasampadā-Kammavācā*, p. 7. Compare also the note above, p. 147.

he was learning a recitation. That brother was so overwhelmed with confusion by his contempt, that he could neither commit to memory, nor recite the passage. In consequence of this conduct he now, though initiated, became dull; he forgot each line he learnt as soon as he learnt the next; and whilst he was trying to learn this one verse four months had passed away.

Then his elder brother said to him: "Roadling, you are not fit for this discipline. In four months you have not been able to learn a single stanza, how can you hope to reach the utmost aim of those who have given up the world? Go away, out of the monastery!" And he expelled him. But Little Roadling, out of love for the religion of the Buddhas, did not care for a layman's life.

Now at that time it was the elder Roadling's duty to regulate the distribution of food to the monks. And the nobleman Jīvaka brought many sweet-scented flowers, and going to his Mango-grove presented them to the Teacher, and listened to the discourse. Then, rising from his seat, he saluted the Buddha, and going up to Great Roadling, asked him, "How many brethren are there with the Teacher?"

"About five hundred," was the reply.

"Will the Buddha and the five hundred brethren come and take their morning meal to-morrow at our house?"

"One called Little Roadling, O disciple, is dull, and makes no progress in the faith; but I accept the invitation for all excepting him."

Little Roadling overheard this, and thought, "Though accepting for so many monks, the Elder accepts in such a manner as to leave me out. Surely my brother's love for me has been broken. What's the good of this displine to me now? I must become a layman, and give alms, and do such good deeds as laymen can." And early the next day he went away, saying he would re-enter the world.

Now the Teacher, very early in the morning, when he surveyed the world, became aware of this matter.[1] And going out before him, he remained walking up and down by the gateway on the road along which Little Roadling would have to pass. And Little Roadling, as he left the house, saw the Teacher, and going up to him, paid him reverence. Then the Teacher said to him, "How now, Little Roadling! whither are you going at this time in the morning?"

"Lord! my brother has expelled me, so I am going away to wander again in the ways of the world!"

"Little Roadling! It was under me that your profession of religion took place. When your brother expelled you, why did you not come to me? What will a layman's life advantage you? You may stay with me!"

And he took Little Roadling, and seated him in front of his own apartment, and gave him a piece of very white cloth, created for the purpose, and said, "Now, Little Roadling, stay here, sitting with your face to the East, and rub this cloth up and down, repeating to yourself the words, "The removal of impurity! The removal of impurity!" And so saying he went, when time was called, to Jīvaka's house, and sat down on the seat prepared for him.[2]

But Little Roadling did as he was desired: and as he did so, the cloth became soiled, and he thought, "This piece of cloth was just now exceeding white; and now, through me, it has lost its former condition, and is become soiled. Changeable indeed are all component things!" And he felt the reality of decay and death, and the eyes of his mind were opened!

[1] The Buddha is frequently represented in the later books as bringing the world before his mind's eye in the morning, and thus perceiving whom he could benefit during the day.

[2] When the daily meal was to be served in the house of some layman, all the monks invited went there as soon as the time was announced by the "call of refection" being set up, and sat themselves down in the order of their seniority.

Then the Teacher, knowing that the eyes of his mind were opened, sent forth a glorious vision of himself, which appeared as if sitting before him in visible form, and saying, "Little Roadling! be not troubled at the thought that this cloth has become so soiled and stained. Within thee, too, are the stains of lust and care and sin; but these thou must remove!" And the vision uttered these stanzas:

> It is not dust, but lust, that really is the stain:
> This—'stain'—is the right word for lust.
> 'Tis the monks who have put away this stain,
> Who live up to the Word of the Stainless One!
>
> It is not dust, but anger, that really is the stain:
> This—'stain'—is the right word for anger.
> 'Tis the monks who have put away this stain,
> Who live up to the Word of the Stainless One!
>
> It is not dust, but delusion, that really is the stain:
> This—'stain'—is the right word for delusion.
> 'Tis the monks who have put away this stain,
> Who live up to the Word of the Stainless One!

And as the stanzas were finished, Little Roadling attained to Arahatship, and with it to the intellectual gifts of an Arahat; and by them he understood all the Scriptures.

Long ago, we are told, he had been a king, who, as he was once going round the city, and the sweat trickled down from his forehead, wiped the top of his forehead with his pure white robe. When the robe became dirty, he thought, "By this body the pure white robe has lost its former condition, and has become soiled. Changeable indeed are all component things!" And so he realized the doctrine of impermanency. It was on this account that the incident of the transfer of impurity brought about his conversion.

But to return to our story. Jīvaka, the nobleman, brought to the Buddha the so-called water of presentation. The Teacher covered the vessel with his hand, and said, "Are there no monks in the monastery, Jīvaka?"

"Nay, my Lord, there are no monks there," said Great Roadling.

"But there are, Jīvaka," said the Master.

Jīvaka then sent a man, saying, "Do you go, then, and find out whether there are any monks or not at the monastery."

At that moment Little Roadling thought, "My brother says there are no monks here; I will show him there are." And he filled the Mango-grove with priests—a thousand monks, each unlike the other—some making robes, some repairing them, and some repeating the Scriptures.

The man, seeing all these monks at the monastery, went back, and told Jīvaka, "Sir, the whole Mango-grove is alive with monks."

It was with reference to this that it is said of him, that

"Roadling, multiplying himself a thousand fold,
Sate in the pleasant Mango-grove till he was bidden to the feast."

Then the Teacher told the messenger to go again, and say, "The Teacher sends for him who is called Little Roadling."

So he went and said so. But from a thousand monks the answer came, "I am Little Roadling! I am Little Roadling!"

The man returned, and said, "Why, Sir, they all say they are called Little Roadling!"

"Then go and take by the hand the first who says 'I am Little Roadling,' and the rest will disappear."

And he did so. And the others disappeared, and the Elder returned with the messenger.[1]

And the Teacher, when the meal was over, addressed Jīvaka, and said, "Jīvaka, take Little Roadling's bowl; he will pronounce the benediction." And he did so. And the Elder, as fearlessly as a young lion utters his challenge, compressed into a short benedictive discourse the spirit of all the Scriptures.

Then the Teacher rose from his seat and returned to the *Wihāra* (monastery), accompanied by the body of mendicants. And when the monks had completed their daily duties, the Blessed One arose, and standing at the door of his apartment, discoursed to them, propounding a subject of meditation. He then dismissed the assembly, entered his fragrant chamber, and lay down to rest.

In the evening the monks collected from different places in the hall of instruction, and began uttering the Teacher's praises,—thus surrounding themselves as it were with a curtain of sweet kamala flowers! "Brethren, his elder brother knew not the capacity of Little Roadling, and expelled him as a dullard because in four months he could not learn that one stanza; but the Buddha, by his unrivalled mastery over the Truth, gave him Arahatship, with the intellectual powers thereof, in the space of a single meal, and by those powers he understood all the Scriptures! Ah! how great is the power of the Buddhas!"

And the Blessed One, knowing that this conversation had arisen in the hall, determined to go there; and rising from his couch, he put on his orange-coloured under garment, girded himself with his belt as it were with lightning, gathered round him his wide flowing robe red as kamala flowers, issued from his fragrant chamber, and

[1] Little Roadling has now become an Elder, a monk of the higher of the two grades.

proceeded to the hall with that surpassing grace of motion peculiar to the Buddhas, like the majestic tread of a mighty elephant in the time of his pride. And ascending the magnificent throne made ready for the Buddha in the midst of the splendid hall, he seated himself in the midst of the throne emitting those six-coloured rays peculiar to the Buddhas, like the young sun when it rises over the mountains on the horizon, and illumines the ocean depths!

As soon as the Buddha came in, the assembly of the mendicants stopped their talking and were silent. The Teacher looked mildly and kindly round him, and thought, "This assembly is most seemly; not a hand nor foot stirs, no sound of coughing or sneezing can be heard! If I were to sit here my life long without speaking, not one of all these men—awed by the majesty and blinded by the glory of a Buddha—would venture to speak first. It behoves me to begin the conversation, and I myself will be the first to speak!" And with sweet angelic voice he addressed the brethren: "What is the subject for which you have seated yourselves together here, and what is the talk among you that has been interrupted?"

"Lord! we are not sitting in this place to talk of any worldly thing: it is thy praises we are telling!" And they told him the subject of their talk. When he heard it the Teacher said, "Mendicants! Little Roadling has now through me become great in religion; now formerly through me he became great in riches."

The monks asked the Buddha to explain how this was. Then the Blessed One made manifest that which had been hidden by change of birth.

Long ago,[1] when Brahmadatta was reigning in Benares, in the land of Kāsi, the Bodisat was born in a treasurer's family; and when he grew up he received the post of treasurer, and was called Chullaka.[2] And he was wise and skilful, and understood all omens. One day as he was going to attend upon the king he saw a dead mouse lying on the road; and considering the state of the stars at the time, he said, "A young fellow with eyes in his head might, by picking this thing up, start a trade and support a wife."

Now a certain young man of good birth, then fallen into poverty, heard what the official said, and thinking, "This is a man who wouldn't say such a thing without good reason," took the mouse, and gave it away in a certain shop for the use of the cat, and got a farthing for it.

With the farthing he bought molasses, and took water in a pot. And seeing garland-makers returning from the forest, he gave them bits of molasses, with water by the ladle-full.[3] They gave him each a bunch of flowers; and the next day, with the price of the flowers, he bought more molasses; and taking a potful of water, went to the flower garden. That day the garland-makers gave him, as they went away, flowering shrubs from which half the blossoms had been picked. In this way in a little time he gained eight pennies.

Some time after, on a rainy windy day, a quantity of dry sticks and branches and leaves were blown down by the wind in the king's garden, and the gardener saw no way of getting rid of them. The young man went and

[1] With this story compare Kathā Sarit Sāgarā, Book VI. vv. 29 and foll.

[2] Pronounce Choollacker with the accent on the first syllable.

[3] 'Uluṇka,' half a cocoa-nut shell, the common form of cup or ladle among the Indian poor.

said to the gardener, "If you will give me these sticks and leaves, I will get them out of the way." The gardener agreed to this, and told him to take them.

Chullaka's pupil[1] went to the children's playground, and by giving them molasses had all the leaves and sticks collected in a twinkling, and placed in a heap at the garden gate. Just then the king's potter was looking out for firewood to burn pots for the royal household, and seeing this heap he bought it from him. That day Chullaka's pupil got by selling his firewood sixteen pennies and five vessels—water-pots, and such-like.

Having thus obtained possession of twenty-four pennies, he thought, "This will be a good scheme for me," and went to a place not far from the city gate, and placing there a pot of water, supplied five hundred grass-cutters with drink.

"Friend! you have been of great service to us," said they. "What shall we do for you?"

"You shall do me a good turn when need arises," said he. And then, going about this way and that, he struck up a friendship with a trader by land and a trader by sea.

And the trader by land told him, "To-morrow a horse-dealer is coming to the town with five hundred horses."

On hearing this, he said to the grass-cutters, "Give me to-day, each of you, a bundle of grass, and don't sell your own grass till I have disposed of mine."

"All right!" cried they in assent, and brought five hundred bundles, and placed them in his house. The horse-dealer, not being able to get grass for his horses

[1] So called ironically, from the apt way in which he had learnt the lesson taught him by Chullaka.

through all the city, bought the young man's grass for a thousand pence.

A few days afterwards his friend the trader by sea told him that a large vessel had come to the port. He thinking, "This will be a good plan," got for eight pennies a carriage that was for hire, with all its proper attendants; and driving to the port with a great show of respectability, gave his seal-ring as a deposit for the ship's cargo. Then he had a tent pitched not far off, and taking his seat gave orders to his men that when merchants came from outside he should be informed of it with triple ceremony.[1]

On hearing that a ship had arrived, about a hundred merchants came from Benares to buy the goods.

They were told, "You can't have the goods: a great merchant of such and such a place has already paid deposit for them."

On hearing this, they went to him; and his footmen announced their arrival, as had been agreed upon—three deep. Each of the merchants then gave him a thousand to become shareholders in the ship, and then another thousand for him to relinquish *his* remaining share: and thus they made themselves owners of the cargo.

So Chullaka's pupil returned to Benares, taking with him two hundred thousand.[2] And from a feeling of

[1] Literally, "with a threefold knock," which I take to mean that the outside attendant announced them to another attendant, he to a third, and the third attendant to their master. The latter thus appeared to be a man of great consequence, as access to him was so difficult, and attended with so much ceremony.

[2] That is, twice a thousand pieces from each of the hundred merchants. But of course he should have paid out of this sum the price of the cargo. It can scarcely be intended to suggest that his acuteness led him to go off without paying for the cargo. The omission must be a slip of the story-teller's.

gratitude, he took a hundred thousand and went to Chullaka the treasurer. Then the treasurer asked him, "What have you been doing, my good man, to get all this wealth?"

"It was by adhering to what you said that I have acquired it within four months," said he: and told him the whole story, beginning with the dead mouse.

And when Chullaka the high treasurer heard his tale, he thought, "It will never do to let such a lad as this get into any one else's hands." So he gave him his grown-up daughter in marriage, and made him heir to all the family estates. And when the treasurer died, he received the post of city treasurer. But the Bodisat passed away according to his deeds.

It was when the Buddha had finished his discourse that he, as Buddha, uttered the following verse:

As one might nurse a tiny flame,
The able and far-seeing man,
E'en with the smallest capital,
Can raise himself to wealth!

It was thus the Blessed One made plain what he had said, "Mendicants! Little Roadling has now through me become great in religion; but formerly through me he became great in riches."

When he had thus given this lesson, and told the double story, he made the connexion, and summed up the Jātaka by concluding, "He who was then Chullaka's pupil was Little Roadling, but Chullaka the high treasurer was I myself."

END OF THE STORY OF CHULLAKA THE TREASURER.

No. 5.

TAṆḌULA-NĀḶI JĀTAKA.

The Measure of Rice.[1]

"*What is the value of a measure of rice,*" *etc.*—This the Teacher told while sojourning at Jetavana, about a monk called Udāyin the Simpleton.

At that time the Elder named Dabba, a Mallian by birth, held the office of steward in the Order.[2] When he issued the food-tickets in the morning, Udāyin sometimes received a better kind of rice, and sometimes an inferior kind. One day when he received the inferior kind, he threw the distribution-hall into confusion, crying out, "Why should Dabba know better than any other of us how to give out the tickets?"

When he thus threw the office into disorder, they gave him the basket of tickets, saying, "Well, then, do you give out the tickets to-day!"

From that day he began to distribute tickets to the Order; but when giving them out he did not know which meant the better rice and which the worse, nor in which

[1] Compare Léon Feer in the *Journal Asiatique*, 1876, vol. viii. pt. ii. pp. 510–525.

[2] The Bhatt' Uddesika, or steward, was a senior monk who had the duty of seeing that all the brethren were provided with their daily food. Sometimes a layman offered to provide it (*e.g.* above, p. 162); sometimes grain, or other food belonging to the monastery, was distributed to the monks by the steward giving them tickets to exchange at the storehouse. The necessary qualifications for the stewardship are said to be: 1. Knowledge of the customs regulating the distribution. 2. A sense of justice. 3. Freedom from ignorance. 4. Absence of fear. 5. Good temper.

storehouse the better was kept and in which the worse. When fixing the turns, too, he did not distinguish to what storehouse each monk's turn had come; but when the monks had taken their places, he would make a scratch on the wall or on the floor, to show that the turn for such and such a kind of rice had come thus far, and for such and such a kind of rice thus far. But the next day there were either more or fewer monks in hall. When they were fewer, the mark was too low down; when they were more, the mark was too high up; but ignoring the right turns, he gave out the tickets according to the signs he had made.

So the monks said to him, "Brother Udāyin! the mark is too high, or too low." And again, "The good rice is in such a storehouse, the inferior rice in such a storehouse."[1]

But he repelled them, saying, "If it be so, why is the mark different? Why should I trust you? I will trust the mark rather!"

Then the boys and novices cast him out from the hall of distribution, exclaiming, "When you give tickets, Brother Udāyin, the brethren are deprived of their due. You are incapable of the office. Leave the place!"

Thereupon a great tumult arose in the hall of distribution. The Teacher heard it, and asked of Ānanda the Elder, "There is a great tumult, Ānanda, in the hall. What is the noise about?"

The Elder told the Successor of the Prophets how it was.

Then he said, "Not now only, Ānanda, does Udāyin by his stupidity bring loss upon others, formerly also he did the same."

[1] I am not sure that I have understood rightly the meaning of *vassagga*,—a word of doubtful derivation, which has only been found in this passage. Possibly we should translate: "The turn for the better rice has come to the monk whose seniority dates from such and such a year, and the turn for the inferior kind to the monk whose seniority dates from such and such a year."

The Elder asked the Blessed One to explain that matter. Then the Blessed One made manifest an occurrence hidden by change of birth.

Long ago, Brahma-datta was king in Benares, in the land of Kāsi. At that time our Bodisat was his Valuer. He valued both horses, elephants, or things of that kind; and jewelry, gold, or things of that kind; and having done so, he used to have the proper price for the goods given to the owners thereof.

Now the king was covetous. And in his avarice he thought, "If this valuer estimates in this way, it will not be long before all the wealth in my house will come to an end. I will appoint another valuer."

And opening his window, and looking out into the palace yard, he saw a stupid miserly peasant crossing the yard. Him he determined to make his valuer; and sending for him, asked if he would undertake the office. The man said he could; and the king, with the object of keeping his treasure safer, established that fool in the post of valuer.

Thenceforward the dullard used to value the horses and elephants, paying no regard to their real value, but deciding just as he chose: and since he had been appointed to the office, as he decided, so the price was.

Now at that time a horse-dealer brought five hundred horses from the northern prairies. The king sent for that fellow, and had the horses valued. And he valued the five hundred horses at a mere measure of rice, and straightway ordered the horse-dealer to be given the measure of rice, and the horses to be lodged in the stable. Then the horse-dealer went to the former valuer, and told him what had happened, and asked him what he should do.

"Give a bribe to that fellow," said he, "and ask him thus: 'We know now that so many horses of ours are worth a measure of rice, but we want to know from you what a measure of rice is worth. Can you value it for us, standing in your place by the king?' If he says he can, go with him into the royal presence, and I will be there too."

The horse-dealer accepted the Bodisat's advice, went to the valuer, and bribed him, and gave him the hint suggested. And he took the bribe, and said, "All right! I can value your measure of rice for you."

"Well, then, let us go to the audience-hall," said he; and taking him with him, went into the king's presence. And the Bodisat and many other ministers went there also.

The horse-dealer bowed down before the king, and said, "I acknowledge, O king, that a measure of rice is the value of the five hundred horses; but will the king be pleased to ask the valuer what the value of the measure of rice may be?"

The king, not knowing what had happened, asked, "How now, valuer, *what* are five hundred horses worth?"

"A measure of rice, O king!" said he.

"Very good, then! If five hundred horses are worth only a measure of rice, what is that measure of rice worth?"

"The measure of rice is worth all Benares, both within and without the walls," replied that foolish fellow.

For the story goes that he first valued the horses at a measure of rice just to please the king; and then, when he had taken the dealer's bribe, valued that measure of rice at the whole of Benares. Now at that time the circumference of the rampart of Benares was twelve leagues, and the land in its suburbs was three hundred leagues in extent. Yet the foolish fellow estimated that so-great city of Benares, together with all its suburbs, at a measure of rice!

Hearing this the ministers clapped their hands, laughing, and saying, "We used to think the broad earth, and the king's realm, were alike beyond price; but this great and famous royal city is worth, by his account, just a measure of rice! O the depth of the wisdom of the valuer! How can he have stayed so long in office? Truly he is just suited to our king!" Thus they laughed him to scorn.

Then the Bodisat uttered this stanza:

> What is a measure of rice worth?
> All Benares and its environs!
> And what are five hundred horses worth?
> That same measure of rice![1]

Then the king was ashamed, and drove out that fool, and appointed the Bodisat to the office of Valuer. And in course of time the Bodisat passed away according to his deeds.

[1] These lines are not in the printed text. But see the Corrigenda; and Léon Feer, in the *Journal Asiatique* for 1876, p. 520.

When the Teacher had finished preaching this discourse, and had told the double story, he made the connexion, and summed up the Jātaka by concluding, "He who was then the foolish peasant valuer was Udāyin the Simpleton, but the wise valuer was I myself."

END OF THE STORY OF THE MEASURE OF RICE.

No. 6.

DEVA-DHAMMA JATAKA.

On True Divinity.[1]

"*Those who fear to sin,*" *etc.*—This the Blessed One told while at Jetavana, concerning a monk of much property.

For a landed proprietor who dwelt at Sāvatthi became a monk, we are told, after the death of his wife. And when he was going to be ordained, he had a hermitage and a kitchen and a storehouse erected for his own use, and the store filled with ghee and rice, and so was received into the Order. And even after he was ordained he used to call his slaves and have what he liked cooked, and ate it. And he was well furnished with all things allowed to the fraternity; he had one upper garment to wear at night and one to wear by day, and his rooms were detached from the rest of the monastery.

One day, when he had taken out his robes and coverlets, and spread them in the cell to dry, a number of brethren from the country, who were seeking for a lodging, came to his cell, and seeing the robes and other things, asked him, "Whose are these?"

"Mine, brother," said he.

"But, brother, this robe, and this robe, and this under

[1] It was on the occasion related in the Introductory Story of this Jātaka, and after he had told the Birth Story, that the Buddha, according to the commentator on that work (Fausböll, pp. 302–305), uttered the 141st verse of the Dhamma-padaŋ. The Introductory Story to No. 32, translated below in this volume, is really only another version of this tale of the luxurious monk.

garment, and this under garment, and this coverlet—are they all yours?"

"Yes; mine indeed," said he.

"Brother, the Buddha has allowed only three sets of robes; yet, though you have entered the Order of the self-denying Buddha, you have furnished yourself thus grandly." And saying, "Come, let us bring him before the Sage," they took him, and went to the Teacher.

When the Teacher saw them, he said, "How is it, mendicants, that you bring this brother here against his will?"

"Lord! this mendicant has much property and a large wardrobe."

"Is this true then, brother, that you have so many things?"

"It is true, O Blessed One!"

"How is it, brother, that you have become thus luxurious? Have not I inculcated being content with little, simplicity, seclusion, and self-control?"

On hearing what the Teacher said, he called out angrily, "Then I will go about in this way!" and throwing off his robe, he stood in the midst of the people there with only a cloth round his loins!

Then the Teacher, giving him support in temptation, said, "But, brother, you had formerly a sense of shame, and lived for twelve years a conscientious life when you were a watersprite. How then, now, having entered the so honourable Order of the Buddhas, can you stand there throwing off your robes in the presence of all the brethren, and lost to all sense of shame?"

And when he heard the Teacher's saying, he recovered his sense of propriety, and robed himself again, and bowing to the Teacher stood respectfully aside.

But the monks asked the Teacher to explain how that was. Then the Teacher made manifest the matter which had been hidden by change of birth.

Long ago Brahma-datta was king in Benares, in the country of Kāsi. And the Bodisat of that time assumed re-existence in the womb of his chief queen; and on the day on which they chose a name for him, they gave him the name of Prince Mahiŋsāsa. And when he could run to and fro, and get about by himself, another son was born, whom they called the Moon Prince.

When he could run to and fro, and get about by himself, the mother of the Bodisat died. The king appointed another lady to the dignity of chief queen. She became very near and dear to the king, and in due course she brought forth a son, and they called his name the Sun Prince.

When the king saw his son, he said in his joy, "My love! I promise to give you, for the boy, whatever you ask!"

But the queen kept the promise in reserve, to be used at some time when she should want it. And when her son was grown up, she said to the king, "Your majesty, when my son was born, granted me a boon. Now give me the kingdom for my son!"

The king said, "My two sons are glorious as flames of fire! I can't give the kingdom to your child alone!" And he refused her.

But when she besought him again and again, he thought to himself, "This woman will surely be plotting some evil against the lads!" And he sent for them, and said, "My boys! when the Sun Prince was born, I granted a boon. And now his mother demands the kingdom for him! I have no intention of giving it to him. But the very name of womankind is cruelty! She will be plotting some evil against you. Do you get away into the forest; and when I am dead, come back and reign in the city that is yours by right!" So, weeping and lamenting, he kissed them on their foreheads, and sent them forth.

As they were going down out of the palace, after taking leave of their father, the Sun Prince himself, who was playing there in the courtyard, caught sight of them. And when he learnt how the matter stood, he thought to himself, "I, too, will go away with my brothers!" And he departed with them accordingly.

They went on till they entered the mountain region of Himālaya. There the Bodisat, leaving the path, sat down at the foot of a tree, and said to the Sun Prince:

"Sun Prince, dear! do you go to yonder pond; and after bathing and drinking yourself, bring us, too, some water in the leaves of the lotus plants."

Now that pond had been delivered over to a water-sprite by Vessavana (the King of the Fairies), who had said to him:

"Thou art hereby granted as thy prey all those who go down into the water, save only those who know what is true divinity. But over such as go not down thou hast no power."

So from that time forth, the water-sprite used to ask all those who went down into the water, what were the characteristic signs of divine beings, and if they did not know, he used to eat them up alive.

Now Sun Prince went to the pond, and stepped down into it without any hesitation. Then the demon seized him, and demanded of him:

"Do you know what is of divine nature?"

"Oh, yes! They call the Sun, and the Moon, Gods," was the reply.

"*You* don't know what is of divine nature," said he, and carrying him off down into the water, he put him fast in his cave.

But the Bodisat, when he found that he was so long in coming, sent the Moon Prince. Him, too, the demon seized and asked him as before:

"Do you know what is of divine nature?"

"Yes, I do. The far-spreading sky is called divine."[1]

"You then don't know what is divine," said he; and he took him, too, and put him in the same place.

When he too delayed, the Bodisat thought to himself, "Some accident must have happened." He himself, therefore, went to the place, and saw the marks of the foot-steps where both the boys had gone down into the water. Then he knew that the pond must be haunted by a water-sprite; and he stood fast, with his sword girded on, and his bow in his hand.

But when the demon saw that the Bodisat was not going down into the water, he took to himself the form of a woodman, and said to the Bodisat:

"Hallo, my friend! you seem tired with your journey. Why don't you get down into the lake there; and have a bath, and drink, and eat the edible stalks of the lotus plants, and pick the flowers, and so go on your way at your ease?"

And as soon as the Bodisat saw him, he knew that he was the demon, and he said,

"It is you who have seized my brothers!"

"Yes, it is I," said he.

[1] The elder brother is more advanced in his theology.

"What for, then?"

"I have been granted all those who go down into this pond."

"What? All!"

"Well; all save those who know what beings are divine. The rest are my prey."

"But have *you* then any need of divine beings?"

"Yes, certainly."

"If it be so, I will tell you who are divine."

"Speak on then; and I shall get to know who have the attributes which are divine."

Then the Bodisat said, "I would teach you regarding this matter; but I am all unclean with my journey." And the water-sprite bathed the Bodisat, and provided him with food, and brought him water, and decked him with flowers, and anointed him with perfumes, and spread out for him a couch in a beautiful arbour.

And the Bodisat seated himself there, and made the water-sprite sit at his feet, and said, "Give ear then attentively, and listen what divine nature is." And he uttered the verse—

> The pure in heart who fear to sin,
> The good, kindly in word and deed—
> These are the beings in the world,
> Whose nature should be called divine.

And when the water-sprite heard that, his heart was touched, and he said to the Bodisat—

"O, Wise Teacher, in you I place my trust. I will give you up one of your brothers. Which shall I bring?"

"Bring me the younger of the two."

"But, Teacher; you who know so well all about the divine nature, do you not act in accordance with it?"

"What do you mean?"

"That neglecting the elder, and telling me to bring the younger of the two, you pay not the honour that is due to seniority."

"I both know, O Demon, what divinity is, and I walk according to it. It is on that boy's account that we came to this forest: for it was for him that his mother begged the kingdom from our father, and our father being unwilling to grant that, sent us away to live in the forest, that we might be safe from danger. The lad himself came all the way along with us. Were I to say, 'An ogre has eaten him in the wilderness,' no one would believe it. Therefore it is that I, to avoid all blame, have told you to bring *him*."

"Verily thou hast spoken well, O Teacher. Thou not only knowest what divinity is, but hast acted as a divinity would."

And when he had thus magnified the Bodisat with believing heart, he brought forth both the brothers and gave them back to him.

Then said the Bodisat to him, "Friend, it is by reason of evil deeds committed by you in some former birth, that you have been born as an ogre, living on the flesh of other beings. And now you still go on sinning. This thine iniquity will prevent thine ever escaping from re-birth in evil states. From henceforth, therefore, put away evil, and do good!"

With these words he succeeded in converting him. And the ogre being converted, the Bodisat continued to live there under his protection. And one day he saw by the conjunction of the stars that his father was dead. So he took the water-sprite with him and returned to Benares, and took upon himself the kingdom. And he made Moon Prince his heir-apparent, and Sun Prince his commander-in-chief. And for the water-sprite he made a dwelling-place in a pleasant spot, and took care that he should be constantly provided with the best of garlands and flowers and food. And he himself ruled his kingdom in righteousness, until he passed away according to his deeds.

The Teacher having finished this discourse spoke on the Four Truths. And when he had done, that monk entered the First Stage of the Path leading to Nirvāna. And the Buddha having told the double story, made the connexion and summed up the Jātaka by concluding, "The then water-sprite was the luxurious monk; the Sun Prince was Ānanda; the Moon Prince was Sāriputta; but the elder brother, the Prince Mahiŋsāsa, was I myself."[1]

[1] The whole of this story, including the introduction, is found also, word for word, in the commentary on the 'Scripture Verses' (Fausböll, pp. 302–305); and the commentator adds that the Buddha then further uttered the 141st verse of that collection:

> Not nakedness, not plaited hair, not dirt,
> Not fasting oft, nor lying on the ground;
> Not dust and ashes, nor vigils hard and stern,
> Can purify that man who still is tossed
> Upon the waves of doubt!

The same verse occurs in the Chinese work translated by Mr. Beal ('The Dhammapada, etc.,' p. 96). Another verse of similar purport has been quoted above (p. 69), and a third will be found in *Āmagandha Sutta* (Sutta Nipāta, p. 168, verse 11). The same sentiment occurs in the *Mahā-Bhārata*, iii. 13445, translated in Muir's 'Metrical Translations from Sanskrit Writers,' p. 75, and in the Northern Buddhist work *Divyāvadāna* (Burnouf, Introduction à l'Histoire du Bouddhisme Indien, p. 313).

END OF THE STORY ABOUT TRUE DIVINITY.

No. 9.[1]

MAKHĀ-DEVA JĀTAKA.[2]

The Story of Makhā Deva.

"*These grey hairs,*" *etc.*—This the Teacher told when at Jetavana, in reference to the Great Renunciation. The latter has been related above in the Nidāna Kathā.[3]

Now at that time the priests as they sat were magnifying the Renunciation of the One Mighty by Wisdom. Then the Teacher entered the assembly, and sat down in his place, and addressed the brethren, saying, "What is the subject on which you are talking as you sit here?"

"On no other subject, Lord! but on your Renunciation," said they.

"Mendicants, not then only did the Successor of the Prophets renounce the world; formerly also he did the same."

The monks asked him to explain how that was. Then the Blessed One made manifest an occurrence hidden by change of birth.

Long ago, in Mithilā, in the land of Videha, there was a king named Makhā Deva, a righteous man, and ruling

[1] For Nos. 7 and 8, see respectively Bhaddasāla Jātaka, Book xii., and Saŋvara Jātaka, Book xi.

[2] Comp. the Makhā-deva Sutta, No. 83 in the Majjhima Nikāya.

[3] See above, pp. 81–83.

in righteousness.[1] Eighty-four thousand years he was a prince, as many he shared in the government, and as many he was sovereign. As such he had lived a long, long time, when one day he said to his barber, "My good barber, whenever you find grey hairs on my head, let me know."

And after a long, long time had passed away, the barber one day found among the jet-black locks one grey hair; and he told the king of it, saying, "There is a grey hair to be seen on your head, O king!"

"Pull it out, then, friend, and put it in my hand!" said he.

So he tore it out with golden pincers, and placed it in the hand of the king. There were then eighty-four thousand years of the lifetime allotted to the king still to elapse. But, nevertheless, as he looked upon the grey hair he was deeply agitated, as if the King of Death had come nigh unto him, or as if he found himself inside a house on fire.[2] And he thought, "O foolish Makhā Deva! though grey hairs have come upon you, you yet have not been able to get rid of the frailties and passions which deprave men's hearts!"[3]

As he thus meditated and meditated on the appearance of the grey hair, his heart burned within him, drops of perspiration rolled down from his body, and his very robes oppressed him and became unbearable. And he thought, "This very day I must leave the world and devote myself to a religious life!"

[1] He is mentioned in the Mahāvaŋsa, p. 8, in a list of the legendary kings of old.

[2] At p. 81, above, the same idea is put into the mouth of Gotama himself.

[3] *Ime kilese.* The use of the determinative pronoun implies that the king is meant to refer to the particular imperfections known as *kilesā.* They are acquisitiveness, ill-temper, dullness of perception, vanity, wrong views, doubt, sloth, arrogance, want of self-respect, and want of respect for public opinion.

Then he gave to the barber a grant of a village whose revenue amounted to a hundred thousand. And he sent for his eldest son, and said to him, "My son! grey hairs have appeared on my head. I am become an old man. I have done with all human hopes; now I will seek heavenly things. It is time for me to abandon the world. Do you assume the sovereignty. I will embrace the religious life, and, dwelling in the garden called Makhā Deva's Mango-park, I will train myself in the characteristics of those who are subdued in heart."

His ministers, when he formed this intention, came to him and said, "What is the reason, O king! of your giving up the world?"

Then the king, taking the grey hair in his hand, uttered this verse—

These grey hairs that have come upon my head
Are angel messengers appearing to me,
Laying stern hands upon the evening of my life!
'Tis time I should devote myself to holy thought!

Having thus spoken, he laid down his sovranty that very day, and became a hermit; and living in the Mango-grove of Makhā Deva, of which he had spoken, he spent eighty-four thousand years in practising perfect goodwill towards all beings, and in constant devotion to meditation. And after he died he was born again in the Brahma heaven; and when his allotted time there was exhausted, he became in Mithilā a king called Nimi, and reunited his scattered family.[1] And after that he became a

[1] The whole story is given below, in the Nimi Jātaka, Book xii.

hermit in that same Mango-grove, and practised perfect goodwill towards all beings, and again returned to the Brahma heaven.

The Teacher, having thus discoursed on the subject that not then only, but formerly too, the Successor of the Buddhas had abandoned the world, proclaimed the Four Truths. Some entered the First Stage of the Path to Nirvāna, some the Second, some the Third. And when the Blessed One had thus told the double story, he established the connexion, and summed up the Jātaka as follows: "The barber of that time was Ānanda, the prince was Rāhula, but Makhā Deva the king was I myself."

END OF THE STORY OF MAKHĀ DEVA.

No. 10.

SUKHAVIHĀRI JĀTAKA.

The Happy Life

"*He whom others guard not,*" *etc.*—This the Teacher told while at the Anūpiya Mango-grove, near the town of that name, about the Elder named Bhaddiya the Happy-minded. Bhaddiya the Happy-minded took the vows when the six young noblemen did so together with Upāli.[1] Of these, Bhaddiya and Kimbila and Bhagu and Upāli became Arahats, Ānanda entered the First Stage of the Road to Nirvāna, Anuruddha attained to the Knowledge of the Past and the Present and the Future, and Devadatta acquired the power of Deep Meditation. The story of the six young noblemen, up to the events at Anūpiya, will be related in the Khaṇḍahāla Jātaka.

Now one day the venerable Bhaddiya called to mind how full of anxiety he had been when, as a king, caring for himself like a guardian angel, and surrounding himself with every protection, he had lolled in his upper chamber on his royal couch: and now how free from anxiety he was, when, as an Arahat, he was wandering, here and there, in forests and waste places. And realizing this change, he uttered an exclamation of joy, "Oh, Happiness! Happiness!"

[1] See the Translator's 'Buddhism,' p. 65, and the authorities there quoted, to which add Culla Vagga, VII. i. 1–4. The name Bhaddiya means the Happy One, and the story has very probably arisen in explanation of the name.

This the monks told the Blessed One, saying, "Bhaddiya is prophesying about Arahatship!"[1]

The Blessed One replied, "Mendicants! not now only is Bhaddiya full of joy; he was so also in a former birth."

The monks requested the Blessed One to explain how that was. Then the Blessed One made manifest an event hidden through change of birth.

Long ago, when Brahma-datta was reigning in Benares, the Bodisat became a wealthy Brāhman of the north-west country. And perceiving the evils of worldly lusts, and the advantages of the religious life, he abandoned the world, and went to the Himālaya region, and adopted the life of a hermit, and practised the Eight Attainments. And the number of his disciples increased greatly, until he was attended by five hundred ascetics.

In the rainy season he left the Himālayas, and attended by the body of ascetics, journeyed through the towns and villages till he came to Benares, and there took up his dwelling-place under the patronage of the king in the royal park. When he had there passed the four rainy months, he took leave of the king. But the king asked him to stop, saying, "You are old, Sir. Why go to the Himālayas? Send your disciples there, but dwell here yourself!"

So the Bodisat gave the five hundred ascetics in charge

[1] The word translated "Happiness" is also a name of Arahatship or Nirvāna (that is, perfect peace, goodness, and wisdom).

to his senior pupil, and sent him away, saying, "You shall go and live with these men in the Himālayas. I will stay here."

Now the senior pupil was a royal devotee who had abandoned a mighty kingdom for the religious life; and having gone through the course of meditation preparatory thereto, had acquired the eight kinds of spiritual insight.

As he was living in the Himālaya region with the ascetics, he one day conceived a desire to see his teacher, and said to the ascetics, "Do you live on quietly here; I am just going to pay my respects to our teacher, and shall be back soon."

Then he went to the place where his teacher was, saluted him, and offered him friendly greeting; and spreading a mat on the floor, lay down by his side.

Just then the king also went to the park to see the teacher, and saluting him, took his seat respectfully on one side. Though the disciple saw the king, he did not get up, but lying there just as he was broke forth into a chant of joy, "Oh, Happiness! Oh, Happiness!"

The king, displeased that the ascetic, on seeing him, had not arisen, said to the Bodisat, "Sir, this ascetic must have enjoyed himself to his heart's content. He lies there, quite at his ease, singing a song!"

"Great king! This ascetic was once a king like you. He is thinking, 'Formerly, as a layman, even when enjoying royal splendour, and guarded by many men with arms in their hands, I had no such joy as this,' and he utters this exclamation of joy in reference to the joys of meditation, and to the happiness of the religious life."

And having thus spoken, the Bodisat further uttered this verse in order to instruct the king in righteousness—

He who needs no others to defend him,
He who has not others to defend,—
He it is who lives at ease, O king!
Untroubled he with yearnings or with lusts.

When the king had listened to this discourse, he was satisfied again; and taking leave, he returned to the palace. And the disciple, too, took his leave, and returned to the Himālaya region. But the Bodisat dwelt there in continued meditation till he died, and he was then reborn in the Brahma heaven.

When the Teacher had preached this discourse, and told the two stories, he established the connexion, and summed up the Jātaka as follows: "The pupil of that time was Bhaddiya the Elder, but the Master of the company of disciples was I myself."[1]

END OF THE STORY ON A HAPPY LIFE.

[1] This story is founded on the similar story told of Bhaddhiya (the same Bhaddiya as the one mentioned in the Introductory Story) in the Culla Vagga, VII. i. 5, 6. The next story but one (the Banyan Deer) is one of those illustrated in the Bharhut sculptures. Both must therefore belong to the very earliest period in Buddhist history.

CHAPTER II. SĪLAVAGGA.

No. 11.

LAKKHAṆA JĀTAKA.

The Story of 'Beauty.'

"*The advantage is to the good.*"—This the Master told while at the Bambu-grove near Rājagaha, about Deva-datta.[1] For on one occasion, when Deva-datta asked for the Five Rules,[2] and could not get what he wanted, he made a schism in the Order, and taking four hundred of the mendicants with him, went and dwelt at the rock called Gayā-sīsa.

Afterwards the minds of these mendicants became open to conviction. And the Master, knowing it, said to his two chief disciples, "Sāriputta! those five hundred pupils of yours adopted the heresy of Deva-datta, and went away with him, but now their minds have become open to conviction. Do you go there with a number of the brethren, and preach to them, and instruct them in the Fruits of the Path of Holiness, and bring them back with you!"

[1] "The story of Deva-datta," adds a gloss, "as far as his appointment as Abhimāra, will be related in the Khaṇḍahāla Jātaka, as far as his rejection as Treasurer, in the Culla-haṃsa Jātaka, and as far as his sinking into the earth, in the Samudda-vānija Jātaka in the 12th Book."

[2] See the translator's 'Buddhism,' p. 76.

They went, and preached to them, and instructed them in the Fruits, and the next day at dawn returned to the Bambu Grove, bringing those mendicants with them. And as Sāriputta on his return was standing by, after paying his respects to the Blessed One, the mendicants exalted him, saying to the Blessed One, "Lord! how excellent appears our elder brother, the Minister of Righteousness, returning with five hundred disciples as his retinue, whereas Deva-datta is now without any followers at all!"

"Not only now, O mendicants! has Sāriputta come in glory, surrounded by the assembly of his brethren; in a former birth, also, he did the same. And not now only has Deva-datta been deprived of his following; in a former birth also he was the same."

The monks requested the Blessed One to explain how that was. Then the Blessed One made manifest a thing hidden by the interval of existence.

Long ago, in the city Rājagaha, in the land of Magadha, there ruled a certain king of Magadha. At that time the Bodisat came to life as a deer, and when he grew up he lived in the forest at the head of a herd of a thousand deer. He had two young ones, named Lakkhaṇa (the Beautifully-marked One, 'Beauty') and Kāḷa (the Dark One, 'Brownie').

When he had become old, he called them, and said, "My beloved! I am old. Do you now lead the herd about." And he placed five hundred of the deer under the charge of each of his sons.

Now in the land of Magadha at crop time, when the

corn is ripening in the fields, there is danger brewing for the deer in the adjoining forest. Some in one place, and some in another, the sons of men dig pit-falls, fix stakes, set traps with stones in them, and lay snares to kill the creatures that would eat the crops. And many are the deer that come to destruction.

So when the Bodisat saw that crop time was at hand, he sent for his sons, and said, "My children! the time of growing crops has come; many deer will come to destruction. We are old, and will get along by some means or another without stirring much abroad. But do you lead your herds away to the mountainous part of the forest, and return when the crops are cut!"

"Very well," said they; and departed with their attendant herds.

Now the men who live on the route they have to follow know quite well, "At such and such a time the deer are wont to come up into the mountains; at such and such a time they will come down again." And lurking here and there in ambush, they wound and kill many deer.

But Brownie, in his dullness, knew not that there were times when he ought to travel and times when he ought not; and he led his herd of deer early and late alike—at dawn, or in evening twilight—past the village gates. The men in different places—some in the open, some in ambush—destroyed, as usual, a number of the deer. So he, by his stupidity, brought many of his herd to destruction, and re-entered the forest with diminished numbers.

Beauty, on the other hand, was learned and clever, and fertile in resource; and he knew when to go on, and when to stay. He approached no village gates; he travelled not by day, nor even at dawn or by evening twilight; but he travelled at midnight, and so he reached the forest without losing a single animal.

There they stayed four months; and when the crops were cut they came down from the mountain-side. Brownie, going back as he had come, brought the rest of the herd to destruction, and arrived alone. But Beauty, without losing even one of his herd, came up to his parent attended by all the five hundred of his deer.

And when the Bodisat saw his sons approaching, he held a consultation with the herd of deer, and put together this stanza,—

> The righteous man hath profit, and the courteous in speech.
> Look there at Beauty coming back with all his troop of kindred,
> Then look at this poor Brownie, deprived of all he had![1]

When he had thus welcomed his son, the Bodisat lived to a good old age, and passed away according to his deeds.

Thus the Master gave them this lesson in virtue in illustration of what he had said, "Not only now, O mendicants! has Sāriputta come in glory, surrounded by the assembly of his brethren; in a former birth, also, he did the same. And not now only has Deva-datta been deprived of his

[1] This verse is quoted by the Dhammapada Commentator, p. 146, where the Introductory Story is substantially the same, though differing in some details. The first line of the verse is curious, as there is nothing in the fable about righteousness or courtesy. It either belonged originally to some other tale, or is made purposely in discord with the facts to hint still more strongly at the absurdity of the worthy deer attempting to make human poetry.

following; in a former birth also he was the same." And he united the two stories, and made the connexion, and summed up the Jātaka as follows: "Then 'Brownie' was Deva-datta, and his attendants Deva-datta's attendants. 'Beauty' was Sāriputta, and his attendants the followers of the Buddha. The mother was the mother of Rāhula, but the father was I myself."

END OF THE STORY ABOUT 'BEAUTY.'

No. 12.

NIGRODHA-MIGA JĀTAKA.

The Banyan Deer.

"*Follow the Banyan deer,*" *etc.*—This the Master told while at Jetavana, about the mother of the Elder named Kumāra Kassapa.[1] She, we are told, was the daughter of a rich merchant of the city of Rājagaha; she was deeply rooted in virtue, and despised all transient things; she had reached her last birth, and in her heart the destiny of future Arahatship shone like a lamp within a translucent pitcher. From the time when she knew her own mind she had no pleasure in a lay life, but was desirous to take the vows. And she said to her parents,—

"Mother, dear! my heart finds no pleasure in household life. I want to take the vows according to that teaching of the Buddha which leads to Nirvāna. Let me be ordained!"

"What is it you are saying, dear? This family is of great wealth, and you are our only daughter. You cannot be allowed to take the vows."

When, after repeated asking, she was unable to obtain her parents' permission, she thought, "Let it be so. When I get to another family, I will make favour with my husband, and take the vows."

And when she grew up, she entered another family as

[1] This Introductory Story is given also as the occasion on which v. 160 of the Dhammapada was spoken (Fausböll, pp. 327 and foll.)

wife, and lived a household life as a virtuous and attractive woman. And in due time she conceived, but she knew it not.

Now in that city they proclaimed a feast. All the dwellers in the city kept the feast, and the city was decked like a city of the gods. But she, up to the time when the feast was at its height, neither anointed herself nor dressed, but went about in her every-day clothes. Then her husband said to her,—

"My dear! all the city is devoted to the feast; yet you adorn yourself not."

"The body, Sir, is but filled with its thirty-two constituent parts. What profit can there be in adorning it? For this body has no divine, no angelic attributes: it is not made of gold, or gems, or yellow sandal-wood; it springs not from the womb of lotus-flowers, white or red; it is not filled with the nectar-balm of holiness. But verily it is born in corruption: it springs from father and mother: its attributes are the decomposition, the wearing away, the dissolution, the destruction, of that which is impermanent! It is produced by excitement; it is the cause of pains, the subject of mournings, a lodging-place for all diseases. It is the receptacle for the action of Karma; foul within, without it is ever discharging: its end is death: and its goal is the charnel-house,—there, in the sight of all the world, to be the dwelling-place of worms and creeping things!"[1]

[1] The thirty-two constituent parts will be found enumerated in the Khuddaka Pāṭha, p. 3, and most of them are mentioned in the following verses, which are not attributed to the 'attractive' young wife, and which sound wooden enough after her spirited outburst. Possibly they are a quotation by this commentator of some monkish rhymes he thinks appropriate to the occasion. The whole of the conversation is omitted in the Dhammapada commentary.

Bound together by bones and sinews,
O'erspread with flesh and integument,
The body is hidden 'neath its skin,—
It seems not as it really is!

"Dear Lord! what should I gain by adorning this body? Would not putting ornaments on it be like painting the outside of a sepulchre?"

"My dear!" replied the young nobleman, "if you think this body so sinful, why don't you become a nun?"

"If you grant me leave, dear husband, I will take the vows this day!"

"Very well, then; I will get you ordained," said he. And giving a donation at a great cost, he took her, with

It is filled inside—the trunk is filled—
With liver, and with abdomen;
With heart and lungs, kidney and spleen;
With mucus, matter, sweat, and fat;
With blood, and grease, and bile, and marrow.

And from each of its nine orifices
Impurity flows ever down:
Rheum from the eye, wax from the ear,
From the nose mucus, vomit from the mouth;
And bile and phlegm do both come out
From the perspiring, dirty frame.

Its hollow head, too, is but filled
With the nerve-substance of the brain.
Yet the fool, whom dullness never leaves,
He thinks it beautiful and bright.

The body causes endless ills;—
Resembles just a upas-tree;
The dwelling-place of all disease,
Is but a mass of misery.

Were the inside of this body
Only visible without,
One would have to take a stick in hand
To save oneself from crows and dogs!

Evil-smelling and impure,
The body's like a filthy corpse;
Despised by those who've eyes to see,
It's only praised by those who're fools!

a numerous retinue, to the nunnery, and had her admitted into the Order of Nuns—but among those who sided with Deva-datta. And she was overjoyed that her wish had been fulfilled, and that she had become a nun.

Now, as she became far gone with child, the nuns noticed the alteration in her person,—the swelling of her hands and feet and back, and the increase in her girth; and they asked her, "Lady, you seem to be with child. How is this?"

"I don't know how it is, ladies; but I have kept the vows."

Then the nuns led her to Deva-datta, and asked him, "Sir! this young lady, after with difficulty gaining her husband's consent, was received into the Order. But now it is evident that she is with child; and we know not whether she became so when she was a laywoman or when she was a nun. What shall we do now?"

Deva-datta, not being a Buddha, and having no forbearance, kindness, or compassion, thought thus: "If people can say, 'A nun of Deva-datta's side is carrying about a child in her womb, and Deva-datta condones it,' I shall be disgraced. I must unfrock this woman!" And without any inquiry, he answered with eagerness, "Go and expel this woman from the Order!"—just as if he were rushing forwards to roll away a mere piece of stone!

When they heard his decision, they arose, and bowed to him, and returned to the nunnery. But the young girl said to the nuns, "Ladies! the Elder, Deva-datta, is not the Buddha. Not under him did I enter the religious life, but under the Buddha himself, who is supreme among men. What I obtained with such difficulty, O, deprive me not of that! Take me, I pray you, and go to the Master himself at Jetavana!"

And they took her; and passing over the forty-five leagues of road which stretched from Rājagaha to that place, they arrived in due course at Jetavana, and saluting the Master, told him the whole matter.

The Teacher thought, "Although the child was conceived when she was still in the world, yet the heretics will have an opportunity of saying, 'The mendicant Gautama has accepted a nun expelled by Deva-datta!' Therefore, to prevent such talk, this case ought to be heard in the presence of the king and his ministers."

So the next day he sent for Pasenadi the king of Kosala, Anātha Piṇḍika the Elder, Anātha Piṇḍika the Younger, the Lady Visākhā the influential disciple, and other well-known persons of distinction. And in the evening, when all classes of disciples had assembled, he said to Upāli the Elder, "Go and examine into this affair of the young nun in the presence of the church!"

The Elder accordingly went to the assembly; and when he had seated himself in his place, called the Lady Visākhā before the king, and gave in charge to her the following investigation: "Do you go, Visākhā, and find out exactly on what day of what month this poor child was received into the Order, and then conclude whether she conceived before or after that day."

The Lady agreed; and having had a curtain hung, made a private examination behind it of the young nun; and comparing the days and months, found out that in truth she had conceived while she was yet living in the world. And she went to the Elder, and told him so; and the Elder, in the midst of the assembly, declared the nun to be innocent.

Thus was her innocence established. And she bowed down in grateful adoration to the assembly, and to the Master; and she returned with the other nuns to the nunnery.

Now, when her time was come, she brought forth a son strong in spirit—the result of a wish she had uttered at the feet of Padumuttara the Buddha. And one day, as the king was passing near the nunnery, he heard the cry of a child, and asked his ministers the reason. They knew of the matter, and said, "O king! that young nun has had a son, and the cry comes from it."

"To take care of a child, Sirs, is said to be a hindrance to nuns in their religious life. Let us undertake the care of it," said he.

And he had the child given to the women of his harem, and brought it up as a prince. And on the naming-day they called him Kassapa; but as he was brought up in royal state, he became known as Kassapa the Prince.

When he was seven years old, he was entered in the noviciate under the Buddha; and when he attained the necessary age, received full orders; and, as time went on, he became the most eloquent among the preachers. And the Master gave him the pre-eminence, saying, "Mendicants! the chief of my disciples in eloquence is Kassapa the Prince." Afterwards, through the Vammīka Sutta, he attained to Arahatship. His mother, the nun, too, obtained spiritual insight, and reached Nirvāna.[1] And Kassapa the Prince became as distinguished in the religion of the Buddhas as the full moon in the midst of the vault of heaven.

Now one day the Successor of the Buddhas, when he had returned from his rounds and taken his meal, exhorted the brethren, and entered his apartment. The brethren, after hearing the exhortation, spent the day either in their day-rooms or night-rooms, and then met together at eventide for religious conversation. And, as they sat there, they exalted the character of the Buddha, saying, "Brethren, the Elder Prince Kassapa, and the

[1] Literally reached the chief Fruit; the benefit resulting from the completion of the last stage of the path leading to Nirvāna; that is, Nirvāna itself. It is a striking proof of the estimation in which women were held among the early Buddhists, that they are several times declared to have reached this highest result of intellectual activity and earnest zeal. Compare the Introductory Story to Jātaka No. 234.

Lady his mother, were nearly ruined by Deva-datta, through his not being a Buddha, and having no forbearance or kindness; but the Supreme Buddha, being the King of Righteousness, and being perfect in kindness and forbearance and compassion, became the means of salvation to them both!"

Then the Master entered the hall with the dignity peculiar to a Buddha, and seating himself, asked them, "What are you sitting here talking about, O mendicants?"

"Lord," said they, "concerning your excellences!" And they told him the whole matter.

"Not now only, O mendicants!" said he, "has the Successor of the Buddhas been a source of salvation and a refuge to these two; formerly also he was the same."

Then the monks asked the Blessed One to explain how that was; and the Blessed One made manifest that which had been hidden by change of birth.

Long ago, when Brahma-datta was reigning in Benares, the Bodisat came to life as a deer. When he was born he was of a golden colour; his eyes were like round jewels, his horns were white as silver, his mouth was red as a cluster of kamala flowers, his hoofs were bright and hard as lacquer-work, his tail as fine as the tail of a Tibetan ox,[1] and his body as large in size as a foal's.

He lived in the forest with an attendant herd of five hundred deer, under the name of the King of the Banyan Deer; and not far from him there dwelt another deer,

[1] *Bos Grunniens.*

golden as he, under the name of the Monkey Deer, with a like attendant herd.

The king of Benares at that time was devoted to hunting, never ate without meat, and used to summon all the townspeople to go hunting every day, to the destruction of their ordinary work.

The people thought, "This king puts an end to all our work. Suppose now in the park we were to sow food and provide water for the deer, and drive a number of deer into it, and close the entrance, and deliver them over to the king."

So they planted in the park grass for the deer to eat, and provided water, and tied up the gate; and calling the citizens, they entered the forest, with clubs and all kinds of weapons in their hands, to look for the deer. And thinking, "We shall best catch the deer by surrounding them," they encircled a part of the forest about a league across. And in so doing they surrounded the very place where the Banyan Deer and the Monkey Deer were living.

Then striking the trees and bushes, and beating on the ground, with their clubs, they drove the herd of deer out of the place where they were; and making a great noise by rattling their swords and javelins and bows, they made the herd enter the park, and shut the gate. And then they went to the king, and said to him:

"O king! by your constant going to the chase, you put a stop to our work. We have now brought deer from the forest, and filled your park with them. Henceforth feed on *them!*" And so saying, they took their leave, and departed.

When the king heard that, he went to the park; and

seeing there two golden-coloured deer, he granted them their lives. But thenceforth he would sometimes go himself to shoot a deer, and bring it home; sometimes his cook would go and shoot one. The deer, as soon as they saw the bow, would quake with the fear of death, and take to their heels; but when they had been hit once or twice, they became weary or wounded, and were killed.

And the herd of deer told all this to the Bodisat. He sent for the Monkey Deer, and said:

"Friend, almost all the deer are being destroyed. Now, though they certainly must die, yet henceforth let them not be wounded with the arrows. Let the deer take it by turns to go to the place of execution. One day let the lot fall upon my herd, and the next day on yours. Let the deer whose turn it is go to the place of execution, put his head on the block, and lie down. If this be done, the deer will at least escape laceration."

He agreed: and thenceforth the deer whose turn it was used to go and lie down, after placing his neck on the block of execution. And the cook used to come and carry off the one he found lying there.

But one day the lot fell upon a roe in the herd of the Monkey Deer who was with young. She went to the Monkey Deer, and said, "Lord! I am with young. When I have brought forth my son, we will both take our turn. Order the turn to pass me by."

"I cannot make your lot," said he, "fall upon the others. You know well enough it has fallen upon you. Go away!"

Receiving no help from him, she went to the Bodisat, and told him the matter. He listened to her, and said, "Be it so! Do you go back. I will relieve you of your turn." And he went *himself*, and put his neck upon the block of execution, and lay down.

The cook, seeing him, exclaimed, "The King of the Deer, whose life was promised to him, is lying in the place of execution. What does this mean?" And he went hastily, and told the king.

The king no sooner heard it than he mounted his chariot, and proceeded with a great retinue to the place, and beholding the Bodisat, said, "My friend the King of the Deer! did I not grant you your life? Why are you lying here?"

"O great king! a roe with young came and told me that the lot had fallen upon her. Now it was impossible for me to transfer her miserable fate to any one else. So I, giving my life to her, and accepting death in her place, have lain down. Harbour no further suspicion, O great king!"

"My Lord the golden-coloured King of the Deer! I never yet saw, even among men, one so full of forbearance, kindness, and compassion. I am pleased with thee in this matter. Rise up! I grant your lives, both to you and to her!"

"But though two be safe, what shall the rest do, O king of men?"

"Then I grant their lives to the rest, my Lord."

"Thus, then, great king, the deer in the park will have gained security, but what will the others do?"

"They also shall not be molested."

"Great king! even though the deer dwell secure, what shall the rest of the four-footed creatures do?"

"They also shall be free from fear."

"Great king! even though the quadrupeds are in safety, what shall the flocks of birds do?"

"Well, I grant the same boon to them."

"Great king! the birds then will obtain peace, but what of the fish who dwell in the water?"

"They shall have peace as well."

And so the Great Being, having interceded with the king for all creatures, rose up and established the king in the Five Precepts,[1] and said, "Walk in righteousness, O great king! Doing justice and mercy to fathers and mothers, to sons and daughters, to townsmen and landsmen, you shall enter, when your body is dissolved, the happy world of heaven!"

Thus, with the grace of a Buddha, he preached the Truth to the king; and when he had dwelt a few days in the park to exhort the king, he went away to the forest with his attendant herd.

And the roe gave birth to a son as beautiful as buds of flowers; and he went playing about with the Monkey Deer's herd. But when its mother saw that, she said, "My son, henceforth go not in his company; you may keep to the Banyan Deer's herd!" And thus exhorting him, she uttered the verse—

> Follow the Banyan Deer:
> Dwell not with the Monkey Deer.
> Better death with the Banyan Deer,
> Than life with the Monkey Deer.[2]

Now after that the deer, secure of their lives, began to eat men's crops. And the men dared not strike them or drive them away, recollecting how it had been granted to them that they should dwell secure. So they met together in front of the king's palace, and told the matter to the king.

[1] See 'Buddhism,' pp. 139, 140.
[2] Quoted by the Dhammapada commentator, p. 329.

"When I was well pleased, I granted to the leader of the Banyan Deer a boon," said he. "I may give up my kingdom, but not my oath! Begone with you! Not a man in my kingdom shall be allowed to hurt the deer."

When the Banyan Deer heard that, he assembled the herds, and said, "Henceforth you are not allowed to eat other people's crops." And so forbidding them, he sent a message to the men: "Henceforth let the husbandmen put up no fence to guard their crops; but let them tie leaves round the edge of the field as a sign."

From that time, they say, the sign of the tying of leaves was seen in the fields, and from that time not a single deer trespassed beyond it; for such was the instruction they received from the Bodisat.

And the Bodisat continued thus his life long to instruct the deer, and passed away with his herd according to his deeds.

The king, too, hearkened to the exhortations of the Bodisat, and then, in due time, passed away, according to his deeds.

The Master, having finished the discourse in illustration of his saying, "Not only now was I the protector of the nun and of Kassapa the Prince; in a former birth I was the same," he fully expounded the Four Truths. And when he had told the double story, he made the connexion, and summed up the Jātaka by saying, "He who was then the Monkey Deer was Deva-datta, his herd was Deva-datta's following, the roe was the nun, her son was Kassapa the Prince, the king was Ānanda, but the royal Banyan Deer was I myself."

END OF THE STORY OF THE BANYAN DEER.

No. 13.

KAṆḌINA JĀTAKA.

The Dart of Love.

[The Introductory Story is the same as that of the Indriya Jātaka in Book VIII.]

Long ago a king of Magadha was reigning in Rājagaha, in the country of Magadha. At the season of harvest the deer suffered much at the hands of the people of Magadha. So they were wont to go away to the forest at the foot of the mountains.

Now a certain mountain stag, who lived in that jungle, made friends with a roe from the inhabited country. And when those deer came down from the mountain-side to return home, he, being caught in the snares of love, went down with them.

Then she said to him, "You, Sir, are but a simple deer of the mountains, and the inhabited country is beset with danger and difficulty. Pray don't go down with us!"

But he, being fallen deep into love for her, would not turn back, and went along with her.

Now when the people of Magadha saw that the time was come for the deer to return from the hills, they used to lie waiting in ambush all along the road. And just where those two were coming on, there stood a certain hunter behind a thicket.

The young roe smelt the smell of a man, and immediately thought, "There'll be some hunter behind there." And she let the foolish stag go on first, and kept back herself. The hunter with one shot from his bow felled the stag there on the spot; but the roe, as soon as she saw he was hit, fled away like the wind.

Then the hunter came out of his ambush, skinned that deer, made a fire, cooked the sweet flesh in the glowing charcoal, ate and drank, and carried off the rest all dropping with blood and gore, and went home to give his children a treat.

Now the Bodisat of that time was a tree fairy, dwelling in that wood. When he saw what had happened, he said to himself,

"Not through father, not through mother, but through lust, has this poor fool of a deer come to his death. In the dawn of passion creatures think themselves in bliss, but they end in losing their limbs in misery, or tasting the grief of all kinds of bonds and blows. What more shameful in this world than that which brings sorrow and death to others? What more despicable than the country where women administer and teach, a land under harem rule? What more wretched than the men who give themselves up to women's control?" And then, whilst all the fairies of the wood cast bouquets before him and cheered him on, he brought the three rebukes into one verse, and made the whole wood ring as he uttered the stanza—

O dreadful barbéd dart of love, that tears men's hearts!
O foolish land, where woman bears the rule!
O stupid men, who fall 'neath woman's power!

[1] When the Master had taught them this story, he proclaimed the Four Truths. And at the conclusion thereof that love-sick monk was converted. And the Master made the connexion, and summed up the Jātaka by saying, "The mountain-deer of that time was the love-sick brother, the roe was his former wife, and the tree fairy, who preached the sermon showing the evil of passion, was I myself."

END OF THE STORY OF THE DART OF LOVE.

[1] The two previous lines should belong, I think, to the explanatory comment.

No. 14.

VĀTA-MIGA JĀTAKA.

The Greedy Antelope.

"*There is nothing worse than greed, they say.*"—This the Master told when he was living at Jetavana about the Elder named Tissa the younger, the keeper of the law concerning food.

For when the Master, we are told, was residing at the Bambu-grove, near Rājagaha, a young man of a very wealthy family of distinction, by name Prince Tissa, went one day to the Bambu-grove, and when he had heard the Teacher's discourse, he became desirous to devote himself to a religious life. And when, on his asking leave to enter the Order, his parents refused their consent, he compelled them to grant it, in the same manner as Raṭṭha-pāla had done, by refusing to eat for seven days.[1] And he then took the vows under the Master.

The Master remained at the Bambu-grove about half a month after receiving him into the Order, and then went to Jetavana. There this young man of family passed his life, begging his daily food in Sāvatthi, and observing all the Thirteen Practices by which the passions are quelled. So under the name of "The Young Tissa who keeps the

[1] The story of *Raṭṭhapāla* is given in the Sutta of that name, translated by Gogerly, J. C. A. S., 1847–1848, p. 95. The same plan was followed by *Sudinna* as related in the Pārājikaŋ, and translated by Coles, J. C. A. S., 1876–1877, p. 187.

law concerning food,"[1] he became as distinguished and famous in Buddhadom as the moon in the vault of heaven.

At that time they were holding festival in Rājagaha, and the parents of the monk put away all the jewelry which had belonged to him in the days of his laymanship into a silver casket; and took the matter to heart, weeping, and saying, "At other festivals our boy used to keep the feast wearing this ornament or this. And now Gotama the Mendicant has taken him, him our only son, away to Sāvatthi! And we know not what fate is falling to him there."

Now a slave-girl coming to the house, and seeing the wife of the lord weeping, asked her, "Why, Lady! do you weep?" And she told her what had happened.

"Well, Lady, what dish was your son most fond of?" said she.

"Such and such a one," was the reply.

"If you grant me full authority in this house, I will bring your son back!" said she.

The Lady agreed, gave her wherewith to pay all her expenses, and sent her forth with a great retinue, saying, "Go now, and by your power bring back my son."

So the girl then went to Sāvatthi in a palankeen, and took up her abode in the street in which the monk was wont to beg. And without letting him see the people who had come from the lord's house, but surrounding herself with servants of her own, she from the very first provided the Elder when he came there with food and drink. Having thus bound him with the lust of taste, she in due course got him to sit down in her house; and when she saw that by giving him to eat she had brought him into her power, she shammed sickness, and lay down in her inner chamber.

Then the monk, when his begging time had come,

[1] This is the third of the Thirteen just alluded to.

arrived on his rounds at the door of the house. An attendant took his bowl, and made him sit down in the house. No sooner had he done so, than he asked, "How is the lady devotee?"

"She is sick, reverend Sir, and wishes to see you," was the reply. And he, bound by the lust of taste, broke his observance and his vow, and went to the place where she was lying. Then she told him why she had come, and alluring him, so bound him by the lust of taste, that she persuaded him to leave the Order. And having brought him into her power, she seated him in her palankeen, and returned to Rājagaha with all her retinue.

And this news became the common talk. And the monks, assembled in the hall of instruction, began to say one to another, "A slave-girl has brought back Young Tissa, the keeper of the law concerning food, having bound him with the lust of taste."

Then the Master, entering the chapel, sat down on his throne, and said, "On what subject are you seated here talking?"

And they told him the news.

"Not now only, O mendicants!" said he, "has this monk, caught by the lust of taste, fallen into her power; formerly also he did the same." And he told a story.

Once upon a time BRAHMA-DATTA, the king of Benares, had a gardener named SANJAYA. Now a swift antelope who had come to the garden took to flight as soon as it saw Sanjaya. But Sanjaya did not frighten it away; and when it had come again and again it began to walk about in the garden. And day by day the gardener used to pluck the various fruits and flowers in the garden, and take them away to the king.

Now one day the king asked him, "I say, friend gardener, is there anything strange in the garden so far as you've noticed?"

"I've noticed nothing, O king! save that an antelope is in the habit of coming and wandering about there. That I often see."

"But could you catch it?"

"If I had a little honey, I could bring it right inside the palace here!"

The king gave him the honey; and he took it, went to the garden, smeared it on the grass at the spot the antelope frequented, and hid himself. When the deer came, and had eaten the honey-smeared grass, it was bound with the lust of taste; and from that time went nowhere else, but came exclusively to the garden. And as the gardener saw that it was allured by the honey-smeared grass, he in due course showed himself. For a few days the antelope took to flight on seeing him. But after seeing him again and again, it acquired confidence, and gradually came to eat grass from the gardener's hand. And when the gardener saw that its confidence was gained, he strewed the path right up to the palace as thick with branches as if he were covering it with mats, hung a gourdful of honey over his shoulder, carried a bundle of grass at his waist, and then kept sprinkling honey-smeared grass in front of the antelope till he led him within the palace.

As soon as the deer had got inside, they shut the door. The antelope, seeing men, began to tremble and quake with the fear of death, and ran hither and thither about the hall. The king came down from his upper chamber, and seeing that trembling creature, said, "Such is the nature of an antelope, that it will not go for a week afterwards to a place where it has seen men, nor its life long to a place where it has been frightened. Yet this one, with just such a disposition, and accustomed only to the jungle, has now, bound by the lust of taste, come to just such a place. Verily there is nothing worse in the world than this lust of taste!" And he summed up the lesson in this stanza:

> "There's nothing worse than greed, they say,
> Whether at home, or with one's friends.
> Through taste the deer, the wild one of the woods,
> Fell under Sanjaya's control."

And when in other words he had shown the danger of greed, he let the antelope go back to the forest.

When the Master had finished this discourse in illustration of what he had said ("Not now only O mendicants! has this monk, caught by the lust of taste, fallen into her power; formerly also he did the same"), he made the connexion, and summed up the Jātaka as follows: "He who was then Sanjaya was this slave-girl, the antelope was the monk, but the king of Benares was I myself."

END OF THE STORY OF THE SWIFT ANTELOPE.

No. 15.

KHARADIYĀ JĀTAKA.

The Deer who would not learn.

"*Though a deer be most swift, O Kharādiyā.*"—This the Master told when at Jetavana, concerning a certain foul-mouthed monk. For that monk, we are told, was abusive, and would take no admonition.

Now the Master asked him, "Is it true what they say, O mendicant! that you are abusive, and will take no admonition?"

"It is true, O Blessed One!" said he.

The Master said, "Formerly also, by your surliness and your refusing to accept the admonition of the wise, you were caught in a snare and came to destruction." And he told a story.

Once upon a time, when Brahma-datta was reigning in Benares, the Bodisat became a stag, and lived in the forest, with a herd for his retinue.

Now his sister-roe (Kharādiyā) pointed out to him her son, and gave him in charge to him, saying, "Brother! this is your nephew. Teach him the devices of the deer."

And he said to his nephew, "Come at such and such a time to learn."

At the appointed time he did not go. And one day as he was wandering about, disregarding seven admonitions given on as many days, and not learning the devices of the deer, he was caught in a snare.

Then his mother went to her brother, and asked, "How now, brother! was your nephew instructed in the devices of the deer?"

"Think no more of that incorrigible fellow!" said the Bodisat. "Your son did not learn the devices of the deer."

And then, to explain his own unwillingness to have anything further to do with him, he uttered this stanza:

> "Though a deer be most swift,[1] O Kharādiyā!
> And have antlers rising point o'er point,
> If he transgress the seventh time,
> I would not try to teach him more!"

But the hunter killed that wilful deer caught in the snare, and, taking his flesh, departed.

The Master having finished this discourse, in illustration of what he had said ("Formerly also, by your surliness and your refusing to accept the admonition of the wise, you were caught in a snare, and came to destruction"), made the connexion, and summed up the Jātaka: "The nephew deer of that time was the abusive monk, the sister was Uppala-vaṇṇā, but the admonishing deer was I myself."

END OF THE STORY OF THE DEER WHO WOULD NOT LEARN.

[1] "'Eight-hoofed,' two hoofs on each foot," explains the commentator. See note on p. 223.

No. 16.

TIPALLATTHA-MIGA JĀTAKA.

The Cunning Deer.

"*I've taught the deer in posture skilled.*"—This the Master told when at the Badarika monastery in Kosambi, about his son Rāhula, who was over-anxious to observe the Rules of the Order.[1]

Once upon a time there was a king of Magadha reigning in Rājagaha. At that time the Bodisat came to life as a stag, and lived in the forest, attended by a herd of deer.

Now his sister brought her son to him, saying, "Brother! instruct this thy nephew in the devices of the deer."

"Very well," said the Bodisat, in assent, and directed his nephew, "Go away now, dear, and on your return at such and such a time you may receive instruction."

And he failed not at the time appointed by his uncle, but went to him and received instruction.

One day as he was wandering about in the wood, he was caught in a snare. And he uttered a cry—the cry

[1] This amusing Introductory Story will scarcely bear translating.

of a captive. Then the herd took to flight, and let the mother know that her son had been caught in a snare. She went to her brother, and asked him,—

"Brother! was your nephew instructed in the devices of the deer?"

"Suspect not your son of any fault," said the Bodisat. "He has well learnt the devices of the deer. Even now he will come back to us and make you laugh for joy." And he uttered this stanza:

I've trained the deer to be most swift,
To drink at midnight only, and, abounding in disguise,
To keep in any posture that he likes.
Breathing through one nostril hid upon the ground,
My nephew, by six tricks at his command
Will yet outdo the foe!

Thus the Bodisat, pointing out how thoroughly his nephew had learnt the devices of the deer, comforted his sister.

But the young stag, when he was caught in the trap, struggled not at all. He lay down on the ground as best he could; stretched out his legs; struck the ground near his feet with his hoofs, so as to throw up earth and grass; let fall his head; put out his tongue; made his body wet with spittle; swelled out his belly by drawing in his breath; breathed through the lower nostril only, holding his breath with the upper; made his whole frame stiff and stark, and presented the appearance of a corpse. Even the bluebottles flew round him, and here and there crows settled!

When the hunter came up, he gave him a blow on the stomach; and saying to himself, "He must have been caught early in the morning, he is already putrid," he loosed the bands which tied him. And apprehending nothing, he began to collect leaves and branches, saying to himself, "I will dress him at once, here on the spot, and carry off the flesh."

But the young stag arose, stood on his feet, shook himself, stretched out his neck, and, swiftly as a cloud driven by a mighty wind, returned to his mother!

The Teacher having finished this discourse, in illustration of his words ("Not now only, mendicants, was Rāhula devoted to instruction; formerly also he was so," etc.), made the connexion, and summed up the Jātaka: "At that time the nephew, the young stag, was Rāhula, the mother was Uppala-vaṇṇā, but the uncle was I myself."

END OF THE STORY OF THE CUNNING DEER.[1]

[1] The verse is very obscure, and the long commentary does not make it clearer. "To keep in any posture that he likes" is literally "having three postures—master of three postures." "Most swift" is in the original "eight-hoofed." If "eight-hoofed" means "with two hoofs on each foot," as the commentator thinks, where would be the peculiarity so creditable to the obedient learner? The last line in the text is so corrupt that the commentator can only suggest three contradictory and improbable explanations. If one could venture to read *chavaŋ kalāhati bhoti*, one might render, "My nephew, lady, can counterfeit a corpse." Mr. Trenckner has been good enough to send me the following suggested translation, "The deer, the threefold cunning (?) fertile in expedients, the cloven-footed, who goes to drink at midnight (! ?) (don't fear for him), lying on one ear, panting on the ground, my nephew, by the six tricks he knows will dodge (the hunter)."

No. 17.

MALUTA JATAKA.

The Wind.

"*Whenever the wind blows,*" *etc.*—This the Master told when at Jetavana, about two Buddhist monks. They, we are told, were living a forest life in the country of Kosala; and one was called DARK and the other called LIGHT. Now one day Light asked Dark, "Brother! at what time does the cold, as some people call it, come on?"

"In the dark half of the month!" said he.

But one day Dark asked Light, "Brother Light! at what time does the so-called cold come on?"

"In the light half of the month!" said he.

And neither of the two being able to solve the knotty point, they went to the Master, and after paying him reverence, asked him, "At what time, Sir, is the cold?"

When the Master had heard their story, he said, "Formerly also, O mendicants! I solved this question for you; but the confusion arising from change of birth has driven it out of your minds." And he told a tale.

Once upon a time two friends, a lion and a tiger, were living in a certain cave at the foot of a hill. At that time the Bodisat, who had devoted himself to the religious life of a hermit, was living at the foot of that same mountain.

Now one day a dispute arose between the friends about the cold. The tiger said it was cold in the dark half of the month, the lion said it was cold in the light half. And as neither of them could solve the difficulty, they asked the Bodisat, and he uttered this stanza:

"It is whenever the wind blows,
In the dark half or in the light.
For cold is caused by wind: and so
You both are right."

Thus the Bodisat pacified the two friends.

When the Master had finished this discourse ("Formerly also," etc.), he proclaimed the Truths. And at the close thereof the two brethren were established in the Fruit of Conversion. The Master made the connexion, and summed up the Jātaka: "He who was then the tiger was Dark, the lion Light, but the ascetic who answered the question was I myself.

END OF THE STORY ABOUT THE WIND.[1]

[1] Compare the Fable of the Two sides of the Shield.

No. 18.

MATAKA-BHATTA JĀTAKA.

On Offering Food to the Dead.

"*If people would but understand.*"—This the Teacher told when at Jetavana, about food offered to the dead.

For at that time people used to kill sheep and goats in large numbers in order to offer what is called "The Feast of the Dead" in honour of their deceased relatives. When the monks saw men doing so, they asked the Teacher, saying, "Lord! the people here bring destruction on many living creatures in order to provide the so-called 'Feast of the Dead.' Can there possibly, Sir, be any advantage in that?"

The Teacher said, "Let not us, O mendicants! provide the Feast of the Dead: for what advantage is there in destroying life? Formerly sages seated in the sky preached a discourse showing the evils of it, and made all the dwellers in Jambu-dīpa give up this practice. But now since change of birth has set in, it has arisen again." And he told a tale.

Once upon a time, when Brahma-datta was reigning in Benares, a Brāhman, a world-famous teacher, accomplished in the Three Vedas, had a goat brought, with the intention of giving the Feast of the Dead, and said to his pupils:

"My lads! take this goat to the river, and bathe it, and hang a garland round its neck, and give it a measure of corn, and deck it out, and then bring it back."

"Very well," said they, and accordingly took it to the river; and when they had bathed it and decorated it, let it stand on the bank.

The goat, seeing in this the effect of his former bad conduct, thought to himself, "To-day I shall be free from that great misery;" and, glad at heart, he laughed a mighty laugh, in sound like the crashing of a jar. Then, thinking to himself, "This Brāhman, by killing me, will take upon himself like misery to that which I had earned," he felt compassion for the Brāhman, and wept with a loud voice.

Then the young Brāhman asked him, "Friend goat! you have both laughed heartily and heartily cried. Pray, what is it makes you laugh, and what is it makes you cry?"

"Ask me about it in your teacher's presence," said he.

They took him back, and told their teacher of this matter. And when he had heard their story, he asked the goat, "Why did you laugh, goat, and why did you cry?"

Then the goat, by his power of remembering former births, called to mind the deeds he had done, and said to the Brāhman, "Formerly, O Brāhman, I had become just such another Brāhman,—a student of the mystic verses of the Vedas; and determining to provide a Feast of the Dead, I killed a goat, and gave the Feast. By having killed that one goat, I have had my head cut off in five hundred births, less one. This is my five hundredth birth, the last of the series; and it was at the thought, 'To-day I shall be free from that great misery,' that I became glad at heart, and laughed in the manner you have heard. Then, again, I wept, thinking, 'I who just by having killed a goat incurred the misery of having five hundred times my head cut off, shall be released to-day from the misery; but this Brāhman, by killing me, will, like me, incur the misery of having his head cut off five hundred times;' and so I wept."

"Fear not, O goat! I will not kill you," said he.

"Brāhman! what are you saying? Whether you kill me or not, I cannot to-day escape from death."

"But don't be afraid! I will take you under my protection, and walk about close to you."

"Brāhman! of little worth is your protection; while the evil I have done is great and powerful!"

The Brāhman released the goat; and saying, "Let us allow no one to kill this goat," he took his disciples, and walked about with it. No sooner was the goat at liberty, than, stretching out its neck, it began to eat the leaves of a bush growing near the ridge of a rock. That very moment a thunderbolt fell on the top of the rock, and a piece of the rock split off, and hit the goat on his outstretched neck, and tore off his head. And people crowded round.

At that time the Bodisat had been born as the Genius of a tree growing on that spot. By his supernatural power he now seated himself cross-legged in the sky in the sight of the multitude; and thinking, "Would that these people, seeing thus the fruit of sin, would abstain from such destruction of life," he in a sweet voice taught them, uttering this stanza:

"If people would but understand
That this would cause a birth in woe,
The living would not slay the living;
For he who taketh life shall surely grieve!"

Thus the Great Being preached to them the Truth, terrifying them with the fear of hell. And when the people had heard his discourse, they trembled with the fear of death, and left off taking life. And the Bodisat, preaching to the people, and establishing them in the Precepts, passed away according to his deeds. The people, too, attending upon the exhortations of the Bodisat, gave gifts, and did other good deeds, and so filled the city of the gods.[1]

The Teacher having finished this discourse, made the connexion, and summed up the Jātaka: "I at that time was the Genius of the tree."

END OF THE STORY ON FOOD OFFERED TO THE DEAD.

[1] That is, by the production at their death of angels as the result of their Karma.

No. 19.

ĀYĀCITA-BHATTA JĀTAKA.

On Offerings given under a Vow.

"*Would you be saved*," *etc.*—This the Teacher told while at Jetavana, about making offerings under a vow to the gods.

At that time, we are told, men about to go on a trading journey used to kill animals, and lay an offering before the gods, and make a vow, saying, "When we have returned in safety and success, we will make an offering to you," and so depart. Then when they returned safe and successful, thinking, "This has happened by the power of the God, they killed animals, and made the offering to release themselves from the vow.

On seeing this, the mendicants asked the Blessed One, "Lord! is there now any advantage in this?" And he told a tale.

Once upon a time, in the land of Kāsi, a landed proprietor in a certain village promised an offering to the Genius of a Banyan-tree standing by the gate of the village. And when he had returned safely, he slew a number of animals; and saying to himself, "I will make myself free from my vow," he went to the foot of the tree.

But the tree-god, standing in a fork of the tree, uttered this stanza:

> Would you be free, you first must die!
> Seeking for freedom thus, is being bound!
> Not by such deeds as these are the wise made free:
> Salvation is the bond of fools!"[1]

Thenceforward men refrained from such life-destroying deeds, and living a life of righteousness filled the city of the gods.

The Teacher, having finished this discourse, made the connexion, and summed up the Jātaka: "I at that time was the Genius of the Tree."

END OF THE STORY ON OFFERINGS GIVEN UNDER A VOW.

[1] That is, in seeking after what they think is salvation (safety from the wrath of a god), fools practise rites and harbour delusions which become spiritual bonds. Death to oneself, and spiritual rebirth, is the only true salvation. The whole parable is a play on the word "*Mutti*," which means both salvation, and the performance of, the being delivered from, a vow.

No. 20.

NAḶAPĀNA JĀTAKA.

The Monkeys and the Demon.

"*He saw the marks of feet,*" *etc.*—This the Teacher told about the Naḷa-canes, when he was living at the Ketaka wood, hard by the Lake of Naḷaka-pāna, after he had come to the village of that name on his tour through Kosala.

At that time the monks, after they had bathed in the Naḷaka-pāna lake, had the canes of the Naḷa-plant brought to them by the novices, for needle-cases. And finding them hollow throughout, they went to the Teacher, and asked him, "Lord! we had Naḷa-canes brought for needle-cases. They are hollow throughout, from root to point. How is this?"

"This, mendicants," said he, "is a former command of mine." And he told a tale.

This was formerly, they say, a densely-wooded forest. And in its lake there was a water-demon, who used to eat whomsoever went down into the water. At that time the Bodisat was a monkey-king, in size like the fawn of a red deer; and attended by a troop of monkeys about eighty thousand in number, he lived in that forest, preserving them from harm.

Now he exhorted the troop of monkeys, saying, "My children! in this forest there are poisonous trees, and pools haunted by demons. When you are going to eat fruits of any kind you have not eaten before, or to drink water you have not drunk before, ask me about it."

"Very well," said they. And one day they went to a place they had not been to before. There they wandered about the greater part of the day; and when, in searching about for water, they found a pond, they sat down without even drinking, and looked forward to the arrival of their king.[1]

When the Bodisat had come, he asked them, "Why, my children, do you take no water?"

"We awaited your arrival," said they.

"It is well, my children!" said the Bodisat; and fixing his attention on the foot-marks close round the edge of the pond, he saw that they went down, but never came up. Then he knew that it was assuredly haunted by demons, and said, "You have done well, my children, not to have drunk the water. This pond is haunted!"

But when the demon of the water saw that they were not going down into it, he assumed the horrible shape of a blue-bellied, pale-faced, red-handed, red-footed creature, and came splashing out through the water, and cried out, "Why do you sit still here? Go down and drink the water!"

But the Bodisat asked him, "Are you the water-demon who haunts this spot?"

"Yes! I am he!" was the reply.

[1] Any one who has seen the restlessness of monkeys in the safe precincts of a Buddhist monastery (or even in the monkey-house at the Zoological Gardens) will appreciate the humour of this description. The Bharhut sculptor, too, has some capital monkeys sitting, like good little boys, and listening to the Bodisat.

"Have you received power over all who go down into the pool?"

"Yes, indeed! I carry off even a bird when it comes down, and I let no one off. You too I will devour, one and all!"

"We shall not allow you to eat us."

"Well, then! drink away!"

"Yes! we shall drink the water too, but we shall not fall into your hands."

"How, then, will you get at the water?"

"You imagine, I suppose, that we must go down to drink. But you are wrong! Each one of us eighty thousand shall take a Naḷa-cane and drink the water of your pond without ever entering it, as easily as one would drink from the hollow stem of a water-plant. And so you will have no power to eat *us!*"

It was when the Teacher as Buddha had recalled this circumstance that he uttered the first half of the following stanza:

> "I saw the marks of feet that had gone down,
> I saw no marks of feet that had returned."

(But then he said to the monkeys)—

> "We'll drink the water through a reed,"

(And turning to the demon, he added)—

> "And yet I'll not become your prey!"

So saying, the Bodisat had a Naḷa-cane brought to him, and appealing in great solemnity to the Ten Great Perfections (generosity, morality, self-denial, wisdom, perseverance, patience, truth, resolution, kindness, and resignation) exercised by him in this and previous births, he blew into the cane.[1] And the cane became hollow throughout, not a single knot being left in it. In this manner he had another, and then another, brought, and blew into it.[2] Then the Bodisat walked round the pond, and commanded, saying, "Let all the canes growing here be perforated throughout." And thenceforward, since through the greatness of the goodness of the Bodisats their commands are fulfilled, all the canes which grew in that pond became perforated throughout.

There are four miracles in this *Kalpa* (the period which elapses between the commencement of the formation of the world and its final destruction) which endure throughout a *Kalpa*—the sign of the hare in the moon will last the whole Kalpa:[3] the place where the fire was extinguished in the Quail-birth will not take fire again through all the Kalpa:[4] the place where the potter lived will remain arid through all the Kalpa: the canes growing round this pond will be hollow through all the Kalpa. These four are called the Kalpa-lasting Wonders.

After giving this command, the Bodisat took a cane and seated himself. So, too, those eighty thousand monkeys took, each of them, a cane, and seated themselves round the pond. And at the same moment as he drew

[1] This solemn appeal to a former good action, if it be true, is often represented as working a miracle, and is called *saccakiriyā*, *i.e.* "truth-act." Childers properly compares 2 Kings i. 10: "If I be a man of God, then let fire come down from heaven, and consume thee and thy fifty. And there came down fire from heaven and consumed him and his fifty." But the miracle, said in the Buddhist scriptures to follow on an appeal of this kind, is usually, as in this case, an assistance to some one in distress. On the Perfections, see above, pp. 54 to 58.

[2] This seems to be a gloss, as the writer adds, "He could not have stopped at that point; so it should not thus be understood."

[3] On this story, see the translator's "Buddhism," pp. 196–198.

[4] On this story, see below, Jātaka No. 35.

the water up into his cane and drank, so, too, they all sat safe on the bank, and drank.

Thus the water-demon got not one of them into his power on their drinking the water, and he returned in sorrow to his own place. But the Bodisat and his troop went back again to the forest.

When the Teacher, having finished this discourse in illustration of his words ("The hollowness of these canes, mendicants, is a former command of mine"), he made the connexion, and summed up the Jātaka, saying: "He who was then the water-demon was Devadatta; the eighty thousand monkeys were the Buddha's retinue; but the monkey king, clever in resource, was I myself."

END OF THE STORY OF NAḶA-PĀNA.

No. 21.

KURUNGA-MIGA JĀTAKA.

The Wily Antelope.

"*The Kurunga knows full well,*" *etc.*—This the teacher told while at Jetavana about Devadatta.

For once when the monks had assembled in the lecture hall, they sat talking of Devadatta's wickedness, saying, "Brother Devadatta has suborned archers, and hurled down a rock, and sent forth Dhanapālaka the elephant; in every possible way he goes about to slay the Sage."

The Teacher came, and sat down on the seat reserved for him, and asked, "What is it, then, Mendicants, you are sitting here talking about?"

"Lord! we were talking about the wickedness of Devadatta in going about to slay you."

The Teacher answered, "Not now only, O mendicants, has Devadatta gone about to slay me; formerly, too, he did the same, and was unsuccessful in his endeavour." And he told a tale.

Once upon a time, when Brahmadatta was reigning in Benares, the Bodisat became A KURUNGA ANTELOPE and lived in his forest home, feeding on fruits. And at one time he was eating the Sepaṇṇi fruit on a heavily-laden Sepaṇṇi-tree.

Now, a deerstalker of that village used to note the tracks of the deer at the foot of the fruit-trees, build himself a platform on the tree above, and seating himself there, wound with a javelin the deer who came to eat the fruit, and make a living by selling their flesh.

On seeing, one day, the foot-marks of the Bodisat at the foot of the Sepaṇṇi-tree, he made himself a platform upon it, and having breakfasted early, he took his javelin with him, went to the wood, climbed up the tree, and took his seat on the platform.

The Bodisat, too, left his lair early in the morning, and came up to eat the Sepaṇṇi-fruits; but without going too hastily to the foot of the tree, he thought to himself, "Those platform-hunters sometimes make their platforms on the trees. I wonder can there be any danger of that kind." And he stopped at a distance to reconnoitre.

But the hunter, when he saw that the Bodisat was not coming on, kept himself quiet, and threw down fruit so that it fell in front of him.

The Bodisat said to himself, "Why, these fruits are coming this way, and falling before me. There must be a hunter up there!" And looking up again and again, he discerned the hunter. Then pretending not to have seen him, he called out, "Hallo, O tree! You have been wont to let your fruit fall straight down, as if you were putting forth a hanging root: but to-day you have given up your tree-nature. So as you have surrendered the characteristics of tree-nature, I shall go and seek my food at the foot of some other tree." So saying, he uttered this stanza:

"The Kurunga knows full well, Sepaṇṇi,
What kind of fruit you thus throw down.
Elsewhere I shall betake myself:
Your fruit, my friend, belikes me not."[1]

Then the hunter, seated as he was on the platform, hurled his javelin at him, calling out, "Away with you! I've lost you this time!"

The Bodisat turned round, and stopped to cry out, "I tell you, O man, however much you may have lost *me* this time, the eight Great Hells and the sixteen Ussada Hells, and fivefold bondage and torment—the result of your conduct—these you have *not* lost!" And so saying, he escaped whither he desired. And the hunter, too, got down, and went whithersoever he pleased.

When the Teacher had finished this discourse in illustration of what he had said ("Not now only, O mendicants, does Devadatta go about to slay me; formerly, also, he did the same"), he made the connexion, and summed up the Jātaka as follows: "He who was then the hunter was Devadatta, but the Kurunga Antelope was I myself."[2]

END OF THE STORY OF THE KURUNGA ANTELOPE.

[1] This verse is quoted by the Dhammapada Commentator, Fausböll, p. 147.

[2] The Commentator on the "Scripture Verses" (p. 331), says that it was at the end of this story that the Buddha uttered the 162nd verse of that Collection—"He who exceeds in wickedness makes himself such as his enemy might desire, (dragging himself down) as the creeper the tree which it has covered."

No. 22.

KUKKURA JĀTAKA.

The Dog who turned Preacher.

"*The dogs brought up in the king's house,*" *etc.*—This the Teacher told, while at Jetavana, about benefiting one's relations. This will be explained in the Bhadda-sāla Jātaka in the Twelfth Book. In confirmation of what is there related, he told a tale.

Once upon a time, when Brahmadatta was reigning in Benares, the Bodisat, in consequence of an act which would have that effect, came to life as a dog, and lived in a great cemetery attended by a troop of several hundred dogs.

Now, one day the king mounted his state-chariot, drawn by milk-white steeds, went to his park, amused himself there the rest of the day, and after sunset returned to the city. And they put the carriage harness, just as it had been used, in the courtyard.

There was rain in the night, and the harness got wet. The royal dogs, too, came down from the flat roof of the palace, and gnawed at the leather work and straps. The next day the servants told the king, "Dogs have got in, O king, through the sliding door, and have eaten the leather work and the straps."

The king, enraged at the dogs, gave orders that dogs should be killed wherever they were seen. So there ensued a wholesale destruction of dogs: and finding there was no safety for them anywhere else, they escaped to the cemetery, and joined themselves to the Bodisat.

The Bodisat asked them the reason of their coming in such numbers together. "People say," was the answer, "that the leather work and the straps of a carriage in the harem have been gnawed by dogs. The king in his anger has commanded all dogs to be destroyed. Extreme is the danger we are in!"

The Bodisat said to himself, "There's no opportunity for dogs from outside to get into a place so guarded. It must be the royal dogs from within the palace that have done this thing. And now nothing happens to the thieves, and the innocent are punished with death. What if I were to make the king see who the real culprits are, and so save the lives of my kinsfolk?"

And he comforted his relations with the words, "Don't you be afraid! I will restore you to safety. Wait here whilst I go and see the king."

Then guiding himself by thoughts of love, he called to mind his Perfections, and uttered a command; saying, "Let none dare to throw a club or a clod at me!" and so unattended he entered the city. And when they saw him, not a creature grew angry at the sight of him.

Now the king, after issuing the order for the destruction of the dogs, sat himself down in the seat of judgment. The Bodisat went straight up to the place, and rushing forwards, ran underneath the king's throne. Thereupon the king's attendants were about to drive him away, but the king stopped them.

After he had rested awhile, he came out from under the throne, and made obeisance to the king, and asked him, " Is it you who are having the dogs slain?"

"Yes; it is I," was the reply.

" What is their fault, O king of men?"

"They have eaten the leathern coverings and straps of my chariot."

" Do you know which ones did it?"

" That we don't know."

"To have all killed wherever they may be found, without knowing for certain who are the culprits that gnawed the leather, is not just, O king!"

" I gave orders for the destruction of the dogs, saying, 'Kill them all wherever they may be found,' because dogs had eaten the carriage leather."

"What then! Do your men kill all dogs, or are there some not punished with death?"

"There are some. The royal dogs in our house are exempt."

"Great king! only just now you were saying you had given orders to kill all dogs, wherever found, because dogs had eaten the carriage-leather; and now you say that the well-bred dogs in your own house have been exempted. Now this being so, you become guilty of partiality and the other shortcomings of a judge.[1] Now, to be guilty of such thing is neither right, nor kingly.

[1] Literally, of the Agatis (things of which a judge, and especially a king, sitting as judge, ought not to be guilty); they are four in number, partiality, ill-will, ignorance, and fear.

It behoves him who bears the name of king to try motives as with a balance. Since the royal dogs are not punished with death, whilst the poor dogs are, this is no sentence of death on all dogs, but slaughter of the weak."

Then the Great Being further lifted up his pleasant voice, and said, "Great king! That which you are doing is not justice;" and he taught the king the Truth in this stanza:

> "The dogs brought up in the king's house,
> The thoroughbreds in birth and strength—
> Not these, but we, are to be killed.
> This is no righteous vengeance; this is slaughter
> of the weak!"

When the king heard what the Bodisat said, he asked, "O Wise One, do you then know who it is has eaten the carriage leather?"

"Yes; I know it," said he.

"Who are they then?"

"It is the thoroughbreds living in your own house."

"But how can we know they are the guilty ones?"

"I will prove it to you."

"Prove it then, O sage!"

"Send for the thoroughbreds, and have a little butter-milk and Dabba grass brought in."

The king did so; and the Great Being said, "Have the grass crushed in the buttermilk, and give the dogs to drink."

The king did so; and each of the dogs, as they drank it, vomited it up,—and bits of leather with it.

Then the king was delighted as with a decision by the all-wise Buddha himself; and gave up his sceptre to the

Bodisat. But the Bodisat preached the law to the king in the ten verses on righteousness, from the story of the Three Birds, beginning—

Walk righteously, O great king! . . . .

And confirming the king in the Five Commandments, and exhorting him thenceforward to be unweary (in well doing), he returned to the king his sceptre.

And the king listened to his exhortation, and granted security to all living creatures; and commanded a constant supply of food, like the royal food, for all the dogs from the Bodisat downwards. And he remained firm in the teaching of the Bodisat, and did works of charity and other good deeds his life long, and after death was reborn in the world of the gods.

Now the Exhortation of the Dog flourished for tens of thousands of years. But the Bodisat lived to a good old age and passed away according to his deeds.

When the Teacher had concluded this discourse, in illustration of his saying ("Not now only, O mendicants, did the Tathāgata act for the benefit of his relatives, formerly also he did so"), he made the connexion, and summed up the Jātaka by saying, "He who was then the king was Ānanda, the others were the Buddha's attendants, but the Dog was I myself."

END OF THE STORY OF THE DOG.

No. 23.

BHOJĀJĀNĪYA JĀTAKA.

The Bhoja Thoroughbred.

"Though fallen on his side," etc.—This the Teacher told when at Jetavana, concerning a monk who had lost heart in the struggle after holiness. For the Master then addressed the monk, and said, "Formerly, O mendicants, the wise were wont to exert themselves unremittingly, and did not give up when they received a check." And he told a tale.

Long ago, when Brahma-datta was reigning in Benares, the Bodisat was born into the family of a thoroughbred Bhoja horse, and became the state charger of the king of Benares. He fed out of a priceless golden dish on the most delicious fine old rice; and he stood in a fragrant perfumed stall, hung round with curtains embroidered with flowers, covered with a canopy painted with golden stars, decked with garlands of sweet-smelling flowers, and furnished with a lamp of fragrant oil that was never extinguished.

Now there was no king who did not covet the kingdom of Benares. On one occasion seven kings surrounded the city, and sent a letter to the king of Benares, saying, "Either give us up the kingdom, or give us battle!"

The king called a council of his ministers, and told them this, and asked them what was to be done.

"You ought not yourself, O king, to go out to battle at once," was the reply. "Send such and such a knight to give battle; and if he fails, we shall know what to do afterwards."

The king sent for him, and said, "Can you give battle, well beloved, to these seven kings?"

"O king," said he, "if I may have the thoroughbred Bhoja charger, I shall be able to fight, not only the seven kings, but the kings of all the continent of India."

"Take the Bhoja or any other charger you like, my trusty friend, and give them battle," said the king.

"Very good, my lord," said he, and took his leave, and went down from the palace, and had the Bhoja brought, and carefully clad in mail. And himself put on all his armour, girt on his sword, mounted the horse, issued from the city, charged like lightning against the first entrenchment, broke through it, took one king alive, galloped back, and delivered him over to the city guard.

Then he started again, broke through the second, then the third, and so took five kings alive; and had broken through the sixth, and had just taken the sixth king prisoner, when the Bhoja thoroughbred received a wound, and blood gushed forth, and he began to be in severe pain.

When the horseman saw the Bhoja was wounded, he made him lie down at the king's gate, loosened his mail, and began to harness another horse.

Whilst the Bodisat lay there as best he could, he

opened his eyes, and saw the knight, and said to himself, "He is harnessing another horse. That horse won't be able to break through the seventh line, or take the seventh king. What I have already done will be lost. The knight, too, who has no equal, will be killed; and the king, too, will fall into the enemy's power. No other horse, save I alone, can break through that remaining line and take the seventh king." And lying there as he was, he sent for the knight, and said—

"O friend! O knight! no other horse, save I alone, will be able to break through the remaining line and take that last king. And I will not myself destroy the deeds I have already done. Have me helped up, and put the armour on to *me*." And so saying, he uttered this stanza:

> "Though fallen on his side,
> And wounded sore with darts,
> The Bhoja's better than a hack!
> So harness *me*, O charioteer!"

Then the knight helped the Bodisat up, bound up his wound, put on all his harness, seated himself on his back, broke through the seventh line, took the seventh king alive, and delivered him over to the king's guard.

They led the Bodisat, too, to the king's gate, and the king went out to see him. Then the Great Being said to the king—

"O Great King! slay not those seven kings. Take an oath from them, and let them go. Let the honour due to me and to the knight be all given to him alone. It is not right to let a warrior come to ruin when he has taken seven kings prisoners and delivered them over to you.

And do you give gifts, and keep the commandments, and rule your kingdom in righteousness and equity!"

And when the Bodisat had thus exhorted the king, they took off his harness. And as they were taking it off, piece by piece, he breathed his last.

Then the king had a funeral performed for him, and gave the knight great honour, and took an oath from the seven kings that they would not rebel against him, and sent them away each to his own place. And he ruled his kingdom in righteousness and equity, and so at the end of his life passed away according to his deeds.

The Teacher added, "Thus, O mendicants, the wise, even in former times, exerted themselves unremittingly, and did not give in when they received a check. How then can you lose heart, after being ordained according to a system of religion so adapted to lead you to salvation! And he then explained the Truths.

When his exhortation was concluded, the monk who had lost heart was established in the Fruit of Arahatship. Then the Teacher made the connexion, and summed up the Jātaka by saying, "The king of that time was Ānanda, the knight was Sāriputta, but the Bhoja thoroughbred was I myself."

END OF THE STORY OF THE BHOJA THOROUGHBRED.

No. 24.

ĀJAÑÑA JĀTAKA.

The Thoroughbred War Horse.

"*At every time, in every place.*"—This also the Master told, while at Jetavana, about that monk who lost heart.[1] But when he had addressed the monk with the words, "The wise in former times, O monk, continued their exertion, even though in the struggle they received a blow," he told this tale.

Long ago, when Brahmadatta was reigning in Benares, seven kings, as before, surrounded the city. Then a warrior who fought from a chariot harnessed two Sindh horses, who were brothers, to his chariot, issued from the city, broke through six lines and took six kings prisoners.

At that moment the eldest of the horses received a wound. The charioteer drove on till he came to the king's gate, took the elder horse out, loosened his harness, made him lie down on his side, and began to harness another horse.

[1] See the last Introductory Story.

When the Bodisat saw this, he thought as before, sent for the charioteer, and lying as he was, uttered this stanza:

"At every time, in every place,
Whate'er may chance, whate'er mischance,
The thoroughbred's still full of fire!
'Tis a hack horse who then gives in!"

The charioteer helped the Bodisat up, harnessed him, broke through the seventh line, and bringing the seventh king with him, drove up to the king's gate and took out the horse.

The Bodisat, lying there on his side, exhorted the king as before, and then breathed his last. The king performed funeral rites over his body, did honour to the charioteer, ruled his kingdom with righteousness, and passed away according to his deeds.

When the Teacher had finished the discourse, he proclaimed the Truths, and summed up the Jātaka (that monk having obtained Arahatship after the Truths) by saying, "The king of that time was Ānanda, the horse the Supreme Buddha."

END OF THE STORY OF THE THOROUGHBRED.

No. 25.

TITTHA JĀTAKA.

The Horse at the Ford.

"*Feed the horse, then, charioteer,*" *etc.*—This the Master told while at Jetavana about a monk who at that time was a co-resident junior under the Minister of Righteousness, but who had formerly been a goldsmith.

For the knowledge of hearts and motives belongs to the Buddhas only, and to no one else; and hence it was that even the Minister of Righteousness[1] prescribed corruption as a subject of meditation for the monk under his rule, through ignorance of his true character.

Now the monk derived no benefit from that religious exercise—for the following reason. He had come to life in five hundred successive births in a goldsmith's house. From the continual sight through so long a period of the purest gold, the idea of impurity was difficult for him to grasp. Four months he spent without being able to get the faintest notion of it.

As the Minister of Righteousness was unable to bestow salvation (Arahatship) on his co-resident junior, he said to himself, "He must be one of those whom only a Buddha can lead to the Truth! We will take him to the Tathāgata." And he led him to the Master.

The Master inquired of Sāriputta why he brought the

[1] A title of honour given to Sāriputta.

monk before him. "Lord! I prescribed a subject of meditation for this brother, but in four months he has failed to get the most elementary notion of it; so I presumed he was one of those men whom only a Buddha can lead to the Truth, and I have brought him to you."

"What was the particular exercise you prescribed for him, Sāriputta?"

"The Meditation on Impurity, O Blessed One!"

"O Sāriputta! you don't understand the hearts and motives of men. Do you go now; but return in the evening, and you shall take your co-resident with you."

Thus dismissing Sāriputta, the Teacher had the monk provided with a better suit of robes, kept him near himself on the begging-round, and had pleasant food given to him. On his return with the monks he spent the rest of the day in his apartment, and in the evening took that brother with him on his walk round the monastery. There, in a mango-grove, he created a pond, and in it a large cluster of lotuses, and among them one flower of surpassing size and beauty. And telling the monk to sit down there and watch that flower, he returned to his apartment.

The monk gazed at the flower again and again. The Blessed One made that very flower decay; and even as the monk was watching it, it faded away and lost its colour. Then the petals began to fall off, beginning with the outermost, and in a minute they had all dropped on the ground. At last the heart fell to pieces, and the centre knob only remained.

As the monk saw this, he thought, "But now this lotus-flower was exquisitely beautiful! Now its colour has gone; its petals and filaments have fallen away, and only the centre knob is left! If such a flower can so decay, what may not happen to this body of mine! Verily nothing that is composite is enduring!" And the eyes of his mind were opened.

Then the Master knew that he had attained to spiritual insight; and without leaving his apartment, sent out an appearance as of himself, saying:

"Root out the love of self,
As you might the autumn lotus with your hand.
Devote yourself to the Way of Peace alone—
To the Nirvāna which the Blessed One has preached!"[1]

As the stanza was over the monk reached to Arahatship; and at the thought of now being delivered from every kind of future life, he gave utterance to his joy in the hymn of praise beginning—

He who has lived his life, whose heart is fixed,
Whose evil inclinations are destroyed;
He who is wearing his last body now,
Whose life is pure, whose senses well controlled—
He has gained freedom!—as the moon set free,
When an eclipse has passed, from Rahu's jaws.

The utter darkness of delusion,
Which reached to every cranny of his mind,
He has dispelled; and with it every sin—
Just as the thousand-ray'd and mighty sun
Sheds glorious lustre over all the earth,
And dissipates the clouds!

. . . .

And he returned to the Blessed One, and paid him reverence. The Elder also came; and when he took leave of the Teacher, he took his co-resident junior back with him.

And the news of this was noised abroad among the brethren. And they sat together in the evening in the Lecture Hall, extolling the virtues of the Sage, and

[1] This is verse No. 285 of the 'Scripture Verses,' *àpropos* of which the commentator tells the same story as is told here.

saying, "Brethren, Sāriputta the Venerable, not possessing the knowledge of hearts and motives, ignored the disposition of the monk under his charge; but the Master, having that knowledge, procured in one day for that very man the blessing of Arahatship, with all its powers! Ah! how great is the might of the Buddhas!"

When the Teacher had come there and had taken his seat, he asked them what they were talking about. And they told him.

"It is not so very wonderful, O monks," said he, "that I now, as the Buddha, should know this man's disposition; formerly also I knew it."

And he told a tale.

Once upon a time Brahmadatta was reigning in Benares, and the Bodisat was his adviser in things spiritual and temporal.

Now somebody took a common hack to be rubbed down at the ford where the king's state charger used to be bathed. The charger was offended at being led down into the water where a hack had been rubbed down, and refused to step into it.

The horsekeeper went and said to the king, "Your majesty! the state charger won't enter the water."

The king sent for the Bodisat, and said, "Do you go, Paṇḍit, and find out why the horse won't go into the water when he is led down to the ford."

"Very well, my Lord!" said he; and went to the ford, and examined the horse, and found there was nothing the matter with it. Then, reflecting what might be the reason, he thought, "Some other horse must have been watered here just before him; and offended at that, he must have refused to enter the water."

So he asked the horsekeepers whether anything had been watered at the ford just before.

"A certain hack, my Lord!" said they.

Then the Bodisat saw it was his vanity that made him wish not to be bathed there, and that he ought to be taken to some other pond. So he said, "Look you, horsekeeper, even if a man gets the finest milky rice with the most delicious curry to eat, he will tire of it sooner or later. This horse has been bathed often enough at the ford here, take him to some other ford to rub him down and feed him." And so saying, he uttered the verse—

"Feed the horse, then, O charioteer,
Now at one ford, now at another.
If one but eat it oft enough,
The finest rice surfeits a man!"

When they heard what he said, they took the horse to another ford, and there bathed and fed him. And as they were rubbing down the horse after watering him, the Bodisat went back to the king.

The king said, "Well, friend! has the horse had his bath and his drink?"

"It has, my Lord!"

"Why, then, did it refuse at first?"

"Just in this way," said he; and told him all.

The king gave the Bodisat much honour, saying, "He understands the motives even of such an animal as this. How wise he is!" And at the end of this life he passed away according to his deeds. And the Bodisat too passed away according to *his* deeds.

When the Master had finished this discourse in illustration of his saying ("Not now only, O mendicants, have I known this man's motive; formerly also I did so"), he made the connexion, and summed up the Jātaka, by saying, "The state charger of that time was this monk, the King was Ānanda, but the wise minister was I myself."

END OF THE STORY OF THE FORD.

No. 26.

MAHILĀ-MUKHA JĀTAKA.

Evil communications corrupt good manners.

"*By listening first to robbers' talk,*" *etc.*[1]—This the Master told when at Jetavana, about Devadatta. Devadatta became well-pleasing to Prince Ajāta-sattu, and had great gain and honour. The Prince had a monastery built for him at Gayā-sīsa, and five hundred vessels-full of food made of the finest old fragment-rice provided for him daily. Through this patronage Devadatta's following increased greatly, and he lived with his disciples in that monastery.

At that time there were two friends living at Rājagaha; and one of them took the vows under the Teacher, the other under Devadatta. And they used to meet in different places, or go to the monasteries to see one another.

Now one day Devadatta's adherent said to the other, "Brother! why do you go daily with toil and trouble to beg your food? Ever since Devadatta was settled at the Gayā-sīsa Monastery he is provided with the best of things to eat. That's the best way to manage. Why do you make labour for yourself? Wouldn't it be much

[1] This Introductory Story is also told as the introduction to Jātakas Nos. 141 and 184.

better for you to come in the morning to Gayā-sīsa and enjoy really good food—drinking our excellent gruel, and eating from the eighteen kinds of dishes we get?"

When he had been pressed again and again, he became willing to go; and thenceforward he used to go to Gayā-sīsa and take his meal, and return early to the Bambu Grove. But it was impossible to keep it secret for ever; and before long it was noised abroad that he went to Gayā-sīsa and partook of the food provided for Devadatta. So his friends asked him if that were true.

"Who has said such a thing?" said he.

"Such and such a one," was the reply.

"Well, it is true, brethren, that I go and take my meals at Gayā-sīsa; but it is not Devadatta, it is the others who give me to eat."

"Brother! Devadatta is a bitter enemy of the Buddhas. The wicked fellow has curried favour with Ajāta-sattu, and won over his patronage by his wickedness. Yet you, who took the vows under a system so well able to lead you to Nirvāna, now partake of food procured for Devadatta by his wickedness. Come! we must take you before the Master!" So saying, they brought him to the Lecture Hall.

The Master saw them, and asked, "What, then! are you come here, O mendicants! bringing this brother with you against his will?"

"Yes, Lord," said they. "This brother took the vows under you, and yet he partakes of the food which Devadatta's wickedness has earned for him."

The Teacher asked him whether this was true what they said.

"Lord!" replied he, "it is not Devadatta, but the others who give me food: *that* I do eat."

Then said the Teacher, "O monk, make no excuse for it. Devadatta is a sinful, wicked man. How then can you, who took the vows here, eat Devadatta's bread, even while devoting yourself to my religion? Yet you always, even when right in those whom you honoured, used to follow also any one you met." And he told a tale.

Long ago, when Brahmadatta was reigning in Benares, the Bodisat became his minister. At that time the king had a state elephant, named 'Girly-face,' who was good and gentle, and would hurt nobody.

Now one day, robbers came at night-time to a place near his stall, and sat down not far from him, and consulted about their plans, saying, "Thus should a tunnel be broken through; thus should housebreaking be carried out; goods should be carried off only after the tunnel or the breach has been made clear and open as a road or a ford; the taker should carry off the things, even with murder, thus no one will be able to stand up against him; robbery must never be united with scruples of conduct, but with harshness, violence, and cruelty." Thus advising and instructing one another, they separated.

And the next day likewise, and so for many days they assembled there, and consulted together. When the elephant heard what they said, he thought, "It is me they are teaching. I am in future to be harsh, violent, and cruel." And he really became so.

Early in the morning an elephant keeper came there. Him he seized with his trunk, dashed to the ground, and slew. So, likewise, he treated a second and a third, slaying every one who came near him.

So they told the king that 'Girly-face' had gone mad, and killed every one he caught sight of. The King sent the Bodisat, saying, "Do you go, Paṇḍit, and find out what's the reason of his having become a Rogue!"[1]

The Bodisat went there, and finding he had no bodily ailment, thought over what the reason could be; and came to the conclusion that he must have become a Rogue after overhearing some conversation or other, and thinking it was meant as a lesson for *him*. So he asked the elephant keepers, "Has there been any talking going on at night time, near the stable?"

"O yes, sir! Some thieves used to come and talk together," was the reply.

The Bodisat went away, and told the king, "There is nothing bodily the matter with the elephant, your Majesty; it is simply from hearing robbers talk that he has become a Rogue."

"Well; what ought we to do now?"

"Let holy devotees, venerable by the saintliness of their lives,[2] be seated in the elephant stable and talk of righteousness."

[1] A "Rogue elephant" is a well-known technical term for a male who has been driven out of the herd, and away from the females, by a stronger than himself; or for a male, who, in the rutting season, has lost his self-command. Such elephants, however gentle before, become exceedingly vicious and wanton.

[2] Literally Samaṇa-Brāhmans, the Samaṇas, or Self-conquering Ones, being those who have given up the world, and devoted themselves to lives of self-renunciation and of peace. Real superiority of caste—true Brāhmanship—is the result, not of birth, but of self-culture and self-control. The Samaṇas are therefore the true Brāhmans, 'Brāhmans by saintliness of life.' The Samaṇas were not necessarily Buddhists, though they disregarded the rites and ceremonies inculcated by the Brāhmans. It would not have answered the king's purpose to send Brāhmans: who are distinguished throughout the Jātakas, not by holiness of life, but by birth; and who would be represented as likely to talk, not of righteousness, but of ritual. I cannot render the compound, therefore, by 'Samaṇas AND Brāhmans,' and I very much doubt whether it ever has that meaning (but see Childers *contra*, under *Samaṇa*). It certainly never has the sense of 'Samaṇas OR Brāhmans.' It was an early Buddhist idea that the only true Samaṇas were those members of the Order who had entered the Noble Path, and the only true Brāhmans those who had reached to the goal of the Noble Path, that is, to Nirvāna. See Mahā Parinibbana Sutta, p. 58.

"Then do so, my friend," said the king. And the Bodisat got holy men to sit near the elephant's stall, telling them to talk of holy things.

So, seated not far from the elephant, they began: "No one should be struck, no one killed. The man of upright conduct ought to be patient, loving, and merciful."

On hearing this, he thought, "It is me these men are teaching; from this time forth I am to be good!" And so he became tame and quiet.

The king asked the Bodisat, "How is it, my friend? Is he quieted?"

"Yes, my Lord! The elephant, bad as he was, has, because of the wise men, been re-established in his former character." And so saying, he uttered the stanza:

> By listening first to robbers' talk,
> 'Girly-face' went about to kill.
> By listening to men with hearts well trained,
> The stately elephant stood firm once more
> In all the goodness he had lost.

Then the king gave great honour to the Bodisat for understanding the motives even of one born as an animal. And he lived to a good old age, and, with the Bodisat, passed away according to his deeds.

The Teacher having finished this discourse, in illustration of what he had said ("Formerly also, O monk, you used to follow any one you met. When you heard what thieves said, you followed thieves; when you heard what the righteous said, you followed them"), he made the connexion, and summed up the Jātaka by saying, "He who at that time was 'Girly-face' was the traitor-monk, the king was Ānanda, and the minister was I myself."

END OF THE STORY ABOUT 'GIRLY-FACE.'[1]

[1] Perhaps 'Woman-face' would be a more literal rendering of the word *Mahilā-mukha*. But as the allusion is evidently to the elephant's naturally gentle character, I have rendered the expression by 'Girly-face.' The exaggeration in this story is somewhat too absurd for Western tastes.

No. 27.

ABHIṆHA JĀTAKA.

The Elephant and the Dog.

"*No longer can he take a morsel even,*" *etc.*—This the Master told when at Jetavana about an old monk and a lay convert.

At Sāvatthi, the story goes, there were two friends. One of them entered the Order, and went every day to get his meal at the house of the other. The other gave him to eat, and ate himself; and went back with him to the monastery, sat there chatting and talking with him till sunset, and then returned to the city. The other, again, used to accompany him to the city gate, and then turn back. And the close friendship between them became common talk among the brethren.

Now one day the monks sat talking in the Lecture Hall about their intimacy. When the Teacher came, he asked them what they were talking about, and they told him. Then he said, "Not now only, O mendicants, have these been close allies; they were so also in a former birth." And he told a tale.

Long ago, when Brahmadatta was reigning in Benares, the Bodisat became his minister.

At that time a dog used to go to the state elephant's

stable, and feed on the lumps of rice which fell where the elephant fed. Being attracted there by the food, he soon became great friends with the elephant, and used to eat close by him. At last neither of them was happy without the other; and the dog used to amuse himself by catching hold of the elephant's trunk, and swinging to and fro.

But one day there came a peasant who gave the elephant-keeper money for the dog, and took it back with him to his village. From that time the elephant, missing the dog, would neither eat nor drink nor bathe. And they let the king know about it.

He sent the Bodisat, saying, "Do you go, Paṇḍit, and find out what's the cause of the elephant's behaviour."[1]

So he went to the stable, and seeing how sad the elephant looked, said to himself, "There seems to be nothing bodily the matter with him. He must be so overwhelmed with grief by missing some one, I should think, who had become near and dear to him." And he asked the elephant-keepers, "Is there any one with whom he is particularly intimate?"

"Certainly, Sir! There was a dog of whom he was very fond indeed!"

"Where is it now?"

"Some man or other took it away."

"Do you know where the man lives?"

"No, Sir!"

Then the Bodisat went and told the king, "There's nothing the matter with the elephant, your majesty; but

[1] So at p. 121 of the Mahāvaṇsa the king sends Mahinda to find out why the state elephant refused his food. Mahinda finds the motive to be that the elephant wants a *Dāgaba* to be built; and the king, "who always gratified the desires of his subjects," had the temple built at once! The author of the Mahāvaṇsa must often have heard the Jātaka stories told, and this among the number.

he was great friends with a dog, and I fancy it's through missing it that he refuses his food."

And so saying, he uttered the stanza:

No longer can he take a morsel even
Of rice or grass; the bath delights him not!
Because, methinks, through constant intercourse,
The elephant had come to love the dog.

When the king heard what he said, he asked what was now to be done.

"Have a proclamation made, O king, to this effect: 'A man is said to have taken away a dog of whom our state elephant was fond. In whose house soever that dog shall be found, he shall be fined so much!'"

The king did so; and as soon as he heard of it, the man turned the dog loose. The dog hastened back, and went close up to the elephant. The elephant took him up in his trunk, and placed him on his forehead, and wept and cried, and took him down again, and watched him as he fed. And then he took his own food.

Then the king paid great honour to the Bodisat for knowing the motives even of animals.

When the Teacher had finished this discourse, and had enlarged upon the Four Truths,[1] he made the connexion and summed up the Jātaka, "He who at that time was the dog was the lay convert, the elephant was the old monk, but the minister paṇḍit was I myself."

END OF THE STORY ON CONSTANCY.

[1] *Note by the Commentator.* "This so-called enforcing (or illustrating) the story by a discourse on the Four Truths is to be understood at the end of every Jātaka; but we only mention it when it appears that it was blessed (to the conversion of some character in the Introductory Story)."

No. 28.

NANDI-VISĀLA JĀTAKA.

The Bull who Won the Bet.

"*Speak kindly.*"—This the Master told when at Jetavana concerning the abusive language of the Six.[1]

For on one occasion the Six made a disturbance by scorning, snubbing, and annoying peaceable monks, and overwhelming them with the ten kinds of abuse. The monks told the Blessed One about it. He sent for the Six, and asked them whether it was true. And on their acknowledging it, he reproved them, saying, "Harsh speaking, O mendicants, is unpleasant, even to animals. An animal once made a man who addressed him harshly lose a thousand." And he told a tale.

Long ago a king of Gandhāra was reigning in Takkasilā, in the land of Gandhāra. The Bodisat came to life then as a bull.

Now, when he was yet a young calf, a certain Brāhman, after attending upon some devotees who were wont to

[1] These "Six" are noted characters in Buddhist legend. They are six bad monks, whose evil deeds and words are said to have given occasion to many a "bye-law," if one may so say, enacted in the Vinaya Pitaka for the guidance of the members of the Buddhist Order of Mendicants.

give oxen to priests, received the bull. And he called it Nandi Visāla, and grew very fond of it; treating it like a son, and feeding it on gruel and rice.

When the Bodisat grew up, he said to himself, "This Brāhman has brought me up with great care; and there's no other ox in all the continent of India can drag the weight I can. What if I were to let the Brāhman know about my strength, and so in my turn provide sustenance for him!"

And he said one day to the Brāhman, "Do you go now, Brāhman, to some squire rich in cattle, and offer to bet him a thousand that your ox will move a hundred laden carts."

The Brāhman went to a rich farmer, and started a conversation thus:

"Whose bullocks hereabout do you think the strongest?"

"Such and such a man's," said the farmer; and then added, "but of course there are none in the whole countryside to touch my own!"

"I have one ox," said the Brāhman, "who is good to move a hundred carts, loads and all!"

"Tush!" said the squire. "Where in the world is such an ox?"

"Just in my house!" said the Brāhman.

"Then make a bet about it!"

"All right! I bet you a thousand he can."

So the bet was made. And he filled a hundred carts (small waggons made for two bullocks) with sand and gravel and stones, ranged them all in a row, and tied them all firmly together, cross-bar to axle-tree.

Then he bathed Nandi Visāla, gave him a measure of scented rice, hung a garland round his neck, and yoked him by himself to the front cart. Then he took his seat on the pole, raised his goad aloft, and called out, "Gee up! you brute!! Drag 'em along! you wretch!!"

The Bodisat said to himself, "He addresses me as a wretch. I am no *wretch!*" And keeping his four legs as firm as so many posts, he stood perfectly still.

Then the squire that moment claimed his bet, and made the Brāhman hand over the thousand pieces. And the Brāhman, minus his thousand, took out his ox, went home to his house, and lay down overwhelmed with grief.

Presently Nanda Visāla, who was roaming about the place, came up and saw the Brāhman grieving there, and said to him,

"What, Brāhman! are you asleep?"

"Sleep! How can I sleep after losing the thousand pieces?"

"Brāhman! I've lived so long in your house, and have I ever broken any pots, or rubbed up against the walls, or made messes about?"

"Never, my dear!"

"Then why did you call me a wretch? It's your fault. It's not my fault. Go now, and bet him two thousand, and never call me a wretch again—I, who am no wretch at all!"

When the Brāhman heard what he said, he made the bet two thousand, tied the carts together as before, decked out Nandi Visāla, and yoked him to the foremost cart.

He managed this in the following way: he tied the pole and the cross-piece fast together; yoked Nandi Visāla on one side; on the other he fixed a smooth piece of timber from the point of the yoke to the axle-end, and wrapping it round with the fastenings of the cross-piece, tied it fast; so that when this was done, the yoke could not move this way and that way, and it was possible for one ox to drag forwards the double bullock-cart.

Then the Brāhman seated himself on the pole, stroked Nandi Visāla on the back, and called out, "Gee up! my beauty!! Drag it along, my beauty!!"

And the Bodisat, with one mighty effort, dragged forwards the hundred heavily-laden carts, and brought the hindmost one up to the place where the foremost one had stood!

Then the cattle-owner acknowledged himself beaten, and handed over to the Brāhman the two thousand; the bystanders, too, presented the Bodisat with a large sum; and the whole became the property of the Brāhman. Thus, by means of the Bodisat, great was the wealth he acquired.

So the Teacher reproved the Six, saying, "Harsh words, O mendicants, are pleasant to no one;" and uttered, as Buddha, the following stanza, laying down a rule of moral conduct:

Speak kindly; never speak in words unkind!
He moved a heavy weight for him who kindly spake.
He gained him wealth; he was delighted with him!

When the Teacher had given them this lesson in virtue ("Speak kindly," etc.), he summed up the Jātaka, "The Brāhman of that time was Ānanda, but Nandi Visāla was I myself."

END OF THE STORY OF THE BULL WHO WON THE BET.

No. 29.

KAṆHA JĀTAKA.

The Old Woman's Black Bull.

"*Whene'er the load be heavy.*"—This the Master told while at Jetavana, about the Double Miracle. That and the Descent from Heaven will be explained in the Birth Story of the Sarabha Antelope, in the Thirteenth Book.

The Supreme Buddha performed on that occasion the Double Miracle, remained some time in heaven, and on the Great Day of the Pavāraṇā Festival[1] descended at the city of Saŋkassa, and entered Jetavana with a great retinue.

When the monks were seated in the Lecture Hall, they began to extol the virtue of the Teacher, saying, "Truly, Brethren! unequalled is the power of the Tathāgata. The yoke the Tathāgata bears none else is able to bear. Though the Six Teachers kept on saying, 'We will work wonders! We will work wonders!' they could not do even one. Ah! how unequalled is the power of the Tathāgata!"

[1] This was a December festival, held to celebrate the close of the season of WAS, the four (or, according to some authorities, three) months of rainy weather, during which the members of the Order had to stay in one place. The Buddha had spent WAS among the angels—not, of course, that he cared to go to heaven for his own sake, but to give the ignorantly happy and deluded angels an opportunity of learning how to forsake the error of their ways. In a subsequent form of this curious legend, whose origin is at present unknown, he is said to have descended into hell with a similar object. See Professor Cowell in the *Indian Antiquary* for 1879.

When the Teacher came there, he asked them what they were discussing, and they told him. Then he said, "O mendicants! who should now bear the yoke that I can bear? For even when an animal in a former birth I could find no one to drag the weight I dragged." And he told a tale.

Long ago, when Brahmadatta was reigning in Benares, the Bodisat returned to life as a bull.

Now, when it was still a young calf, its owners stopped a while in an old woman's house, and gave him to her when they settled their account for their lodging. And she brought him up, treating him like a son, and feeding him on gruel and rice.

He soon became known as "The old woman's Blackie." When he grew up, he roamed about, as black as collyrium, with the village cattle, and was very good-tempered and quiet. The village children used to catch hold of his horns, or ears, or dewlaps, and hang on to him; or amuse themselves by pulling his tail, or riding about on his back.

One day he said to himself, "My mother is wretchedly poor. She's taken so much pains, too, in bringing me up, and has treated me like a son. What if I were to work for hire, and so relieve her distress!" And from that day he was always on the look out for a job.

Now one day a young caravan owner arrived at a neighbouring ford with five hundred bullock-waggons. And his bullocks were not only unable to drag the carts across, but even when he yoked the five hundred pair in a row they could not move one cart by itself.

The Bodisat was grazing with the village cattle close to the ford. The young caravan owner was a famous judge of cattle, and began looking about to see whether there were among them any thoroughbred bull able to drag over the carts. Seeing the Bodisat, he thought he would do; and asked the herdsmen—

"Who may be the owners, my men, of this fellow? I should like to yoke him to the cart, and am willing to give a reward for having the carts dragged over."

"Catch him and yoke him then!" said they. "He has no owner hereabouts."

But when he began to put a string through his nose and drag him along, he could not get him to come. For the Bodisat, it is said, wouldn't go till he was promised a reward.

The young caravan owner, seeing what his object was, said to him, "Sir! if you'll drag over these five hundred carts for me, I'll pay you wages at the rate of two pence for each cart—a thousand pieces in all."

Then the Bodisat went along of his own accord. And the men yoked him to the cart. And with a mighty effort he dragged it up and landed it safe on the high ground. And in the same manner he dragged up all the carts.

So the caravan owner then put five hundred pennies in a bundle, one for each cart, and tied it round his neck. The bull said to himself, "This fellow is not giving me wages according to the rate agreed upon. I shan't let him go on now!" And so he went and stood in the way of the front cart, and they tried in vain to get him away.

The caravan owner thought, "He knows, I suppose, that the pay is too little;" and wrapping a thousand pieces in a cloth, tied them up in a bundle, and hung that round his neck. And as soon as he had got the bundle with a thousand inside he went off to his 'mother.'

Then the village children called out, "See! what's that round the neck of the old woman's Blackie?" and began to run up to him. But he chased after them, so that they took to their heels before they got near him; and he went straight to his mother. And he appeared with eyes all bloodshot, utterly exhausted from dragging over so many carts.

"How did you get this, dear?" said the good old woman, when she saw the bag round his neck. And when she heard, on inquiry from the herdsmen, what had happened, she exclaimed, "Am I so anxious, then, to live on the fruit of your toil, my darling! Why do you put yourself to all this pain?"

And she bathed him in warm water, and rubbed him all over with oil, and gave him to drink, and fed him up with good food. And at the end of her life she passed away according to her deeds, and the Bodisat with her.

When the Teacher had finished this lesson in virtue, in illustration of that saying of his ("Not now only, O mendicants, has the Bodisat been excellent in power; he was so also in a former birth"), he made the connexion, and, as Buddha, uttered the following stanza:

Whene'er the load be heavy,
Where'er the ruts be deep,
Let them yoke 'Blackie' then,
And he will drag the load!

Then the Blessed One told them, "At that time, O mendicants, only the Black Bull could drag the load." And he then made the connexion and summed up the Jātaka: "The old woman of that time was Uppala-vaṇṇā, but 'the old woman's Blackie' was I myself."

END OF THE STORY OF THE OLD WOMAN'S BLACK BULL.[1]

[1] It will be observed that the old woman's 'Blackie' could understand what was said to him, and make his own meaning understood; but he could not speak.

No. 30.

MUṆIKA JĀTAKA.

The Ox who Envied the Pig.

"*Envy not Muṇika.*"—This the Master told while at Jetavana, about being attracted by a fat girl. That will be explained in the Birth Story of Nārada-Kassapa the Younger, in the Thirteenth Book.

On that occasion the Teacher asked the monk, "Is it true what they say, that you are love-sick?"

"It is true, Lord!" said he.

"What about?"

"My Lord! 'tis the allurement of that fat girl!"

Then the Master said, "O monk! she will bring evil upon you. In a former birth already you lost your life on the day of her marriage, and were turned into food for the multitude." And he told a tale.

Long ago, when Brahma-datta was reigning in Benares, the Bodisat came to life in the house of a landed proprietor in a certain village as an ox, with the name of 'Big-red.' And he had a younger brother called 'Little-red.' And all the carting work in the household was carried on by means of the two brothers.

Now there was an only daughter in that family, and she was asked in marriage for the son of a man of rank in a neighbouring city. Then her parents thinking, "It will do for a feast of delicacies for the guests who come to the girl's wedding," fattened up a pig with boiled rice. And his name was 'Sausages.'

When Little-red saw this, he asked his brother, "All the carting work in the household falls to our lot. Yet these people give us mere grass and straw to eat; while they bring up that pig on boiled rice! What can be the reason of that fellow getting that?"

Then his brother said to him, "Dear Little-red, don't envy the creature his food! This poor pig is eating the food of death! These people are fattening the pig to provide a feast for the guests at their daughter's wedding. But a few days more, and you shall see how these men will come and seize the pig by his legs, and drag him off out of his sty, and deprive him of his life, and make curry for the guests!" And so saying, he uttered the following stanza:

"Envy not 'Sausages!'
'Tis deadly food he eats!
Eat your chaff, and be content;
'Tis the sign of length of life!"

And, not long after, those men came there; and they killed 'Sausages,' and cooked him up in various ways.

Then the Bodisat said to Little-red, "Have you seen 'Sausages,' my dear?"

"I have seen, brother," said he, "what has come of the food poor Sausages ate. Better a hundred, a thousand times, than his rice, is our food of only grass and straw and chaff; for it works no harm, and is evidence that our lives will last."

Then the Teacher said, "Thus then, O monk, you have already in a former birth lost your life through her, and become food for the multitude." And when he had concluded this lesson in virtue, he proclaimed the Truths. When the Truths were over, that love-sick monk stood fast in the Fruit of Conversion. But the Teacher made the connexion, and summed up the Jātaka, by saying, "He who at that time was 'Sausages' the pig was the love-sick monk, the fat girl was as she is now, Little-red was Ānanda, but Big-red was I myself."

END OF THE STORY OF THE OX WHO ENVIED THE PIG.[1]

[1] If *Muṇika*, the name of the Pig, is derived from the root MAR (B. R. No. 2)—as I think it must be, in spite of the single ṇ—it is a verbal noun derived from a past participle, meaning 'cut into small pieces.' The idea is doubtless of the small pieces of meat used for curry, as the Indians had no sausages. I could not dare to coin such a word as 'Curry-bit-ling,' and have therefore preserved the joke by using a word which will make it intelligible to European readers.

This well-told story is peculiarly interesting as being one of those Indian stories which have reached Europe independently of both the 'Kalilag and Dimnag' and the 'Barlaam and Josaphat' literature. Professor Benfey (pp. 228-229 of his Introduction to the Pañca Tantra) has traced stories somewhat analogous throughout European literature; but our story itself is, he says, found almost word for word in an unpublished Hebrew book by Berachia ben Natronai, only that two donkeys take the place of the two oxen. Berachia lived in the twelfth or thirteenth century, in Provence.

One of the analogous stories is where a falcon complains to a cock, that, while he (the falcon) is so grateful to men for the little they give him that he comes and hunts for them at their beck and call, the cock, though fed up to his eyes, tries to escape when they catch him. "Ah!" replies the cock, "I never yet saw a falcon brought to table, or frying in a pan!" (Anvar i Suhaili, p. 144; Livre des Lumières, p. 112; Cabinet des Fées, xvii. 277; Bidpai et Lokman, ii. 59; La Fontaine, viii. 21). Among the so-called Æsop's Fables is also one where a calf laughs at a draught ox for bearing his drudgery so patiently. The ox says nothing. Soon after there is a feast, and the ox gets a holiday, while the calf is led off to the sacrifice (James's Æsop, No. 150).

Jātaka No. 286 is the same story in almost the same words, save (1) that the pig's name is there *Sālūha*, which means the edible root of the water-lily, and might be freely rendered 'Turnips'; and (2) that there are three verses instead of one. As special stress is there laid on the fact that 'Turnips' was allowed to lie on the *heṭṭhā-mañca*, which I have above translated 'sty,' it is possible that the word means the platform or seat in front of the hut, and under the shade of the overhanging eaves,—a favourite resort of the people of the house.

CHAPTER IV. KULĀVAKAVAGGA.

No. 31.

KULĀVAKA JĀTAKA.

On Mercy to Animals.

"Let the Nestlings in the wood."—This the Master told while at Jetavana, about a monk who drank water without straining it.

Two young monks who were friends, it is said, went into the country from Sāvatthi; and after stopping as long as it suited them in a certain pleasant spot, set out again towards Jetavana, with the intention of joining the Supreme Buddha.

One of them had a strainer, the other had not; so they used to strain water enough at one time for both to drink.

One day they had a dispute; and the owner of the strainer would not lend it to the other, but strained water himself, and drank it. When the other could not get the strainer, and was unable to bear up any longer against his thirst, he drank without straining. And in due course they both arrived at Jetavana; and after saluting the Teacher, took their seats.

The Teacher bade them welcome, saying, "Where are you come from?"

"Lord! we have been staying in a village in the land of Kosala; and we left it to come here and visit you."

"I hope, then, you are come in concord."

The one without a strainer replied, "Lord! this monk quarrelled with me on the way, and wouldn't lend me his strainer!"

But the other one said, "Lord! this monk knowingly drank water with living things in it without straining it!"

"Is it true, O monk, as he says, that you knowingly drank water with living creatures in it?"

"Yes, Lord! I drank the water as it was."

Then the Teacher said, "There were wise men once, O monk, ruling in heaven, who, when defeated and in full flight along the mighty deep, stopped their car, saying, 'Let us not, for the sake of supremacy, put living things to pain;' and made sacrifice of all their glory, and even of their life, for the sake of the young of the Supaṇṇas."

And he told a tale.[1]

Long ago a king of Magadha was reigning in Rājagaha, in the land of Magadha.

At that time the Bodisat (just as he who is now Sakka was once born in the village of Macala in Magadha) was born in that very village as a nobleman's son. On the naming-day they gave him the name of Prince Magha, and when he grew up he was known as 'Magha the young Brāhman.'

His parents procured him a wife from a family of equal

[1] The following tale is told, with some variations, in the course of the commentary on verse 30 of the Dhammapada (pp. 186 and foll.); but the Introductory Story is there different.

rank; and increasing in sons and daughters, he became a great giver of gifts, and kept the Five Commandments.

In that village there were as many as thirty families; and one day the men of those families stopped in the middle of the village to transact some village business. The Bodisat removed with his feet the lumps of soil on the place where he stood, and made the spot convenient to stand on; but another came up and stood there. Then he smoothed out another spot, and took his stand there; but another man came and stood upon it. Still the Bodisat tried again and again with the same result, until he had made convenient standing-room for all the thirty.

The next time he had an open-roofed shed put up there; and then pulled that down, and built a hall, and had benches spread in it, and a water-pot placed there. On another occasion those thirty men were reconciled by the Bodisat, who confirmed them in the Five Commandments; and thenceforward he continued with them in works of piety.

Whilst they were so living they used to rise up early, go out with bill-hooks and crowbars in their hands, tear up with the crowbars the stones in the four high roads and village paths, and roll them away, take away the trees which would be in the way of vehicles, make the rough places plain, form causeways, dig ponds, build public halls, give gifts, and keep the Commandments—thus, in many ways, all the dwellers in the village listened to the exhortations of the Bodisat, and kept the Commandments.

Now the village headman said to himself, "I used to have great gain from fines, and taxes, and pot-money, when these fellows drank strong drink, or took life, or broke the other Commandments. But now Magha the young Brāhman has determined to have the Commandments kept, and permits none to take life or to do anything else that is wrong. I'll make them keep the Commandments with a vengeance!"

And he went in a rage to the king, and said, "O king! there are a number of robbers going about sacking the villages!"

"Go, and bring them up!" said the king in reply.

And he went, and brought back all those men as prisoners, and had it announced to the king that the robbers were brought up. And the king, without inquiring what they had done, gave orders to have them all trampled to death by elephants!

Then they made them all lie down in the court-yard, and fetched the elephant. And the Bodisat exhorted them, saying, "Keep the Commandments in mind. Regard them all—the slanderer, and the king, and the elephant—with feelings as kind as you harbour towards yourselves!"

And they did so.

Then men led up the elephant; but though they brought him to the spot, he would not begin his work, but trumpeted forth a mighty cry, and took to flight. And they brought up another and another, but they all ran away.

"There must be some drug in their possession," said the king; and gave orders to have them searched. So they searched, but found nothing, and told the king so.

"Then they must be repeating some spell. Ask them if they have any spell to utter."

The officials asked them, and the Bodisat said there was. And they told the king, and he had them all called before him, and said, "Tell me that spell you know!"

Then the Bodisat spoke, and said, "O king! we have no other spell but this—that we destroy no life, not even of grass; that we take nothing which is not given to us; that we are never guilty of unchastity, nor speak falsehood, nor drink intoxicants; that we exercise ourselves in love, and give gifts; that we make rough places plain, dig ponds, and put up rest-houses—this is our spell, this is our defence, this is our strength!"

Then the king had confidence in them, and gave them all the property in the house of the slanderer, and made him their slave; and bestowed too the elephant upon them, and made them a grant of the village.

Thenceforward they were left in peace to carry on their works of charity; and they sent for a builder and had a large rest-house put up at the place where the four roads met. But as they no longer took delight in womankind, they allowed no woman to share in the good work.

Now at that time there were four women in the Bodisat's household, named Piety, Thoughtful, Pleasing, and Well-born. Piety took an opportunity of meeting the builder alone, and gave him a bribe, and said to him, "Brother! manage somehow to give me a share in this rest-house."

This he promised to do, and before doing the other work he had a piece of timber dried and planed; and bored it through ready for the pinnacle. And when it was finished he wrapped it up in a cloth and laid it aside. Then when the hall was finished, and the time had come for putting up the pinnacle, he said,—

"Dear me! there's one thing we haven't provided for!"

"What's that?" said they.

"We ought to have got a pinnacle."

"Very well! let's have one brought."

"But it can't be made out of timber just cut; we ought to have had a pinnacle cut and planed, and bored some time ago, and laid aside for use."

"What's to be done now then?" said they.

"You must look about and see if there be such a thing as a finished pinnacle for sale put aside in any one's house."

And when they began to search, they found one on Piety's premises; but it could not be bought for money.

"If you let me be partaker in the building of the hall, I will give it you?" said she.

"No!" replied they, "it was settled that women should have no share in it."

Then the builder said, "Sirs! what is this you are saying? Save the heavenly world of the Brahma-angels, there is no place where womankind is not. Accept the pinnacle; and so will our work be accomplished!"

Then they agreed; and took the pinnacle and completed their hall with it.[1] They fixed benches in the hall, and set up pots of water in it, and provided for it a constant supply of boiled rice. They surrounded the hall with a wall, furnished it with a gate, spread it over with sand inside the wall, and planted a row of palmyra-trees outside it.

And Thoughtful made a pleasure ground there; and so

[1] The commentator on the "Scripture Verses" adds an interesting point—that there was an inscription on the pinnacle, and that the Bodisat put up a stone seat under a tree outside, that all who went in might read the letters, and say, "This hall is called the Hall of Piety."

perfect was it that it could never be said of any particular fruit-bearing or flowering tree that it was not there!

And Pleasing made a pond there, covered with the five kinds of water-lilies, and beautiful to see!

Well-born did nothing at all.[1]

And the Bodisat fulfilled the seven religious duties—that is, to support one's mother, to support one's father, to pay honour to age, to speak truth, not to speak harshly, not to abuse others, and to avoid a selfish, envious, niggardly disposition.

> That person who his parents doth support,
> Pays honour to the seniors in the house,
> Is gentle, friendly-speaking, slanders not;
> The man unselfish, true, and self-controlled,
> Him do the angels of the Great Thirty Three
> Proclaim a righteous man!

Such praise did he receive; and at the end of his life he was born again in the heaven of the Great Thirty Three, as Sakka, the king of the Gods, and there, too, his friends were born again.

At that time there were Titans dwelling in the heaven of the Great Thirty Three.

And Sakka said, "What is the good to us of a kingdom shared by others?"

And he had ambrosia given to the Titans to drink, and

[1] The "Scripture Verses" commentator (p. 189) avoids the curious abruptness of this rather unkind remark by adding that the reason for this was that Well-born's being the Bodisat's niece and servant, she thought she would share in the merit of *his* part in the work.

when they became like drunken men, he had them seized by the feet and thrown headlong upon the precipices of Mount Sineru.

They fell just upon "The abode of the Titans;" a place so called, upon the lowest level of Sineru, equal in size to the Tāva-tiŋsa heaven. In it there is a tree, like the coral-tree in Sakka's heaven, which stands during a kalpa, and is called "The variegated Trumpet-Flower Tree."

When they saw the Trumpet-Flower Tree in bloom, they knew, "This is not our heaven, for in heaven the Coral-Tree blossoms."

Then they said, "That old Sakka has made us drunk, and thrown us into the great deep, and taken our heavenly city!"

Then they made resolve, "We'll war against him, and win our heavenly city back again!"

And they swarmed up the perpendicular sides of Sineru like so many ants!

When Sakka heard the cry, "The Titans are up!" he went down the great deep to meet them, and fought with them from the sky. But he was worsted in the fight, and began to flee away along the summit of the southern vault of heaven in his famous Chariot of Glory a hundred and fifty leagues in length.[1]

Now as his chariot went rapidly down the great deep, it passed along the Silk Cotton Tree Forest, and along its route the silk cotton trees were cut down one after another like mere palmyra palms, and fell into the great deep. And as the young ones of the Wingéd Creatures tumbled over and over into the great deep, they burst

[1] Vejayanta. Compare what is said above, p. 97, of Māra's *vāhana*, Giri-mekhala.

forth into mighty cries. And Sakka asked his charioteer, Mātali—

"What noise is this, friend Mātali? How pathetic is that cry!"

"O Lord! as the Silk Cotton Tree Forest falls, torn up by the swiftness of your car, the young of the Wingéd Creatures, quaking with the fear of death, are shrieking all at once together!"

Then answered the Great Being, "O my good Mātali! let not these creatures suffer on our account. Let us not, for the sake of supremacy, put the living to pain. Rather will I, for their sake, give my life as a sacrifice to the Titans. Stop the car!"

And so saying, he uttered the stanza—

"Let the Nestlings in the Silk Cotton Wood
Escape, O Mātali, our chariot pole.
Most gladly let me offer up my life:
Let not these birds, then, be bereft of offspring!"

Then Mātali, the charioteer, on hearing what he said, stopped the car, and returned towards heaven by another way. But as soon as they saw him stopping, the Titans thought, "Assuredly the Archangels of other world-systems must be coming; he must have stopped his car because he has received reinforcements!" And terrified with the fear of death, they took to flight, and returned to the Abode of the Titans.

And Sakka re-entered his heavenly city, and stood in the midst thereof, surrounded by the hosts of angels from both the heavens.[1] And that moment the Palace of Glory burst through the earth and rose up a thousand leagues

[1] That is, his own angels and those of the archangel Brahma.

in height. And it was because it arose at the end of this glorious victory that it received the name of the Palace of Glory.

Then Sakka placed guards in five places, to prevent the Titans coming up again,—in respect of which it has been said—

Between the two unconquerable cities
A fivefold line of guards stands firmly placed
Of Snakes, of Winged Creatures, and of Dwarfs,
Of Ogres, and of the Four Mighty Kings.

When Sakka had thus placed the guards, and was enjoying the happiness of heaven as king of the angels, Piety changed her form of existence, and was re-born as one of his attendants. And in consequence of her gift of the pinnacle there arose for her a jewelled hall of state under the name of 'Piety,' where Sakka sat as king of the angels, on a throne of gold under a white canopy of state, and performed his duties towards the angels and towards men.

And Thoughtful also changed her form of existence, and was re-born as one of his attendants. And in consequence of her gift of the pleasure-ground, there arose for her a pleasure-ground under the name of 'Thoughtful's Creeper Grove.'

And Pleasing also changed her form of existence, and was re-born as one of his attendants. And in consequence of her gift of the pond, there arose for her a pond under the name of 'Pleasing.'

But since Well-born had done no act of virtue, she was

re-born as a female crane in a pool in a certain forest. And Sakka said to himself, "There's no sign of Well-born. I wonder where she can have got to!" And he considered the matter till he discovered her.

Then he went to the place, and brought her back with him to heaven, and showed her the delightful city with the Hall of Piety, and Thoughtful's Creeper Grove, and the Pond of Pleasing. And he then exhorted her, and said—

"These did works of charity, and have been born again as my attendants; but you, having done no such works, have been re-born as an animal. Henceforward live a life of righteousness!"

And thus confirming her in the Five Commandments, he took her back, and then dismissed her. And from that time forth she lived in righteousness.

A few days afterwards, Sakka went to see whether she was able to keep good, and he lay on his back before her in the form of a fish. Thinking it was dead, the crane seized it by the head. The fish wagged its tail.

"It's alive, I think!" exclaimed she, and let it go.

"Good! Good!" said Sakka, "You are well able to keep the Commandments." And he went away.

When she again changed her form of existence, she was born in a potter's household in Benares. Sakka, as before, found out where she was, and filled a cart with golden cucumbers, and seated himself in the middle of the village in the form of an old woman, calling out, "Buy my cucumbers! Buy my cucumbers!"

The people came up and asked for them.

"I sell," said she, "only to those who live a life of righteousness. Do you live such a life?"

"We don't know anything about righteousness. Hand them over for money!" said they.

"I want no money; I will only give to the righteous," was her reply.

"This must be some mad woman!" said they, and left her.

But when Well-born heard what had happened, she thought, "This must be meant for me!" and went and asked for some cucumbers.

"Do you live a righteous life, lady?" was the question.

"Certainly, I do," said she.

"It's for your sake that I brought these here," replied the old woman; and leaving all the golden cucumbers, and the cart too, at the door of the house, she departed.

And Well-born still continued in righteousness to the end of that life; and when she changed her existence, she became the daughter of a Titan named 'The Son of Misunderstanding;' but in consequence of her virtue she became exceeding beautiful.

When she was grown up, her father assembled the Titans together that his daughter might choose for a husband the one she liked best. Sakka was looking about as before to find out where she was; and when he discovered it, he took the form of a Titan, and went to the place,—thinking that when choosing a husband, she might take him.

Then they led Well-born in fine array to the meeting place, and told her to choose whomsoever she liked as her husband. And when she began to look at them, she saw

Sakka, and by reason of her love to him in the former birth, she was moved to say, "This one is my husband," and so chose him.

And he led her away to the heavenly city, and gave her the post of honour among great multitudes of houris; and at the end of his allotted time, he passed away according to his deeds.

When the Teacher had finished this discourse, he reproved the monk, saying, "Thus, O monk, formerly wise men, though they held rule in heaven, offered up their lives rather than destroy life; but you, though you have taken the vows according to so saving a faith, have drunk unstrained water with living creatures in it!" And he make the connexion, and summed up the Jātaka, by saying, "He who at that time was Mātali the charioteer was Ānanda, but Sakka was I myself."

END OF THE STORY ON MERCY TO ANIMALS.[1]

[1] In this story we have a good example of the way in which the current legends, when adopted by the Buddhists, were often so modified as to teach lessons of an effect exactly contrary to those they had taught before. It is with a touch of irony that Sakka is made to conquer the Titans, not by might, but through his kindness to animals.

No. 32.

NACCA JĀTAKA.

The Dancing Peacock.

"*Pleasant is your cry.*"—This the Master told when at Jetavana, about the luxurious monk. The occasion is as above in the Story on True Divinity.[1]

The Teacher asked him, "Is this true, O monk, what they say, that you are luxurious?"

"It is true, Lord," said he.

"How is it you have become luxurious?" began the Teacher.

But without waiting to hear more, he flew into a rage, tore off his robe and his lower garment, and calling out, "Then I'll go about in this way!" stood there naked before the Teacher!

The bystanders exclaimed, "Shame! shame!" and he ran off, and returned to the lower state (of a layman).

When the monks were assembled in the Lecture Hall, they began talking of his misconduct. "To think that one should behave so in the very presence of the Master!" The Teacher then came up, and asked them what they were talking about, as they sat there together.

"Lord! we were talking of the misconduct of that monk, who, in your presence, and in the midst of the disciples, stood there as naked as a village child, without

[1] See above, p. 178.

caring one bit; and when the bystanders cried shame upon him, returned to the lower state, and lost the faith!"

Then said the Teacher, "Not only, O monks, has this brother now lost the jewel of the faith by immodesty; in a former birth he lost a jewel of a wife from the same cause." And he told a tale.

Long ago, in the first age of the world, the quadrupeds chose the Lion as their king, the fishes the Leviathan, and the birds the Golden Goose.[1]

Now the royal Golden Goose had a daughter, a young goose most beautiful to see; and he gave her her choice of a husband. And she chose the one she liked the best.

For, having given her the right to choose, he called together all the birds in the Himālaya region. And crowds of geese, and peacocks, and other birds of various kinds, met together on a great flat piece of rock.

The king sent for his daughter, saying, "Come and choose the husband you like best!"

On looking over the assembly of the birds, she caught sight of the peacock, with a neck as bright as gems, and a many-coloured tail; and she made the choice with the words, "Let this one be my husband!"

So the assembly of the birds went up to the peacock, and said, "Friend Peacock! this king's daughter having to choose her husband from amongst so many birds, has fixed her choice upon you!"

[1] How this was done, and the lasting feud which the election gave rise to between the owl and the crow, is told at length in Jataka No. 270. The main story in Book III. of the Pañca Tantra is founded on this feud.

"Up to to-day you would not see my greatness," said the peacock, so overflowing with delight that in breach of all modesty he began to spread his wings and dance in the midst of the vast assembly,—and in dancing he exposed himself.

Then the royal Golden Goose was shocked!

And he said, "This fellow has neither modesty in his heart, nor decency in his outward behaviour! I shall not give my daughter to him. He has broken loose from all sense of shame!" And he uttered this verse to all the assembly—

"Pleasant is your cry, brilliant is your back,
Almost like the opal in its colour is your neck,
The feathers in your tail reach about a fathom's length,
But to such a dancer I can give no daughter, sir, of mine!"

Then the king in the midst of the whole assembly bestowed his daughter on a young goose, his nephew. And the peacock was covered with shame at not getting the fair gosling, and rose straight up from the place and flew away.

But the king of the Golden Geese went back to the place where he dwelt.

When the Teacher had finished this lesson in virtue, in illustration of what he had said ("Not only, O monks, has this brother now lost the jewel of the faith by immodesty, formerly also he lost a jewel of a wife by the same cause"), he made the connexion, and summed up the Jātaka, by saying, "The peacock of that time was the luxurious monk, but the King of the Geese was I myself."

END OF THE STORY ABOUT THE DANCING PEACOCK.[1]

[1] This fable forms one of those illustrations of which were carved in bas relief round the Great Tope at Bharhut. There the fair gosling is represented just choosing the peacock for her husband; so this tale must be at least sixteen hundred years old. The story has not reached Europe; but it is referred to in a stanza occurring in, according to Benfey, the oldest recension of the Pañca Tantra contained in the Berlin MS. See Benfey, i. § 98, p. 280; and Kahn, 'Sagwissenschaftliche Studien,' p. 69.

The word *Haŋsa*, which I have here translated Goose, means more exactly a wild duck; and the epithet '*Golden*' is descriptive of its beauty of colour. But the word *Haŋsa* is etymologically the same as our word Goose (compare the German Gans); and the epithet 'golden,' when applied to a goose, being meaningless as descriptive of outward appearance, gave rise to the fable of the Goose with the Golden Eggs. The latter is therefore a true 'myth,' born of a word-puzzle, invented to explain an expression which had lost its meaning through the progress of linguistic growth.

No. 33.

SAMMODAMĀNA JĀTAKA.

The sad Quarrel of the Quails.

"*So long as the birds but agree.*"—This the Master told while at the Banyan Grove, near Kapilavatthu, concerning a quarrel about a *chumbat* (a circular roll of cloth placed on the head when carrying a vessel or other weight).

This will be explained in the Kuṇāla Jātaka. At that time, namely, the Master admonishing his relations, said, "My lords! for relatives to quarrel one against another is verily most unbecoming! Even animals once, who had conquered their enemies so long as they agreed, came to great destruction when they fell out with one another." And at the request of his relatives he told the tale.

Long ago, when Brahmadatta was reigning in Benares, the Bodisat came to life as a quail; and lived in a forest at the head of a flock many thousands in number.

At that time there was a quail-catcher who used to go to the place where they dwelt, and imitate the cry of a quail; and when he saw that they had assembled together, he would throw his net over them, get them all into a heap by crushing them together in the sides of the net, and stuff them into his basket; and then going home, he used to sell them, and make a living out of the proceeds.

Now one day the Bodisat said to the quails, "This fowler is bringing our kith and kin to destruction! Now I know a stratagem to prevent his catching us. In future, as soon as he has thrown the net over you, let each one put his head through a mesh of the net, then *all* lift it up *together*, so as to carry it off to any place we like, and then let it down on to a thorn bush. When that is done, we shall each be able to escape from his place under the net!"

To this they all agreed; and the next day, as soon as the net was thrown, they lifted it up just in the way the Bodisat had told them, threw it on a thorn bush, and got away themselves from underneath. And whilst the fowler was disentangling his net from the bush, darkness had come on. And he had to go empty-handed away.

From the next day the quails always acted in the same manner: and he used to be disentangling his net till sundown, catching nothing, and going home empty-handed.

At last his wife said to him in a rage, "Day after day you come here empty-handed! I suppose you've got another establishment to keep up somewhere else!"

"My dear!" said the fowler, "I have no other establishment to keep up. But I'll tell you what it is. Those quails are living in harmony together; and as soon as I cast my net, they carry it away, and throw it on a thorn-bush. But they can't be of one mind for ever! Don't you be troubled about it. As soon as they fall out, I'll come back with every single one of them, and that'll bring a smile into your face!" And so saying, he uttered this stanza to his wife:

> "So long as the birds but agree,
> They can get away with the net;
> But when once they begin to dispute,
> Then into my clutches they fall!"

And when only a few days had gone by, one of the quails, in alighting on the ground where they fed, trod unawares on another one's head.

"Who trod on *my* head?" asked the other in a passion.

"I didn't mean to tread upon you; don't be angry," said the other; but he was angry still. And as they went on vociferating, they got to disputing with one another in such words as these: "Ah! it was you then, I suppose, who did the lifting up of the net!"

When they were so quarrelling, the Bodisat thought, "There is no depending for safety upon a quarrelsome man! No longer will these fellows lift up the net; so they will come to great destruction, and the fowler will get his chance again. I dare not stay here any more!" And he went off with his more immediate followers to some other place.

And the fowler came a few days after, and imitated the cry of a quail, and cast his net over those who came together. Then the one quail cried out:

"The talk was that the very hairs of your head fell off when you heaved up the net. Lift away, then, now!"

The other cried out, "The talk was that the very feathers of your wings fell out when you heaved up the net. Lift away, then, now!"

But as they were each calling on the other to lift away,

the hunter himself lifted up the net, bundled them all in in a heap together, crammed them into his basket, and went home, and made his wife to smile.

When the Master had finished this lesson in virtue, in illustration of what he had said ("Thus, O king, there ought to be no such thing as quarrelling among relatives; for quarrels are the root of misfortune"), he made the connexion, and summed up the Jātaka, "He who at that time was the foolish quail was Deva-datta, but the wise quail was I myself."

END OF THE STORY OF THE SAD QUARREL OF THE QUAILS.[1]

[1] Professor Benfey, in the Introduction to his Pañca Tantra (vol. i. p. 304), and Professor Fausböll in the Journal of the Royal Asiatic Society for 1870, have dealt with the history of this story. It has not been found in Europe, but occurs in somewhat altered form in the Mahā-bhārata (Book V. vv. 2455 and foll.), in the first Book of the Hitopadesa, and in the second Book of the Pañca Tantra. The Buddhist story is evidently the origin of the others.

No. 34.

MACCHA JĀTAKA.

The Fish and his Wife.

"*'Tis not the heat, 'tis not the cold.*"—This the Master told when at Jetavana, about being tempted back by one's former wife.

For on that occasion the Master asked the monk, "Is it true, then, that you are love-sick?"

"It is true, Lord!" was the reply.

"What has made you sad?"

"Sweet is the touch of the hand, Lord! of her who was formerly my wife. I cannot forsake her!"

Then the Master said, "O Brother! this woman does you harm. In a former birth also you were just being killed through her when I came up and saved you." And he told a tale.

Once upon a time, when Brahmadatta was reigning in Benāres, the Bodisat became his private chaplain.

At that time certain fishermen were casting their nets into the river. Now a big fish came swimming along playing lustily with his wife. She still in front of him smelt the smell of a net, and made a circuit, and escaped it. But the greedy amorous fish went right into the mouth of the net.

When the fishermen felt his coming in they pulled up the net, seized the fish, and threw it alive on the sand, and began to prepare a fire and a spit, intending to cook and eat it.

Then the fish lamented, saying to himself;

"The heat of the fire would not hurt me, nor the torture of the spit, nor any other pain of that sort; but that my wife should sorrow over me, thinking I must have deserted her for another, that is indeed a dire affliction!"

And he uttered this stanza—

> "'Tis not the heat, 'tis not the cold,
> 'Tis not the torture of the net;
> But that my wife should think of me,
> 'He's gone now to another for delight.'"

Now just then the chaplain came down, attended by his slaves, to bathe at the ford. And he understood the language of all animals. So on hearing the fish's lament, he thought to himself:

"This fish is lamenting the lament of sin. Should he die in this unhealthy state of mind, he will assuredly be reborn in hell. I will save him."

And he went to the fishermen, and said—

"My good men! don't you furnish a fish for us every day for our curry?"

"What is this you are saying, sir?" answered the fishermen. "Take away any fish you like!"

"We want no other: only give us this one."

"Take it, then, sir."

The Bodisat took it up in his hands, seated himself at

the river-side, and said to it, "My good fish! Had I not caught sight of you this day, you would have lost your life. Now henceforth sin no more!"

And so exhorting it, he threw it into the water, and returned to the city.

When the Teacher had finished this discourse, he proclaimed the Truths. At the end of the Truths the depressed monk was established in the fruit of conversion. Then the Teacher made the connexion, and summed up the Jātaka: "She who at that time was the female fish was the former wife, the fish was the depressed monk, but the chaplain was I myself."

END OF THE STORY OF THE FISH AND HIS WIFE.[1]

[1] This story has several points of affinity with the one above, No. 13 (pp. 211–213), on the stag who came to his death through his thoughtless love for the roe.

No. 35.

VAṬṬAKA JĀTAKA.

The Holy Quail.

"*Wings I have that will not fly.*"—This the Master told when journeying through Magadha about the going out of a Jungle Fire.

For once, when the Master was journeying through Magadha, he begged his food in a certain village in that land; and after he had returned from his rounds and had finished his meal, he started forth again, attended by the disciples. Just then a great fire arose in the jungle. Many of the monks were in front, many of them behind. And the fire came spreading on towards them, one mass of smoke and flame. Some of the monks being unconverted were terrified with the fear of death; and called out—

"Let's make a counter-fire, so that the conflagration shall not spread beyond the space burnt out by that."

And taking out their fire-sticks they began to get a light.

But the others said, "Brethren, what is this you are doing? 'Tis like failing to see the moon when it has reached the topmost sky, or the sun as it rises with its thousand rays from the eastern quarter of the world; 'tis like people standing on the beachy shore and perceiving not the ocean, or standing close to Sineru and seeing not that mighty mountain, for you—when journeying along in company with the greatest Being in earth or heaven—to call out, 'Let *us* make a counter fire,' and to take no notice of the supreme, the Buddha! You know not the power of the Buddhas! Come, let us go to the Master!"

And they all crowded together from in front, and from behind, and went up in a body near to the Mighty by Wisdom.

There the Master stopped, surrounded by the whole body of disciples.

The jungle fire came on roaring as if to overwhelm them. It came right up to the place where the Great Mortal stood, and then—as it came within about sixteen rods of that spot—it went out, like a torch thrust down into water, leaving a space of about thirty-two rods in breadth over which it could not pass!

Then the monks began to magnify the Teacher, saying;

"Oh! how marvellous are the qualities of the Buddhas! The very fire, unconscious though it be, cannot pass over the place where the Buddhas stand. Oh! how great is the might of the Buddhas!"

On hearing this the Teacher said—

"It is not, monks, through any power I have now that the fire goes out on reaching this plot of ground. It is through the power of a former act of mine. And in all this spot no fire will burn through the whole kalpa, for that was a miracle enduring through a kalpa."[1]

Then the venerable Ānanda folded a robe in four, and spread it as a seat for the Teacher. The Teacher seated himself; and when he had settled himself cross-legged, the body of disciples seated themselves reverently round him, and requested him, saying—

"What has now occurred, O Lord, is known to us. The past is hidden from us. Make it known to us."

And the Teacher told the tale.

[1] See above, p. 235.

Long ago the Bodisat entered upon a new existence as a quail in this very spot, in the land of Magadha; and after having been born in the egg, and having got out of the shell, he became a young quail, in size like a big partridge.[1] And his parents made him lie still in the nest, and fed him with food they brought in their beaks. And he had no power either to stretch out his wings and fly through the air, nor to put out his legs and walk on the earth.

Now that place was consumed year after year by a jungle fire. And just at that time the jungle fire came on with a mighty roar and seized upon it. The flocks of birds rose up, each from his nest, and flew away shrieking. And the Bodisat's parents too, terrified with the fear of death, forsook the Bodisat, and fled.

When the Bodisat, lying there as he was, stretched forth his neck, and saw the conflagration spreading towards him, he thought: "If I had the power of stretching my wings and flying in the air, or of putting out my legs, and walking on the ground, I could get away to some other place. But I can't! And my parents too, terrified with the fear of death, have left me all alone, and flown away to save themselves. No other help can I expect from others, and in myself I find no help. What in the world shall I do now!"

But then it occurred to him, "In this world there is such a thing as the efficacy of virtue; there is such a thing as the efficacy of truth. There are men known as omniscient Buddhas, who become Buddhas when seated under the Bo-tree through having fulfilled the Great Virtues in the long ages of the past; who have gained

[1] Bheṇḍuka.

salvation by the wisdom arising from good deeds and earnest thought, and have gained too the power of showing to others the knowledge of that salvation; who are full of truth, and compassion, and mercy, and long-suffering; and whose hearts reach out in equal love to all beings that have life. To me, too, the Truth is one, there seems to be but one eternal and true Faith. It behoves me, therefore—meditating on the Buddhas of the past and on the attributes that they have gained, and relying on the one true faith there is in me—to perform an Act of Truth; and thus to drive back the fire, and procure safety both for myself, and for the other birds."

Therefore it is said (in the Scriptures)—

"There's power in virtue in the world—
In truth, and purity, and love!
In that truth's name I'll now perform
A mystic Act of Truth sublime.

Then thinking on the power of the Faith,
And on the Conquerors in ages past,
Relying on the power of the Truth,
I then performed the Miracle!"

Then the Bodisat called to mind the attributes of the Buddhas who had long since passed away; and, making a solemn asseveration of the true faith existing in himself, he performed the Act of Truth, uttering the verse—

"Wings I have that will not fly,
Feet I have that will not walk;
My parents, too, are fled away!
O All-embracing Fire—go back!"[1]

[1] It is difficult to convey the impression of the mystic epithet here used of fire. *Jātaveda* must mean "he who possesses (or perhaps possesses the

Then before him and his Act of Truth the Element went back a space of sixteen rods; but in receding it did not return to consume the forest; it went out immediately it came to the spot, like a torch plunged into water.

Therefore it is said—

> "For me and for my Act of Truth
> The great and burning fire went out,
> Leaving a space of sixteen rods,
> As fire, with water mixed, goes out."

And as that spot has escaped being overwhelmed by fire through all this *kalpa*, this is said to be 'a kalpa-enduring miracle.' The Bodisat having thus performed the Act of Truth, passed away, at the end of his life, according to his deeds.

When the Teacher had finished this discourse, in illustration of what he had said ("That this wood is not passed over by the fire is not a result, O monks, of my present power; but of the power of the Act of Truth I exercised as a new-born quail"), he proclaimed the Truths. At the conclusion of the Truths some were Converted, some reached the Second Path, some the Third, some the Fourth. And the Teacher made the connexion, and summed up the Jātaka, "My parents at that time were my present parents, but the King of the Quails was I myself."

END OF THE STORY OF THE HOLY QUAIL.[1]

knowledge of) all that is produced." It is used not infrequently in the Vedic literature as a peculiarly holy and mystical epithet of Agni, the personification of the mysterious element of fire, and seems to refer to its far-reaching, all-embracing power.

[1] This story is referred to as one of the 'kalpa-enduring miracles' in Jātaka No. 20 above, p. 235.

No. 36.

SAKUṆA JĀTAKA.

The Wise Bird and the Fools.

"*The earth-born tree.*"—This the Master told when at Jetavana, about a monk whose hut was burned.

A certain monk, says the tradition, received from the Teacher a subject for meditation, and leaving Jetavana, took up his abode in a dwelling in a forest near a border village, belonging to the people of Kosala.

Now in the very first month his hut was burned down; and he told the people, saying, "My hut is burnt down, and I live in discomfort."

"Our fields are all dried up now," said they; "we must first irrigate the lands." When they were well muddy, "We must sow the seed," said they. When the seed was sown, "We must put up the fences," was the excuse. When the fences were up, they declared, "There will be cutting, and reaping, and treading-out to do." And thus, telling first of one thing to be done and then of another, they let three months slip by.

The monk passed the three months in discomfort in the open air, and concluded his meditation, but could not bring the rest of his religious exercise to completion. So when Lent was over he returned to the Teacher, and saluting him, took his seat respectfully on one side.

The Teacher bade him welcome, and then asked him,

"Well, brother, have you spent Lent in comfort? Have you brought your meditation to its conclusion?"

He told him what had happened, and said, "As I had no suitable lodging, I did not fully complete the meditation."

"Formerly, O monk," said the Teacher, "even animals were aware what was suitable for them, and what was not. Why did not you know it?"

And he told a tale.

Long ago, when Brahma-datta was reigning in Benāres, the Bodisat came to life again as a bird, and lived a forest life, attended by a flock of birds, near a lofty tree, with branches forking out on every side.

Now one day dust began to fall as the branches of the tree rubbed one against another. Then smoke began to rise. The Bodisat thought, on seeing this,—

"If these two branches go on rubbing like that they will send out sparks of fire, and the fire will fall down and seize on the withered leaves; and the tree itself will soon after be consumed. We can't stop here; we ought to get away at once to some other place." And he addressed the flock in this verse:

> "The earth-born tree, on which
> We children of the air depend,
> It, even it, is now emitting fire.
> Seek then the skies, ye birds!
> Behold! our very home and refuge
> Itself has brought forth danger!"

Then such of the birds as were wise, and hearkened to

the voice of the Bodisat, flew up at once with him into the air, and went elsewhere. But such as were foolish said one to another, "Just so! Just so! He's always seeing crocodiles in a drop of water!" And paying no attention to what he said, they stopped there.

And not long afterwards fire was produced precisely in the way the Bodisat had foreseen, and the tree caught fire. And smoke and flames rising aloft, the birds were blinded by the smoke; they could not get away, and one after another they fell into the fire, and were burnt to death!

When the Teacher had finished this discourse with the words, "Thus formerly, O monk, even the birds dwelling on the tree-tops knew which place would suit them and which would not. How is it that you knew it not?" he proclaimed the Truths. At the conclusion of the Truths the monk was established in Conversion. And the Teacher made the connexion, and summed up the Jātaka, "The birds who at that time listened to the voice of the Bodisat were the followers of the Buddha, but the Wise Bird was I myself."

END OF THE STORY OF THE WISE BIRD AND THE FOOLS.

No. 37.

TITTIRA JĀTAKA.

The Partridge, Monkey, and Elephant.

"*'Tis those who reverence the aged.*"—This the Master told on the road to Sāvatthi about Sāriputta being kept out of a night's lodging.

For when Anātha Piṇḍika had finished his monastery, and sent word to the Teacher, the latter left Rājagaha and arrived at Vesali; and after resting there a short time, he set out again on the road to Sāvatthi.[1]

On that occasion the pupils of the Six went on in front, and before lodgings had been taken for the Elders, occupied all the places to be had, saying,—

"This is for our superior, this for our instructor, and these for us."

The Elders who came up afterwards found no place to sleep in. Even Sāriputta's pupils sought in vain for a lodging-place for the Elder. So the Elder having no lodging passed the night either walking up and down, or sitting at the foot of a tree, not far from the place where the Teacher was lodged.

In the early morning the Teacher came out and coughed. The Elder coughed too.

"Who's there?" said the Teacher.

"'Tis I, Lord; Sāriputta," was the reply.

[1] See above, p. 130.

"What are you doing here, so early, Sāriputta?" asked he.

Then he told him what had happened; and on hearing what the Elder said, the Teacher thought,—

"If the monks even now, while I am yet living, show so little respect and courtesy to one another, what will they do when I am dead?" And he was filled with anxiety for the welfare of the Truth.

As soon as it was light he called all the priests together, and asked them—

"Is it true, priests, as I have been told, that the Six went on in front, and occupied all the lodging-places to the exclusion of the Elders?"

"It is true, O Blessed One!" said they.

Then he reproved the Six, and addressing the monks, taught them a lesson, saying,—

"Who is it, then, O monks, who deserves the best seat, and the best water, and the best rice?"

Some said, "A nobleman who has become a monk." Some said, "A Brāhman, or the head of a family who has become a monk." Others said, "The man versed in the Rules of the Order; an Expounder of the Law; one who has attained to the First Jhāna, or the Second, or the Third, or the Fourth." Others again said, "The Converted man; or one in the Second or the Third Stage of the Path to Nirvāna; or an Arahat; or one who knows the Three Truths; or one who has the Sixfold Wisdom."[1]

When the monks had thus declared whom they each thought worthy of the best seat, and so on, the Teacher said:

"In my religion, O monks, it is not the being ordained from a noble, or a priestly, or a wealthy family; it is not being versed in the Rules of the Order, or in the general or the metaphysical books of the Scriptures; it is not the attainment of the Jhānas, or progress in the Path of

[1] See the translator's 'Buddhism,' pp. 108 and 174–177 (2nd edition).

Nirvāna, that is the standard by which the right to the best seat, and so on, is to be judged. But in my religion, O monks, reverence, and service, and respect, and civility, are to be paid according to age; and for the aged the best seat, and the best water, and the best rice are to be reserved. This is the right standard; and therefore the senior monk is entitled to these things. And now, monks, Sāriputta is my chief disciple; he is a second founder of the Kingdom of Righteousness, and deserves to receive a lodging immediately after myself. He has had to pass the night without a lodging at the foot of a tree. If you have even now so little respect and courtesy, what will you not do as time goes on?"

And for their further instruction he said:

"Formerly, O monks, even animals used to say, 'It would not be proper for us to be disrespectful and wanting in courtesy to one another, and not to live on proper terms with one another. We should find out who is eldest, and pay him honour.' So they carefully investigated the matter, and having discovered the senior among them, they paid him honour; and so when they passed away, they entered the abode of the gods."

And he told a tale.

Long ago there were three friends living near a great Banyan-tree, on the slope of the Himālaya range of mountains—a Partridge, a Monkey, and an Elephant. And they were wanting in respect and courtesy for one another, and did not live together on befitting terms.

But it occurred to them, "It is not right for us to live in this manner. What if we were to cultivate respect towards whichever of us is the eldest?"

"But which is the eldest?" was then the question;

until one day they thought, "This will be a good way for finding it out;" and the Monkey and the Partridge asked the Elephant, as they were all sitting together at the foot of the Banyan-tree—

"Elephant dear! How big was this Banyan Tree at the time you first knew it?"

"Friends!" said he, "When I was little I used to walk over this Banyan, then a mere bush, keeping it between my thighs; and when I stood with it between my legs, its highest branches touched my navel. So I have known it since it was a shrub."

Then they both asked the Monkey in the same way. And he said, "Friends! when I was quite a little monkey I used to sit on the ground and eat the topmost shoots of this Banyan, then quite young, by merely stretching out my neck. So that I have known it from its earliest infancy."

Then again the two others asked the Partridge as before. And he said—

"Friends! There was formerly a lofty Banyan-tree in such and such a place, whose fruit I ate and voided the seeds here. From that this tree grew up: so that I have known it even from before the time when it was born, and am older than either of you!"

Thereupon the Elephant and the Monkey said to the clever Partridge—

"You, friend, are the oldest of us all. Henceforth we will do all manner of service for you, and pay you reverence, and make salutations before you, and treat you with every respect and courtesy, and abide by your counsels. Do you in future give us whatever counsel and instruction we require."

Thenceforth the Partridge gave them counsel, and kept them up to their duty, and himself observed his own. So they three kept the Five Commandments; and since they were courteous and respectful to one another, and lived on befitting terms one with another, they became destined for heaven when their lives should end.

"The holy life of these three became known as 'The Holiness of the Partridge.' For they, O monks, lived in courtesy and respect towards one another. How then can you, who have taken the vows in so well-taught a religion, live without courtesy and respect towards one another? Henceforth, O monks, I enjoin upon you reverence, and service, and respect, according to age; the giving of the best seats, the best water, and the best food according to age; and that the senior shall never be kept out of a night's lodging by a junior. Whoever so keeps out his senior shall be guilty of an offence."

It was when the Teacher had thus concluded his discourse that he, as Buddha, uttered the verse—

"'Tis those who reverence the old
That are the men versed in the Faith.
Worthy of praise while in this life,
And happy in the life to come."

When the Teacher had thus spoken on the virtue of paying reverence to the old, he established the connexion, and summed up the Jātaka, by saying, "The elephant of that time was Moggallāna, the monkey Sāriputta, but the partridge was I myself."

END OF THE STORY OF THE PARTRIDGE, THE MONKEY, AND THE ELEPHANT.[1]

[1] This Birth Story, with the same Introductory Story, is found, in nearly identical terms, in the Culla Vagga (vi. 6). The story, therefore, is at least as old as the fourth century B.C. Jātaka No. 117 is also called the Tittira Jātaka.

No. 38.

BAKA JĀTAKA.

The Cruel Crane Outwitted.

"*The villain though exceeding clever.*"—This the Master told when at Jetavana about a monk who was a tailor.

There was a monk, says the tradition, living at Jetavana, who was exceeding skilful at all kinds of things that can be done to a robe, whether cutting out, or piecing together, or valuing, or sewing it. Through this cleverness of his he was always engaged in making robes, until he became known as 'The robe-maker.'

Now what used he to do but exercise his handicraft on some old pieces of cloth, so as to make out of them a robe soft and pleasant to the touch; and when he had dyed it, he would steep it in mealy water, and rub it with a chank-shell so as to make it bright and attractive, and then lay it carefully by. And monks who did not understand robe work, would come to him with new cloths, and say—

"We don't understand how to make robes. Be so kind as to make this into a robe for us."

Then he would say, "It takes a long time, Brother, before a robe can be made. But I have a robe ready made. You had better leave these cloths here and take that away with you."

And he would take it out and show it to them.

And they, seeing of how fine a colour it was, and not noticing any difference, would give their new cloths to the tailor-monk, and take the robe away with them, thinking it would last. But when it grew a little dirty, and they washed it in warm water, it would appear as it really was, and the worn-out places would show themselves here and there upon it. Then, too late, they would repent.

And that monk became notorious, as one who passed off old rags upon anybody who came to him.

Now there was another robe-maker in a country village who used to cheat everybody just like the man at Jetavana. And some monks who knew him very well told him about the other, and said to him—

"Sir! there is a monk at Jetavana who, they say, cheats all the world in such and such a manner."

"Ah!" thought he, "'twould be a capital thing if I could outwit that city fellow!"

And he made a fine robe out of old clothes, dyed it a beautiful red, put it on, and went to Jetavana. As soon as the other saw it, he began to covet it, and asked him—

"Is this robe one of your own making, sir?"

"Certainly, Brother," was the reply.

"Sir! let me have the robe. You can take another for it," said he.

"But, Brother, we village monks are but badly provided. If I give you this, what shall I have to put on?"

"I have some new cloths, sir, by me. Do you take those and make a robe for yourself."

"Well, Brother! this is my own handiwork; but if you talk like that, what can I do? You may have it," said the other; and giving him the robe made of old rags, he took away the new cloths in triumph.

And the man of Jetavana put on the robe; but when a few days after he discovered, on washing it, that it was made of rags, he was covered with confusion. And it became noised abroad in the order, "That Jetavana robe-maker has been outwitted, they say, by a man from the country!"

And one day the monks sat talking about this in the Lecture Hall, when the Teacher came up and asked them what they were talking about, and they told him the whole matter.

Then the Teacher said, "Not now only has the Jetavana robe-maker taken other people in in this way, in a former birth he did the same. And not now only has he been outwitted by the countryman, in a former birth he was outwitted too." And he told a tale.

Long ago the Bodisat was born to a forest life as the Genius of a tree standing near a certain lotus pond.

Now at that time the water used to run short at the dry season in a certain pond, not over large, in which there were a good many fish. And a crane thought, on seeing the fish—

"I must outwit these fish somehow or other and make a prey of them."

And he went and sat down at the edge of the water, thinking how he should do it.

When the fish saw him, they asked him, "What are you sitting there for, lost in thought?"

"I am sitting thinking about you," said he.

"Oh, sir! what are you thinking about us?" said they.

"Why," he replied; "there is very little water in this pond, and but little for you to eat; and the heat is so great! So I was thinking, 'What in the world will these fish do now?'"

"Yes, indeed, sir! what *are* we to do?" said they.

"If you will only do as I bid you, I will take you in

my beak to a fine large pond, covered with all the kinds of lotuses, and put you into it," answered the crane.

"That a crane should take thought for the fishes is a thing unheard of, Sir, since the world began. It's eating us, one after the other, that you're aiming at!"

"Not I! So long as you trust me, I won't eat you. But if you don't believe me that there is such a pond, send one of you with me to go and see it."

Then they trusted him, and handed over to him one of their number—a big fellow, blind of one eye, whom they thought sharp enough in any emergency, afloat or ashore.

Him the crane took with him, let him go in the pond, showed him the whole of it, brought him back, and let him go again close to the other fish. And he told them all the glories of the pond.

And when they heard what he said, they exclaimed, "All right, Sir! You may take us with you."

Then the crane took the old purblind fish first to the bank of the other pond, and alighted in a Varaṇa-tree growing on the bank there. But he threw it into a fork of the tree, struck it with his beak, and killed it; and then ate its flesh, and threw its bones away at the foot of the tree. Then he went back and called out—

"I've thrown that fish in; let another come!"

And in that manner he took all the fish, one by one, and ate them, till he came back and found no more!

But there was still a crab left behind there; and the crane thought he would eat him too, and called out—

"I say, good crab, I've taken all the fish away, and put them into a fine large pond. Come along. I'll take you too!"

"But how will you take hold of me to carry me along?"

"I'll bite hold of you with my beak."

"You'll let me fall if you carry me like that. I won't go with you!"

"Don't be afraid! I'll hold you quite tight all the way."

Then said the crab to himself, "If this fellow once got hold of fish, he would never let them go in a pond! Now if he should really put me into the pond, it would be capital; but if he doesn't—then I'll cut his throat, and kill him!" So he said to him—

"Look here, friend, you won't be able to hold me tight enough; but we crabs have a famous grip. If you let me catch hold of you round the neck with my claws, I shall be glad to go with you."

And the other did not see that he was trying to outwit him, and agreed. So the crab caught hold of his neck with his claws as securely as with a pair of blacksmith's pincers, and called out, "Off with you, now!"

And the crane took him and showed him the pond, and then turned off towards the Varaṇa-tree.

"Uncle!" cried the crab, "the pond lies that way, but you are taking me this way!"

"Oh, that's it, is it!" answered the crane. "Your dear little uncle, your very sweet nephew, you call me! You mean me to understand, I suppose, that I am your slave, who has to lift you up and carry you about with him! Now cast your eye upon the heap of fish-bones lying at the root of yonder Varaṇa-tree. Just as I have eaten those fish, every one of them, just so I will devour you as well!"

"Ah! those fishes got eaten through their own stupidity," answered the crab; "but I'm not going to let you eat *me.* On the contrary, it is *you* that I am going to destroy. For you in your folly have not seen that I was outwitting you. If we die, we die both together; for I will cut off this head of yours, and cast it to the ground!" And so saying, he gave the crane's neck a grip with his claws, as with a vice.

Then gasping, and with tears trickling from his eyes, and trembling with the fear of death, the crane beseeched him, saying, "O my Lord! Indeed I did not intend to eat you. Grant me my life!"

"Well, well! step down into the pond, and put me in there."

And he turned round and stepped down into the pond, and placed the crab on the mud at its edge. But the crab cut through its neck as clean as one would cut a lotus-stalk with a hunting-knife, and then only entered the water!

When the Genius who lived in the Varaṇa-tree saw this strange affair, he made the wood resound with his plaudits, uttering in a pleasant voice the verse—

"The villain, though exceeding clever,
Shall prosper not by his villany.
He may win indeed, sharp-witted in deceit,
But only as the Crane here from the Crab!"

When the Teacher had finished this discourse, showing that "Not now only, O mendicants, has this man been outwitted by the country robe-maker, long ago he was outwitted in the same way," he established the connexion, and summed up the Jātaka, by saying, "At that time he was the Jetavana robe-maker, the crab was the country robe-maker, but the Genius of the Tree was I myself."

END OF THE STORY OF THE CRUEL CRANE OUTWITTED.[1]

[1] This fable is a great favourite. It was among those translated into the Syriac and Arabic, and has been retained in all the versions of the Kalila and Dimna series, while it occurs in the Arabian Nights, and in the story-books of the Northern Buddhists and of the Hindus. It has been already traced through all the following story-books (whose full titles, and historical connexion, are given in the Tables appended to the Introduction to this volume).

Kalilag und Dimnag, pp. 12, 13.
Sylvestre de Sacy, chapter v.
Wolf, vol. i. p. 41.
Anvār i Suhaili, p. 117.
Knatchbull, pp. 113–115.
Symeon Seth (Athens edition), p. 16.
John of Capua, c. 4 b.
'Ulm' German text, D. V. b.
The Spanish version, xiii. 6.
Firenzuola, p. 39.
Doni, p. 59.
Livre des Lumières, p. 92.
Cabinet des Fées, xvii. p. 221.
Livre des Merveilles (du Meril in a note to Batalo, p. 238).
Contes et Fables Indiennes de Bidpai et de Lokman, i. p. 357.
La Fontaine, x. 4.
Arabian Nights (Weil, iv. 915).
Pañca Tantra, i. 7 (comp. ii. 58).
Hitopadesa, iv. 7 (Max Müller. p. 118).
Kathā Sarit Sāgara Tar. lx. 79–90.
Dhammapada, p. 155.

Professor Benfey has devoted a long note to the history of the story (Introduction to the Pañca Tantra, i. 174, § 60), and I have only succeeded in adding, in a few details, to his results. The tale is told very lamely, as compared with the Pāli original, in all those versions I have been able to consult. It is strange that so popular a tale was not included by Planudes or his successors in their collections of so-called Æsop's Fables.

No. 39.

NANDA JĀTAKA.

Nanda on the Buried Gold.

"*The golden heap, methinks.*"—This the Master told while at Jetavana, about a monk living under Sāriputta.

He, they say, was meek, and mild of speech, and served the Elder with great devotion. Now on one occasion the Elder had taken leave of the Master, started on a tour, and gone to the mountain country in the south of Magadha. When they had arrived there, the monk became proud, followed no longer the word of the Elder; and when he was asked to do a thing, would even become angry with the Elder.

The Elder could not understand what it all meant. When his tour was over, he returned again to Jetavana; and from the moment he arrived at the monastery, the monk became as before. This the Elder told the Master, saying,—

"Lord! there is a mendicant in my division of the Order, who in one place is like a slave bought for a hundred, and in another becomes proud, and refuses with anger to do what he is asked."

Then the Teacher said, "Not only now, Sāriputta, has the monk behaved like that; in a former birth also, when in one place he was like a slave bought for a hundred, and in another was angrily independent."

And at the Elder's request he told the story.

Long ago, when Brahma-datta was reigning in Benāres, the Bodisat came to life again as a landowner. He had a friend, also a landowner, who was old himself, but whose wife was young. She had a son by him; and he said to himself,—

"As this woman is young, she will, after my death, be taking some husband to herself, and squandering the money I have saved. What, now, if I were to make away with the money under the earth?"

And he took a slave in the house named Nanda, went into the forest, buried the treasure in a certain spot of which he informed the slave, and instructed him, saying, "My good Nanda! when I am gone, do you let my son know where the treasure is; and be careful the wood is not sold!"

Very soon after he died; and in due course his son became of age. And his mother said to him, "My dear! your father took Nanda the slave with him, and buried his money. You should have it brought back, and put the family estates into order."

And one day he accordingly said to Nanda, "Uncle! is there any money which my father buried?"

"Yes, Sir!" said he.

"Where is it buried?"

"In the forest, Sir."

"Then come along there." And taking a spade and a bag, he went to the place whereabouts the treasure was, and said, "Now, uncle, where is the money?"

But when Nanda had got up on to the spot above the treasure, he became so proud of it, that he abused his young master roundly, saying, "You servant! You son of a slave-girl! Where, then, did you get treasure from here?"

The young master made as though he had not heard the abuse; and simply saying, "Come along, then," took him back again. But two or three days after he went to the spot again; when Nanda, however, abused him as before.

The young man gave him no harsh word in reply, but turned back, saying to himself,—

"This slave goes to the place fully intending to point out the treasure; but as soon as he gets there, he begins to be insolent. I don't understand the reason of this. But there's that squire, my father's friend. I'll ask him about it, and find out what it is."

So he went to the Bodisat, told him the whole matter, and asked him the reason of it.

Then said the Bodisat, "On the very spot, my young friend, where Nanda stands when he is insolent, there must your father's treasure be. So as soon as Nanda begins to abuse you, you should answer, 'Come now, slave, who is it you're talking too?' drag him down, take the spade, dig into that spot, take out the treasure, and then make the slave lift it up and carry it home!" And so saying he uttered this verse—

> "The golden heap, methinks, the jewelled gold,
> Is just where Nanda, the base-born, the slave,
> Thunders out swelling words of vanity!"

Then the young squire took leave of the Bodisat, went home, took Nanda with him to the place where the treasure was, acted exactly as he had been told, brought back the treasure, put the family estates into order; and following the exhortations of the Bodisat, gave gifts, and did other good works, and at the end of his life passed away according to his deeds.

When the Teacher had finished this discourse, showing how formerly also he had behaved the same, he established the connexion, and summed up the Jātaka, "At that time Nanda was the monk under Sāriputta, but the wise squire was I myself."

END OF THE STORY OF NANDA ON THE BURIED GOLD.[1]

[1] In the so-called Æsop's Fables are several on the text that a haughty spirit goeth before a fall; for instance, 'The Charger and the Ass,' 'The Bull and the Frog,' and 'The Oats and the Reeds'; but this is the only story I know directed against the pride arising from the temporary possession of wealth.

No. 40.

KHADIRANGĀRA JĀTAKA.

The Fiery Furnace.

"*Far rather will I fall into this hell.*"—This the Master told while at Jetavana, about Anātha Piṇḍika.

For Anātha Piṇḍika having squandered fifty-four thousands of thousands in money on the Buddhist Faith about the Monastery, and holding nothing elsewhere in the light of a treasure, save only the Three Treasures (the Buddha, the Truth, and the Order), used to go day after day to take part in the Three Great Services, once in the morning, once after breakfast, and once in the evening.

There are intermediate services too. And he never went empty-handed, lest the lads, and the younger brethren, should look to see what he might have brought. When he went in the morning he would take porridge; after breakfast ghee, butter, honey, molasses, and so on; in the evening perfumes, garlands, and robes. Thus offering day after day, the sum of his gifts was beyond all measure. Traders, too, left writings with him, and took money on loan from him up to eighteen thousands of thousands, and the great merchant asked it not again of them. Other eighteen thousands of thousands, the property of his family, was put away and buried in the river bank; and when the bank was broken in by a storm they were washed away to the sea, and the brazen pots rolled just as they were—closed and sealed—to the bottom of the ocean. In his house again a constant supply of rice was ordered to be kept in readiness for five hundred members of the Order, so that the Merchant's house was to the Order like a public pool dug where four high roads meet; and he stood to them in the place of father and mother. On that account even the Supreme Buddha himself used to go to his residence; and the Eighty Chief Elders also; and the number of other monks coming and going was beyond measure.

Now his mansion was seven stories high, and there were seven great gates to it, with battlemented turrets over them; and in the fourth turret there dwelt a fairy who was a heretic. When the Supreme Buddha entered the house, she was unable to stop up above in the turret, but used to bring her children downstairs and stand on the ground floor; and so she did when the Eighty Chief Elders, or the other monks were coming in or going out.[1]

And she thought, "So long as this mendicant Gotama and his disciples come to the house, there is no peace for me. I can't be eternally going downstairs again and again, to stand on the ground floor; I must manage so that they come no more to the house."

So one day, as soon as the chief business manager had retired to rest, she went to him, and stood before him in visible shape.

"Who's there?" said he.

"It's I; the Fairy who dwells in the turret over the fourth gate."

"What are you come for?"

"You are not looking after the Merchant's affairs. Paying no thought to his last days, he takes out all his money, and makes the mendicant Gotama full of it. He undertakes no business, and sets no work on foot. Do

[1] It is a great breach of etiquette for an inferior to remain in any place above that where his superior is.

you speak to the Merchant so that he may attend to his business; and make arrangements so that that mendicant Gotama and his disciples shall no longer come to the place."

But the other said to her, "O foolish Fairy! the Merchant in spending his money spends it on the religion of the Buddhas, which leadeth to salvation. Though I should be seized by the hair, and sold for a slave, I will say no such thing. Begone with you!"

Another day the Fairy went to the Merchant's eldest son, and persuaded him in the same manner. But he refused her as before. And to the Merchant himself she did not dare to speak.

Now by constantly giving gifts, and doing no business, the Merchant's income grew less and less, and his wealth went to ruin. And as he sank more and more into poverty, his property, and his dress, and his furniture, and his food were no longer as they had been. He nevertheless still used to give gifts to the Order; but he was no longer able to give of the best.

One day when he had taken his seat, after saluting the Teacher, he said to him, "Well, householder! are gifts still given at your house?"

"They are still being given, Lord," said he, "but only a mere trifle of stale second day's porridge."

Then said the Master to him, "Don't let your heart be troubled, householder, that you give only what is unpleasant to the taste. For if the heart be only right, a gift given to Buddhas, or Pacceka Buddhas,[1] or their disciples, can never be otherwise than right. And why? Through the greatness of the result. For that he who can cleanse his heart can never give unclean gifts is declared in the passage—

[1] One who has the power of gaining salvation for himself; but not of giving others the knowledge of it. The Birth Story to which this is an Introduction is about a gift to a Pacceka Buddha.

If only there be a believing heart,
There is no such thing as a trifling gift
To the Mortal One, Buddha, or his disciples.
There is no such thing as a trifling service
To the Buddhas, to the Illustrious Ones;
If you only can see the fruit that may follow,
E'en a gift of stale gruel, dried up, without salt!

And again he said to him, "Householder! although the gift you are giving is but poor, you are giving it to the Eight Noble Beings.[1] Now when I was Velāma, and gave away the Seven Treasures, ransacking the whole continent of India to find them, and kept up a great donation, as if I had turned the five great rivers into one great mass of water, yet I attained not even to taking refuge in the Three Gems, or to keeping the Five Precepts, so unfit were they who received the gifts. Let not your heart be troubled, therefore, because your gifts are trifling." And so saying, he preached to him the Velāmika Sutta.

Now the Fairy, who before had not cared to speak to the Merchant, thinking, "Now that this man has come to poverty, he will listen to what I say," went at midnight to his chamber, and appeared in visible shape before him.

"Who's there?" said the Merchant on seeing her.

"'Tis I, great Merchant; the Fairy who dwells in the turret over the fourth gate."

"What are you come for?"

"Because I wish to give you some advice."

"Speak, then."

"O great Merchant! you take no thought of your last days. You regard not your sons and daughters. You have squandered much wealth on the religion of Gotama

[1] *Ariya-puggalas*, the persons who, by self-culture and self-control, have entered respectively on the Four Stages, and have reached the Four Fruits of the Noble Eightfold Path.

the mendicant. By spending your money for so long a time, and by undertaking no fresh business, you have become poor for the sake of the mendicant Gotama. Even so you are not rid of the mendicant Gotama. Up to this very day the mendicants swarm into your house. What you have lost you can never restore again; but henceforth neither go yourself to the mendicant Gotama, nor allow his disciples to enter your house. Turn not back even to behold the mendicant Gotama, but attend to your own business, and to your own merchandize, and so re-establish the family estates."

Then said he to her, "Is this the advice you have to offer me?"

"Yes; this is it."

"He whose power is Wisdom has made me immovable by a hundred, or thousand, or even a hundred thousand supernatural beings such as you. For my faith is firm and established like the great mountain Sineru. I have spent my wealth on the Treasure of the Religion that leads to Salvation. What you say is wrong; it is a blow that is given to the Religion of the Buddhas by so wicked a hag as you are, devoid of affection. It is impossible for me to live in the same house with you. Depart quickly from my house, and begone elsewhere!"

When she heard the words of the converted, saintly disciple, she dared not stay; and going to the place where she dwelt, she took her children by the hand, and went away. But though she went, she determined, if she could get no other place of abode, to obtain the Merchant's forgiveness, and return and dwell even there. So she went to, the guardian god of the city, and saluted him, and stood respectfully before him.

"What are you come here for?" said he.

"Sir! I have been speaking thoughtlessly to Anātha Piṇḍika; and he, enraged with me, has driven me out from the place where I dwelt. Take me to him, and persuade him to forgive me, and give me back my dwelling-place."

"What is it you said to him?"

"'Henceforth give no support to the Buddha, or to the Order of Mendicants, and forbid the mendicant Gotama the entry into your house.' This, Sir, is what I said."

"You said wrong. It was a blow aimed at religion. I can't undertake to go with you to the Merchant!"

Getting no help from him, she went to the four Archangels, the guardians of the world. And when she was refused by them in the same manner, she went to Sakka, the King of the Gods, and telling him the whole matter, besought him urgently, saying, "O God! deprived of my dwelling-place, I wander about without a shelter, leading my children by the hand. Let me in your graciousness be given some place where I may dwell!"

And he, too, said to her, "You have done wrong! You have aimed a blow at the religion of the Conqueror. It is impossible for me to speak on your behalf to the Merchant. But I can tell you one means by which the Merchant may pardon you."

"It is well, O God. Tell me what that may be!"

"People have had eighteen thousands of thousands of money from the Merchant on giving him writings. Now take the form of his manager, and without telling anybody, take those writings, surround yourself with so many young ogres, go to their houses with the writings in one hand, and a receipt in the other, and stand in the centre of the house and frighten them with your demon power, and say, 'This is the record of your debt. Our Merchant said nothing to you in byegone days; but now he is fallen into poverty. Pay back the moneys which you had from him.' Thus, by displaying your demon power, recover all those thousands of gold, and pour them into the Merchant's empty treasury. There was other wealth of his buried in the bank of the river Aciravatī, which, when the river-bank was broken, was washed away to the sea. Bring that back by your power, and pour it into his treasury. In such and such a place, too, there is another treasure of the sum of eighteen thousands of thousands, which has no owner. That too bring, and pour it into his empty treasury. When you have undergone this punishment of refilling his empty treasury with these fifty-four thousands of thousands, you may ask the Merchant to forgive you."

"Very well, my Lord!" said she; and agreed to what he said, and brought back all the money in the way she was told; and at midnight entered the Merchant's bed-chamber, and stood before him in visible shape.

"Who's there?" said he.

"It is I, great Merchant! the blind and foolish Fairy who used to dwell in the turret over your fourth gate. In my great and dense stupidity, and knowing not the merits of the Buddha, I formerly said something to you; and that fault I beg you to pardon. For according to the word of Sakka, the King of the Gods, I have performed the punishment of filling your empty treasury with fifty-four thousands of thousands I have brought—the eighteen thousands of thousands owing to you which I have recovered, the eighteen thousands of thousands lost in the sea, and eighteen thousands of thousands of ownerless money in such and such a place. The money you spent on the monastery at Jetavana is now all restored. I am in misery so long as I am allowed no place to dwell in. Keep not in your mind the thing I did in my ignorance, but pardon me, O great Merchant!"

When he heard what she said, Anātha Piṇḍika thought, "She is a goddess, and she says she has undergone her punishment, and she confesses her sin. The Master shall consider this, and make his goodness known. I will take her before the Supreme Buddha." And he said to her, "Dear Fairy! if you wish to ask me to pardon you, ask it in the presence of the Buddha!"

"Very well. I will do so," said she. "Take me with you to the Master!"

To this he agreed. And when the night was just passing away, he took her, very early in the morning, to the presence of the Master; and told him all that she had done.

When the Master heard it, he said, "You see, O householder, how the sinful man looks upon sin as pleasant, so long as it bears no fruit; but when its fruit ripens, then he looks upon it as sin. And so the good man looks upon his goodness as sin so long as it bears no fruit; but when its fruit ripens, then he sees its goodness." And so saying, he uttered the two stanzas in the Scripture Verses:

The sinner thinks the sin is good,
So long as it hath ripened not;
But when the sin has ripened, then
The sinner sees that it was sin!

The good think goodness is but sin,
So long as it hath ripened not;
But when the good has ripened, then
The good man sees that it was good!

And at the conclusion of the verses the Fairy was established in the Fruit of Conversion. And she fell at the wheel-marked feet of the Teacher, and said, "My Lord! lustful, and infidel, and blind as I was, I spake wicked words in my ignorance of your character. Grant me thy pardon!"

Then she obtained pardon both from the Teacher and from the Merchant.

On that occasion Anātha Piṇḍika began to extol his own merit in the Teacher's presence, saying, "My Lord! though this Fairy forbad me to support the Buddha, she could not stop me; and though she forbad me to give gifts, I gave them still. Shall not this be counted to my merit, O my Lord?"

But the Teacher said, "You, O householder, are a Converted person, and one of the Elect disciples. Your faith is firm, you have the clear insight of those who are walking in the First Path. It is no wonder that you were not turned back at the bidding of this weak Fairy. But that formerly the wise who lived at a time when a Buddha had not appeared, and when knowledge was not matured, should still have given gifts, though Māra, the Lord of the angels of the Realms of Lust, stood in the sky, and told them to give no gifts; and showing them a pit full of live coals eighty cubits deep, called out to them, 'If you give the gift, you shall be burnt in this hell'—that was a wonder!"

And at the request of Anātha Piṇḍika, he told the tale.

Long ago, when Brahma-datta was reigning in Beṇāres, the Bodisat came to life in the family of the Treasurer of Benāres, and was brought up in much luxury, like a prince. And he arrived in due course at years of discretion; and even when he was but sixteen years old he had gained the mastery over all branches of knowledge.

At the death of his father he was appointed to the office of Treasurer, and had six Gift-halls built,—four at the four gates, and one in the midst of the city, and one at the entrance to his mansion. And he gave Gifts, and kept the Precepts, and observed the Sabbath-days.

Now one day when pleasant food of all sweet tastes was being taken in for the Bodisat at breakfast-time, a Pacceka Buddha, who had risen from a seven days' trance, saw that the time had come for him to seek for food.

And thinking he ought to go that day to the door of the Benāres Treasurer's house, he washed his face with water from the Anotatta lake, and used a toothpick made from the betel-creeper, put on his lower robe as he stood on the table-land of Mount Manosilā, fastened on his girdle, robed himself, took a begging-bowl he created for the purpose, went through the sky, and stood at the door of the house just as the breakfast was being taken in to the Bodisat.

As soon as the Bodisat saw him, he rose from his seat, and looked at a servant who was making the preparations.

"What shall I do, Sir?" said he.

"Bring the gentleman's bowl," said his master.

That moment Māra the Wicked One was greatly agitated, and rose up, saying, "It is seven days since this Pacceka Buddha received food. If he gets none to-day, he will perish. I must destroy this fellow, and put a stop to the Treasurer's gift."

And he went at once and caused a pit of live coals, eighty fathoms deep, to appear in the midst of the house. And it was full of charcoal of Acacia-wood; and appeared burning and flaming, like the great hell of Avīci. And after creating it, he himself remained in the sky.

When the man, who was coming to fetch the bowl, saw this, he was exceeding terrified, and stopped still.

"What are you stopping for, my good man?" asked the Bodisat.

"There is a great pit of live coals burning and blazing in the very middle of the house, Sir!" said he. And as people came up one after another, they were each overcome with fear, and fled hastily away.

Then thought the Bodisat, "Vasavatti Māra must be

exerting himself with the hope of putting an obstacle in the way of my almsgiving. But I am not aware that I can be shaken by a hundred or even a thousand Māras. This day I will find out whether my power or Māra's—whether my might or Māra's—is the greater."

And he himself took the dish of rice just as it stood there ready, and went out, and stood on the edge of the pit of fire; and looking up to the sky, saw Māra, and said—

"Who are you?"

"I am Māra," was the reply.

"Is it you who created this pit of fire?"

"Certainly, I did it."

"And what for?"

"Simply to put a stop to your almsgiving, and destroy the life of that Pacceka Buddha!"

"And I'll allow you to do neither the one nor the other. Let us see this day whether your power or mine is the greater!" And still standing on the edge of the pit of fire, he exclaimed—

"My Lord, the Pacceka Buddha! I will not turn back from this pit of coal, though I should fall into it headlong. Take now at my hands the food I have bestowed, even the whole of it." And so saying, he uttered the stanza:

"Far rather will I fall into this hell
Head downwards, and heels upwards, of my own
Accord, than do a deed that is unworthy!
Receive then, Master, at my hands, this alms!"

And as he so said, he held the dish of rice with a firm grasp, and walked right on into the fiery furnace!

And that instant there arose a beautiful large lotus-flower, up and up, from the bottom of the depth of the fiery pit, and received the feet of the Bodisat. And from it there came up about a peck of pollen, and fell on the Great Being's head, and covered his whole body with a sprinkling of golden dust. Then standing in the midst of the lotus-flower, he poured the food into the Pacceka Buddha's bowl.

And he took it, and gave thanks, and threw the bowl aloft; then rose himself into the sky, in the sight of all the people; and treading as it were on the clouds whose various shapes formed a belt across the heavens, he passed away to the mountain regions of Himālaya.

Māra too, sorrowing over his defeat, went away to the place where he dwelt.

But the Bodisat, still standing on the lotus, preached the Law to the people in praise of charity and righteousness; and then returned to his house, surrounded by the multitude. And he gave gifts, and did other good works his life long, and then passed away according to his deeds.

The Teacher then concluded this discourse in illustration of his words, "This is no wonder, O householder, that you, having the insight of those who are walking in the First Path, should now have been unmoved by the Fairy; but what was done by the wise in former times, that was the wonder." And he established the connexion, and summed up the Jātaka, by saying, "There the then Pacceka Buddha died, and on his death no new being was formed to inherit his Karma; but he who gave alms to the Pacceka Buddha, standing on the lotus after defeating the Tempter, was I myself."

END OF THE STORY OF THE FIERY FURNACE.[1]

[1] This story is quoted in 'Strange Stories from a Chinese Studio,' translated by Herbert A. Giles, vol. i. p. 396.

END OF BOOK I. CHAPTER IV.

INDEX.

THE names mentioned in the Tables following the Introduction are not included in this Index, as the Table in which any name should occur can easily be found from the Table of Contents. The names of the Jātakas as far as published in Mr. Fausböll's text are included in this Index, the reference being to the number of the story; all the other references are to the pages in this volume.

In Pāli pronounce vowels as in Italian, consonants as in English (except c = *ch*, ñ = *ny*, ŋ = *ng*), and place the accent on the long syllable. This is a rough rule for practical use. Details and qualifications may be seen in my manual 'Buddhism,' pp. 1, 2.

Made in the USA
Las Vegas, NV
23 October 2024

536019e4-f336-4f08-bcce-af9cc68bf380R01